THE JEW OF MALTA

A Critical Reader

Edited by
Robert A Logan

The Arden Shakespeare

1 3 5 7 9 10 8 6 4 2

First published in 2013 by The Arden Shakespeare

Copyright © Robert A Logan and contributors 2013

The Arden Shakespeare is an imprint of Bloomsbury Publishing Plc

The Arden Shakespeare
Bloomsbury Publishing Plc
49–51 Bedford Square
London WC1B 3DP

www.ardenshakespeare.com

Hardback ISBN: 9781441169396
Paperback ISBN: 9781441110794
EPUB ISBN: 9781408191538
EPDF ISBN: 9781408191545

Available in the USA from Bloomsbury Academic & Professional,
175 Fifth Avenue/3rd Floor, New York, NY 10010.

A CIP catalogue record for this book is available from the British Library

This book is produced using paper that is made from wood grown
in managed, sustainable forests. It is natural, renewable and recyclable.
The logging and manufacturing processes conform to the environmental
regulations of the country of origin.

Printed and bound in India

THE JEW OF MALTA

Arden Early Modern Drama Guides

Series Editors:
Andrew Hiscock
University of Wales, Bangor, UK and Lisa Hopkins,
Sheffield Hallam University, UK

Arden Early Modern Drama Guides offers practical and accessible
introductions to the critical and performative contexts of key
Elizabethan and Jacobean plays. Each guide not only introduces
the text's critical and performance history but also provides
students with an invaluable insight into the landscape of current
scholarly research through a keynote essay on the state of the art
and newly commissioned essays of fresh research from different
critical perspectives.

CONTENTS

ACKNOWLEDGEMENTS

Unquestionably, the first debt of gratitude has to be to the eight scholars who contributed chapters of such unwavering excellence that I'm convinced this collection of essays will continue to generate intellectual curiosity and stimulation for years to come. Students, teachers and scholars interested in Marlowe and *The Jew of Malta* will find the chapters fresh, provocative and exciting, for not only is their content exceptionally strong but so also is the range of approaches, a feature that extends beyond consideration of this play exclusively to Renaissance drama generally.

The Marlowe Society of America has provided encouragement and inspiration to all Marlowe scholars for over a half of a century and should be thanked for their consistent, active support. Less abstractly, I want to make clear how grateful I am to Lisa Hopkins and Andrew Hiscock for their unfailingly cheerful encouragement in enlisting me and guiding me through the editorial process and for their critical acuity in reading the manuscript before its final version.

My strongest expression of gratitude is due to my partner, John Wright, who with customary generosity has provided intellectual and emotional support and been instrumental in making sure that I had the time needed to devote to what we both understand is an admirable endeavour.

SERIES INTRODUCTION

The drama of Shakespeare and his contemporaries has remained at the very heart of English curricula internationally and the pedagogic needs surrounding this body of literature have grown increasingly complex as more sophisticated resources become available to scholars, tutors and students. This series aims to offer a clear picture of the critical and performative contexts of a range of chosen texts. In addition, each volume furnishes readers with invaluable insights into the landscape of current scholarly research as well as including new pieces of research by leading critics.

This series is designed to respond to the clearly identified needs of scholars, tutors and students for volumes which will bridge the gap between accounts of previous critical developments and performance history and an acquaintance with new research initiatives related to the chosen plays. Thus, our ambition is to offer innovative and challenging Guides which will provide practical, accessible and thought-provoking analyses of Early Modern Drama. Each volume is organized according to a progressive reading strategy involving introductory discussion, critical review and cutting-edge scholarly debate. It has been an enormous pleasure to work with so many dedicated scholars of Early Modern Drama and we are sure that this series will encourage you to read 400-year-old playtexts with fresh eyes.

Andrew Hiscock and Lisa Hopkins

TIMELINE

February 1564: Birth of Christopher Marlowe.

26 February 1564: Christopher Marlowe is christened at St. George's, Canterbury.

14 January 1579–ca. December 1580: Christopher Marlowe is a scholar at the King's school, Canterbury.

17 March 1581: Marlowe matriculates at Cambridge University (Corpus Christi).

7 May 1581: Marlowe is formally elected to receive the Archbishop Parker scholarship at Cambridge.

1581–6: Marlowe is believed to be involved in secret service for the government.

July–August 1582: Marlowe's first absence from Cambridge.

April–June 1583: Marlowe is absent from Cambridge again.

Spring 1584: Marlowe completes requirements for the BA degree.

July 1584–ca. 25 February 1586: Marlowe is absent from Cambridge five times.

1585–6: *Dido, Queene of Carthage*, perhaps written with Thomas Nashe and the translations of Ovid's *Amores* and *The First Book of Lucan* are thought to belong to the university period. However, like 'The Passionate Shepherd to his Love', they cannot be dated precisely.

31 March 1587: Marlowe is admitted to candidacy for the MA degree.

29 June 1587: Privy Council intervenes with a letter to the Cambridge authorities, praising Marlowe's 'good service' to the queen and petitioning that his degree be granted on schedule.

1587–8: Marlowe's *Tamburlaine*, Parts 1 and 2 is performed to acclaim in London; his association with the Admiral's Men, their celebrated leading actor Edward Alleyn, and theatrical manager Philip Henslowe begins.

1588–93: Marlowe writes *Doctor Faustus* (1588?), *The Jew of Malta* (1589?), *The Massacre at Paris* (1592?), *Edward II* (1592–3?) and *Hero and Leander* (early 1593?); the precise order of composition is uncertain.

18 September 1589: Marlowe is imprisoned with Thomas Watson for participation in a street brawl/swordfight in which William Bradley is killed.

19 September 1589: The coroner's jury finds that Marlowe withdrew from combat and that Watson killed Bradley in self-defense.

1590: Publication of *Tamburlaine*, Parts 1 and 2. Marlowe may also have written *The Jew of Malta* (although both earlier and later dates have been proposed).

1591: Marlowe and Thomas Kyd share the same workroom, as well as the patronage of Ferdinando Stanley, Lord Strange, whose players, Lord Strange's Men, perform their plays.

February 1592–June 1596: Henslowe's *Diary* lists 36 performances of *The Jew of Malta*, attesting its popularity.

26 January 1592: Marlowe is accused of counterfeiting money in the Netherlands by Richard Baines, but is apparently released.

9 May 1592: Marlowe is bound over to keep the peace.

15 September 1592: Marlowe fights William Corkine in Canterbury; after suits and countersuits, the case is dismissed on 9 October.

12 May 1593: Thomas Kyd is arrested on suspicion of libel and imprisoned; papers containing heretical opinions, which Kyd later attributes to Marlowe, are found in Kyd's rooms.

18 May 1593: The Privy Council issues a warrant for Marlowe's arrest.

20 May 1593: Marlowe is called before the Privy Council and is instructed to give his 'daily attendance'; he is not imprisoned.

30 May 1593: Marlowe is killed by Ingram Frizer at the house of Widow Eleanor Bull in Deptford. According to witnesses, Marlowe attacked Frizer after a heated 'public' dispute over the 'reckoning', or bill.

1 June 1593: The coroner's jury finds that Frizer acted in self-defense; Marlowe is buried in the churchyard of St. Nicholas's Church, Deptford.

17 May 1594: *The Jew of Malta* is entered in the Stationers' Register but the earliest printed edition of the play to survive is the quarto of 1633 (see below).

1594: Publication of *Dido, Queen of Carthage* and *Edward II*, both bearing Marlowe's name as author.

1594: Publication of *The Massacre at Paris*.

1598: Publication of *Hero and Leander*; Marlowe is identified as the author.

1599: The Bishop of London and the Archbishop of Canterbury order a public burning of Marlowe's translation of *Ovid's Elegies*.

1600: *Lucan's First Book*, a classical translation, is published with Marlowe identified as author.

1604: The A-Text of *Doctor Faustus* is published.

1616: The B-Text of *Doctor Faustus* is published.

1633: *The Jew of Malta* is published, with a dedication by Thomas Heywood; Marlowe is identified as author, and praised in the prologue as 'the best of Poets in that age'.

NOTES ON CONTRIBUTORS

Bruce E. Brandt is a Professor of English at South Dakota State University. He received his BA and MA from the University of Denver and his PhD from Harvard University. His most recent publications are 'Christopher Marlowe Studies: Bibliography, 2000–2009', in *Marlowe Studies: An Annual*, 1 (2011): pp. 193–277, and 'The Critical Backstory', in *Doctor Faustus: A Critical Guide* (London: Continuum, 2010), pp. 17–41. Other publications include *Christopher Marlowe in the Eighties: An Annotated Bibliography of Marlowe Criticism from 1978 through 1989* (West Cornwall, CT: Locust Hill Press, 1992), *Christopher Marlowe and the Metaphysical Problem Play* (Salzburg: Universität Salzburg, Institut für Anglistik und Amerikanistik, 1985), and articles and notes on topics ranging from Shakespeare to Ursula Le Guin. Complementing his Marlowe scholarship, he has long been active in the Marlowe Society of America, having served as membership chair, editor, vice-president and president.

Sara Munson Deats, Distinguished University Professor at the University of South Florida, is former President of the Marlowe Society of America and has published approximately 50 essays on Marlowe, Shakespeare and the early modern drama in referred journals and anthologies. In addition, Professor Deats has published ten books. These include a feminist study of Marlowe's plays entitled *Sex, Gender, and Desire in the Plays of Christopher Marlowe* (1996), for which she received the Roma Gill Award for Outstanding Contribution to Marlowe scholarship. She has also edited a collection of essays on *Antony and Cleopatra* for Routledge Press (2005) and has edited with Robert Logan two collections of essays on Christopher Marlowe, entitled: *Marlowe's Empery: Expanding His Critical Contexts* (2002) and, most recently, *Placing*

Christopher Marlowe's Plays: Fresh Critical Contexts (2008), plus, most recently, *A Critical Guide to 'Doctor Faustus'* for Continuum Press. In addition, Professor Deats has co-edited with Lagretta Lenker five books relating literature to social issues. She is currently working on her eleventh book, *The Faust Legend on Stage and Screen.*

Andrew Duxfield is an Associate Lecturer at Sheffield Hallam University. He is the winner of the 2009 Hoffman Prize for distinguished publication on Christopher Marlowe, and his published essays include '*Doctor Faustus* and Renaissance Hermeticism', in this series' corresponding title on *Doctor Faustus*, '*Doctor Faustus* and the Failure to Unify', in *Early Modern Literary Studies*, and 'Modern Problems of Editing: The Two Texts of Marlowe's *Doctor Faustus*', in *Literature Compass*. He has delivered a number of lectures and conference papers on Marlowe, and is working on a book on unity and ambiguity in the plays.

Roslyn L. Knutson, Emerita Professor of English at the University of Arkansas at Little Rock, is the author of *Playing Companies and Commerce in Shakespeare's Time* (Cambridge University Press, 2001) and *The Repertory of Shakespeare's Company, 1594–1613* (University of Arkansas Press, 1991). She has published on theatre history in numerous journals, annuals and essay collections. Her current projects include a repertorial analysis of the commercial theatrical marketplace in 1587–93, when the plays of Christopher Marlowe were new; and the wiki-style *Lost Plays Database* (www.lostplays.org), which she co-edits with David McInnis (University of Melbourne).

Robert A. Logan teaches at the University of Hartford where he is Chair of the Arts and Sciences English department. He has also served as Director of the University's Humanities Center, and, from 1999–2003, was President of The Marlowe Society of America. Professor Logan has written several articles and book chapters on Marlowe and Shakespeare, served as guest editor, published numerous reviews and has co-edited with Sara Munson

Deats two collections of essays: *Marlowe's Empery: Expanding His Critical Contexts* (2002) and *Placing the Plays of Christopher Marlowe: Fresh Cultural Contexts* (2008). In 2007, he published a critical work entitled *Shakespeare's Marlowe: The Influence of Christopher Marlowe on Shakespeare's Artistry*. The book won the 2009 Roma Gill Prize for the best new work in Marlowe studies. He was the general editor for a series of six volumes on each of the University Wits (Robert Greene, Christopher Marlowe, Thomas Nashe, Thomas Lodge, John Lyly, George Peele), published in 2011, and was himself author/editor of the volume on Christopher Marlowe. At present, he is finishing up a book entitled: *Measuring Up: Shakespeare, 'Antony and Cleopatra', and Paradigms of Fame.*

Ian McAdam teaches courses on dramatic and non-dramatic early modern literature at the University of Lethbridge, Alberta, Canada. He is the author of *The Irony of Identity: Self and Imagination in the Drama of Christopher Marlowe* (Delaware, 1999) and *Magic and Masculinity in Early Modern English Drama* (Duquesne, 2009). He is currently working on a project tentatively entitled 'Marlowe, Shakespeare, and the Secular Christ'.

Kirk Melnikoff is an Associate Professor of English at the University of North Carolina at Charlotte. He is editor of *Robert Greene* (Ashgate, 2011) and co-editor of *Writing Robert Greene: New Essays on England's First Notorious Professional Writer* (Ashgate, 2008). He is currently finishing a monograph on Elizabethan publishing practices and the development of English literature in the vernacular.

Sarah K. Scott is Associate Professor of English at Mount St. Mary's University where she teaches courses in Shakespeare, early modern poetry and drama, and cultural, gender, and sexuality studies. She is the author of essays on Dekker, Marlowe, Marston and Middleton as well as co-editor of *Christopher Marlowe the Craftsman: Lives, Stage, and Page*. She serves as assistant editor of the New Variorum Shakespeare *Julius Caesar.*

M. L. Stapleton is Chapman Distinguished Professor of English at Indiana University-Purdue University, Fort Wayne. He is the editor of the New Variorum Shakespeare *Julius Caesar* and *Marlowe Studies*: *An Annual*. His most recent book is *Spenser's Ovidian Poetics* (2009).

INTRODUCTION

Robert A. Logan

Along with the increase in scholarship and criticism written about Christopher Marlowe and his works during the twentieth and twenty-first centuries has come an imposing surge in the number of disagreements surrounding his plays and poetry.[1] Vying for the Marlovian play with the greatest amount of controversy is *The Jew of Malta*. It may well be, however, that the controversy exists as a modern rather than an early modern phenomenon. One could posit that the popularity of the play when it was first out of the gate could be perceived as a sign that audiences did not find it a source of contentiousness. Probably, however, its initial theatre audiences did not scrutinize either the events of the play or the characterization of its protagonist with the analytical depth of modern scholars and critics. This likelihood would also vitiate the counterargument that the popularity of the play can be attributed to the considerable number of instantaneous disputes it evoked, especially concerning the figure of Barabas.

No evidence exists to tell us when *The Jew of Malta* was first performed or, specifically, how its initial audiences reacted to it. Nevertheless, Philip Henslowe's *Diary* records 36 performances of *The Jew of Malta* between February 1592 and June 1596.[2] Because this figure tops the number of recorded performances of any other stage play in the 1590s, scholars have concluded that it was extremely popular. A comment by N. W. Bawcutt gives support to this supposition: 'Between February and June 1592 there were ten performances at intervals of less than a fortnight, all earning good sums of money'.[3] At the end of June 1592, because of the plague, the theatres were shut down by order of the Privy Council. On 29 December, they reopened until 1 February 1593, during which time *The Jew of Malta* was performed three times; the theatres then closed down again for the remainder of the year. Scholars have speculated that the play's next period of popularity – in June and July of 1594 (four performances in June, two in July) – may have been caused by the execution of the Queen's Jewish physician, Roderigo Lopez, on 7 June 1594. Later that year, however, the drama fell victim apparently to a period of neglect that continued into 1595, a year without any recorded performances. Even so, it was back on the boards in 1596 with eight performances during the first six months. Bawcutt points out that Henslowe's list of properties indicates that the play continued to be performed into the late 1590s.[4]

To keep the popularity of *The Jew of Malta* in a realistic contextual perspective, we need to understand that it did not make the list of the 12 top-grossing plays recorded in Henslowe's *Diary* during the period from 1592–7.[5] We know less today about the more popular plays than about *The Jew of Malta* because only two of the texts on the list have survived.[6] Consequently, the popularity of Marlowe's play, apart from its quality as a drama, may seem greater to us now than it seemed to those in the final decade of the sixteenth century simply because we lack information about lost and unknown plays. Even if box-office receipts give us a short-term measure of the popularity of Marlowe's play, they reveal almost nothing about its reputation over the course of time – unless they suggest that its initial welcome garnered a popular esteem that guaranteed its chances of surviving well into the future. More particularly, in 1633, a publisher, Nicholas Vavasour, had the text printed, indicating that the play had acquired a popularity or familiarity widespread enough to be considered an investment that, as a book, would turn a profit. The readership may or may not have first been attracted by performances of the play (of which we have no record). The best measure of *The Jew of Malta*'s long-term renown is, of course, reflected in the effectiveness of its influence.[7] The play did not have the contemporary impact on drama of the *Tamburlaine* plays.[8] In fact, in England, the only recorded performance after 1601 until the twentieth century, excluding those mentioned on the title page of the 1633 quarto, is Edmund Kean's

1818 production of Samson Penley's adaptation in which Barabas becomes a tragic figure victimized by a thoroughly corrupt society. The 1633 text depicts a wealthy, evil Jewish merchant set at odds with his Christian society and alienated from Malta's other Jews, a villain who resists stereotyping as either a Jew or a Vice figure. In spite of Penley's 1818 revision, the 1633 text managed to stay afloat long enough to become by the twentieth century a curricular fixture in schools. At the same time, the play also began to enjoy a revival among reading and viewing audiences that has lasted to the present day.

Because line 3 of the Prologue to *The Jew of Malta* makes reference to the assassination of the Duke of Guise, which occurred on 23 December 1588, scholars assume that the play was written within the following year or so. Although the chronology of Marlowe's plays is uncertain, this proposed date would place the play after *Dido, Queen of Carthage*, the two *Tamburlaine* plays, and *Doctor Faustus*[9]– that is, at the beginning of the second half of Marlowe's dramatic output. The play was entered in the Stationers' Register on 17 May 1594, but if it was printed, no extant copy of it has ever been found. The play was entered again on 20 November 1632 to a different stationer and printed in 1633 in a quarto version that Bawcutt argues convincingly is 'a foul papers text of high authority'.[10] According to the quarto's title page and Thomas Heywood's dedicatory letter to Thomas Hammon, the play had already been performed before the King and Queen at court and at the Cockpit Theatre.[11] In the Prologue to the latter production, Heywood[12] mentions that Marlowe was 'the best of poets in that age / The Malta Jew had being' (ll.2–3) and that Edward Alleyn, 'the best of actors' (l.4), first played the lead role. In his Prologue to Charles I and Queen Henrietta, Heywood says a bit defensively that, even though the play was written many years ago, it was 'in that age thought second unto none' (l.4) and that their majesties will find the Machiavellian character of Barabas of particular interest.[13] Thus, writing almost half a century after the play was composed, Heywood does not so much as hint at anything like our current controversy over the play.

The Jew of Malta is unique among Marlowe's plays in not having a clear and definite source. It could, of course, be that Marlowe drew upon a narrative source or several sources of which we have no knowledge. The play does not reflect any specific event from Mediterranean history, although the Turks did lay siege to Malta in 1551 and 1565 – but not at all in the manner that the play portrays the event. As for the figure of Barabas, no candidate from life has ever been found as a model, although it is clear that Marlowe's knowledge of history, politics, religion and current events all played a part in influencing him as he composed the play.[14] His knowledge of previous characterizations of Jews, including stereotypical notions based on cultural myths and assumptions, may also have contributed to his portrayal of Barabas. But, again, it is difficult to pin down direct sources.[15] As James Shapiro points out, Marlowe was familiar with some of the nastier myths about Jews: for example, he was evidently acquainted with 'an unusually persistent belief that a hereditary feature transmitted by Jews was their stench',[16] which Marlowe depicts with an ironic reversal when Lodowick asks Barabas why he walks away from him and Barabas replies sardonically, ''tis a custom held with us, / That when we speak with gentiles like to you, / We turn into the air to purge ourselves' (*JM* 2.2.45–7) and again later when Barabas, seeing Friar Bernardine and Friar Jacomo approach, says to Ithamore, 'I smelt 'em ere they came' (*JM* 4.1.23). In a second example of an ugly myth, the playwright shows himself well aware of 'the belief that Jews abducted children and killed them, using their blood for ritual purposes'.[17] Marlowe dramatizes this myth in the scene in which Friar Bernardine tells Friar Jacomo that Barabas has done 'a thing that makes me tremble to unfold' (*JM* 3.6.48) and Jacomo asks, 'What, has he crucified a child' (*JM* 3.6.49). These pieces of evidence tell us that Marlowe absorbed definite influences, but they do not reveal specific sources.

Nevertheless, there is an endless fascination among scholars who are ever eager to find sources and influences for the play. In the present volume, M. L. Stapleton opens a new door on the subject by linking Marlowe's well-known familiarity with the views and actions of the Ovidian persona of the *Amores* with Barabas's behaviour. Stapleton contends with extensive detail and nuanced arguments that Marlowe's translation of the *Amores*, the *Elegies*, gave the poet/playwright an understanding of the personality of the Ovidian lover that could only have helped him in defining the individual traits and activities of Barabas, as well as in his use of language.

The controversies that swirl around *The Jew of Malta* break down into three categories: (1) the extent of Marlowe's familiarity with Niccolò Machiavelli and his works as they bear on his use of the persona Machevill[18] in the Prologue and Machiavelli as a guiding force in determining characterizations and events during the course of the play; (2) the difficulties encountered in attempting to characterize the genre of the play; and (3) the problems one faces in arriving at a coherent understanding of the character of Barabas, including the differences in his portrayal in the first two and last three acts of the play and his part in the complex Maltese world of politics, religion and economics.

The Machevill of the Prologue lacks the requisite authenticity of details that would verify Marlowe's first-hand familiarity with Machiavelli's writings.[19] A discrepancy existed in Elizabethan and Jacobean England between the real Machiavelli – a Florentine diplomat and civil servant, as well as a writer of history, political philosophy and drama – and the distorted common image that demonized him as a proponent of tyranny and atheism; concomitantly, a similarly inaccurate image of his writings as handbooks on these subjects prevailed. Because the Florentine's books were banned in England, contorted views of him and his writings were free to flourish. Machevill, who may possibly be the first stage impersonation of Machiavelli in English drama,[20] could well be a reflection of such fictionalized views. Whether he was or was not the first, we recognize that Marlowe sought to surprise and engage his audience by beginning the play with a sensationalized figure that would then linger in the shadows throughout the play as the potential spirit behind the actions and attitudes of not just Barabas, but Ferneze, del Bosco, and Selim-Calymath as well.

At the beginning of the Prologue, Machevill implies that the Duke of Guise, the egregiously villainous Catholic protagonist of Marlowe's *The Massacre at Paris*, was a disciple of Machiavelli (*JM* Prologue 3); but there is no evidence to substantiate such a claim, thus making the charge an anti-Catholic invention of Marlowe's own fashioning.[21] Moreover, when Machevill says, 'I count religion but a childish toy' (*JM* Prologue 14), we know that this view differs from the pragmatic attitude that Machiavelli actually held towards the essential usefulness of religion.[22] What we do not know is whether Marlowe knew it. Furthermore, when Machevill tells us that Barabas 'smiles to see how full his bags are crammed, / Which money was not got without my means' (*JM* Prologue 31–2), we are puzzled, because nothing in the play that follows identifies or supports such a 'means'. To clarify, but at the risk of also oversimplifying matters, we might say that Barabas mirrors, albeit in extreme ways, the misleading images and views of Machiavelli promulgated among Elizabethans and Jacobeans, whereas, more often than not, Ferneze manifests the actual principles of the Florentine political philosopher even if his motive is self-interest rather than concern for the well-being of Malta. Barabas lacks the drive for power that so interests Machiavelli, and Machiavelli lacks the attraction to infinite riches that motivates many of Barabas's actions. Whatever we make finally of Marlowe's knowledge of Machiavelli and the reasons for the playwright's use of him in the drama, we can see that he darkens with pessimism the practical means and consequences that the real Machiavelli optimistically believed would better the political state.

The Christians in the play are Catholic and, therefore, Marlowe's criticisms of them would have been music to the Protestant ears of his initial audiences, as would the criticisms of the Jews, another religious sect that was anathema to those who upheld the state religion.[23] Marlowe parodies both Christian and Jewish religious hypocrisy, especially the absence of religious moral principles to which the characters presumably subscribe. He dramatizes a world in which those who are greedy for power, money, and, as Friar Bernadine reveals, sex (*JM* 1.2.327 and 3.6.41) are, in fact, devoid of moral scruples. In the course of the play, Marlowe generalizes beyond any particular sect the criticisms of the characters' lack of morals, beginning with Machevill's generalized pronouncement, 'I count religion but a childish toy' (114). Apart from any consideration of how far from the ethical roots of their religion the characters have strayed, in itself a criticism of the ineffectiveness of all religion, Marlowe makes clear that their behaviour is motivated by the power politics and materialistic interests intensified by the drama's Mediterranean setting: namely, pressures on the island of Malta created from without by the Turks and the Spanish in their desire for control. The Prologue, however, warns specifically of the dangers of Catholicism and with pointed irony and fatalism: 'Though some speak openly against my books, / Yet will they read me, and thereby attain / To Peter's chair' (ll. 10–12). In establishing his closest affiliation with Machiavelli's interests but with a cynical perspective, Machevill also affirms the absoluteness of power as the basis of a ruler's political authority: 'Might first made kings, and the laws were then most sure / When like the Draco's they were writ in blood' (ll. 20–1). Finally, the Prologue suggests that Machiavelli's pernicious doctrinal influence has found its way to the shores of England (ll. 1–4, 29). In case Marlowe's audiences were in any doubt, the Prologue informs them that the attitudes and actions of humankind in Malta are no different from those in England where similar power plays in the guise of religious rectitude and as a consequence of material greed have overturned any pretense to either a healthy sociopolitical or personal scheme of values. This seemingly hopeless situation is the true tragedy portrayed in *The Jew of Malta*. It is not, as Machevill personalizes it, 'the tragedy of a Jew' (l. 30).

The question Machevill's statement raises, however, is what is the genre of the play? The 1633 title page calls the drama 'The Famous Tragedy of the Rich Jew of Malta', but it is as difficult to see how this is so as it is to see how Machevill's statement obtains. The conventional notion of tragedy as a fall from high estate might seem to fit the two attributions of tragedy, except that Barabas is endlessly resourceful and keeps reinventing his high estate, often delighting more in the means than the ends. Discussion of the issue of genre has gained in prominence ever since T. S. Eliot made his well-known comments on the subject:[24]

> If one takes the *Jew of Malta* not as a tragedy or as a 'tragedy of blood' [i.e., a revenge tragedy], but as a farce, the conclud-ing act becomes intelligible; and if we attend with a careful ear to the versification, we find that Marlowe develops a tone to suit this farce, and even perhaps that this tone is his most powerful and mature tone. I say farce, but with the enfeebled humour of our times the word is a misnomer; it is the farce of the old English humour, the terribly serious, even savage comic humour, the humour, which spent its last breath in the decadent genius of Dickens.[25]

Eliot focuses on the exaggerated events of the final act of the play that evoke laughter and even sneers from an audience, laughter at the campy, 'savage' notion of constructing a large cauldron with the intention of boiling Turks in it; and he is scornful of both Barabas's inexplicable decision to double-cross Calymath and form a pact with Ferneze, and Ferneze's to double-cross Barabas. In contrast to our response to Ferneze's convincing final act of treachery, it is difficult to accept realistically the Jew's foolish decision to restore the former governor's power. The uncertainty of our response in comprehending Barabas's motives here and elsewhere makes understandable our inability to categorize the genre of the play. However, this may well be part of an overall strategy, Marlowe's desire to dislodge us from familiar, even hackneyed responses to dramatic productions. The implication is that it would be silly to try in a conventional manner to pigeon-hole the play; we should instead sit back and allow the actions of the moment to take hold of us without concern for assigning an all-encompassing abstract label to them. In effect, the play jostles us into responding without being moored to a single, let alone a narrow, generic perspective. Marlowe facilitates this implicit directive through the episodic nature of the plot, through the diversity of tones with which he presents the events, and through the sudden surprises in Barabas's actions and reactions. At times, we are surer of our response than we are at other times. In the second scene of the play, we are invited to feel a serious loathing towards the Christians (especially Ferneze) for unjustly persecuting the Jews, especially Barabas, as a consequence of their own failings.[26] In Act 4, scene 4, however, where Barabas disguises himself as a French musician with a lute and carries in his hat a nosegay whose odour is lethal, we experience a scene that contains Eliot's 'savage comic humour'. We may laugh at Barabas's lame role-playing and his ability to gull Bellamira, Pilia-Borza and even Ithamore, but, as Eliot's word 'savage' suggests, given the context of revenge and wholesale murder, there is also a sharp edge of seriousness to the scene. We understand this edge, but do we feel it – in the same way that we feel the evil of Iago or Edmund? Does our eagerness to be entertained by Barabas override or hold in suspension our moral sense?[27]

Marlowe's shifts from realistic to non-realistic characterizations and episodes do not appear to be a deliberate subversion of traditional patterns of generic distinction but, more broadly, an attempt to overturn his spectators' conventional moral and dramaturgical expectations through shock and surprise – but also often with comic irony. It is this means of encouraging a responsive open-mindedness that gives freshness to the theatrical experience and, thereby, makes the play memorable. If the playwright creates inconsistencies, ambivalences and ambiguities along the way, so much the better, for they act as dramaturgical devices that can only help to keep an audience engaged.[28] The tendency among scholars and critics has been to try to link the play with traditions that are familiar – for example, the Vice figure of medieval drama, revenge tragedy, Protestant anti-Catholic propaganda, and, as we have seen, the influence of Machiavelli and the anti-Machiavellians. But the play is defiant in its resistance to source studies and to upholding standard claims and dictates of established religious and political institutions. Nor does the play allow us to sustain a clear, balanced moral perspective. The portrayal of power politics uses ethnic and religious differences to justify treacherous betrayals and the ruthless assertions of absolute control. Ferneze's reasoning for taking money from the Jews (1.2.37–162) and Del Bosco's for defying the Turks (2.2) are, respectively, cases in point. The upshot is that we lack a moral compass to guide us in the course of our responses to the political, religious and cultural differences in the play. Invariably, issues of politics, religion and ethnicity pull us back to the shortcomings, weaknesses and failings of humankind. And, to be sure, we are left with a bitter taste in our mouths at the ultimate resurgence of Ferneze and the ugly hypocrisy of his final statement, the last words of the play: 'So march away, and let due praise be given / Neither to fate nor fortune, but to heaven' (5.5.122–3). Instead of being upset at the death of Barabas, our distress is directed towards the irremediable conditions that permit Ferneze and power politics to thrive. The play is therefore unable to resolve the confusion of issues that it has presented, because it has not located a value system from which to proceed. Without such a system, we are also unable to place the label of a genre on the play.

Central to any discussion of *The Jew of Malta* is the difficulty one has responding to the protagonist.[29] We have already seen that Barabas oscillates between being a realistic and non-realistic figure. Reading and viewing audiences have discovered that it is not possible to stereotype him as a Vice figure, a Machiavellian, a Jew or a merchant. Considered from a literary perspective, he belongs to a long line of tricksters, resourceful role players whose adherence to the laws and norms of society is always questionable. The tricksters range from clever criminals to people of all classes who live by their wits, characters from whom we are enough detached to enjoy their means without becoming emotionally upset by their ends. Barabas expresses the credo of the kind of trickster that he is when he exclaims, in contrast to his fellow Jews, 'Barabas is born to better chance, / And framed of finer mould than common men, / That measure naught but by the present time' (1.2.223–5). Barabas is a narcissist ('Assure yourselves I'll look unto (*Aside*) myself' – 1.1.172 and '*Ego mihimet sum semper proximus*' [I am always nearest to myself] – 1.1.188) – alienated from everyone, including his daughter and the Jewish community. With regard to the latter, he exclaims scornfully:

> See the simplicity of these base slaves,
> Who for the villains have no wit themselves,
> Think me to be a senseless lump of clay
> That will with every water wash to dirt! (1.2.215–19)

Unlike Shylock, Barabas never mentions a Leah and so is not humanized in the same way as the Venetian usurer. Marlowe's protagonist lives by the rules of self-interest with which he instructs Ithamore:

> Hast thou no trade? Then listen to my words,
> And I will teach thee that shall stick by thee:
> First, be thou void of these affections,
> Compassion, love, vain hope, and heartless fear;
> Be moved at nothing, see thou pity none,
> But to thyself smile when the Christians moan. (2.3.171–6)

Barabas becomes more hardhearted and ruthless as the play develops but he is always without humanity, an emotional void.

As critics have long posited, there are noticeable differences between the first two acts of the play and the last three acts. After Act 2, Barabas becomes less reflective and more staunchly a victimizer than a victim; moreover, the number of events increases and several incidents are exaggerated to produce multiple instances of irony. I am reminded of the break in *Measure For Measure* at 3.1.152 where the play turns away from potential tragedy – from raising serious issues and presenting in-depth characterizations – to become a comedy of intrigue. Although Barabas becomes more trickster than merchant in Acts 3–5, his hard-heartedness, energy, resourcefulness and tendency to shy away from power remain constant. His views on power are stated early in the play when he speaks about his alien status as a Jew 'wealthier far than any Christian' (1.1.127):

> I must confess we [Jews] come not to be kings.
> That's not our fault: alas, our number's few,
> And crowns come either by succession,
> Or urged by force; and nothing violent
> Oft have I heard tell, can be permanent.
> Give us a peaceful rule, make Christians kings,
> That thirst so much for principality. (1.1.128–34)

This view is the closest we can come to understanding why, at the end of the play, he foolishly makes a bargain with Ferneze for money rather than power. Even if Barabas's motives still leave us scratching our heads in bewilderment, especially given his attitude towards violence and his desire for a 'peaceful rule', his discomfort in his power as governor and his attempt to sell his power for money both suggest that, in spite of differences between the two parts of the play, lines of continuity in the characterization of the Jew do exist. Moreover, the dim sociopolitical view of a soulless materialistic society has been sustained as a binding force between the early and late portions of the play.

Whether Marlowe's depiction of Barabas's alien status, self-promoted by the Jew, has both an aesthetic and moral basis is questionable, but it certainly works as a device for engaging an audience. We have seen that Barabas is variously both a realistic and non-realistic figure, but at times we have little understanding of how to respond to him. For example, it is difficult to know just how factual the autobiographical catalogue of crimes is that he recites to Ithamore (2.3.179–205). Is he putting on a show for his recently purchased slave in order to enlist him as a villainous partner in crime? If so, is the list more fiction than fact? Is his list of crimes so exaggerated that it invokes the laughter of comic irony rather than a moral response?

What we can be sure of is that, like Marlowe (who is pulling the strings), Barabas understands that he lives in a wholly materialistic society where buying and selling constitute the prevalent *modus vivendi*. Marlowe's heavy use of asides not only suggests the sudden shifts of attitude in Barabas that make him intriguing to an audience, but they also suggest, not without bitter irony, the prevalence and vital importance of deception and double standards in a functioning materialistic society. That deception is a necessary rule of thumb in this society becomes clear when Barabas distinguishes between honest and dishonest dissembling:

> As good dissemble that thou never mean'st
> As first mean truth, and then dissemble it;
> A counterfeit profession is better
> Than unseen hypocrisy. (1.2.292–5)

The irony in this passage and in passages throughout the play is, to invoke Eliot again, 'savage comic humour'. As a well-sustained perspective, it appears to be the strongest element of continuity in the play, intensifying the grim hopelessness of establishing Barabas's 'peaceful rule' in the midst of political, religious and cultural differences.

Because we lack the necessary information, it would be presumptuous to attempt to assert the impact of *The Jew of Malta* on the development of English drama. Yet, the controversy that the play has given rise to among scholars and critics since the opening decades of the twentieth century suggests that at the very least Marlowe opened up new ways of thinking about characterization and genre, enhanced by such devices as purposeful ambivalence and ambiguity. In subverting dramaturgical conventions, he enabled those playwrights who followed him to think outside the box. The essays that make up this volume make that point loud and clear.

Bruce Brandt's chapter, 'The Critical Backstory', views with precise meticulousness evidence of what he calls 'the critical fortunes of *The Jew of Malta*', moving from the play's earliest entries in Philip Henslowe's *Diary* to the various critical perspectives that emerge at the end of the twentieth century. He breaks his discussion into the following topics: the play's date and early reception, its text, its sources, the Bible, Marlowe and Machiavelli, Jewish stereotypes and anti-Semitism, *The Jew of Malta* and *The Merchant of Venice*, the decline and revival of Marlowe's literary reputation, the roots of modern criticism, romanticism and savage farce and the criticism of the later twentieth century. Although admittedly selective rather than comprehensive, Brandt's astute synopses present a remarkably thorough portrayal of over four centuries of the critical landscape.

Sara Munson Deats's chapter on the performance history of *The Jew of Malta* is the most complete survey of the stagings of the play to date. Written with scrupulous attention to detail and clarity, Deats investigates the wide-ranging differences in the ways various directors have chosen to focus on both the comic and serious elements of the play. She also displays a scholarly thoroughness and precision in examining over 80 reviews of performances of the play. The results of her study enable her to come to several conclusions about the text itself. For example, in what has become in productions an issue of the play's attitude towards Jews, she deduces from her analysis that '*The Jew of Malta* is perhaps the most sophisticated and ironic burlesque of anti-Semitism ever written'.

Andrew Duxfield picks up where Bruce Brandt's chapter left off, bringing us up to date on the state of the art of criticism since the twentieth century. Duxfield is sensitive to the changing trends in literary criticism generally, and he brings his considerable knowledge to bear on his contemplation of *The Jew of Malta*. He makes clear that his chapter aims 'to provide a narrative account of trends and patterns in discussion of the play, and also provide an easily navigable reference resource which can be dipped into for specific items of information'. He breaks the chapter into three sections: an overview of central critical issues; an annotated bibliography of a broad selection of each year's offerings; an extensive and invaluable year-by-year bibliography of the twenty-first-century's publications. The chapter's incisiveness and clarity only add to its admirable usefulness for students and scholars.

Roslyn L. Knutson takes up a long-neglected topic in her essay on '*The Jew of Malta* in Repertory'. With a richness of detail and thoroughness, she places the play in the intriguing, wide-ranging context of theatre history. In explaining chronologically its performances by various companies, she convincingly strikes down speculations that have hardened erroneously into facts. These include new information about the likelihood of provincial performances of the play, the venues of such performances, the play's repertorial competition and its marketing influence. With the solidity of documentary evidence, the chapter handsomely separates fact from fiction, making clear the play's staying power from its beginnings in the public theatre to its production before royalty almost a half century later.

Ian McAdam takes up the familiar issue of the connections between *The Jew of Malta* and *The Merchant of Venice*. However, he gives his study of influence a freshness and complexity by treating the issues, emanating from Marlowe's subversive tendencies, that make the two plays controversial – namely, 'the political/economic and the psychological/theological levels of meaning'. Contending that the two plays cast aspersions on both mercantile aggressiveness and religious hypocrisy, McAdam links these cultural concerns with an increasing anxiety in masculine self-fashioning and control, aided by the disappearance of a strong religious sense of right and wrong. He finds that this anxiety enables both dramatists to establish with subtlety a homoerotic subtext.

Kirk Melnikoff takes a new approach to *The Jew of Malta* by viewing its first entry into the Stationers' Register as an occasion to study its earliest emergence in the context of print culture – specifically, as a print commodity in 1594. Rejecting the notion that the Register's entry by Ling and Millington indicates that they decided to finance an edition of the play because of Marlowe's name recognition, he finds that the intended first publication arises out of the complex of political, moral and literary views of Ling and Millington. He concludes his argument by delineating in the text the views that might have drawn the two publishers to band together to attempt to publish the play. His essay opens a door on the play that has not been opened before. With well-supported, documentary evidence, he makes several astute observations that set the popularity of the play in an arresting light.

The volume concludes with Sarah K. Scott's survey of those resources that will be most helpful to students and teachers of the play as well as to scholars. As she says, 'The following discussion presents an array of scholarship that includes editions, critical essays, critical companions, and media-based resources to encourage meaningful and productive classroom examination of Marlowe's provocative play.' Readers will find most useful her annotated bibliography of books, journal articles, essays in edited collections and media resources. With regard to media resources, Scott wisely cautions that students need to be discriminating in availing themselves of websites, especially those that make 'false claims' or appear to encourage 'ahistorical thinking'. Overall, this chapter offers valuable resources for both teaching strategies and critical perspectives.

ONE

The Critical Backstory

Bruce E. Brandt

Nearly four and a quarter centuries ago, Marlowe's Machevill strode out upon the stage 'to present the tragedy of a Jew', ambiguously asking the audience to 'grace him as he deserves'.[1] Looking at how Barabas and the play have since been graced, this chapter traces the critical fortunes of *The Jew of Malta* from that beginning to the end of the twentieth century. It examines the play's date and early reception, its text, its sources, the Bible, Marlowe and Machiavelli, Jewish stereotypes and anti-Semitism, *The Jew of Malta* and *The Merchant of Venice*, the decline and revival of Marlowe's literary reputation, the roots of modern criticism, romanticism and savage farce and the criticism of the later twentieth century. Such an overview is necessarily selective rather than comprehensive, and is far from doing justice to the full range of scholarship that has been devoted to the play.

Date and Early Reception

Although *The Jew of Malta* cannot be precisely dated, it was necessarily written prior to 26 February 1592, when Philip Henslowe's *Diary* (his account book) records the receipt of 50 shillings for a performance by the Lord Strange's Men. The play's première may have been earlier, for Henslowe's entry was not marked with his 'ne' for new.[2] Machevill's statement 'And now the Guise is dead', spoken at the beginning of the Prologue, provides a *terminus a quo* for the play, since the assassination of the Duke of Guise occurred on 23 December 1588. Machevill's phrasing suggests that the Guise's death was relatively recent, and most scholars have concluded that the play was written in 1589 or 1590. John Bakeless provides a lengthy list of such opinions running from John Payne Collier in 1831 to Rupert Taylor in 1936 (pp. 329–30), and all later editors have concurred.

The play was well received. Henslowe records 36 performances between February 1592 and June 1596, at which time he ceased recording individual plays. Moreover, a list of stage properties written on 10 March 1598, includes a cauldron for the *Jew*, and on 19 May 1601, the Diary lists expenses 'to buy diverse things for the *Jew of Malta*', including payments to a tailor. Some scholars have thought that these later expenditures could point to a revival, but Bawcutt observes they may simply mean various props and costumes were becoming worn from frequent use.[3] Gill suggests that it was the play's frequent performances that account for the word 'famous' in the title as it was entered into the Stationers' Register in 1594: *The Famous Tragedy of the Rich Jew of Malta* (p. xvi). That is, it was the play itself that was famous. Its popularity was doubtlessly enhanced by the performance in the title role of Edward Alleyn, whom S. P. Ceresano dubs England's first 'superstar' actor.[4] Judging from Thomas Heywood's 'The Epistle Dedicatory' and 'The Prologue to the Stage, at the Cockpit' in the 1633 quarto of *The Jew of Malta*, she concludes that the memory of Alleyn's performance could still be invoked in high praise of the play 29 years after his retirement from the stage in 1604 (pp. 55–6). Frequent literary and dramatic allusions further attest to the play's familiarity and rich impact throughout the 1590s and the first decade of the seventeenth century (Bakeless, pp. 367–75).

The Text

Given the early popularity of *The Jew of Malta* and the value now attached to Marlowe's literary production, it is amazing to think how perilously close the play came to being lost to posterity, for it was not printed until 1633, 40-some years after it was written. The play had been entered in the Stationers' Register in 1594, but for some reason the intended publication did not occur.[5]

The 1633 quarto reflects Thomas Heywood's revival of the play for performance at Court and at the Cockpit. It was entered in the Stationers' Register on 20 November 1632 to be published by Nicholas Vavasour and was printed in 1633 by John Beale.[6]

The 40-year gap between the time of writing and publication certainly raises the possibility of revision, and early criticism, by and large, perceived the text as deficient. For example, in 1910 Tucker Brooke concluded that 'Undoubtedly the 1633 quarto presents the tragedy in a form sadly corrupted and altered from that in which it left the hands of Marlowe'.[7] Brooke perceived at least two revisions, one for a 1601 revival and one when Heywood revived the play. Similarly, John Bakeless felt that although the overall form of the play was Marlowe's, 'the play has been badly mangled, and there is some doubt how much of its latter half is really his' (pp. 330–1). He thought it probable that Thomas Heywood's revival occasioned the alterations, and that Heywood himself was most likely the adapter. Early Romantic criticism (see below) was particularly insistent that the first two acts of the play were superior to the final three, and perceived in this aesthetic judgement evidence of co-authorship or textual corruption. Una Ellis-Fermor thought the play's first two acts 'contain the most strongly-imagined and sparingly-executed study that Marlowe ever made', but that the next two acts seem not to have been written by him.[8] Even at mid-century F. P. Wilson argued that 'To suppose that the same man who wrote the first two acts was wholly responsible for the last three is revolting to sense and sensibility', an opinion quoted approvingly by Irving Ribner in 'Marlowe's Tragic Glass' and echoed in his edition of Marlowe's plays.[9]

However, later criticism has reversed this perception of an imperfect text. Leo Kirschbaum refuted the idea that Heywood had added the friar scenes to the play by noting that *Titus Andronicus*'s allusion to the scene where the dead body of Friar Barnadine is propped up means that this action was part of the play as performed in 1592, 'And that the text as we have it must substantially be as Marlowe left it'.[10] J. C. Maxwell then demonstrated that despite its printing errors *The Jew of Malta* is not

textually corrupt, and that any aesthetic disappointment one has
with the last three acts cannot be blamed on revision.[11] Moreover,
it is now clear that the printing is not as bad as earlier critics
perceived. Bawcutt describes the quarto as being 'a very ordinary piece of book production, with about fifty trivial and obvious misprints involving single letters, the omission of several
single words, and anything between sixty and a hundred words
requiring emendation' (*Jew*, p. 38). He finds that some oddities
of layout and lineation suggest that the type was set by formes.
Bowers notes that a combination of worn type and light inking
means that determining the pointing often requires comparing a
number of copies (p. 255). The extensive collations by Bawcutt
and Bowers reveal no substantive textual cruxes. Arguments based
on spelling and vocabulary also confirm the integrity of the text.
George Coffin Taylor's analysis of Marlowe's characteristic use of
the word 'now' to begin lines and speeches shows that revision by
Heywood or anyone else is unlikely.[12] Robert Welsh likewise maintains that spelling evidence weakens the case for any revision by
Heywood.[13] Similarly, looking at certain colloquialisms and con-
tractions common in some authors after 1600, D. J. Lake confirms
that Heywood's hand is not visible in the text of *The Jew of Malta*,
although he suggests that Thomas Dekker introduced some of his
own stylistic mannerisms when copying the text at the beginning
of the seventeenth century.[14] The conclusions of modern editors
concerning the underlying text from which the 1633 Quarto was
printed similarly confirm the text's integrity. Bowers believes that
the underlying manuscript was likely the promptbook or a transcript of the promptbook, while Leo Kirschbaum, Richard Van
Fossen and Bawcutt suggest that the text is based on an authorial
or scribal manuscript.[15]

Strangely, the question of why Heywood and Vavasour would
have chosen, respectively, to perform and publish such an old play
has not been much discussed until the present day. Earlier critics
such as Bakeless perceived that the long gap in time might have
motivated Heywood to spruce up 'the quaint text of an earlier day'
for the 'up-to-date seventeenth-century audience at the court of

Charles I' (331). Bawcutt, although he defends the text's integrity, hears an apologetic tone in Heywood's Prologue and Epilogue for the court performance, 'as though the play was now regarded as old-fashioned and unlikely to appeal to Charles I and his courtiers'. He assumes that Heywood felt that 'it still had some popularity for less sophisticated audiences' (p. 2). However, very recently the argument has been advanced that there was a point to the revival, and that Charles and the court were indeed the intended audience. John Parker proposes that because of its age, *The Jew of Malta*'s revival and publication was a way of safely protesting against the Catholic sympathies of Charles I, while Zachary Lesser argues that Nicholas Vavasour, the publisher, would have seen it as addressing current theological controversies in line with his pro-Laudian sympathies.[16]

Sources

Unlike Marlowe's other plays, for which specific historical or literary sources can be identified, *The Jew of Malta* is essentially original with Marlowe, who drew on material from a wide variety of sources. Nine such sources or analogues for *The Jew of Malta* are reprinted in Vivien Thomas and William Tydeman's *Christopher Marlowe: The Plays and their Sources*.[17] However, as Bawcutt emphasizes, 'Marlowe often made comparatively brief use in the play of a plot-incident, historical event, or idea which can be repeatedly paralleled in earlier writers, so that it is impossible to say confidently that he followed any particular version' (p. 4). In Gill's judgement, the hunt for sources has primarily served to 'confirm the originality of Marlowe's invention' (p. xi). The play obviously draws on historical events such as the siege of Malta and alludes to the Turkish siege of Rhodes, but Marlowe freely adapts the history to his dramatic purposes. Malta, for example, did not pay tribute to the Turks, and the statement that 'not a man survived' was not true of the defenders of Rhodes (Bawcutt, *Jew*, p. 5). What Marlowe may have known about Malta itself is an intriguing question. Gill is convinced that 'Marlowe seems to have known a lot about the island of Malta, its geography, and its recent history' (pp. ix–x). Lisa Hopkins concurs, arguing 'that *The Jew of Malta* is informed by a very precise set of perceptions of the island and its role in the history of Europe and of Christendom, and that where it does actually deviate from historical truth it does so in the service of a very specifically formulated aesthetic, representational and political agenda'.[18]

A model for Barabas may have been Joseph Nasi, an extremely wealthy Jew who became an influential figure in the court of the Turkish emperor Selim II, who made him Duke of Naxos, a conquered Christian island. The similarities to Barabas were pointed out by Leon Kellner in 1887, and in 1929 Ethel Seaton identified sources from which Marlowe could have learned of Nasi.[19] Other wealthy and notorious Jews have been suggested as models for Barabas, such as David Passi and Alvaro Mendes, but Bawcutt notes that the parallels are fewer and that he has 'not discovered any printed allusions to them early enough for Marlowe to have read' (pp. 8–9). Other possible sources for aspects of *The Jew of Malta* include Anne Dowriche's narrative poem *The French History*, in which Randall Martin discerns parallels between Dowriche's Catherine de Medici and Marlowe's Machevill and Barabas as well as his Guise in *The Massacre at Paris*. He suggests that Dowriche's Catherine can be seen as the prototype for the stage Machiavel, a creation usually credited to Marlowe.[20] News pamphlets were clearly a source of inspiration for Marlowe when he wrote *The Massacre at Paris*. In one such pamphlet William Harrison finds several suggestive details that could relate to *The Jew of Malta*, including disguise, poisoned nuns and poisoned flowers.[21] More recently, Michael Brennan has identified two previously unexamined English newsletters describing the siege of Malta which would still have been in circulation or in libraries in the 1590s.[22] Other reading may also have affected Marlowe. H. D. Purcell perceives a number of parallels indicating that Marlowe's conception of Barabas was influenced by George Whetstone's *English Myrror*.[23] Bawcutt observes that Foxe's *Acts and Monuments* relates an incident where Christians lured Turkish soldiers into a monastery outside the city and blew it up (p .4). Kocher looks at a well-known poisoning episode in sixteenth-century legal history in which one Richard Rose or Rouse poisoned the porridge served to the Bishop of Rochester's household, killing 17 members of the Bishop's family as well as a large number of alms seekers. This incident led to the passing of a law in which the penalty for poisoning was being boiled to death. Since *The Jew of Malta* uses both the crime and the penalty, but at different points in the play, Kocher sees not only a source, but deduces that the depictions of the poisoned nuns and the death of Barabas were written by the same author, another sign of the play's textual integrity.[24] Finally, *The Jew of Malta* is richly informed by the Bible, by Machiavelli and by Marlowe's use of Jewish stereotypes, each of which requires separate discussion.

The Bible

Recognition and appreciation of Marlowe's biblical knowledge and its role in *The Jew of Malta* steadily increased during the twentieth century. Bakeless, writing in the 1940s, held that this play provides the clearest evidence of Marlowe's biblical reading, pointing simply to his use of the Book of Job when depicting Barabas's behaviour in adversity (pp. 354–6). James Sims' *Dramatic Uses of Biblical Allusion in Marlowe and Shakespeare* identifies a threefold pattern of reversal in Marlowe's use of biblical allusions in *Doctor Faustus* and *The Jew of Malta*, noting that Marlowe will give the words of a righteous person to an evil person, show a character espousing values which are the opposite of those in the passage alluded to or alter the meaning of the passage quoted.[25] A more massive compendium, R. M. Cornelius's *Christopher Marlowe's Use of the Bible* concludes that Marlowe believed in Christianity, that his biblical references are careful and accurate, and that his plays reflect Christian truths. Cornelius identifies over a thousand biblical references in Marlowe's works, including 157 in *The Jew of Malta*.[26] Sara Deats re-examines the play's allusions to Scripture and demonstrates 'Marlowe's use of Biblical parody both as a

strategy for uniting the disparate sequences of the play and as a
pointer to the typological norms underlying the play's satire on
the mercantile and Machiavellian *zeitgeist* of Malta'.[27] Exploring
the effect that the Calvinist doctrine of election had on the expectations of the Elizabethan audience and the evolution of tragedy,
Martha Tuck Rozett's *The Doctrine of Election and the Emergence of
Elizabethan Tragedy* shows that Marlowe focuses on issues that are
ambiguous in a Calvinistic context, or about which his audience
might feel apprehension. She suggests that there would have been
a kind of dualism in the audience's response to Barabas because
'In an age which equated heroism with bold action and viewed the
elect as resolute and unyielding, the revenger's decision to take
action was an ambiguous one indeed'.[28] Finally, two interesting
studies explore antecedents for specific moments in *The Jew of
Malta*. First, Catherine Brown Tkacz relates the pit containing
a cauldron which Barabas has prepared for Calymath to the Old
Testament's seven references to someone falling into a pit he had
prepared for another, showing that in the history of biblical commentary the image of the pit had become linked to three of the specific crimes committed by Barabas: murder, fraud and betrayal.[29]
Secondly, Ruth Hanusa discerns that Barabas's aside while talking
to Lodowick, 'but ere he shall have her, / I'll sacrifice her on a pile
of wood' (2.3.52–3), alludes to Jephthah's sacrifice of his daughter
in Judges 11 rather than to Abraham's sacrifice of Isaac.[30]

Marlowe and Machiavelli

An important and much debated question in Marlovian criticism
over the last century has been whether Marlowe himself knew
the difference between the opinions he attributed to Machevill in
the opening Prologue and the actual opinions of Machiavelli, the
Florentine philosopher, social scientist and patriot. In 1897 Edward
Meyer promulgated the idea that English anti-Machiavellianism
derived from Innocent Gentillet's *Contre-Machiavel*, a work which
was written in 1576 to discredit Machiavelli and which greatly
distorted him.[31] Meyer perceived numerous points of Marlowe's

indebtedness to Gentillet, and his argument proved highly influential. Bakeless's discussion of the *Jew of Malta*, for example, relies on Meyer (347–53), and while H. M. Bennett thought that Marlowe knew both Machiavelli and Gentillet, he accepted that most of the material for *The Jew of Malta* derived from the latter.[32] Meyer's thesis was supplanted when Mario Praz in 1928 and Felix Raab in 1964 demonstrated that Elizabethan access to Machiavelli's works was much greater than once thought.[33] Irving Ribner argued that 'There is ample evidence that Machiavelli's own writings were widely read in sixteenth-century England, both in the original and in excellent translations, and we know that in many quarters his ideas were highly respected'.[34] He saw Marlowe closely following Machiavellian ideas in *Tamburlaine*, but not in *The Jew of Malta*. He proposed instead that Barabas, the stage 'Machiavel' popularized by Marlowe and Kyd, descended from Seneca and the morality Vice, and not from Machiavelli. Bawcutt complicated the argument in 1970 in a survey of writings about Machiavelli that could have been (but not necessarily were) known to Marlowe. Rather than finding a simple dichotomy between Machiavelli and the popular stage 'Machiavel', Bawcutt insists on the complexity of the sixteenth-century understanding of Machiavelli, emphasizing that 'we are not forced to choose between Machiavelli on the one side and his opponents on the other as sources for Elizabethan knowledge'.[35] However, he does maintain that 'There is little evidence in *The Jew of Malta* to indicate clearly that Marlowe had a first-hand knowledge of Machiavelli's writings' (p. 33). Paul Kocher also finds nothing in the play that resembles anything actually written by either Machiavelli or Gentillet.[36]

If Marlowe's knowledge of Machiavelli thus seems highly feasible, although not entirely provable, what should be made of his engagement, or lack of engagement, with Machiavellian ideas in *The Jew of Malta*? Early in the twentieth century Una Ellis-Fermor felt certain that Marlowe knew Machiavelli's *The Prince*, and that it appealed to him because of Machiavelli's 'vigilant cynicism' and 'the sinister cold-bloodedness' of his book (93). In short, what appealed to Marlowe was not Machiavelli's ideas but 'his

undeviating independence of spirit', with which Marlowe imagi-
natively identified (p. 92). She thought that Marlowe's infatuation
with Machiavelli lessened as he moved towards *Edward II*. Armed
with a better understanding of sixteenth-century Machiavellian
thought and Marlowe's canon, and possessed of a less Romantic
view of Marlowe's mind, Antonio D'Andrea's analysis of *Jew
of Malta*'s Prologue concludes that Marlowe had no particular
interest in Machiavelli's political reasoning or doctrines 'apart
from the use that could be made of them in the theatre'.[37] He was
concerned only with the stage impact of the speech that he gave to
Machevill. Also focusing on dramaturgical effectiveness, Howard
Babb argues that the play is an 'artistic whole' and that its emphasis on 'policy' contributes to its unity. He notes that the loaded
term appears 13 times, serving as a running critique of the play's
portrayal of 'religious hypocrisy and governmental expedience'.[38]
More recent criticism tends to find a deeper engagement with
Machiavellian doctrine, and judges that Marlowe is not simply
reflecting Machiavellian thought, but responding to it critically.
Catherine Minshull finds that although Machevill introduces
Barabas as one of his favoured disciples, his behaviour diverges
widely from the description of Machiavellianism actually given
in the Prologue. In this she sees one of Marlowe's large-scale
structural ironies: he plays with his audience's expectations, 'not
only by introducing a character to them as a "Machiavellian" who
turns out to be profoundly uninterested in Machiavellian political and military theory, but also by presenting them unexpectedly
with a real Machiavellian in the character of Ferneze'. However,
she observes that *The Jew of Malta* helped to establish the stereotype of the Machiavel because 'Marlowe's audience mistook
his caricature of a Machiavellian villain for the real thing'.[39] Luc
Borot argues that despite the way Machiavelli is portrayed in the
Prologue, *The Jew of Malta* reveals Marlowe's direct knowledge of
his theories: the play's various rulers and aspirants to rule reflect
the full range of Machiavelli's considerations concerning monarchy, aristocracy and democracy: 'The play repeats Machiavelli's
judgment that the three forms of regime are equal; but Marlowe

is convinced that they are equally evil.' Hence, Malta becomes 'a parody of the ideal forms of government dreamt of by the humanists'.[40] Carol Heffernan suggests that Marlowe identified with Machiavelli's idealistic aspirations and 'critical, analytic impulse which led to the questioning of orthodox creeds and standards'.[41] She uses Barabas as a vehicle for criticizing religious and ethical values and shows him longing to separate himself from the corrupt world which he disdains. However, Marlowe does not endorse this separation: it does society no good and the play shows Barabas's deterioration – 'There is no exit from the corruption of Malta' (p. 107). Bob Hodge analyses Marlowe's interpretation of Machiavelli from a Marxist perspective. He finds that Barabas, Ferneze and Calymath all 'make mistakes which Machiavelli specifically discusses, and all suffer the consequences which Machiavelli predicted'.[42] However, Marlowe's more radical critique sees economic classes where Machiavelli saw only the political classes of ruler and ruled, and in such scenes as Barabas's conflation of his daughter and his gold, Marlowe explores 'the psychic consequences of the reduction of human relationships to a system of commodities' (p. 18).

Jewish Stereotypes and Anti-Semitism

The question of a Jewish presence in Elizabethan London was long fraught with contention. Many prominent Victorian historians denied that there were any Jews in England at that time, perhaps in part from a too credulous reading of the early chronicle histories, but perhaps also from anti-Semitism and a concern for the purity of England's Anglo-Saxon heritage. James Shapiro's *Shakespeare and the Jews* provides a judicious overview of what we now know about the Jewish population of Renaissance England and early modern English attitudes towards Jews. Although Jews had officially been expelled from England in the thirteenth century, Shapiro shows that many aspects of the Expulsion, including its date, the numbers affected and the reasons for it, are less clear-cut than was once thought.[43] Moreover, 'archival research over the past hundred years makes it clear that small numbers of Jews began drifting back into England almost immediately after the Expulsion, and began to arrive in larger numbers during the Tudor period' (p. 62). By Marlowe's day the Jewish population included a small London community of 80 or 90 Portuguese *Marranos* or *Conversos* (p. 72). The entire Jewish population was not large. Shapiro finds that the total number of Jews in Marlowe's England fluctuated but was 'probably never more than a couple of hundred at any given time in the whole country' (p. 76). Still, he concludes that 'Elizabethans curious about Jewish practices would not have had far to seek in London to speak with those raised as Jews' (p. 70). Certainly Bakeless, in the mid-twentieth century, was convinced that both Marlowe and Shakespeare must have known practicing Jews, for while he sees Barabas and Shylock as villains, he also sees them as possessed of 'family affection, a habit of quoting the Old Testament, clannishness, religious strictness, and dietary observances', traits which would be observed in actual individuals (362). Wilbur Sanders, in contrast, insists that 'The Jews known to have been present in sixteenth- and seventeenth-century London were prosperous merchants, some of them trained advisors of the government, and in no significant way related to the Shylocks and Barabas's of the stage'. Rather, he thinks that the stereotypical portrayal of these characters was 'unconstrained by the facts of experience'.[44] Peter Berek determines that Marranism is the form of Jewishness that most strongly influenced the drama of the 1590s, for Marranos 'are plausible representations of the idea that identity is not stable and can be created by individuals themselves'.[45] However, he goes on to argue that while Marlowe's own interest may have been sparked by the self-fashioning of the Marrano, the source of the hostile Jewish portraits in subsequent Elizabethan drama is Barabas and not Elizabethan social and religious history. The play may ironically show that the Christians are no better than Barabas, but 'for Marlowe, unlike his predecessors, the Jewishness of Barabas is part of the essence of his evil, and not just an accidental accompaniment. Barabas is monstrous because he is a Jew; other villains are evil insofar as they are like him' (p. 137). Certainly the large nose characterizing the stage Jew and other usurers seems to have started with Marlowe's Barabas.[46] Modern productions often seek ways to respond to this anti-Semitism, a process that began when Edmund Kean played Barabas at Drury Lane in 1818, the first English revival since the seventeenth century. The script was adapted by Samson Penley, who strove to lessen Barabas's cruelty and who added a Prologue denying any intention 'To cast opprobrium o'er the Hebrew name'.[47] As Thomas Dabbs notes, the decision was in line with the then current tendency to portray Jews sentimentally rather than anti-Semitically, a change that perhaps reflected London's changing demographics: 'The population expansion in London included, by the end of the eighteenth century, the arrival of twenty thousand Jews from the Continent, most of whom were destitute'.[48] An interesting late-twentieth-century response is Stevie Simkin's production which used a frame play to depict Nazi soldiers and interned Jews producing Marlowe's play in Warsaw, 1939. For Simkin, 'Our ability to recognize Marlowe's Jew as a constructed one – and to retain that awareness as we track his progress through the play, may open a new perspective on the play's anti-Semitism' and allow us to 'find space to re-appropriate *The Jew of Malta* to challenge rather than simply to reinforce racial stereotype and prejudice'.[49]

Critics have frequently suggested that Marlowe did not use 'Jew' in a modern sense. Reading *The Jew of Malta* in the context of the morality tradition, Douglas Cole observes that 'For the Christian of the Elizabethan age, as for the Christian of centuries previous, "Jew" and "Turk" were familiar epithets applied not only to opponents of Christianity but also to those Christians who acted as the non-Christian was imagined to behave'.[50] Barabas is literally a Jew, but he is also a 'Jew' in this figurative sense, characterized, by 'greed, egoism, infidelity, and worldliness', as are 'most of the characters in the play' (Cole, p. 134). G. K. Hunter goes much further in asserting that for Marlowe 'Jew' was a moral or theological category rather than a racial or ethnographic one.[51]

The 'Jew' is one who chooses worldly values above Christian ones, and Hunter sees Marlowe as using the theological ironies of his portrayal of Barabas to condemn the hypocrisy of the Christians (p. 235). Alan C. Dessen also observes that the sixteenth century could understand Jewishness as referring not to race or religion so much as to a spiritual or moral condition. He demonstrates that Robert Wilson's *Three Ladies of London*, Marlowe's *The Jew of Malta* and Shakespeare's *The Merchant of Venice* use this understanding, as personified in the stage Jew, as a means of challenging 'the professions of supposedly Christian London or Malta or Venice'.[52]

One does not, of course, have to abandon more literal notions of Jewishness or anti-Semitism to argue that the play indicts others besides the Jews. Jean-Marie Maguin finds that *The Jew of Malta* is deeply anti-Semitic and that 'Marlowe, through his play, offers an excellent instance of the complementarity between ideological prejudice and racial hatred'.[53] However, he notes in conclusion that Marlowe's sarcasm applies to all groups in Malta, and may even be self-reflexive, especially in the play's linking of Barabas and atheism. Likewise, Charles Peavy acknowledges the stereotypical anti-Semitism of Marlowe's portrayal of Barabas, but interprets the play as being primarily a satiric attack on Catholicism.[54] Discussing Marlowe's influence on Shakespeare, Thomas Cartelli argues against those who see *The Merchant of Venice* as anti-Semitic with positively portrayed Christians, noting that while Marlowe's play may not be free from anti-Semitism, it dissolves cultural differences in the common desire for gold and shows how Ferneze's 'duplicity relativizes and, finally, neutralizes the viciousness of Barabas'.[55] Referencing Marx, Stephen Greenblatt also perceives that Marlowe finds the figure of the Jew to be useful as 'an embodiment for a Christian audience of all they loathe and fear, all that appears stubbornly, irreducibly different'.[56] For Greenblatt, Marlowe never relinquishes this anti-Semitic stereotype or Barabas's conventional role as a villain who undoes himself, but the hostility he excites is directed against Christian society. The world of Malta is 'hag-ridden by the power of money and given over to the slave market' (p. 205). Jerry Philips similarly draws on Marx to explore 'the complex relationship between the trope of cannibalism, the economics of capitalism, and the poetics of the literary text'. [57] In *The Jew of Malta* and *The Merchant of Venice*, he finds that 'the demonization of the Jewish merchant/usurer provides a grammar of images – eloquent of disease, malign intelligence, disguise, temptation, and conspiracy – which (even in our time) overtly and covertly informs the rhetoric of anti-capitalism' (p. 199). David H. Thurn perceives that *The Jew of Malta* 'raises in an exemplary way the vexing question of how best to theorize the mutual determination of the economic and cultural spheres in early modern England'.[58] He finds that the play both depicts aspects of the prehistory of capitalism and suggests the limitations of the containment and exchange models used by new historicism and its critics to explain its ideological effects. A part of the ideological currency upon which Marlowe draws is the popular, stereotypical image of the Jew (p. 164). Daryl W. Palmer, by looking at writings by merchants in Richard Hakluyt's *Principal Navigations*, discovers connections between cultural categories that 'we assume to be distinct, such as commerce and ethnicity, people and things, documentation and performance'.[59] He observes that 'Marlowe endows his villainous merchant with immoderation and comic excrescence bred in the confines of the morality tradition', but 'that Barabas himself asks his listeners to think about Jews as a distinct group with its own ethnic version of political desire: "I must confesse we come not to be Kings"' (p. 49). Finally, Lloyd Edward Kermode envisions Barabas, like other figures of the male Jew in the drama of the 1590s, as 'an outsider, a stranger, an objective commentator and subversive critic, willing to fight against the sociopolitical system represented on the stage'.[60] He connects the dramatic effectiveness of such characters with the siting of the theatres outside the city walls, arguing that their location both intensifies the drama's potentiality for subversive damage while cushioning the city from its influential power (p. 215).

The Jew of Malta and *The Merchant of Venice*

Parallels are often discerned between *The Jew of Malta* and Shakespeare's *The Merchant of Venice*. Much of this scholarship focuses on Shakespeare rather than Marlowe, explicating the ways in which the earlier work may have served as a source for or been an influence on *The Merchant of Venice*. However, a number of interesting studies have examined the two plays comparatively. Early in the century William Poel proposed that while Barabas and Shylock share many similarities, the two plays differ markedly in their depictions of Christianity. Marlowe, he asserts, 'attacks Christianity wantonly and aggressively, not only by portraying Barabas's contempt for the Christians, but by making the Christians contemptible in themselves'.[61] *The Merchant of Venice* is Shakespeare's rebuttal of this vision of Christianity. Writing a half century later, Irving Ribner perceives no direct relationship between the two plays. Rather, he observes that comparing the two provides insight 'into the vast gulf which divides the two major Elizabethan dramatists'.[62] The difference is that between love and affirmation and hatred and negation: 'Shakespeare's play involves a conflict between gold, the evanescent, meaningless value of this world, and love, the permanent value of heaven, and in this conflict it is love that triumphs, whereas in Marlowe's play love – in the fidelity of Abigail, and in Barabas' need for companionship – breeds only greater destruction' (p. 47). Arthur Humphreys argues that both plays interrogate society's motives: 'Marlowe sees these, apart from some redeeming gleams in minor characters, as the manipulation of power, wealth being its sinews and intrigue its method. Shakespeare's interpretation is quite different. *The Merchant of Venice* celebrates human goodness, not uncritically, for no unblemished world exists, yet responding movingly to what goodness can be among men and women'.[63]

Michael Echeruo maintains that both plays are anti-Semitic in the theological sense discussed above and asks how it could be otherwise, since the creative imagination is 'conditioned by the expectations of its audience'. Even if a play questions or rejects these implications, it 'cannot escape addressing itself to' them.[64] That the play would have been seen as anti-Semitic underlies Margaret Hotine's speculation that political influence was behind the revival of *The Jew of Malta* in 1594. Recalling Essex's sponsorship of a *Richard II* revival the day before his rebellion, she observes that Dr Lopez's troubles may not have been known outside of court circles prior to 5 February, but the revival occurred on 4 February. Essex, who was pushing the case against Lopez even though the Queen was reluctant to pursue it, may have believed that the revival would generate popular support. She also speculates that the play's next revival, in 1596, may have fanned the anti-Semitism created by the Lopez trial and that *The Merchant of Venice* is a 'counterblast' to this anti-Semitism.[65]

Maurice Charney argues that '*The Merchant of Venice* is so radically different from *The Jew of Malta* because Shakespeare was so intensely aware of his powerful rival: 'Without directly imitating Marlowe, he is attempting to surpass him in writing a tragic-comic play about an overweening Jew. Shakespeare tempers Marlowe's splendid rhetoric with a wide variety of unheroic, wheedling, and malicious touches that make Shylock less grand than Barabas but more dramatically compelling. On his side, Marlowe was trying to discover in Shakespeare a more theatrical, more character-oriented, and less rhetorical way of writing plays'.[66] James Shapiro also probes Shakespeare's engagement with Marlowe as a literary rival. He views Shakespeare as using a strategy of containment in which he attempts 'to evoke, then reject and exclude what he borrows from Marlowe'.[67] Although he had earlier made use of *The Jew of Malta* in writing *Titus Andronicus* and *Richard III*, Shapiro asserts that Shakespeare does not successfully contain Marlowe's influence in *The Merchant of Venice*. Rather, Marlowe's work 'threatens to expose the limitations of Shakespeare's art' (pp. 107–8). Belmont is revealed to be much like Venice, collapsing distinctions as they are collapsed in *The Jew of Malta*: '*The Merchant* is thus much more Marlovian than its Romantic plot would lead us to believe, especially in its capacity to invite doctrinal readings while subverting the religious, judicial, social, and economic practices and ideologies upon which those doctrines are founded' (p. 109).

The Roots of Modern Criticism

Tastes in drama and literature inevitably change, and as John Shawcross comments, the ethos of seventeenth-century theatre and poetic was 'antithetical to that of the Elizabethan age'.[68] By the late seventeenth century Marlowe was not only out of fashion but largely forgotten. The sole Restoration edition of any of Marlowe's plays was the 1663 quarto of *Doctor Faustus*, which interestingly incorporates a new scene that uses material from *The Jew of Malta*.[69] The next printing of a Marlowe play did not occur until 1744, when *Edward II* was included in Robert Dodsley's *Old Plays*, 'the first extensive and comprehensive collection of old plays in English history' and 'perhaps the single most important event in the critical rediscovery of Renaissance drama' (Dabbs, p. 25). In 1780, a full century and a half after its initial publication, Isaac Reed, the editor of the second edition of *Old Plays*, added *The Jew of Malta* to the collection (Dabbs, p. 27). Unfortunately, the biographical information then available reflected Thomas Beard's description of Marlowe's scurrility and blasphemy, Antony Wood's allegation that Marlowe had died in a brawl over a serving woman, and the accusations found in the Baines note, which had been published by Joseph Ritson in 1782.[70] Hence, despite a growing appreciation of his work, Marlowe's presumed lifestyle made him 'far too socially unacceptable for his works to gain public approval from established scholars or critics' (Dabbs, p. 30).

The situation altered in the early nineteenth century and critics began to speak openly of Marlowe's poetic and dramatic strengths. Charles Lamb included generous extracts from Marlowe in his *Specimens of English Dramatic Poets who Lived about the Time of Shakespeare*, and William Hazlitt paid tribute to Marlowe in his 'Lectures chiefly on the Dramatic Literature of the Age of Elizabeth'.[71] Marlowe's plays began to appear in other play collections, and in 1818 *The Jew of Malta* was adapted for performance on the London stage, the first production of Marlowe in a century and a half. His literary rehabilitation is both manifest and solidified by the appearance of William Pickering's three-volume edition of Marlowe's *Works*, whose unsigned preface praised Marlowe as 'the only pre-Shakespearean poet to make "an impression upon the hearts of the audience"' and praising the purity of his poetic inspiration. In roughly a decade, as Dabbs observes, Marlowe had been transformed from a debauched atheist to 'Kit' Marlowe, whose 'familiar appellation' could be seen 'as evidence of a kind disposition, or a companionable nature' (pp. 47–8).

By the mid-nineteenth century, James Broughton, John Payne Collier and Alexander Dyce had indeed begun to uncover a more accurate portrait of Marlowe's biography, although many of their findings 'were ignored, overlooked, or distorted in some way by historians, teachers, and critics who were pressed by larger theoretical or ideological concerns' (Dabbs, p. 51). The ideological pressure affecting public and scholarly impressions of Marlowe arose from two conflicting trends in mid- to late-Victorian thought. The first was the identification of Marlowe with the excesses and idealism which the Victorians attached to Romantic thought. Writers such as A. C. Swinburne, J. A. Symonds and Havelock Ellis saw Marlowe as a rebel and free thinker or sceptic, driven as Symonds said, by 'l'amour de l'impossible'.[72] The second trend grew out of the Victorian efforts to educate the middle and working classes, a movement which required a morally solid canon. One result of the need to see Marlowe as a morally affirming writer was the ascendancy of *Doctor Faustus*. Earlier in the century precedence had been given to *Edward II* and *The Jew of Malta*. However, teaching these plays meant confronting the issues of homosexuality and anti-Semitism, while *Doctor Faustus* could be read as affirming that the wages of sin are death.

The continuing impact of these nineteenth-century assessments of Marlowe on later criticism has been debated. Irving Ribner, assessing the state of Marlowe studies on the occasion of Marlowe's 400th birthday, concluded that 'Modern criticism of Marlowe generally has avoided the excesses of his nineteenth-century Romantic idolators'.[73] Harry Levin, writing on the same occasion, judged that our reading of Marlowe is less naive than it was in the nineteenth century.[74] Millar Maclure, a few years later, concurred that 'critical tools have been sharpened, made more numerous and subtle by accretions from other disciplines, and that this process has effectively undercut that prevailing and stultifying nineteenth-century assumption that the plays and poems are wholly expressions of the personality of their maker' (p. 23). However, the still later criticism of Dabbs and Kenneth Friedenreich emphasizes that the Victorian construction of Marlowe continues to colour modern interpretations of Marlowe.[75] Both critics urge the necessity of freeing ourselves from these nineteenth-century perceptions.

Romanticism and Savage Farce

The influence of the nineteenth-century construction of Marlowe on twentieth-century Marlowe criticism of *The Jew of Malta* is particularly evident in the vision of Marlowe as a highly subjective artist who projects his own scepticism and intellectual frustrations into his plays. Una Ellis-Fermor, the most prominent early-twentieth-century exponent of this Romantic perspective, sees the plays as mirrors of Marlowe's own rebellious mind. For her, *The Jew of Malta* is where 'we begin to recognize in Marlowe the man whose trenchant exposure of shams is revealed in the document known as the Baines libel' (p. 97). As discussed above, her perspective colours her perception of the integrity of the text, for not distinguishing between Marlowe and his protagonist and reading the initial portrayal of Barabas as one truly 'framed of finer mould than common men' (line 1.2.223) makes it difficult, if not impossible, to correlate the opening with the comic intrigue of the later acts. With modifications, this notion of the subjectivity of Marlowe's drama persists throughout the century. By the mid-century it is evident in Paul Kocher's *Christopher Marlowe*, which adjudges him to be 'one of the most highly subjective playwrights of his age' (p. 4) and finds *The Jew of Malta* to be 'a criticism of Christian life and principles' (p. 120). Harry Levin's magisterial *The Overreacher*, a title that alludes both to Marlowe's 'style, which is so emphatically himself', and to his protagonists, takes Marlowe criticism in new directions, but retains a sense of Marlowe as rebel.[76] At the century's end both Stephen Greenblatt's seminal *Renaissance Self-Fashioning* and Ian McAdam's *The Irony of Imagination* argue that 'Marlowe is deeply implicated in his heroes'.[77]

A radically different understanding of the play's dynamic appeared early in the century. In a brief essay on Marlowe's use of blank verse, T. S. Eliot describes the play as misunderstood and says that it should be perceived as farce rather than tragedy – farce being not the 'enfeebled humour' of his own day, but 'the terribly serious, even savage comic humour' found in Dickens and Ben Jonson's *Volpone*.[78] Resistance to Eliot's suggestion persisted throughout the first half of the century.[79] H. S. Bennett's 1931 edition of *The Jew of Malta*, for example, dismissively finds that 'This view seems to postulate considerable powers of detachment from contemporary taste and practice on the part of Marlowe' (p. 17) and M. C. Bradbrook curtly concludes that it fails to explain the play's obvious change of tone after the second act.[80] However, as textual criticism demolished the idea of a corrupt text, criticism became 'more sympathetic to Eliot's view of the play'.[81] Thus, M. M. Mahood's thesis that Marlowe's plays record the disintegration of humanism straightforwardly defines *The Jew of Malta* as a savage farce. Levin urges that the play be accepted as an artistic whole and lauds Eliot's connection of the play's grotesqueries with those of *Volpone*, and Erich Segal interprets *The Jew of Malta*'s farce as comic *Schadenfreude*.[82]

The Later Twentieth Century

Marlowe studies blossomed in the second half of the twentieth century, both in quantity and in variety of critical approaches.[83] Recognition of *The Jew of Malta* as ironic comedy rather than as failed tragedy was reinforced by identification of Barabas with the Vice figure of the morality drama. Acknowledging the cogency of

Eliot's classification, Bernard Spivack maintains in *Shakespeare and the Allegory of Evil* that 'The play is racked by its seriocomic extremes because on the one hand, through the genius of its author, it presses towards the heights of Elizabethan tragedy; on the other, through its chief figure, it inherits the "tragical mirth" of the morality drama'.[84] Spivack's focus on the morality roots of the Elizabethan drama is also seen in Douglas Cole's *Suffering and Evil in the Plays of Christopher Marlowe* and David Bevington's *From Mankind to Marlowe*, both appearing in 1962 but drawing quite different conclusions.[85] For Cole, Marlowe's plays are religiously orthodox, reflecting both Marlowe's theological training and the religious perspective of the moralities, and Barabas is an incarnation of evil. Bevington discerns that Marlowe's debts to the moralities are to dramatic structure rather than theology. 'The Vice', he finds, 'has been secularized in the person of Barabas', and as the play's 'characteristic ambiguity' derives from its 'combination of secular material and moral structure' (pp. 225, 233). Robert Jones also finds that 'Marlowe uses the morality play's tactics of alienating us from the malicious knave who entertains us'.[86]

The growing perception of *The Jew of Malta* as an artistic whole led critics to seek unifying themes in the play and to look for underlying motivations for Barabas's behaviour. Thus, Nan Cooke Carpenter identifies Barabas's desire for wealth as the main theme of the play. Alan Friedman believes that the play is unified 'by Barabas's decreasing ability to circumscribe events', and Don Beecher sees in the play 'an attempt to revitalize through contemporary modes and idioms the powerful symbolic drama of the Middle Ages'.[87] In *The Overreacher*, Levin suggests that Barabas 'is conscious of being hated and wants to be loved', a thematic idea echoed by a number of critics (p. 78). J. W. Flosdorf identifies love and hate as the structurally unifying themes of the play, Ribner states that 'the source of Barabas' failure' can be found 'in his human need for love', and Bruce Brandt maintains that Barabas, understanding neither, 'is betrayed by his longing for love and by his desire for a stable world'.[88] John Cutts interprets Marlowe's heroes as all, in one way or another, overcompensating for feelings of inadequacy and construes Barabas's infinite riches as 'his compensation for unattainable kingship' and his little room as 'his make-do kingdom'.[89] Dale Priest concludes that Ithamore serves as a dramatic paradigm for Barabas's transformation from villain to fool, a transvaluation that he perceives to be the play's central idea.[90] Psychological criticism, of course, locates the underlying motivations of the protagonist within the playwright. Writing near the century's end, Constance Brown Kuriyama emphasizes Marlowe's homosexuality and asserts that 'Barabas is precisely the kind of hero we might expect Marlowe to turn to once he had abandoned hope of achieving any kind of phallic mastery, and had ceased trying to reconcile his personal goals and ideals with those dictated by his society'.[91] For Matthew Proser, the issue is the way in which aggressiveness disrupts Marlowe's creative process. *The Jew of Malta* marks the point at which 'Marlowe has distanced himself sufficiently from the quandary of his anguish and rage [. . .] to allow his inventiveness to flourish'.[92]

A number of studies in the late sixties and seventies explicated Marlowe's plays in terms of irony or social satire. Reacting against the older notion that the play is disjointed, Eric Rothstein argues that *The Jew of Malta* is skilfully constructed, exploiting thematic parodies of scripture, parent–child relationships, friendship and pastoral. He notes that every character that trusts another is betrayed, including Barabas, who is betrayed by Abigail, Ithamore and Ferneze.[93] Wilbur Sanders challenges historicist readings that confine Shakespeare and Marlowe within the limits of 'Renaissance man' or an 'Elizabethan world picture'. His chapter on *The Jew of Malta* focuses on Marlowe's satiric undercutting of anti-Semitism, Machiavellism and mercantile greed, and complains that Marlowe's 'technique of ironic inversion' imposes limitations 'on the play's grasp of human realities' (p. 43). His humour ultimately succumbs 'to a certain brittle and defensive hardness, which tries to hold the real world, as it were, at arms' length' (59). W. L. Godshalk finds that Marlowe is a severely moral artist whose vision culminates in *The Jew of Malta*. Barabas, like all of Marlowe's protagonists, 'is destroyed [. . .] by the unnatural evil

of which he has become a part'.[94] Charles Masinton discerns that
Marlowe is preoccupied throughout his work with human limitations and corruption, and that *The Jew of Malta* is ultimately 'a
satire against the shameless cant, religious prejudice and affected
virtue of the Christians'.[95] Concentrating on Marlowe's ironic
style, Judith Weil maintains 'that Marlowe mocks his heroes in
a remarkably subtle fashion'.[96] She reads *The Jew of Malta* as an
expanded proverb in the Wisdom tradition and contends that
while 'the follies of Malta are both plausible and amusing', they
are 'calculated to remind the audience of its *own* folly' (p. 49).

Marlowe's questioning of cultural values and ideology remained
a strong component of Marlowe studies in the eighties and nineties.
Stephen Greenblatt's *Renaissance Self-Fashioning*, which inaugurated new historicism, finds that Marlowe's heroes self-consciously
fashion themselves in opposition to authority and that identity in
Marlowe 'is achieved through a subversive identification with the
alien', a pattern most clearly seen in *The Jew of Malta* (p. 203).
Simon Shepherd urges that through their problematizing of theatrical pleasure Marlowe's texts question both 'the values within
conservative nationalist Protestantism' and 'the way that theatre
affirmed these values'.[97] In particular, he sees that *The Jew of Malta*
'deconstructs the ideological positions around nation and religion
in contemporary London' (p. 176). Emily Bartels similarly perceives a subversive questioning of Renaissance England's imperi-
alist self-fashioning in Marlowe's recurrent use of aliens such as
Barabas, a Machiavellian Maltese Jew.[98] Roger Sales looks closely
at the execution of Barabas and finds that 'this ending may have
been provocative, and therefore potentially subversive, because
it encouraged spectators both to recognize and to question the
ways in which power was choreographed on the Elizabethan scaffold'.[99] Reappraising Elizabethan antitheatrical polemics and the
social psychology of the Elizabethan audience, Thomas Cartelli
determines that Elizabethan playgoers sought pleasure rather than
moral enrichment, and that 'In *The Jew of Malta* Marlowe offers
a free-form approach to theatrical representation which encourages the audience's unqualified engagement with the fantasies of

power, play, and moral abandon that he cultivates'.[100] Theatricality and subversion are likewise explored by Darryll Grantley, who views *The Jew of Malta* and *Doctor Faustus* as interrogating 'religious and other terms of power [. . .] by re-producing them as theatrical constructs'.[101] For Clare Harraway, *The Jew of Malta* interrogates the very nature of genre by initially identifying itself as tragedy and 'then proceeding to complicate and to contradict this pronouncement throughout the rest of the play'.[102] Finally, tracing a motif of teasing or tantalization throughout Marlowe's writings, Fred Tromly observes that *The Jew of Malta* subversively links the covetousness stereotypically associated with Jews to the Christians, and then turns 'the idea of Tantalian covetousness against his audience by suggesting that its appetite for moral and theatrical stereotypes [. . .] is itself a manifestation of avarice'.[103]

The last two decades of the twentieth century also brought an interest in feminist approaches to Marlowe. Barbara Baines perceives that Marlowe's plays embody a pattern of suppressing feminine qualities for the sake of achieving a masculine ideal, and that this pattern differs from play to play, becoming more sophisticated as Marlowe matures as an artist. In *The Jew of Malta* and *The Massacre at Paris*, she finds that 'masculine power becomes unmitigated, diabolical aggression'.[104] Jeremy Tambling's exploration of power and patriarchy in *The Jew of Malta* includes comparison to *The Merchant of Venice*. He observes that Abigail is not Machiavellian and that her 'sense of her culture cannot be taken at face value.[105] At issue is sexual difference: the way the woman is constructed within male discourse, the lack of ways in which she can construct herself save through the values of the nunnery, itself thoroughly permeated by the presence of the male' (p. 97). He urges that Malta, 'for the preservation of its ideological character' projects onto Barabas, Abigail and Ithamore 'that which threatens its unity of being and sense of self' (p. 105). He concludes that 'A feminist critique of the play would have to register a fascination with male power and narcissism at its heart, complicit in allowing Abigail her early death (p. 109). For Ren Draya, Abigail's lack of power as a Jew, as a female, and as a daughter exemplifies the silencing of women in Renaissance drama', but that she is none-theless the moral centre of the play. Although courageous, glib and able to dissemble like her father, she is his antithesis. Elizabethans would have found her final conversion sincere and that 'she dies a Christian martyr'.[106]

The Future Beckons

As this brief historical overview has shown, the blossoming of Marlowe studies in the last half of the twentieth century has revealed infinite riches in this little play. Readers and scholars of *The Jew of Malta* have come to appreciate Marlowe's creative engagement with his sources, to understand Marlowe as an ironic artist rather than as a naively subjective writer and to discover that the play richly repays study from the perspective of modern criti-cal approaches. Returning to Machevill's tantalizing request to grace Barabas 'as he deserves', which introduced this chapter, the period between the late eighteenth-century rediscovery of *The Jew of Malta* and the end of the twentieth century has indeed found a play that deserves much grace. That this interest and regard will continue seems highly likely.

TWO

The Performance History

SARA MUNSON DEATS

Few works of literature have been called as many names as
Marlowe's tragical, comical, farcical dramatic hybrid *The Jew of
Malta*. Although the title page of the 1633 quarto proclaims the
work a tragedy – 'The Tragical History of the Rich Jew of Malta' –
the drama conforms to few of the criteria normally associated with
this genre, and the play's farcical and satiric elements are undeniable. Not only genre but also authorship and text, as well as the
nature of both Marlowe's protagonist and his antagonist – Barabas
and Ferneze – have sparked vociferous debate. One of the central
problems concerns Barabas. Many critics have asserted that the
play breaks in half, with the first two acts depicting a potentially
tragic figure in the proud yet abused magnifico of Malta, whereas
the last three acts degenerate into farce. Some commentators even
posit dual authorship to explain this marked disjunction in tone.
Another dilemma concerns the vexing question of the play's anti-
Semitism. Is the drama inescapably anti-Semitic, as some critics
have insisted? Or does the play explode anti-Semitic stereotypes,
revealing the pharisaical Christians to be more rapacious, opportunistic and bigoted than the Jew whom they have stigmatized with
these traits? Clearly, any director undertaking to stage this dramatic conundrum must address these issues and make a number of
crucial decisions concerning genre, tone and characterization.

The Initial Production

The dating of Christopher Marlowe's *The Jew of Malta* is perhaps
the least controversial aspect of this much-debated play. Unless

one posits the Prologue as a belated addition, then Machevill's reference to the death of the Guise on 23 December 1588 establishes the play's *terminus a quo*. Philip Henslowe's first recorded performance of the play at the Rose Theatre on 26 February 1591 sets the play's *terminus ad quem*. Moreover, Machevill's allusion, 'And now the Guise is dead', presenting the assassination of the Guise as a fairly recent event, has led scholars to date the composition of the play between 1589 and 1590.[1] Theatre history affirms that the flamboyant star of the Admiral's Men, Edward Alleyn, played Barabas with a large false nose (and perhaps also a red wig), and textual evidence supports this assumption. Henslowe's record of 36 performances between February 1592 and June 1596, all drawing credible remuneration, validates the popularity of the play;[2] indeed, according to Henslowe's records, the total number of performances would be 'equaled by no other play of Marlowe's, as far as we know', 'although it must be remembered that we have no record of *Edward II* or *Dido*, as these did not belong to Henslowe'.[3] Although Henslowe's detailed records of individual plays cease after 1597, references in his inventory of 1598 to 'a caudern for the Jew' (p. 321) and later in 1601 to 'more things for the Jewe of malta' (p. 170) suggest that the play continued to be performed until the early seventeenth century. Moreover, allusions to the play in later dramas attest to the influence of *The Jew of Malta* on contemporary audiences of the late sixteenth and early seventeenth centuries.[4] However, since Roslyn Knutson's essay in this collection treats the earlier productions of the play in their repertorial context, I will proceed to discuss revivals of the play in the seventeenth, nineteenth and twentieth centuries.

Pre-Twentieth Century Productions

Although *The Jew of Malta* (henceforth referred to as *The Jew)* was entered in the Stationers' Register on 17 May 1594, the earliest extant edition dates to 1633. Two Prologues and an Epilogue added by Thomas Heywood indicate that Queen Henrietta's Company performed the play around 1633 at both the Cockpit

Theatre and the Court. These Prologues also affirm the former popularity of the play 'writ many years agone, / And in that age, thought second unto none' ('The Prologue Spoken at Court', 3–4) and laud the author Marlowe as 'the best of poets in that age' and the star Edward Alleyn, who originally played Barabas, as 'the best of actors' ('The Prologue to the Stage, at the Cockpit', 2, 4). 'The Prologue to the Stage' also identifies Richard Perkins, a popular and versatile performer of the period, as the leading actor impersonating 'Our Jew this day' ('The Prologue to the Stage', 12–13). Both the 'Prologue' and the 'Epilogue' adopt a conventional apologetic tone for presenting such an old-fashioned play, expressing the fear that the play may be 'Too tedious' and may 'wrong' the king's 'princely patience' ('Epilogue', 2, 3).[5] However, John Parker argues that far from being an anachronism, the play was revived because it addressed topical issues, not anti-Semitism, in this case, but rather anti-clericalism. According to Parker, 'the play's typically Tudor attack on monasticism and religious hypocrisy' was adapted to a 'specifically Caroline form of politico-religious dissent'; 'its revival was an attempt [. . .] to use explicitly dated material as a means of contesting publicly [. . .] the increasingly Catholic appearance of Charles's regime'.[6] Apparently Heywood was acutely aware, as many contemporary directors are not, that the play presents not a censure of the Jews but a biting satire of the hypocrisy and materialism of early modern society. Although we have no record of audience response to the revival of Marlowe's tragical black comedy, evidence confirms that the play continued to be performed until the closing of the theatres in 1642 (Bawcutt, p. 3).

After 1642 *The Jew* disappeared from the English stage for over 150 years until its revival by the famous actor/manager Edward Kean. On Passover, 24 April 1818, Kean opened *The Jew* in Drury Lane Theatre to mixed reviews, much condemnation of the play but almost universal praise for Kean's performance and the richly costumed and opulently staged production. The *Times* critic, although deploring the play as a 'tissue of unmingled horror', praised Kean's ability to 'illumine and render tolerable so dark a portrait as that of Barabas',[7] while another reviewer, although censuring the play, lauded the 'wonderful powers' which enabled Kean to 'overbear all obstacles in the production'.[8] From all accounts the Drury Lane revival, featuring a cast of 21 speaking parts, was 'lavishly mounted, with new scenery, dresses, and decorations'. No false nose and red wig for Kean; instead, Barabas wore luxurious robes, and his noble Arab profile and small moustache and beard bestowed an air of nobility. A contemporary print of act IV, scene iv shows T. P. Cook as Pilia Borza 'drinking in raffish doublet and hose with a Pistolian hat decked with tatty feathers', Mr Harley, an impressive Ithamore garbed in an elaborately sashed tunic and Miss Boyce as BellAmira 'resplendent in tiara and eardrops, necklace and pearl bracelet'.[9]

The only play by Marlowe to be revived between 1675 and 1896, *The Jew* initially appears a surprising choice considering the often-virulent censure levelled at the drama by nineteenth-century critics. However, the events of Kean's career offer insight into the actor's decision to stage Marlowe's controversial play. Several years earlier, on 26 January 1814, Kean's debut as a sympathetic, even tragic Shylock catapulted him to stardom; clearly, he sought to recapture this success in his portrait of a tortured and sympathetic Barabas, like his Shylock deformed by society's injustice into a tormented murderer.

To achieve this sanitized Barabas, Marlowe's original script had to be considerably honed and Kean enlisted Samson Penley to purge the more hostile attacks on Barabas and his most offensive actions.[10] The Prologue, in which Machevill identifies Barabas as his chief disciple, became the first victim of Penley's editorial amputation; although many commentators find this Prologue trenchantly ironic in light of the Machiavellian behaviour of all of the Christians and many of the Turks, this irony was evidently lost on Kean and Penley. Barabas's exaggerated catalogue of his villainies was also abbreviated and delivered as an aside intended as a kind of audition of Ithamore for the role of assistant villain, a view endorsed by a number of contemporary critics and strongly approved by the reviewers of Kean's production, one of whom observed: 'Barabas is made (aside) to feign that he has done all this, in order to try Ithamore's disposition. This is a very happy thought; and the answer of Ithamore is not less so'.[11] Most significantly, Penley drastically reduced the body count resulting from Barabas's revenge. Everything related to Barabas's most atrocious acts, his poisoning of the nuns and the murder of his own daughter, ended on the cutting room floor: Abigail died of natural causes, and Barabas expressed appropriate paternal grief at her demise. Moreover, Penley's script omitted all of the farcical tomfoolery with the Friars; Barabas causes the death of only one Friar, strangled offstage by Ithamore. Additionally, Penley replaced Barabas's grotesque plummet into the boiling cauldron with a more dignified death from a volley of shots fired by Maltese troops. Evidently finding the poetry of the Romantic sub-plot uninspiring, Penley purloined language from *Edward II* to romanticize both the scenes between the two lovers, Abigail and Mathias, and those between the two rivals for Abigail's affection, Mathias and Lodowick. Finally, Penley bowdlerized most of the sexual innuendo and with it the caustic satire of Catholic promiscuity and obscenity,[12] thereby expurgating not only the play's savage farce but also its mordent satire of Christian hypocrisy. However, throughout the centuries, commentators have caviled at the disjunction in the play between the tragic first acts and the farcical last ones; for some, therefore, Kean restored the appropriate tone of Marlowe's 'misdirected masterpiece', a tragedy manqué,[13] although, in so doing, he also eliminated the medley of tones that arguably makes *The Jew* such a singular work of art.

What remained was a tragic figure, 'a noble alien monstrously wronged and magnificently revenged', 'a credible member of the human race twisted into a grotesque caricature of villainy by the pressures of society and his own deep-seated sense of injustice' (Smith, p. 10), and Kean played the role to the hilt. Critics found his performance remarkable for its 'striking passages', ranging from the 'fine and sepulchral' tones of his second act lament to his 'absolute delirium of drunken joy' when he recovers his stolen gold to his 'spirit of insatiable revenge'.[14] However, although much ameliorated, to nineteenth-century reviewers Barabas remained 'unnatural', the 'boldest picture of cunning and revenge ever beheld',[15] 'violent, raving, and fiendish'.[16] Thus, Kean's impressive histrionics and Penley's careful pruning proved insufficient to save the production; even whitewashed, Marlowe's scathing satire remained unacceptable to the Romantic sensibility of the nineteenth century and the play closed after eleven performances.[17]

Twentieth-Century Productions[18]

In 1922, the pendulum swung in the opposite direction. The production of *The Jew* at the Phoenix Society, the first professional revival in the twentieth century, offered a reaction to Kean's 1818 interpretation. Perhaps influenced by T.S. Eliot's seminal 1919 essay, which oxymoronically described *The Jew* as a serious, savage farce,[19] director Allen Wade transformed Kean's 'tragedy' into rollicking slapstick. Rejecting the events of the play as incredible and the characters as exaggerated, Wade sought to distance the audience from Marlowe's grotesque fable by presenting the play as 'a monstrous farce, a careless burlesque of human speech and human action',[20] all performed with an 'admirable slickness that left the audience gasping'.[21] This boisterous burlesque stressed the physical action of the play while minimizing characterization, flattening the dramatis personae into stereotypes. According to one reviewer, 'Even the many murders contrived by Barabbas [sic] cannot drag a tear from our eyes, because we do not believe in him or them'.[22] Amid all of this hilarity, Baliol Holloway, 'a rich and picturesque Barabas'[23] 'fought splendidly for his tragedy',[24] but to no avail, as the farcical production reduced the complex portrait of Barabas (part tragic hero, part scheming Machiavel, part comic Vice) into a Satanic 'monster of iniquity',[25] 'a superlatively vindictive villain', who 'howled in harmony with the lines allotted him'.[26] Reviewers praised the able cast, particularly the 'remarkable performance' of Ernest Thesiger as the ragged Ithamore,[27] who savoured some 'sublime moments with that truly admirable woman, Miss Margaret Yarde as Bellamira',[28] as well as the fine acting of Isabel

Jeans, a charming Abigail, whose early death was a heavy loss.[29] Apparently, the play was a rousing success and the audience found everything wildly amusing, guffawing at the poisoning of the nuns and tittering at Barabas's many asides, but amid all of the merriment the corrosive satire of the play was erased. Thus, although the production certainly captured the farcical elements of the play, it neglected the savage, satiric aspects that arguably give the drama its significance. One reviewer observed that the 'house was full of laughter' and 'of such a good laughter that one were a fool to frown upon it'. However, after admitting that 'Ithamore was in all worlds, even Marlowe's own, intended for laughter, and the Jew himself has many a twist of the lip', the reviewer perceptively wondered if the deaths of Abigail, the mourning over Lodowick and Mathias, even the final burning of Barabas, were 'intended to be as amusing as the Phoenix chose to make them'?[30] As James L. Smith observes, both Kean and Wade did Marlowe a disservice: 'Kean squeezed all the tragedy out of his partial reading of the play; the Phoenix left much of Eliot's savage farce untouched [. . .] in each case the performances were justly praised, and the play unjustly damned'(Smith, pp. 211–13).

The production presented by the Marlowe Players at the University of Reading in 1954 appears to have comprehended the satirical intent of the play much better than many professional companies. Ian Calder, Secretary and Treasurer of the Marlowe Players, simultaneously directed and starred in the play. His programme notes explained that 'Marlowe's play deliberately ridiculed while simultaneously exploiting the Elizabethan prejudice against Machiavels and Jews'; Calder further insisted that Ferneze, not Barabas, is the true Machiavel of the play and that all of Barabas's disasters result from his failure to heed Machiavelli's dictums, a view long endorsed by critics.[31] Although, according to the *Times* reviewer, the production achieved a rare unity of purpose, demonstrating that the satirical elements permeate the play from beginning to end, it sacrificed any attempt at psychological realism or sympathy for its hero and reduced Barabas to an 'intentional caricature' of the villain. Ultimately, as with the Phoenix production

30 years earlier, the risible elements prevailed over the satiric, producing a play judged 'uproariously funny' and not much more.[32]

1964 marked the quatercentenary of Marlowe's birth and several productions mounted to honour the occasion sought to reconcile the disparate tragical, comical, farcical modes of the play.

The first of these productions, directed by Donald Bain with Michael Baxter as Barabas, was appropriately staged at The Marlowe Theatre in Canterbury, the playwright's birthplace. Depicting Barabas as 'slightly larger than life', Baxter attempted to harmonize the sympathetic and ludicrous elements of the Jew's character. According to one reviewer, Baxter 'introduced into his reading a deliberate element of ham, but blended it with enough subtlety, enough isolation and love to make him nearly always sympathetic'; another commented that Baxter created a 'magnificent villain', one whom 'the audience took to its heart'.[33] Moreover, sensitive to the satiric elements in the play, one critic suggested that 'Paying lip service to the canons of the day, Marlowe was probably sending up the establishment in much the same way as today's fashion, and creating excellent popular theatre at the same time'.[34] Reviewers praised the highly mobile set and the professional performances not only of Baxter but of John Hollis as Ithamore, Jane Asher as Abigail, and Gillian Martell as the courtesan BellAmira. However, the unfortunate decision to dress Baxter as the traditional Jew with red hair and gabardine degraded Barabas into 'a caricature of avarice and persecution mania', lessening audience empathy, blunting the satirical thrust of the play and reducing what might have been a 'dangerous' evening into only a piece of 'lively entertainment'.[35]

A month later, Peter Cheeseman directed the Victoria Theatre revival at Stoke-on-Trent with Bernard Gallagher starring as Barabas, the dramatist Alan Ayckbourn trebling as Machevill, Del Bosco, and one of the three Jews, and Peter Mason achieving a disarming combination of 'naivety and cunning' as the slave Ithamore.[36] Cheeseman staged the play in the round, employing the simple set and rapid pace of the early modern stage, thereby accommodating Marlowe's tendency to change location in the middle of a scene. Cheeseman denied the disjunctive tone of the play, interpreting it as a precursor of modern 'black comedy', as he stated in his programme notes:

> This is just the kind of humour we can now encompass, the humour of
> the sick joke, and the black comedy. Its mood is extravagant. There is
> violence in the atmosphere, in the subject matter, and in the switchback
> motion from tragedy to comedy within the joke itself. Poisoning a whole
> nunnery with a doped rice pudding is just such a gag.

Within this black comedy, Cheeseman envisioned Barabas as both satirist and target of satire, neither the tragic figure of Kean nor the villainous caricature of the Phoenix Theatre, rather a kind of 'crazy gangster' who gains audience sympathy because of the manifest injustices that he has suffered. Cheeseman insisted, 'When Barabas makes the fateful decision to do evil to those who did [it to] him, we are right behind him'.[37] As the charismatic Barabas, Gallagher received mixed reviews. Peter Roberts of *Plays and* Players praised Gallagher's ability to steer 'a sensible course' between 'tearing a villainous passion to tatters' and 'playing for subdued inward, sardonic comment'.[38] However, other critics objected that although attired in the dignified costume of a successful merchant rather than the stereotypic garb of the stage Jew, Gallagher failed to achieve the desired balance between comic villain and psychologically believable revenger. Although Barabas did experience 'moments of real anguish' in the beginning of the play, his suffering was brief.[39] According to the reviewer for the *Guardian*, 'sweeping around [in] a black cloak like a vulture, cackling like Dracula, licking his chops in exaltation as he succeeds in poisoning an entire nunnery with a mess of pottage' Barabas was reduced to 'a magnificent caricature'.[40] Ultimately, the majority of the critics judged the play more of a 'bloody farce', albeit a genuinely funny one, than the 'black comedy' that Cheeseman clearly intended (Nightingale).

Apparently Clifford Williams, who directed the Royal Shakespeare Company in Marlowe's play, first at the Aldwych Theatre in London in 1964 and later at Stratford-upon-Avon in 1965, achieved greater equipoise in balancing black comedy with satiric bite. The *Times* reviewer relished the 'mixed form' of the play as 'no more than the theatrical camouflage masking the play's real dramatic purpose': Marlowe's use of 'the figure of the Jew to attack hypocrisy in Christian society'. Although admitting that 'No one could accuse Marlowe of painting a flattering portrait of the Machiavellian Jew', the reviewer insisted that throughout the play 'one grows a good deal more fond of him [Barabas] than any other character'.[41] Rejecting the anti-Semitism of the play, another reviewer remarked, 'the only discrimination is against the human race. The Jew is a quadruple-dyed villain [. . .] the Muslims are paltry, extortioners; the Christian gentlemen cowardly swindlers; the monks and nuns lecherous hypocrites'.[42] Hugh Leonard of *Plays and Players* feigned scepticism that such a relevant play could have been written in the sixteenth century, noting 'tongue in cheek': 'The whole play shrieks of the contemporary, and it sends up the stage conventions of the 16th century with a degree of sophistication which simply did not exist in Shakespearean times'.[43] Critics generally praised Clive Revill's ability to encompass Barabas's oxymoronic personae through 'verve and expertise' (Leonard), to be simultaneously sinister and funny,[44] grotesque and credible, 'horrible but loveable', as Williams conceived him.[45] According to Leonard, Revill's portrayal was 'a miracle of control', 'the most remarkable performance to be seen in London' at the time (*Plays and Players*). A number of other actors, at the beginning of memorable careers, received commendation, including Glenda Jackson as a 'delightfully predatory' 'snake-haired courtesan'[46] and 'Ian Richardson as a spell-binding Ithamore, a depraved Ariel, or a Puck smitten with rabies'.[47]

In 1965, Williams restaged the play, honing and tightening the script and recasting some of the principal roles while retaining both Ralph Koltai's highly effective mobile setting in sun-baked Malta and the blend of black comedy and trenchant satire that had made the Aldwych revival such a success. In the new production, Eric Porter, who had already been cast as Shylock in *The Merchant of Venice*, took the title role of Barabas; Peter McEnery replaced Ian Richardson as Ithamore; and Patsy Byrne assumed the part of BellAmira previously played by Glenda Jackson. Williams explained that he had not originally intended to make the two 'Jewish plays' a joint project and that only after the success of *The Jew* in London did he conceive of 'its inclusion in the Stratford season to tie in some ways with the projected *Merchant* revival'. However, from the beginning he had decided to stress the differences rather than the similarities between the two plays.[48] Although Williams's directorial vision remained the same in the two productions, the two actors playing the title role created widely diverse portraits of the Jew of Malta. Clive Revill, attired in simple Jewish gabardine bereft of ornament with a stove-pipe hat, pointed beard and carefully combed dark red hair, embodied the stereotypic portrait of the frugal Jew.[49] Conversely, perhaps to distinguish his Maltese magnifico Barabas from his drab Jewish usurer Shylock, Eric Porter, bejewelled with rings and chains, wore 'an elaborate rich gown', and 'a mantle of thick piled fur' (Smith, p. 20), his opulent costume depicting a man of position and authority. Moreover, Porter combined his 'villainous dignity'[50] with more than a hint of grandeur, through this gravitas creating 'a worthy and potentially tragic representative of a stricken and persecuted race'.[51] Most reviewers found Revill more entertaining, Porter more formidable, but apparently both actors successfully fashioned a multi-faceted portrait of 'a positively endearing person', simultaneously 'totally unprincipled', 'keenly ironic, intelligent, and amusing'.[52] As Charles Landstone commented, even though a murderer and a schemer, 'in a world of rogues, he [Barabas] manages to attract all the sympathies'.[53] Concerning the other cast changes, although reviewers deplored the loss of the 'pure, lyrical line and athletic grace' of Ian Richardson's 'psychotic Ithamore',[54] they cheered Patsy Byrne's 'zestfully wicked'

BellAmira, 'a marvelous parody of provocation run to seed'.[55] Ultimately, reviewers praised the production's ability to balance farce and serious intention, to satirize its satirist 'without blunting the edge of his satire'. As Robert Speaight summarized, although the Jew sinks into his cauldron, 'the arrows of anti-clericism have found their mark, and the Sovereign Order [of Malta] is second to none in the niceties of Realpolitik'.[56]

Perhaps inevitably, reviewers focused on the parallels and contrasts in Williams's Jewish diptych. Clyde Farnsworth of the *New York Times* found the pairing of the two plays effective,[57] whereas the reviewer of the *London Times* deplored the lack of 'organic connection between the two productions'.[58] Clearly, Williams stressed the differences rather than the similarities between *The Jew* and *The Merchant*. Porter portrayed Barabas expansively as a magnificent magnet, power-hungry and intimidating from the very beginning, while depicting Shylock as a shabby Jewish usurer, tormented into vengefulness by the personal and professional threats of the Christians. According to Farnsworth, 'The Stratford audience seemed to enjoy the fire, brilliance, and cynicism of Barabas more than the anguished writhing of Shylock' (*New York Times*). The majority of the critics judged *The Merchant* a competent but not very exciting production of an often-viewed play while lauding *The Jew* as a fascinating foray into black comedy.[59] One reviewer even suggested that 'Shakespeare [was] shown up by Marlowe'.[60]

Despite the success of the 1964 RSC productions, during the next two decades few professional companies attempted to mount this problematic play. However, in 1985 the American Shakespeare Repertory, a dynamic, young off-Broadway group, boldly accepted the challenge. The director Douglas Overtoom presented the drama as an unequivocal satire of political opportunism, religious hypocrisy and anti-Semitism. The cast enacted the drama of betrayal and murder on a bare stage decorated only with raised platforms and large canvas tapestries, the limitations of space enhancing the play's claustrophobic constriction, literally enclosing Marlowe's verbal riches in a little room. The costumes represented a mélange of styles, with Barabas wearing the gray flannel suit of a modern business tycoon, the competing political factions accoutered in the livery of third-world military regimes, the religious orders garbed in traditional habits and BellAmira dressed (or undressed) in the slinky costume of a cabaret singer, with the Weimar Republic nuances reinforced by the beat of German cabaret music. The starkness of the set and the farrago of costumes highlighted the topicality of Marlowe's mordant satire. Paul Rubin enacted the charismatically evil Barabas with panache and zest; the consummate impersonator, his Barabas showed no deterioration, only revelation. As Barabas romped through his various masquerades, moving from grandiose tycoon to wrathful avenger to smirking Vice, the tone of the play modulated to an accompanying key, segueing from trenchant satire to broad farce to music hall burlesque in the bravura boasting match and the BellAmira scenes. The last acts became increasingly vaudevillian, stripping Barabas's death (in an electric chair, not a cauldron) of tragic significance. Overtoom's version presented Ferneze as the authentic Machiavel; Ferneze spoke Machevill's Prologue and at crucial points in the dialogue donned a mask to make patent his 'unseen hypocrisy'. As Ferneze, Roger K. Benhtel gave a fine performance, his controlled and sinister vice contrasting neatly with Barabas's gusto in villainy. In the surprisingly effective BellAmira-Pilia Borza-Ithamore interlude, Overtoom depicted Ithamore as a tatterdemalion Ariel counterbalancing Barabas's infernal Prospero, and his wooing of BellAmira offered a lubricious travesty of courtly love. However, the ASR version was unable to resist the ubiquitous temptation to reduce the play to farce, often submerging Marlowe's subtle ironies in slapstick mirth. Moreover, in order to maintain the tone of dark farce, the production deflated the play's two most admirable characters. The Friar's gross necrophilic abuse of her corpse (the only lapse of taste in the show) rendered laughable the death of Abigail, whereas the play reduced Calymath, the only character in the drama who keeps his word, to a ranting demagogue. Despite these minor flaws, however, the production was undoubtedly a success and I regret that this provocative revival was almost totally ignored by the New York media.[61]

Perhaps buoyed by the successful pairing of *The Jew* and *The Merchant* in 1964, in 1987 the Royal Shakespeare Company again presented the two plays in tandem, although this time with different directors, different casts and different venues (*The Merchant* in the RSC main theatre, *The Jew* in the smaller Swan), rendering the relationship between the two plays tenuous. Even more than its 1965 antecedent, the 1987 revival stressed the satiric elements of the play. Sensitive to the 'functional ambiguity' of a play written at a time of stringent censorship, Irving Wardle commented: 'Under cover of displaying a gross and palpable Jewish villain, Marlowe succeeds in exposing his nominally virtuous Christian adversaries as the real enemy'.[62]

The success of the production at the Swan owed much to its staging and costumes. Bob Crowley's spectacular set, initially a tower of packing cases, transformed first into the rooms in Barabas's house, complete with Danaë-like showers of gold. It then metamorphoses into the market place, the diabolical drawbridge for the final trap, the fiery pit complete with cauldron, and, in a final irony, into a cathedral. Like the ARC 1985 production, the RSC revival also adopted a potpourri of anachronistic costumes to stress the contemporary relevance of Marlowe's play. As Wardle noted, Barabas, jaunty in a Homburg and striped jacket, opened the play as 'a genial merchant with no more than a wry mistrust for his overlords' (*Times*). The production attired the rest of the 'rogues gallery' as third world soldiers: Calymath as an Afghan rebel; Martin del Bosco as a Mogol warrior; and Lodowick as an ex-colonial in puttees.[63]

Consonant with the satiric focus of the production, without omitting any of Barabas's atrocities or wicked asides, Alun Armstrong may well have created the most sympathetic Barabas ever to fret and strut across a stage. Critics largely agreed that Armstrong's 'ripe and detailed performance' generated 'great good-will in the audience' and aligned them with Barabas 'against the hypocritical Christians',[64] as well as immediately establishing a rapport with the audience.[65] I attended the play and agree that Armstrong achieved a visceral bonding with the spectators, like the medieval Vice figure speaking directly to the audience while inviting its complicity in his struggle against his adversaries, a complicity easily granted, partially because the audience had seen him mightily abused and partially because of the vitality, zest and schadenfreude with which he pursued his revenge.[66] However, Kyle also maintained an appropriate Brechtian distance, and few tears were shed when Barabas plunged into the fiery cauldron. Reviewers also universally praised the competent supporting cast with John Carlisle as Ferneze singled out for particular plaudits; indeed the treatment of Ferneze provided one of the most innovative aspects of the production. Carlisle doubled as the 'icily ruthless Governor Ferneze' and Machevill, 'soaring from hell to speak the prologue'. However the audience remained unaware of this double casting until the play's denouement when, as the Governor delivered his 'unctuous praise to heaven', he stripped off a wig and rubber mask to reveal the face of Machevill, just as a plaster Madonna descended from the flies.[67] An audience member need not recall Machiavelli's dictum that it is better to appear religious than to be so to comprehend the irony, for Kyle made evident what is implied throughout the play: Ferneze, with his pious platitudes and his opportunistic scheming, is the true Machiavel.[68]

Unlike so many productions in which rowdy farce totally engulfed savage satire, the revival at the Swan balanced a medley of tones: the serious satire of the opening scenes between Ferneze and Barabas, Abigail's poignant mourning over her dead lover, Barabas's rollicking farce in the centre section, Ithamore's surprisingly lyrical address to BellAmira,[69] and the ironic denouement complete with smirking Machevill, descending Madonna, and expanding cathedral. Although most reviewers agreed that this careful orchestration of theatrical timbres achieved a variety often lacking in revivals of the play, Peter Kemp demurred that the production often stressed the comic at the expense of the satiric, thus reducing Marlowe's 'fierce farce about human villainy to stagey roguishness'.[70] As to the anti-Semitism of the play, commentators disagreed. Sean

French, although acknowledging the play's biting satire of Christian Malta, nevertheless remained disturbed by the anti-Semitic archetypes embodied in Barabas 'that can be seen almost unchanged in Nazi propaganda films'.[71] Conversely, David Nathan of the *Jewish Chronicle*, although granting that the play could be seen as anti-Semitic, added that 'it is also anti-Christian and anti-Moslem. Indeed, it is anti-everything except a good laugh'.[72]

Emboldened by the two successful RSC productions, producers in both London and New York became more willing to stage a work that many considered anti-Semitic, and the 1990s enjoyed several professional or semi-professional mountings of Marlowe's tragical black comedy.

Reviewers acclaimed Michael Grandage's 1999 production at the Almeida Theatre in London for achieving an admirable balance between satire, farce and poignancy. Clearly Grandage was alert to the mordant irony and satiric thrust of the drama and 'the play's staging, in a bleak bare Malta, where nothing except greed, lust, double dealing, and murder flourish, captures just the sense of moral vacancy that Marlowe must have intended'.[73] Moreover, Michael Billington insisted that Ian McDiarmid as Barabas constantly reminded the audience that 'Barabas's villainy is a means of exposing his victims' pride and prejudices'[74] and Matt Wood added that 'Barabas isn't any less moral than the Christians that surround him; he's merely wilier and more of a cut-up'.[75] Like Alun Armstrong in the 1987 RSC production, McDiarmid maintained 'a complicity with the audience that Shylock never achieves, enlisting if not our approval, at least our amused sympathy' (Billington); 'he is our best friend but the Maltese citizenry's worst enemy' (Wood). Nevertheless, Grandage leavened the play's trenchant satire with rambunctious farce. Billington observed that 'Skittish, whimsical and often downright camp, McDiarmid is great fun to watch even if his comic facility sometimes needs to be reined in', and Wood commented that 'this gifted actor does nothing by halves'; he 'is both amazing as well as somewhat wearing'. Reviewers also awarded accolades to the strong supporting cast: Adam Levy's remarkable performance as the lean Ithamore,[76] Poppy Miller's 'almost hysterical integrity' in the role of Abigail and Polly Hemingway's striking performance as the aging courtesan Bell Amira.[77] Although following the format established in the 1987 RSC revival, Grandage's production apparently discovered new levels of meaning in the text. Billington found McDiarmid's Barabas 'sexually drawn to his lethal sidekick, Ithamore', a love relationship touted by Kate Kellaway as one of the most intriguing innovations in the plot. Conversely, in Laurie Maguire's interpretation, the production highlighted the touching father/daughter affiliation, with Barabas depicted as a man suffering not from the deprivation of his riches but from the emotional loss of his beloved daughter. Indeed, according to Maguire, Barabas lived for his daughter, and his tone became tender, even rapturous, when he spoke of 'the lodestone' of his life Abigail. Thus the betrayal first of Abigail and then of Ithamore, Abigail's surrogate, became too much for Barabas to bear, and the parallel positioning of the dead bodies of Abigail and Ithamore accentuated Barabas's double bereavement.[78]

In an interview with Terry Grimley, Grandage insisted that *The Jew* is not an anti-Semitic play, since 'Everyone in it is as corrupt and hypocritical as everyone else',[79] and most reviewers agreed that the play's 'bravura display' took 'the sting out of the play's racial offensiveness' (Billington) and that 'as McDiarmid plays him, Barabas subverts the very stereotypes that he embodies'.[80] Moreover, the denouement of the play evoked images that militated against the play's alleged anti-Semitism and aroused sympathy for Barabas. At the play's conclusion, Barabas 'fell into his cauldron not as a medieval Vice-figure descending into hell-mouth, nor as an outwitted overreacher comically plunging to a barbecue, but as a Jewish father heroically resisting a Nazi death-oven' (Maguire, p. 6), and as Ferneze pronounced his final sanctimonious lines, 'Barabas's face appeared at the porthole cut in the boiling cauldron',[81] recalling the gas chambers of the holocaust.

Perhaps less successful but still noteworthy, the Marlowe Project produced the play at the Musical Theatre Works in New York in November 1999. Directed by Jeff S. Dailey, the 12-person ensemble was attired in period costumes, the men in doublet and hose, 'the priests, nuns, and Turks in appropriately ornamental garb'. The set was stark, consisting of platforms for Abigail's balcony and Barabas's notorious trap, behind which Barabas disappeared as he plummeted into the cauldron.[82] The histrionic abilities of the ensemble received mixed reviews. Henry Traeger praised Bart Shattuck's 'virtuoso performance' as Barabas and the torrid love scenes between Travis Taylor as the slave Ithamore and Eszter Biro as the prostitute BellAmira, as well as Dana Gotlieb's superb impersonation of Abigail (pp. 2–3). Conversely, Doug DeVita complained that 'the production never took on a tone, energy, or style of its own, settling for a certain high-school seriousness that was at frustrating odds with the furious action of Marlowe's imaginative, corrosive script'.[83] However, both reviewers agreed that the escalated tempo of the entire production failed to take into consideration the modern audience's unfamiliarity with long Marlovian lines; thus, both the play's splendid poetry and its savage satire were often obscured.

Apparently even less successful was the production directed by Maurice Edward and performed at the Shakespeare Center of New York in March of 1999. Walter Goodman of the *New York Times* complained that Owen S. Rackleff as Barabas lacked the sportive glee that should make the villain entertaining to watch in all his nefarious machinations; instead, Rackleff's Barabas fumed a lot but rarely sparkled. Moreover, 'to this Elizabethan drama set in the 1930's (presumably so that the soldiers of Malta can wear [Mussolini-like] black shirts with all that they signify), Rackleff brought a Victorian heaviness'. Goodman applauded Charles Geyer's Ithamore, portrayed as 'a chortling and acrobatic cretin with a romantic bent' as the one original performance in the otherwise pedestrian production.[84]

Experimental Productions

Although seldom performed, *The Jew*, like so many early modern dramas, has experienced its share of experimental revivals; some highly inventive, some revealing, some simply wacko.

In 1984, the Nervous Theatre Group staged the play at the Bridge House in London. Andy Johnson directed the modern dress cast of four men who doubled all the roles. I have found no reviews attesting to the effectiveness or lack of effectiveness of this experiment.

Many reviewers agreed that by presenting Barabas as a sympathetic figure and by minimizing his Jewishness, the 1987 RSC production successfully nullified the alleged anti-Semitism of the play but at the cost of ignoring the play's serious ideological problems. In his 1996 production with a student cast at King Alfred's University College in Winchester, Stevie Simkin sought to direct a revival of *The Jew* that would 'confront rather than efface its problematic ideological status' and would foreground the problem of 'performed ethnicity' that the play introduces. To achieve this goal, Simkin appropriated the popular early modern convention of a 'play within a play', transforming Marlowe's text into a performance staged in a factory in Nazi-occupied Warsaw in 1939, in which the Nazi soldiers assumed the roles of the Maltese Christians while compelling the Jewish citizens to take the Jewish parts and the non-Jewish Poles to play the other roles. Although the Nazis intended to humiliate the Jews by forcing them to perform in an anti-Semitic play, the Jewish actors exploited the moments in the text that evoke sympathy for Barabas and his countrymen in order to explode as well as to parody the play's Jewish stereotypes. The denouement of the drama departed totally from the original text. Barabas escaped from the smoke-filled container (reminiscent of the Nazi gas chambers), removed his costume and joined his fellow actors who had already stripped to their street clothes. Only Ferneze, who imposed rigid ethnic identities throughout the play, proved unable to discard either his 1939 character or his Elizabethan persona, but remained imprisoned in his costume, a magnificent Elizabethan robe thrown over a Nazi uniform.[85] Through these various subversive strategies, Simkin sought to highlight both the anti-Semitism of the original play and the drama's interrogation of that anti-Semitism and to explore the degree to which 'ethnic identities can be constructed, imposed, and resisted'.[86]

In the very same year, 1996, the Irondale Ensemble project, devoted to improvisations on classical texts, conflated Marlowe's play with the famous 1892 strike against one of Andrew Carnegie's steel mills in 'Andrew Carnegie Presents *The Jew of Malta*', performed at the Theatre for the New City in New York. In this adaptation, Carnegie merged into Marlowe's 'dark hero' Barabas, whose murder and treachery exceeded 'even management's harshness to labor 100 years ago'. Ably directed by Jim Niesen, the entire saga was enacted against a set of smokestacks, shacks, offices, a river and a drawbridge. D. J. R. Bruckner of the *New York Times* found some of the innovations amusing, as when Carnegie, instead of contriving to boil his adversary in a cauldron as in Marlowe, 'plots to shove his foe into a steel mill's Bessemer converter works'. Apparently, although the fit between Barabas and Carnegie verged on the procrustean, Marlowe's treatment of Machiavelli's concepts allowed the company to draw moral lessons about the crushing of the unions by the steel magnates of the day.[87]

An even more wildly experimental production, staged at the Edinburgh Festival in 2005 by the *Theatro della Contraddizione* from Milan and directed by Marco Maria Linzi and Julio Maria Martino, accoutred the characters in 'ghoulish, leathery masks' reflecting their religious affiliation – Jewish, Christian, Muslim – while the actors moved like frenzied puppets, shrieking their lines with terrifying fervour. Moreover, their thick Italian accents often rendered their lines unintelligible. To add to the confusion, the role of Barabas was performed by several actors, often present on stage simultaneously.[88] Rachel Lynn Bradley complained that this extremely pretentious performance – 'an avant-guard performance art junkie's dream' – murdered *The Jew* in 'a production that incorporated movement, dance, and really bad acting'. She singled out Abigail as the 'only performer who was remotely sympathetic'.[89]

Foreign Productions

Referring to *The Jew*, Lois Potter suggests that 'The more visually expressive style of the non-English speaking theatre perhaps makes it easier to subvert an unacceptable meaning without sub-verting the play itself'.[90] Two foreign productions, one presented in France and one in Vienna, exemplify this statement.

The French revival, directed by Bernard Sobel for the *Ensemble Théâtrale de Gennevilliers* and performed at the Théâtre *de la Renaissance* in Paris, first in 1978 and again in 1999, emphasized the metadramatic aspects of the play identified by many contem-porary critics but largely ignored in productions of the play. After the confiscation of his wealth by the Maltese Christians, Barabas began his transformation from the 'grand cosmopolitan trader' of the first acts to the 'gleeful killer' of the later ones, and Sobel accentuated this metamorphosis through costume change. A trap door opened from which a hand emerged holding a large cardboard nose. Barabas, bearded, bespectacled and dignified, put on the nose, removed his beard, assumed a humpback posture and limp like Richard III, and before the eyes of the audience morphed into a grotesque caricature of the Jew. Moreover, after Barabas's plummet into the cauldron, a curtain fell, again punctuating the theatricality of his role (Potter, p. 271). Through these devices, the play made clear that Barabas's caricature of the monstrous Jew of medieval folklore was a role forced upon him by his anti-Semitic society.

The majority of the twentieth-century productions surveyed in this chapter presented *The Jew* as a combination of 'black farce' and mordant satire, with Barabas's revenge on the Maltese Christians often played for laughs. However, Peter Zadek's inno-vative 2002 version in Vienna starring the famous German actor Gerd Voss transmuted the play into 'the tragedy of a Jew', as described by Machevill in the Prologue. As Michael Billington observed, Zadek also converted the play into a twenty-first cen-tury rather than an early modern tragedy through his deployment of modern dress, contemporary music and anachronistic refer-ences (Barabas includes Alan Greenspan, the highly influential, long-time director of the US Federal Reserve Bank, among his list of prominent Jews). 'On his initial appearance, the hero also strips off a grotesque mask of the kind that Nazi propagandists [. . .] used to characterize Jewish features'. Through these devices

Zadek situated the play within a contemporary political context, exploding the play's surface anti-Semitism by revealing the human being behind the stereotype as a tragic victim of society. Billington praised Voss's performance as the 'amiable, Homburg-hatted Jew driven to murderous revenge by the injustice of the fascist Maltese governor'. The production did not minimize Barabas's maniacal villainy; rather it contextualized Barabas's amorality within 'a society where Jews are routinely stereotyped, plundered, and sacrificed'. Thus Zadek's production offered 'a radical reappraisal of the play by daring to take it seriously'.[91]

Twenty-First-Century Productions

In 2007, The Theatre for a New Audience in New York initiated America's first tandem production of *The Jew* and *The Merchant*, this time staged with a single cast but different directors and wildly dissimilar styles. As with the paired productions by the RSC in 1964 and 1987, reviewers regretted the lack of any connection between the two plays;[92] even though J. Murray Abraham doubled as Barabas and Shylock, his disparate interpretation of the two roles made comparison difficult. The critical judgement of the 1964 pairing overwhelmingly favoured Williams's highly innovative *Jew* over his somewhat pedestrian *Merchant*.[93] Conversely, although critics universally admired Darko Tresnjak's probing, frequently riveting modern-dress *Merchant*, they found David Herskovits's slapstick, period-costumed *Jew* disappointing and trivial.[94]

Commentators agreed that Herskovits fell victim to the pitfall that has plagued revivals of *The Jew* from the 1922 Phoenix Theatre production to the present, the temptation to allow farce to inundate the show, engulfing the drama's corrosive satire and dazzling poetry. Herskovits's 'haphazard romp' reduced all the characters, even Barabas, to 'dopey cartoons', sporting 'silly mustaches, silly costumes and silly wigs'.[95] Even an actor of Abraham's stature was unable to transcend the mindless buffoonery of the production. As Charles Isherwood observed, 'Although reviled as a Jew, the character of Barabas was deployed by Marlowe to expose the brutality and hypocrisy of a world ruled by supposedly pious Christians'. However, 'in this toothless staging, the fatal passions for power, vengeance, and violence [. . .] come across as so much clowning'. Only Arnie Burton received universal plaudits for his turn as the ghoulishly delightful Ithamore.[96] Irene Dash also complained of the production's lack of unity and coherence (p. 18). I attended the play and although I can almost lip-sync the drama's familiar lines, I found both the action and the language difficult to follow amid the performance's breakneck pace and the actors' slapstick mugging to the audience. Michael Basile further remarked on the 'helter-skelter mixing of style and aesthetic': the historically accurate set and lavish costumes were juxtaposed with anachronistic actions and music, as with the two friars' inappropriate samurai stick fight accompanied by a melody reminiscent of *Fiddler on the Roof* (p. 114). Finally, Eyse Sommer deplored the production's distasteful gimmickry, including the friars' necrophilic abuse of Abigail's corpse (shades of the 1985 ASR production) and Pilia Borgia's gratuitous masturbation of Ithamore. Maryann Feola spoke for critical consensus when she summarized: 'In lieu of Marlowe's poetry and dramatic complexity, this production presented revenge tragedy and dark humor à la "Saturday Night Live"' (p. 3).

In 2009, Seth Duerr introduced a second pairing of the two plays by the York Shakespeare Company at the Jewish Community Center in Manhattan. Duerr explained his rationale for coupling the plays and perhaps for presenting them during Hanukkah:

> Both plays have been wrongly accused of being anti-Semitic, as a
> persecuted Jew at each of their centers resorts to revenge. It is the
> majority of the characters, not the playwrights themselves, who alienate
> these Jews (along with all outsiders to their culture), forcing them to

convert or forfeit all their goods. We are exploring these plays
at the

JCC to get at the heart of why they are so misunderstood, to
reveal the

intolerance of the other characters for what it is, and to grasp
why these

stories of bigotry are still, unfortunately, relevant.[97]

I found only two reviews of these paired productions and both
commentators agreed that Duerr's versions vindicated the two
plays from the slur of anti-Semitism. Both revivals stressed the
'outsider' status of the Jews and other nationalities, not only
Barabas and Shylock but also Ithamore and the Prince of Aragon,
who, according to Huessan Ibish, the productions '"othered" to
the hilt with extravagant accents and preposterous costumes',
thereby enlisting sympathy for the alienated outsiders.[98] Ibish
agreed with Duerr that in *The Jew* 'Marlowe effectively kills the
notion that his stereotypically "bad" Jew is any worse – or better – than the Christians or Muslims surrounding him', adding
that Duerr's 'straightforward and uncut production [. . .] bears
out this case quite clearly'. Chris Harcum concurred: 'In the end
we learn that Christians, Muslims, and Jews are capable of doing
bad things for their own self-aggrandizement, including murder. Feigned morals be damned'.[99] Duerr's interpretation of *The
Merchant* also presented Shylock, like Barabas, as 'a wronged man
belonging to a wronged people who came by his vengeful rage
honestly' (Ibish). By depicting both Jewish characters as alienated
victims of society's prejudices, Duerr, alone among the directors
of the four tandem productions surveyed in this chapter, gave significance to the pairing of the two 'Jewish' plays.

Duerr's revival of *The Jew* adopted the simple staging characteristic of the early modern theatre, the set consisting of an
occasional table or chair with the male actors primarily attired in
contemporary black suits and shirts. As in early modern staging,
the minimal set and costumes put the focus on the actors and
on Marlowe's language (Harcum). Duerr's semi-professional

cast received mixed reviews. Harcum commented that 'While this company is strong in attacking the mountain of words, the sense of what is happening is mostly missing', putting the burden on the audience who must try to understand the language and follow the action. Conversely, Ibish, while admitting that occasionally the cast failed to achieve the full potential of the play, praised the overall performances as 'engaging and very sound'. Both reviewers extolled Paul Rubin, who reprised the part that he played with such verve and panache in the 1985 ASR revival, for his brilliant performance in the Herculean role of Barabas, finding him 'likeable one minute and a psychopath another' (Harcum), both comic and entertaining (Ibish). Thus, despite the company's limitations – spare set, simple costumes, semi-professional actors – the two critics who reviewed the dramas agreed that Duerr succeeded in his primary goals: removing the stigma of anti-Semitism from both plays while discovering a significant nexus between them.

What next? Although there have been a number of highly successful stagings of Marlowe's controversial play, there has never been a film version. Although I doubt that *The Jew* will be playing at the neighbourhood multiplex any time soon, a film version is in production, directed by Douglas Morse with Seth Duerr as Barabas. This film is scheduled for release in 2013 and should be available for showing at home or in the classroom.

Other Productions in Brief

Although many critics might dismiss the drama as an historical artefact belonging in a dusty library, *The Jew* has proven surprisingly vital in the theatre; indeed, as I hope that this survey has confirmed, the play is much more fascinating on the stage than on the page. This theatrical effectiveness is further documented by the following list of lesser-known productions, many of them occurring in universities or colleges or in local repertory theatres. Many of these productions, like those surveyed in this chapter, demonstrate that rather than being an anti-Semitism drama, *The*

Jew of Malta is perhaps the most sophisticated and ironic burlesque of anti-Semitism ever written.

1907: The first production of the play in the United States was presented at Williams College in Massachusetts.

1940: The Yale Dramatic Association staged the play in tandem with *A Massacre at Paris*. Both were directed by Burt Shevelowe.

1956: The Cambridge Theatre Group presented a farcical version of the play, produced and directed by John Stow with Tom Rosenthal in the title role.

1960: Tavistock Repertory Company performed the play at the Tower Theatre in Canterbury.

1964 and 1966: The play was twice acted at Merseyside Unity Theatre in Liverpool.

1966: The Marlowe Society of Chislehurst, Kent, mounted a production at Toynbee Hall, London.

1971: The Theatre Mobile staged a production of the play in London.

1975: John Chapman directed the play for The Marlowe Society of Cambridge University at the Arts Theatre in Cambridge.

1984: Oracle Productions produced the play, directed by Peter Benedict, at the Donmar Warehouse, London.

1984: The Hull University Drama Department performed the play, directed by Ben Watt.

1986: The play was staged at the Netherbowe Theatre in Edinburgh.

1993: The Cambridge Arts Trust presented the play at the Mumford Theatre in Cambridge.

2008: The Hall for Cornwall staged *Barabas*, adapted from Marlowe's *The Jew of Malta*, with Joseph Mydell as Barabas and Ery Nzaramba as Ithamore.

2011: The most recent production of the play was directed by Tibor Egervari with the students of the University of Ottawa. From all accounts, the director took a play that many consider to be anti-Semitic and turned the show into a parody presenting anti-Semitism as ridiculous.

THREE

The State of the Art: Current Critical Research

Andrew Duxfield

The Jew of Malta is a play which has enjoyed a significant proportion of its critical attention in relatively recent years. While the play
is not as widely discussed as Marlowe's most famous work, *Doctor
Faustus*, changing trends in literary criticism have helped to lay the
foundations for the resurgence of interest in what was one of the
major popular successes of Elizabethan theatre. With its focus on
culturally marginalized figures, its cynical depiction of the nature
of power politics and capitalist commerce, its dramatization of the
meeting and meshing of racially and culturally disparate groups,
and with its pathologically merciless protagonist, *The Jew of Malta*
has provided fertile ground for a variety of critical approaches –
from New Historicist to Marxist to Psychoanalytical – since literary theory began to expand critical horizons beyond the traditional
canon in the late 1970s.[1] This chapter will provide a survey of the
development of this rich variety of critical approaches since the
turn of the twenty-first century. The aim of the piece is to provide
a narrative account of trends and patterns in discussion of the play,
and also to provide an easily navigable reference resource that can
be dipped into for specific items of information. As such, it will
be structured in three sections. The first will offer an overview
of some of the central issues that have received critical attention
since the year 2000, identifying particular trends, continuities with
and breaks from earlier critical practice, and suggesting directions
which commentary on the play might profitably take in the future.
Naturally, there are a number of critical issues which have been
covered recently that I will not have space to cover in this section;
with that in mind, the second section will provide a year-by-year

account of a broad selection of the work published on *The Jew of Malta* in the relevant period, incorporating brief summaries of each item, from which the reader may identify further trends or individual items of particular interest. The third section will provide an extensive bibliography, also organized by year, providing full reference details for twenty-first-century critical publications that discuss the play.

Critical Tendencies

Money, Marginality and Multiculturalism

The central focus of criticism on *The Jew of Malta* continues to be the representation of Barabas as considered against early modern conceptions of Jews and Jewishness. On the whole, discussion has moved beyond the question of whether the play endorses or satirizes anti-Semitic prejudice to a more nuanced consideration of the position of Barabas as a resident stranger in Malta, and of the opportunities, as well as obstacles, that this position presents; Andrew Hiscock and Julia Reinhard Lupton in particular examine this.[2] Richard Wilson and Daniel Vitkus, meanwhile, both consider the play in terms of the intermediary role often played by prominent Mediterranean Jews in international trade and diplomacy,[3] and the significance of international trade in the play continues to garner particular critical attention.[4] Discussions of politics, religion, commerce and race in *The Jew of Malta* have become largely intertwined in recent years, and the dynamic relationship among these complex factors continues to produce revealing readings.

Genre

The genre of *The Jew of Malta* has been a point of debate since T. S. Eliot accounted for its apparently disjointed nature by remarking that readers were making the mistake of reading it as a tragedy, when it might be more suitably described as a farce.[5] This issue has continued to produce interesting comment in the twenty-first century, with a range of positions being adopted. Lagretta Tallent

Lenker and Anna Beskins, for instance, both argue for the play's tragic status, while Ruth Lunney examines the play in terms of its direct inheritance from late medieval morality drama and Sarah Scott argues that the play anticipates the city comedy that later flourished on the Jacobean stage.[6] Clare Harraway, meanwhile, uses the play as an instance to argue that genre is itself a fluid concept which will always be undermined.[7] However much these suggestions might seem to contradict one another, collectively they reveal something both about the complexity of the play and about the constant state of evolution in which English drama proceeded in the late sixteenth century. More consideration of how Marlowe fits into that evolution might well aid our understanding both of his work and of the period as a whole.[8]

Machiavelli

Most commentaries on *The Jew of Malta* pass some comment on the philosophy of Niccolò Machiavelli, and to the reputation of that philosophy in Elizabethan England. Most readings tend to echo the argument of Catherine Minshull, who in 1982 argued that the great irony of the play is that its real Machiavellian turns out to be Ferneze, not Barabas.[9] No dedicated considerations of the play's appropriation of Machiavelli have appeared in recent years, but Patrick Cheney's recent republican reading of Marlowe's work breathed life into the topic by considering the play alongside Machiavelli's *Discourses*, rather than his more (in)famous political treatise, *The Prince*.[10] Cheney's work demonstrates that there is more to consider about the play's Machiavellianism.

1633

While *The Jew of Malta* is certainly an Elizabethan play, the earliest extant text dates from 1633, some 40 or so years after the play was first being performed on the London stage. Discussion of this fact has tended to focus on its implications in terms of the authorial integrity of the text, and on the extent to which Thomas Heywood may have had a hand in the writing of it. What critics have recently begun to ask, however, is why 1633 was an apt time for the publication of this play; Zachary Lesser and John Parker arrive at rather different conclusions after considering how the play might have spoken to the religious tensions of the time, and Lucy Munro examines the reputation of the play during the Caroline period.[11] Considering the play in a Caroline context offers an insight into the conditions that produced the only textual manifestation of it that we have access to, and further work in this area would be more than worthwhile.

Marlowe and Shakespeare

Critical discussion of Marlowe was once severely limited by a propensity to discuss his body of work only as it relates to Shakespeare's, that is as that of a primitive dramatic precursor or inferior rival. This is especially true with respect to *The Jew of Malta*, which has often been analysed as a less sophisticated prototype of *The Merchant of Venice*.[12] Now that Marlowe criticism has for some time been liberated from this approach, critics such as Robert Logan have been keen to reconsider the dramatic relationship between the two playwrights on less value-based terms.[13] There is undoubtedly room for more light to be shed on the play, and on Marlowe studies more generally, by this approach, whether Marlowe is read alongside Shakespeare or other contemporaries of his; one might profitably consider his plays in relation to those of other dramatists who wrote for the Admiral's Men, for instance.

Biography

Since as early as 1597, when Thomas Beard's providential account of Christopher Marlowe's death was published, Marlovian biography has been a subject of fascination for readers and critics alike, and has been profoundly influential on critical readings of his plays.[14] The twenty-first century has thus far seen an extraordinary flurry of interest in Marlowe biography, with four book-length biographies and a section of a collection of essays in its first six years alone.[15] These works tend to blend biographical and critical practice, conducting readings of the literary texts that are informed by the life and drawing conclusions about the life that are based on readings of the texts. In opposition to this, a more sceptical strain of criticism has emerged in recent years, exemplified by essays by J. A. Downie and Lukas Erne which stress just how little we actually know about Marlowe's life and highlight the potential circularity of reading the texts in terms of a biography that has in large part been constructed through inferences from the texts.[16] There are some indications that the latter viewpoint is now generally holding sway; no full-length biography of Marlowe has appeared since 2005, and a number of critical works published on Marlowe in recent years have made a point of distancing themselves from the biographical approach.[17] It is unlikely that there will ever be a lack of scholarly interest in the biography of such an undeniably fascinating figure, but one might expect to see a clearer distinction in future Marlowe studies between biographical scholarship and literary criticism.

Critical Work on *The Jew of Malta* since 2000

The first year of the twenty-first century was a busy one for Marlowe studies, with four new books appearing, and *The Jew of Malta* approached in a number of ways. Lisa Hopkins's *Christopher Marlowe: A Literary Life* provides an account of the dramatist's life through biographically infused readings of his works. Hopkins historicizes *The Jew of Malta* in terms of early modern Maltese politics, and in particular the great siege of 1565, in which the Christian knights who governed the island successfully repelled Ottoman forces. Clare Harraway's *Re-Citing Marlowe*, by contrast, eschews biographically informed criticism, instead providing a deconstructionist reading of Marlowe's plays, emphasizing through discussion of them the incapacity of language to produce stable meaning. In her chapter on *The Jew of Malta*, Harraway makes use of the play to illuminate a discussion of genre, in which she argues that, like the racial and political categories of Marlowe's Malta, its boundaries are always subject to infiltration and renegotiation. Downie and Parnell's essay collection *Constructing Christopher Marlowe* contains a number of re-examinations of the ways in which our sense of Marlowe has been fashioned by critical and biographical narrative rather than verifiable facts relating to his life, of which there are precious few. Janet Clare's contribution to the volume, 'Marlowe's "Theatre of Cruelty"', pays particular attention to *Tamburlaine*, but also includes discussion of *The Jew of Malta* and other plays. Clare proposes a Marlovian dramaturgy in which ideology is diminished and emphasis is placed on the aesthetic. The essay goes on to identify Marlowe's aesthetic with Antonin Artaud's 'theatre of cruelty', which proposed a theatrical method based more on extreme sensual experience than on accurate psychological representation. Completing the year's round of books, Stevie Simkin's *A Preface to Marlowe* is an introductory companion to the dramatist's life and works, supplementing individual readings of each of the plays with a brief biography, accounts of key historical contexts and performance histories. The year's journal articles included Eric C. Brown's 'Violence, Ritual, and the Execution of Time in Marlowe's *The Jew of Malta*', which focuses on time in the play, and in particular on Barabas's control of it and manipulation of others through it. Emphasizing the ritual and sacrificial significance of time, Brown argues that Barabas's death, indirectly occasioned by his own devising, represents his achievement of complete control over time, since it marks the beginning of a new cycle in which Ferneze will replicate his own behaviour. David Webb, in '"Pageants truly played": Self-dramatization and Naturalistic Character in *The Jew of Malta*', challenges the position current in New Historicist and Cultural Materialist criticism that the early modern subject was an entirely social construct. Focusing on the ways in which characters dramatize themselves in the play, and referring to developments in evolutionary psychology, Webb argues that there is a place in modern criticism for the consideration of an early modern self that is at least in part essential. Mark Hutchings's note '"In Thrace; Brought up in Arabia": *The Jew of Malta*, II.iii.131' argues that Ithamore's account of his origins suggests that he is a former Christian who has undergone an enforced conversion to Islam. This status, Hutchings argues, adds another aspect to the fragile links between individuals and their religious professions in the play.

2001 produced a comparatively sparse offering of critical material. Stevie Simkin followed his work of the previous year with another companion work. *Marlowe: The Plays* is an instalment in the Palgrave 'Analysing Texts' range, and provides examples of close reading of passages from the plays which are organized by theme. Ceri Sullivan's note 'Silver in *The Jew of Malta*' reads the contempt with which Bellamira and Barabas hold the coin of the realm in the context of sixteenth-century economic developments brought about by Elizabeth's re-coining of the currency and the influx of silver from the new world which meant that silver was the precious metal least likely to represent good value.

2002 proved a more fruitful year, particularly with respect to biography. Constance B. Kuriyama's *Christopher Marlowe: A Renaissance Life* offers an account of Marlowe's life through reinterpretation of source documents, and treads carefully when it comes to contentious issues like the dramatist's putative career in espionage and the circumstances surrounding his death. A less cautious approach is taken by Charles Nicholl in the revised edition of his captivating, if speculative, account of Marlowe's demise, *The Reckoning: The Murder of Christopher Marlowe*. The revised edition contains an Epilogue in which some of the conclusions reached in the original publication are reconsidered. The year also provided a substantial contribution to criticism, with two more monographs and a collection of essays published. Ruth Lunney's *Marlowe and the Popular Tradition: Innovation in the English Drama before 1595* sets out to read Marlowe's dramatic oeuvre not in terms of the personality or politics of its author, but rather in the context of the dramatic tradition from which it emerged. Lunney examines how Marlowe's plays utilize and manipulate expectations that audiences would have accrued from direct experience of late morality drama, and in her chapter on *The Jew of Malta* examines in detail the play's appropriation of, and experimentation with, the vice figure. Sara Munson Deats and Robert A. Logan's *Marlowe's Empery: Expanding His Critical Contexts* provides a rich variety of critical material on Marlowe's work, focusing on genre, early modern culture and the plays in performance. In one of the essays in the collection, '"I know she is a courtesan by her attire": Clothing and Identity in *The Jew of Malta*', Randall Nakayama discusses the capacity of clothing to signify identity, citing as a context early modern sumptuary regulations which restricted individuals to attire appropriate to their social station. Alan Shepard examines the plays in terms of contemporary militaristic discourse and concepts of nationhood and heroism in his book *Marlowe's Soldiers: Rhetorics of Masculinity in the Age of the Armada*. Having identified a pervasive anxiety in Elizabethan martial writing about the pernicious effects of rising mercantilism, Shepard examines the opposition between war and commerce in *The Jew of Malta*, finding it not to be an entirely clear-cut dichotomy. A comparable line of enquiry is taken by A. D. Nuttall in his journal article 'Christopher Marlowe: Iron and Gold', the title of which alludes to an address to the commons by Francis Bacon in which he pondered which was the real source of power: might (iron), or wealth (gold). Nuttall begins by offering reflections on reductionism in a scientific context, and goes on to suggest that Marlowe, in contrast to Shakespeare, is a reductionist poet; everything in *Tamburlaine*, he suggests, boils down to iron, and everything in *The Jew of Malta* to gold. Finally, Joan Ozark Holmer's 'Jewish Daughters: The Question of Philo-Semitism in Elizabethan Drama', which appears in a collection of essays on *The Merchant of Venice*, argues that the representations of the daughters of the central Jewish figures in *The Merchant of Venice* and *The Jew of Malta* – Jessica and Abigail respectively – exhibit on the part of Shakespeare and Marlowe a philo-Semitism that has as yet gone unacknowledged.

2003 was a quieter year, but nonetheless one which saw the emergence of interesting new commentary on the play, the republication of important work and a further addition to the recent flurry of biographical activity. Roy Kendall's *Christopher Marlowe and Richard Baines: Journeys through the Elizabethan*

Underground approaches Marlowe's life via that of Richard Baines, his co-arrestee in the coining incident in Flushing, and the author of the incriminating note which still heavily influences the perception of the dramatist's personality. Avraham Oz's *Marlowe*, part of the 'New Casebook' series, brings together a wide range of significant work on Marlowe from the latter part of the twentieth century, including Stephen Greenblatt's seminal essay on *The Jew of Malta*, 'Marlowe, Marx and Anti-Semitism'. Daniel Vitkus's book, *Turning Turk: English Theatre and the Multicultural Mediterranean, 1570–1630*, provides an insight into English involvement in Mediterranean trade and relations with the Ottoman Empire, and examines how the drama of the period both registers and contributes to anxieties about cross-cultural interaction. In a chapter entitled 'Machiavellian Merchants', Vitkus focuses on the mediatory role played by Jews in Anglo-Ottoman relations as a context for readings of *The Jew of Malta* and a number of other plays, emphasizing the instability of racial and cultural boundaries within them. Two journal articles concentrate on Barabas as responding to the constraints of the society within which he lives. In 'A Society of One: Reading *The Jew of Malta* through Serres's Theory of Exchange', Shawn Smith provides a reading of the play which accounts for Barabas's apparent villainy as a strategy for self-preservation. Making use of Serres's theory, according to which a just society functions through exchanges of equivalent value, Smith argues that Barabas, already ostracized by his society and the victim of an act of state-sponsored theft, enacts in return a series of 'broken' exchanges of which he is the only beneficiary, ensuring in the process his own self-sufficiency. B. R. Menpes's 'The Bondage of Barabas: Thwarted Desire in *The Jew of Malta*' similarly depicts Barabas's actions as determined by the immoral world he occupies, with the ultimate result being his alienation from his identity as a merchant and irrevocable drive towards murder and revenge. In a short note entitled 'How Drunken Was Barnadine', J. J. M. Tobin makes some suggestions for the derivation of the name of the character Barnadine in Shakespeare's *Measure for*

Measure, eliminating in the process the friar of the same name in *The Jew of Malta* as a source.

The standout contribution to Marlowe criticism in 2004 was Patrick Cheney's *Cambridge Companion to Christopher Marlowe*, a substantial collection which combines dedicated essays on each of Marlowe's major texts with essays on biographical, textual, stylistic and cultural issues relevant to his work. Chapters in the collection which touch upon *The Jew of Malta* include: Kate Chedgzoy's 'Marlowe's Men and Women: Gender and Sexuality', which discusses the tension between Abigail's desire for orderly union and Barabas's manipulation of her sexuality in ways which benefit his private interests; Laurie Maguire's 'Marlovian Texts and Authorship', which examines the possibility of textual corruption in the 1633 text of the play; Lois Potter's 'Marlowe in Theatre and Film', which offers a brief performance history of the play; Garrett Sullivan's 'Geography and Identity in Marlowe', which considers Barabas's somewhat un–Marlovian attachment to a single, enclosed geographical space; and Paul Whitfield White's 'Marlowe and the Politics of Religion', which discusses the play's representation of Judaism and Catholicism as equally false religions. In a chapter dedicated specifically to *The Jew of Malta*, Julia Reinhard Lupton complicates the commonplace Self/Other dichotomy by examining the multiple kinds of fellowship that emerge in the marginal spaces of Marlowe's Malta. Lupton historicizes the play's fascination with liminality, noting the resonance between Barabas's interstitial identity and the ambiguous status of the London liberties, which, located outside the jurisdiction of the puritan City Fathers, provided a location in which the theatre and other illicit forms of entertainment could flourish. Other work published in 2004 adopts a similar approach to Lupton's. Andrew Hiscock, in a chapter of his book *The Uses of This World: Thinking Space in Shakespeare, Marlowe, Cary and Jonson*, focuses on the physically and culturally marginal spaces occupied and created by Barabas. Like Lupton, Hiscock observes the necessity of Barabas's liminal position in order for him to negotiate the power politics of the island. A chapter of Zachary Lesser's book

Renaissance Drama and the Politics of Publication: Readings in the English Book Trade considers the play from the position of its 1633 publication, and specifically in relation to the growing theological controversy between Puritan and increasingly ceremonial official modes of worship. Lesser argues that *The Jew of Malta* is one of a number of plays published at the time by Nicholas Vavasour which could be construed as demonstrating sympathy with the official position. 2004 also saw the trend for Marlowe biography continue to gather pace, with the publication of David Riggs's *The World of Christopher Marlowe*, a comprehensive biography which includes readings of the works against relevant periods of the dramatist's life.

The interest in biography appeared to reach its high water mark in 2005, as Park Honan's much anticipated *Christopher Marlowe: Poet and Spy* was published. Honan's biography follows a similar pattern to Riggs's, and pays particular attention Marlowe's university years and the possibility of an acquaintance with Shakespeare. Lisa Hopkins's *A Christopher Marlowe Chronology* presents an alternative form of biography, listing by date literary, political and cultural events that directly or indirectly affected Christopher Marlowe's life, career and reputation. The year's critical offering was less substantial than that of 2004. Richard Wilson, in 'Another Country: Marlowe and the Go-Between', focuses on the liminal position of the Jew in early modern European civic society, particularly in the role of mediator in international and intercultural trade. Barabas, located on the multicultural island of Malta at the geographical centre of the Mediterranean, is perfectly poised to take advantage of this position. Foreign dramatic settings often reflect domestic concerns, of course, and Wilson here suggests that Barabas's position as go-between, situated between Ferneze's knights and the forces of Selim-Calymath, reflects that of Elizabethan England in the ongoing struggle between Catholic Spain and the Ottoman Empire. Roger E. Moore's essay, "'I'll Rouse My Senses, and Awake Myself'": Marlowe's *The Jew of Malta* and the Renaissance Gnostic Tradition', provides an unconventional interpretation of the play which reads Barabas's grossly

cavalier attitude to human life as deriving from an adherence to
Gnostic thought (i.e. the mystical belief that the human soul,
mired in the tainted materiality of the body, can achieve divine
ascension through self-knowledge and knowledge of God). This
Gnostic Barabas's disdain for the material (his counting house full
of gold, Moore argues, serves as a signifier of spiritual rather than
material wealth) is such that he finds no value in earthly life, either
others' or his own, and undergoes a form of symbolic apotheosis
when his body is burned away at the end of the play. Julia Reinhard
Lupton's book *Citizen-Saints* offers a chapter on *The Jew of Malta*
that develops further her discussion of the play in the previous
year's *Cambridge Companion*.

2006 produced a healthy variety of approaches to the play. Two
essays relate the play to discussions of biographical issues. David
Riggs's 'The Poet in the Play: Life and Art in *Tamburlaine* and *The
Jew of Malta*' suggests a correlation between the ironic tone of the
play and the duplicitous nature of the activities Marlowe may well
have undertaken in his possible role as a government intelligencer.
Lisa Hopkins's note 'In a little room: Marlowe and *The Allegory
of the Tudor Succession*' proposes that Barabas's famous 'infinite
riches' soliloquy may be an allusion to an inscription on Lucas
de Heere's iconographical 1572 painting of the Tudor monarchs,
given by Elizabeth I to Francis Walsingham as a gift, which begins
with the line 'A face of mvche nobillitye loe in a litle roome'. The
allusion, Hopkins suggests, might imply a cynicism on Marlowe's
part towards the iconography surrounding Elizabeth, and towards
her increasing sponsorship of mercantile travel. Early modern
mercantilism is also a central concern of Daniel Vitkus's 'Turks
and Jews in *The Jew of Malta*', which argues that the play, with its
duplicitous characters rubbing shoulders with Jews and Ottoman
Turks, registered contemporary anxieties about the potentially cor-
rupting effect that growing Mediterranean trade and the resultant
increase in intercultural contact might have on English society. In
'*The Jew of Malta* and the Diabolic Power of Theatrics', Arata Ide
reads the play, with a dissimulating interloper as its central figure,
as capitalizing on contemporary paranoia about the internal threat

posed by Jesuit missionaries, whom popular broadside polemic identified with equivocation and dishonesty. That the Christian characters in the play turn out to exhibit villainy comparable with that of Barabas highlights, Ide suggests, the fictions inherent in Elizabethan propaganda.

Two books were published in 2007 which offered significant contributions on *The Jew of Malta*. John Parker's *The Aesthetics of Antichrist: From Christian Drama to Christopher Marlowe* argues that medieval Christian drama is more complex and ambiguous than is commonly acknowledged. In presenting his thesis Parker traces the representation of the antichrist figure from early Christian times through to Marlowe's drama, culminating in a chapter in which Marlovian protagonists are read against figures who occupy an ambiguous space between Christ and antichrist; Tamburlaine is discussed alongside the apostle Paul, Faustus with the Elizabethan mystic Simon Magus and Barabas is paired with his biblical namesake. Robert A. Logan's book *Shakespeare's Marlowe: The Influence of Christopher Marlowe on Shakespeare's Artistry* looks at the aesthetic relationship between the two dramatists' work in the light of modern studies in intertextuality, and aims to go beyond the commonplace construction of the 'rivalry' between the two playwrights in order to consider more fully the artistic and dramaturgical echoes of Marlowe's work in the Shakespeare canon. Alongside a variety of other comparative readings, Logan provides a fresh perspective on a much studied dramatic relationship in a chapter entitled '"For a tricksy word / Defy the matter": The Influence of *The Jew of Malta* on *The Merchant of Venice*'. Articles published in the same year included Anna Beskins's note 'From Jew to Nun: Abigail in Marlowe's *The Jew of Malta*', which takes issue with the notion, upheld by many critics since T. S. Eliot's commentary on the play early in the twentieth century, that the carnage in the latter half of the play is farcical in nature. Beskins argues that Abigail's death at the hands of her father, in particular, is tragic, and, given that she is 14 years old, reflects contemporary anti-Semitic notions of Jews as child murderers. In '"Iygging vaines" and "riming mother wits": Marlowe, Clowns and the Early

Frameworks of Dramatic Authorship', Kirk Melnikoff examines clownage in *Faustus* and *The Jew of Malta*, arguing that, rather than having dispensed with the trivialities of popular theatre, as the Prologue to *Tamburlaine* states, Marlowe's plays exhibit a more nuanced and developed form of clowning, Ithamore's role in *The Jew of Malta* being a case in point. Leeds Barroll, in his essay 'Mythologizing the Ottoman: *The Jew of Malta* and *The Battle of Alcazar*', contrasts the significant martial and political power exercised by the Ottoman Empire during the lifetime of playwrights such as Marlowe with the markedly less formidable representation of Ottoman power on the Elizabethan stage. Plays like *The Jew of Malta*, Barroll suggests, undersell the Ottoman threat, not out of ignorance but as an act of escapist evasion.

2008 saw the publication of a wealth of Marlowe scholarship, with *The Jew of Malta* receiving plenty of critical attention. Lisa Hopkins's *Christopher Marlowe, Renaissance Dramatist* is an introduction to the author and his work, which offers a brief biography alongside a history of the plays in performance and accounts of the various ways in which they have been critically approached. Hopkins examines both how the plays exhibit the influence of the scholarly education of their author and how they dramatise the transgressive desire to stretch horizons and break boundaries. Hopkins also published an essay in 2008 entitled 'Christopher Marlowe and the Succession to the English Crown'. Hopkins here identifies succession concerns in *The Jew of Malta* and a number of Marlowe's other plays, as well as personal associations between the dramatist and contemporary figures who had an interest in the politics of the succession. The most substantial of the year's contributions to Marlowe studies was the essay collection *Placing the Plays of Christopher Marlowe: Fresh Cultural Contexts*, edited by Sara Munson Deats and Robert A. Logan, which contains five essays that deal directly with *The Jew of Malta*. Stephanie Moss's 'Edmund Kean, Anti-Semitism and *The Jew of Malta*' concentrates on the response to an early-nineteenth-century revival of the play, directed by and starring Edmund Kean, which closed early amid reviews which, while appreciating Kean's performance, lambasted his choice of material as too savage for an enlightened age. Moss reads the response to the production as revealing an anxiety about the disparity between the self-projection of polite society as enlightened and egalitarian and the reality of widespread prejudice concealed by that projection. In a section of the book devoted to exploration of the family in Marlowe's plays, Lagretta Tallent Lenker's 'The Hopeless Daughter of a Hapless Jew: Father and Daughter in *The Jew of Malta*' examines the relationship between Barabas and Abigail, suggesting, like Beskins in 2007, that the death of Abigail does not mark the descent of the play into farce. Lenker reads Barabas's lack of verbal response to his daughter's death as the ineloquence of emotional agony rather than nonchalance, while arguing that his increasing cruelty once she is gone represents a comment on the patriarchal system. The same section of the collection also includes Merry G. Perry's 'Masculinity, Performance, and Identity: Father/Son Dyads in Christopher Marlowe's Plays', which examines father and son relationships (both biological and figurative – Barabas and Ithamore are treated as a father/son dyad, for example) in the plays in the light of recent masculinity studies. Like Lenker, Perry suggests that Marlowe's plays problematize the patriarchal system, in this case through the severity with which rebellions against patriarchal authority are stamped out. William Hamlin's 'Misbelief, False Profession and *The Jew of Malta*' examines the play's use of the unusual and ambiguous word 'misbelief', which refers both to misguided belief and the absence of belief, and upon the effect of Barabas's own misbelief; his apparent absence of belief provides him the space to construct an independently fashioned identity, but ultimately his downfall is secured by the fact that misbelief becomes for him a form of belief in itself. In 'Barabas and Charles I', John Parker identifies the complaints of the dispossessed Barabas against the Christian knights with those found in Protestant polemic against the Catholic Church. With this in mind, the publication of the play in 1633, around which time a number of plays of anti-Catholic sentiment were being revived amidst unrest over Charles I's policy over Church reform, becomes particularly topical, Parker suggests.

A good range of work also appeared in journals and other essay collections during 2008, including two essays which took a psychoanalytical approach. Lars Engle's 'Oedipal Marlowe, Mimetic Middleton' applies Freudian and Girardian models of demystification – Oedipal and mimetic, respectively – to readings of various works (including *The Jew of Malta*) by Marlowe and Middleton. Engle concludes that Marlowe's work concerns itself more with the Oedipal model, in which the subject strives to overthrow repression that is the legacy of something past, while Middleton's plays work to a mimetic model, according to which all desires originate in imitation of others' desires, and according to which human rivalry is thus inevitable. In 'Maltese Psycho: Tragedy and Psychopathology in *The Jew of Malta*', Mathew Martin argues that Barabas offers an example of psychosis – in Lacanian terms, the defiant disavowal of the threat of castration. In Martin's reading, Barabas's murderousness and defiance of his society amount to an ongoing attempt to construct a self who is the agent, and not the victim, of castration. Lea Knudsen Allen considers *The Jew of Malta* in its international context. Through examining the dramatizing of the exotic in play, '"Not every man has the luck to go to Corinth": Accruing Exotic Capital in *The Jew of Malta* and *Volpone*' argues that objects accumulate a symbolic value by virtue of having travelled from one place to another. Allen ends with a reading of the constitutive effect of the exotic on the identity of early modern London, arguing that the city cumulatively accrues cultural capital through exchange and contact with Mediterranean spaces. 2008 saw *The Jew of Malta* feature to a limited extent in a number of essays which focused mainly on Shakespeare's *The Merchant of Venice*. These included Aaron Kitch's 'Shylock's Sacred Nation', which focuses on the role of Jews in early modern Mediterranean trade, and argues that Marlowe's play stresses the importance of mercantilism. A chapter of Lara Bovilsky's book *Barbarous Play: Race on the English Renaissance Stage*, entitled 'Exemplary Jews and the Logic of Gentility' discusses the representation of Jewishness in *The Merchant of Venice*, highlighting its dramatic inheritance from Marlowe's play. Joan Fitzpatrick, in 'Early Modern Dietaries and the Jews: *The Jew of Malta* and *The Merchant of Venice*', states a case for the importance of food in both plays, although primarily in Shakespeare's, with reference to Jewish dietary laws and contemporary treatises on dietary matters.

2009 was a quiet year in terms of publications on *The Jew of Malta*, but did see the publication of a significant book-length study in the form of Patrick Cheney's *Marlowe's Republican Authorship: Lucan, Liberty, and the Sublime*. Cheney reads Marlowe's works alongside his translation of the first book of Lucan's republican-spirited epic *Pharsalia*, and identifies a strain of sympathy with republican ideas running through the Marlowe canon. Cheney's book includes a chapter which examines intertextual echoes between *Pharsalia* and *Edward II*, *The Massacre at Paris* and *The Jew of Malta*, focusing particularly on civil struggles between republicanism and tyranny. The chapter makes an interesting contribution to the long running discussion of Machiavellianism in *The Jew of Malta* by focusing more on *The Discourses* than *The Prince*, with which it is more commonly associated. The year's other relevant work was Lucy Munro's 'Marlowe on the Caroline Stage', which examines the reception and reproduction of Elizabethan and Jacobean drama in the Caroline period, focusing particularly on the 1633 edition of *The Jew of Malta* and its paratextual matter. Munro argues that Marlowe's work still exerted influence in the Caroline period, and had not yet become a mere object of nostalgia.

2010 saw a resurgence in interest in the play, as two more significant books were published. Clayton G. Mackenzie's *Deathly Experiments: A Study of Icons and Emblems of Mortality in Christopher Marlowe's Plays* argues that critical commentary on early modern drama would benefit from a more nuanced understanding of visual culture in the period. Applying this logic to Marlowe's drama, Mackenzie considers the intertextual relationships between the plays and popularly accessible images such as those in emblem books, stained glass windows and church murals. In his chapter on *The Jew of Malta*, Mackenzie considers Barabas's arrogance regarding the fate of his ships alongside a contemporary emblematic depiction of fortune as a ship in stormy seas, and goes on to read the protagonist's demise in the light of depictions of infernal punishment in medieval 'doom' murals. Providing a substantial proportion of the year's Marlowe criticism was Sarah Scott and Michael Stapleton's collection *Christopher Marlowe the Craftsman: Lives, Stage, and Page*, which contains two essays on the play. Ruth Lunney, in 'Speaking to the Audience: Direct Address in the Plays of Marlowe and his Contemporaries', argues that *The Jew of Malta* is a landmark play in terms of its use of direct address to the audience, both quantitatively speaking – more characters address the audience more frequently than in earlier drama – and qualitatively speaking, in the sense that what had hitherto been overwhelmingly a comic device or tool for the convenient relation of plot is employed by Marlowe to much more complex and disruptive effect. Sarah Scott provides a fresh angle on the generic status of the play in her essay '*The Jew of Malta* and the Development of City Comedy', which builds on the work of scholars such as G. K. Hunter and Brian Gibbons, who have noted certain affinities of the play with the City Comedy but stopped short of categorizing it as such on the grounds that it is not sufficiently comic in its overall tone. Scott employs Gibbons's own generic criteria to argue that, with its incessant irony and perverse morality, Marlowe's darkly comic play might indeed be considered an early example of the genre. In the year's other notable contribution to discussion of the play, James Harmer's note, 'Toying With Religion in the Prologue to *The Jew of Malta*', identifies in Machevill's boast 'I count religion but a childish toy / And hold there is no sin but ignorance' (Prologue, 14–15)[18] an allusion to contemporary English translations of Calvin. This allusion, Harmer suggests, adds an extra layer of complexity to the already dense web of associations emanating from this notorious stage archetype; not only is Machevill identified with continental *Realpolitik*, Catholicism and Judaism, but now, problematically, with reformed theology as well.

2011 produced another collection of landmark essays in the form of Robert Logan's collection, *Christopher Marlowe*, which contains reprints of Stephen Greenblatt's 'Marlowe and the Will to Absolute Play', Alfred Harbage's 'Innocent Barabas' and Edward L. Rocklin's 'Marlowe as Experimental Dramatist: The Role of the Audience in *The Jew of Malta*'.

Bibliography

Biographies

Honan, P., *Christopher Marlowe: Poet and Spy* (Oxford: Oxford University Press, 2005).

Hopkins, L., *Christopher Marlowe: A Literary Life* (Basingstoke: Palgrave, 2000).

Hopkins, L., *A Christopher Marlowe Chronology* (Basingstoke: Palgrave, 2005).

Kendall, R., *Christopher Marlowe and Richard Baines: Journeys through the Elizabethan Underground* (Madison, NJ: Fairleigh Dickinson University Press; Cranbury, NJ: Associated University Presses, 2003).

Kuriyama, C. B., *Christopher Marlowe: A Renaissance Life* (Ithaca, NY: Cornell University Press, 2002).

Nicholl, C., *The Reckoning: The Murder of Christopher Marlowe*, revised edn (London: Vintage, 2002).

Riggs, D., *The World of Christopher Marlowe* (London: Faber & Faber, 2004).

Editions

Lynch, S. J., ed., *The Jew of Malta, with Related Texts* (Indianapolis: Hacket, 2009).

Siemon, J. R., ed., *The Jew of Malta*, 3rd edn (London: Methuen, 2009).

Collections of Essays

Cheney, P., ed., *The Cambridge Companion to Christopher Marlowe* (Cambridge: Cambridge University Press, 2004).

Deats, S. M. and Logan R. A., eds, *Marlowe's Empery: Expanding His Critical Contexts* (Newark, DE: University of Delaware Press, 2002).

—, eds, *Placing the Plays of Christopher Marlowe: Fresh Cultural Contexts* (Aldershot: Ashgate, 2008).

Downie, J. A. and Parnell, J. T., eds, *Constructing Christopher Marlowe* (Cambridge: Cambridge University Press, 2000).

Logan, R. A., ed., *Christopher Marlowe* (Aldershot: Ashgate, 2011).

Oz, A., ed., *Marlowe (New Casebooks)* (Basingstoke: Palgrave, 2003).

Scott, S. K. and Stapleton, M. L., eds, *Christopher Marlowe the Craftsman: Lives, Stage, and Page* (Aldershot: Ashgate, 2010).

2000: Individual Essays

Brown, E. C., 'Violence, Ritual and the Execution of Time in Marlowe's *The Jew of Malta*', *Cahiers Elisabethains: Late Medieval and Renaissance Studies*, 58 (2000), pp. 15–29.

Clare, J., 'Marlowe's "theatre of cruelty"', in *Constructing Christopher Marlowe*, ed. J. A. Downie and J. T. Parnell (Cambridge: Cambridge University Press, 2000), pp. 74–87.

Craik, R., 'The Lion in "Burbank" and Charles Lamb', *Yeats Eliot Review: A Journal of Criticism and Scholarship*, 16.4 (2000), pp. 31–2.

Ferguson, D., '"Neither a Borrower nor a Lender Be": Polonius's Borrowings from Marlowe's Barabas', *Conference of College Teachers of English Studies*, 65 (2000), pp. 55–60.

Hutchings, M., '"In Thrace; Brought up in Arabia": *The Jew of Malta*, II.iii.131', *Notes and Queries*, 47.4 (2000), pp. 428–30.

Webb, D., '"Pageants Truly Played": Self-Dramatization and Naturalistic Character', in *The Jew of Malta*, *Renaissance Forum: An Electronic Journal of Early Modern Literary and Historical Studies*, 5.1 (2000), n.p.

2000: Books

Downie, J. A. and Parnell, J. T., eds, *Constructing Christopher Marlowe* (Cambridge: Cambridge University Press, 2000).

Harraway, C., *Re-Citing Marlowe: Approaches to the Drama* (Aldershot: Ashgate, 2000).

Hopkins, L., *Christopher Marlowe: A Literary Life* (Basingstoke: Palgrave, 2000).

Simkin, S., *A Preface to Marlowe* (London: Longman, 2000).

2001: Individual Essays

Rosen, A., 'Into the Ghetto: Representing Jewish Space in Elizabethan England', *JTD: Journal of Theatre and Drama*, 7–8 (2001), pp. 95–104.

Sullivan, C., 'Silver in *The Jew of Malta*', *Notes and Queries*, 48.3 (2001), p. 265.

2001: Books

Simkin, S., *Marlowe: The Plays* (Basingstoke: Palgrave, 2001).

2002: Individual Essays

Holmer, J. O., 'Jewish Daughters: The Question of Philo-Semitism in Elizabethan Drama', in *The Merchant of Venice: New Critical Essays* (London: Routledge, 2002), pp. 107–143.

Kang, S-J., 'Christopher Marlowe and the Politics of Transgression', *Journal of English Language and Literature / Yongo Yongmunhak*, 48.3 (2002), pp. 639–64 (In Korean; English summary).

Nakayama, R., '"I know she is a courtesan by her attire": Clothing and Identity in *The Jew of Malta*', in *Marlowe's Empery: Expanding His Critical Contexts*, ed. S. M. Deats and R. A. Logan (Newark, DE: University of Delaware Press, 2002), pp. 150–63.

Nuttall, A. D., 'Christopher Marlowe: Iron and Gold', *Comparative Criticism: An Annual Journal*, 24 (2002), pp. 37–51.

2002: Books

Deats, S. M. and Logan, R. A., eds, *Marlowe's Empery: Expanding His Critical Contexts* (Newark, DE: University of Delaware Press, 2002).

Kuriyama, C. B., *Christopher Marlowe: A Renaissance Life* (Ithaca, NY: Cornell University Press, 2002).

Lunney, R., *Marlowe and the Popular Tradition: Innovation in the English Drama Before 1595* (Manchester: Manchester University Press, 2002).

Nicholl, C., *The Reckoning: The Murder of Christopher Marlowe*, revised edn (London: Vintage, 2002).

Shepard, A., *Marlowe's Soldiers: Rhetorics of Masculinity in the Age of the Armada* (Aldershot: Ashgate, 2002).

2003: Individual Essays

Faini, P., 'Abigail, Jessica e il "tradimento" del padre', in *Le Forme Del Teatro: VII, La posa eroica di Ofelia, Saggi sul personaggio femminile nel teatro elisabettiano* (Rome: Storia e Letteratura, 2003), pp. 79–91.

Menpes, B. R., 'The Bondage of Barabas: Thwarted Desire in *The Jew of Malta*', *Parergon: Journal of the Australian and New Zealand Association for Medieval and Early Modern Studies*, 20.1 (2003), pp. 65–84.

Smith, S., 'A Society of One: Reading *The Jew of Malta* through Serres's Theory of Exchange', *Examplaria: A Journal of Theory in Medieval and Renaissance Studies*, 15.2 (2003), pp. 419–50.

Tobin, J. J. M., 'How Drunken Was Barnadine?', *Notes and Queries*, 50.1 (2003), pp. 46–7.

2003: Books

Kendall, R., *Christopher Marlowe and Richard Baines: Journeys through the Elizabethan Underground* (Madison, NJ: Fairleigh Dickinson University Press, 2003).

Oz, A., ed., *Marlowe (New Casebooks)* (Basingstoke: Palgrave, 2003).

Vitkus, D., *Turning Turk: English Theater and the Multicultural Mediterranean, 1570–1630* (New York: Palgrave Macmillan, 2003).

2004: Individual Essays

Boehrer, B., 'Disorder in the House of God: Disrupted Worship in Shakespeare and Others', *Comparative Drama*, 38.1 (2004), pp. 83–103.

Chedgzoy, K., 'Marlowe's Men and Women: Gender and Sexuality', in *The Cambridge Companion to Christopher Marlowe*, ed. P. Cheney (Cambridge: Cambridge University Press, 2004), pp. 245–61.

Freller, T., 'Malta im englischen Drama der Shakespeare-Epoche: Handels-und Reiseverkehr als Ursachen literarischer Phänomene-diskutiert am Beispiel von Christopher Marlowes *The Jew of Malta*', *Anglia: Zeitschrift für Englische Philologie*, 122.3 (2004), pp. 404–34 (English summary).

Lupton, J. R., '*The Jew of Malta*', in *The Cambridge Companion to Christopher Marlowe*, ed. P. Cheney (Cambridge: Cambridge University Press, 2004), pp. 144–57.

Maguire, L. E., 'Marlovian Texts and Authorship', in *The Cambridge Companion to Christopher Marlowe*, ed. P. Cheney (Cambridge: Cambridge University Press, 2004), pp. 41–54.

Potter, L., 'Marlowe in Theatre and Film', in *The Cambridge Companion to Christopher Marlowe*, ed. P. Cheney (Cambridge: Cambridge University Press, 2004), pp. 262–81.

Sullivan, G. A. Jr., 'Geography and Identity in Marlowe', in *The Cambridge Companion to Christopher Marlowe*, ed. P. Cheney (Cambridge: Cambridge University Press, 2004), pp. 231–44.

White, P. W., 'Marlowe and the Politics of Religion', in *The Cambridge Companion to Christopher Marlowe*, ed. P. Cheney (Cambridge: Cambridge University Press, 2004), pp. 70–89.

Wilson, R., 'Tragedy, Patronage, and Power', in *The Cambridge Companion to Christopher Marlowe*, ed. P. Cheney (Cambridge: Cambridge University Press, 2004), pp. 207–30.

2004: Books

Bertram, B., *The Time is out of Joint: Skepticism in Shakespeare's England* (Newark: University of Delaware Press, 2004).

Cheney, P., ed., *The Cambridge Companion to Christopher Marlowe* (Cambridge: Cambridge University Press, 2004).

Hiscock, A., *The Uses of This World: Thinking Space in Shakespeare, Marlowe, Cary and Jonson* (Cardiff: University of Wales Press, 2004).

Riggs, D., *The World of Christopher Marlowe* (London: Faber & Faber, 2004).

2005: Individual Essays

Moore, R. E., '"I'll Rouse My Senses, and Awake Myself": Marlowe's *The Jew of Malta* and the Renaissance Gnostic Tradition', *Religion and Literature*, 37.3 (2005), pp. 37–58.

Tamaizumi, Y., 'Hitsujikai no hen'yo (jo): Marlowe kara Cotton e', *Eigo Seinen / Rising Generation*, 151.5 (2005), pp. 273–7.

Wilson, R., 'Another Country: Marlowe and the Go-Between', in *Renaissance Go-Betweens: Cultural Exchange in Early Modern Europe*, ed. W. von Koppenfels (Berlin: de Gruyter, 2005).

2005: Books

Honan, P., *Christopher Marlowe: Poet and Spy* (Oxford: Oxford University Press, 2005).

Hopkins, L., *A Christopher Marlowe Chronology* (Basingstoke: Palgrave, 2005).

Lupton, J. R., *Citizen-Saints: Shakespeare and Political Theology* (Chicago: University of Chicago Press, 2005).

2006: Individual Essays

Hopkins, L., '"In a Little Room": Marlowe and *The Allegory of the Tudor Succession*', *Notes and Queries*, 53.4 (2006), pp. 442–4.

Ide, A., '*The Jew of Malta* and the Diabolic Power of Theatrics in the 1580s', *SEL: Studies in English Literature, 1500–1900*, 46.2 (2006), pp. 257–79.

Riggs, D., 'The Poet in the Play: Life and Art in *Tamburlaine* and *The Jew of Malta*', in *Shakespeare, Marlowe, Jonson: New Directions in Biography*, ed. T. Kozuka and J. R. Mulryne (Aldershot: Ashgate, 2006), pp. 205–24.

Umunç, H., 'On Her Majesty's Secret Service: Marlowe and Turkey', *Belleten*, 70.259 (2006), pp. 903–18.

Vitkus, D., 'Turks and Jews in *The Jew of Malta*', in *Early Modern English Drama: A Critical Companion*, ed. G. A. Sullivan Jr., P. Cheney and A. Hadfield (Oxford: Oxford University Press, 2006), pp. 61–72.

2006: Books

Kozuka, T. and Mulryne, J. R., eds, *Shakespeare, Marlowe, Jonson: New Direction in Biography* (Aldershot: Ashgate, 2006).

Sullivan, G. A. Jr., Cheney, P. and Hadfield A., eds, *Early Modern English Drama: A Critical Companion* (Oxford: Oxford University Press, 2006).

2007: Individual Essays

Barroll, L., 'Mythologizing the Ottoman: *The Jew of Malta* and *The Battle of Alcazar*', in *Remapping the Mediterranean World in Early Modern English Writings*, ed. G. V. Stanivukovic (Basingstoke: Palgrave, 2007), pp. 117–30.

Beskins, A., 'From Jew to Nun: Abigail in Marlowe's *The Jew of Malta*', *Explicator*, 65.3 (2007), pp. 133–6.

Eriksen, R., 'Insula est Melita: Marlowe's Urban Comedy and the Poetics of Predation', in *Urban Preoccupations: Mental and Material Landscapes* (Pisa: Fabrizio Serra, 2007), pp. 123–42.

Melnikoff, K., '"[I]ygging Vaines" and "Riming Mother Wits": Marlowe, Clowns and the Early Frameworks of Dramatic Authorship', *Early Modern Literary Studies: A Journal of Sixteenth- and Seventeenth-Century English Literature*, Special Issue 16 (2007), n.p.

Wilson, R., 'Another Country: Marlowe and the Go-Between', in *Remapping the Mediterranean World in Early Modern English Writings*, ed. G. V. Stanivukovic (Basingstoke: Palgrave, 2007), pp. 131–56.

2007: Books

Logan, R. A., *Shakespeare's Marlowe: The Influence of Christopher Marlowe on Shakespeare's Artistry* (Aldershot: Ashgate, 2007).

Parker, J., *The Aesthetics of Antichrist: From Christian Drama to Christopher Marlowe* (Ithaca, NY: Cornell University Press, 2007).

Stanivukovic, G. V., ed., *Remapping the Mediterranean World in Early Modern English Writings* (Basingstoke: Palgrave, 2007).

2008: Individual Essays

Allen, L. K., '"Not Every Man Has the Luck to Go to Corinth": Accruing Exotic Capital in *The Jew of Malta* and *Volpone*', in *Global Traffic: Discourses and Practices of Trade in English Literature and Culture from 1550 to 1700* (Basingstoke: Palgrave, 2008), pp. 95–114.

Engle, L., 'Oedipal Marlowe, Mimetic Middleton', *Modern Philology*, 105.3 (2008), pp. 417–36.

Fitzpatrick, J., 'Early Modern Dietaries and the Jews: *The Merchant of Venice and The Jew of Malta*', in *Shakespeare's World / World Shakespeares*, ed. R. Fotheringham, C. Jansohn and R. S. White (Newark, DE: University of Delaware Press, 2008), pp. 98–107.

Hamlin, W. H., 'Misbelief, False Profession, and *The Jew of Malta*', in *Placing the Plays of Christopher Marlowe: Fresh Cultural Contexts* ed. S. M. Deats and R. A. Logan (Aldershot: Ashgate, 2008), pp. 125–34.

Hopkins, L., 'Christopher Marlowe and the Succession to the English Crown', *Yearbook of English Studies*, 38.1–2 (2008), pp. 183–98.

Kitch, A., 'Shylock's Sacred Nation', *Shakespeare Quarterly*, 59.2 (2008), pp. 131–55.

Lenker, L. T., 'The Hopeless Daughter of a Hapless Jew: Father and Daughter in Marlowe's *The Jew of Malta*', *Placing the Plays of Christopher Marlowe: Fresh Cultural Contexts*, ed. S. M. Deats and R. A. Logan (Aldershot: Ashgate, 2008), pp. 63–73.

Martin, M. R., 'Maltese Psycho: Tragedy and Psychopathology in *The Jew of Malta*', *Lit: Literature Interpretation Theory*, 19.4 (2008), pp. 367–87.

Moss, S., 'Edmund Kean, Anti-Semitism, and *The Jew of Malta*', in *Placing the Plays of Christopher Marlowe: Fresh Cultural Contexts*, ed. S. M. Deats and R. A. Logan (Aldershot: Ashgate, 2008), pp. 43–59.

Parker, J., 'Barabas and Charles I', in *Placing the Plays of Christopher Marlowe: Fresh Cultural Contexts*, ed. S. M. Deats and R. A. Logan (Aldershot: Ashgate, 2008), pp. 167–81.

Perry, M. G., 'Masculinity, Performance, and Identity: Father/Son Dyads in Christopher Marlowe's Plays', in *Placing the Plays of Christopher Marlowe: Fresh Cultural Contexts*, ed. S. M. Deats and R. A. Logan (Aldershot: Ashgate, 2008), pp. 93–110.

2008: Books

Bovilsky, L., *Barbarous Play: Race on the English Renaissance Stage* (Minneapolis, MN: University of Minnesota Press, 2008).

Deats, S. M. and Logan, R. A., eds, *Placing the Plays of Christopher Marlowe: Fresh Cultural Contexts* (Aldershot: Ashgate, 2008).

Hopkins, L., *Christopher Marlowe, Renaissance Dramatist* (Edinburgh: University of Edinburgh Press, 2008).

2009: Individual Essays

Munro, L., 'Marlowe on the Caroline Stage', *Shakespeare Bulletin: A Journal of Performance Criticism and Scholarship*, 27.1 (2009), pp. 39–50.

2009: Books

Cheney, P., *Marlowe's Republican Authorship: Lucan, Liberty, and the Sublime* (Basingstoke: Palgrave, 2009).

2010: Individual Essays

Harmer, J., 'Toying with Religion in the Prologue to *The Jew of Malta*', *Notes and Queries*, 57.3 (2010), pp. 352–5.

Lunney, R., 'Speaking to the Audience: Direct Address in the Plays of Marlowe and His Contemporaries', in *Christopher Marlowe the Craftsman: Lives, Stage, and Page*, ed. S. K. Scott and M. L. Stapleton (Aldershot: Ashgate, 2010), pp. 109–22.

Scott, S. K., '*The Jew of Malta* and the Development of City Comedy: "The Mean Passage of a History"', in *Christopher Marlowe the Craftsman: Lives, Stage, and Page*, ed. S. K. Scott and M. L. Stapleton (Aldershot: Ashgate, 2010), pp. 91–108.

2010: Books

MacKenzie, C. G., *Deathly Experiments: A Study of Icons and Emblems of Mortality in Christopher Marlowe's Plays* (New York: AMS, 2010).

Scott, S. K. and Stapleton, M. L., eds, *Christopher Marlowe the Craftsman: Lives, Stage, and Page* (Aldershot: Ashgate, 2010).

2011: Books

Logan, R. A., ed., *Christopher Marlowe* (Aldershot: Ashgate, 2011).

FOUR

New Directions: *The Jew of Malta* in Repertory

ROSLYN L. KNUTSON

The first concrete evidence of the existence of *The Jew of Malta* is also a record of its repertorial context. The play is entered in the book of accounts kept by Philip Henslowe, theatrical entrepreneur and owner of the Rose playhouse, who, on 19 February 1592, began to list the offerings there by the players of Lord Strange. *The Jew of Malta* is the seventh play named; it opens the second full week of performances: 'R*eceive*d at the Jewe of malltuse th*e* 26 of febreary*e* 1591 [1592] . . . . . . ls'.[1] But the play was not then new. Its initial appearance on stage was probably a couple of years earlier, 1589 or 1590, probably in repertory with other scripts acquired by players under the patronage of Charles Howard, Lord Admiral.[2] Due to Henslowe's book of accounts (familiarly known as the *Diary*), the performance history of *The Jew of Malta* is readily traceable from that 1592 run into May of 1601. Likewise the *Diary* provides the repertorial context for companies performing the play at the Rose and the Fortune playhouses. However, after 1601 there is nothing to indicate continued theatrical activity until its publication in 1633 with a title page advertising a performance 'BEFORE THE KING AND QVEENE, IN HIS MAJESTIES Theatre at *White-Hall*, by her Majesties Servants at the *Cock-pit*'.[3] The title page adds that the play was '*Written by* CHRISTOPHER MARLO'. The dedicatory epistle and Prologues by Thomas Heywood printed with the text confirm recent performances by the company of Queen Henrietta Maria at court and the Cockpit playhouse (known also as the Phoenix). After this revival, the life of *The Jew of Malta* on the early modern stage apparently came to a close. It is the purpose of this essay to re-examine that life in terms of repertorial commerce. This approach incidentally concerns company owners and performance venues in London and the provinces, but the primary focus here is how well *The Jew of Malta* plays with others. The dynamics of Marlowe's play in repertory with the holdings of its owner-of-the-moment and across company lines provide snapshots of an early modern English theatrical marketing strategy in the making as companies accommodate its enduring commercial appeal to shifts in theatrical fashion.

1589 and the Lord Admiral's Players

Digests of the stage history of *The Jew of Malta* in single-play editions often start with the entry in Henslowe's *Diary* in February 1592 (as above). Then, after a brief look backward to several plays with Jews as characters, the focus moves ahead to 1594 and the sensational coincidence of the execution of Roderigo Lopez in June with performances of Marlowe's play at the Newington and Rose playhouses. However, the initial commercial environment for *The Jew of Malta* was 1589. Initial repertorial questions therefore inquire into the companies in operation, their venues, their holdings and the cultural energies to which those holdings might have responded. It matters also where Marlowe was and what he knew of the playhouse world. According to biographical sources, Marlowe was in London in the fall of 1589; on 18 September he was embroiled in a swordfight with William Bradley; Thomas Watson, who reportedly intervened on Marlowe's behalf, killed Bradley. Marlowe and Watson were committed to Newgate on 18 September 1589, and a document from the prison calendar establishes that both men had lodgings in the parish of Norton Folgate. Both men were exonerated when they appeared at the Newgate Sessions on 3 December.[4] Two recently published lawsuits imply that Marlowe was also in London in 1587 and 1588.[5] From this evidence, it is reasonable to assume that Marlowe, being in London in the year or two leading up to the stage debut of *The Jew of Malta*, could have monitored the Admiral's men and theatrical activity in general with some regularity.[6]

And there were many venues to monitor. Adjacent to Norton Folgate were two playhouses in St. Leonard Shoreditch, the Theatre and the Curtain, which had been built in 1576 and 1577 respectively.[7] South along the Shoreditch High Road past Bishopsgate to the area of Ludgate Hill and Eastcheap, there were four inns noted for playing: the Bull, the Bell, the Cross Keys and the Bell Savage. Further south across London Bridge and to the west was a third playhouse, the Rose, newly built in 1587 (*The Jew of Malta* played there in February 1592, if not also earlier). And a mile or so south beyond London Bridge was the playhouse at Newington, which was in use by 1577 (*The Jew of Malta* played there in June 1594, if not also earlier). Theatre historians know much less about the companies and their offerings at these venues in the late 1580s than Marlowe did. However, one set of documents places the Admiral's men at the Theatre in November 1590: a lawsuit in the Court of Chancery in 1589–90 filed against James Burbage by the widow of his partner in building the Theatre, John Brayne.[8] In that suit, John Alleyn, who is better known as the elder brother of Edward Alleyn but who was a player in his own right, testified that he had gone to Burbage in November 1590 to collect money owed him and his company from performances at the Theatre. In this testimony Alleyn threatened to 'complain to their [the players'] lord and master, the Lord Admiral' if Burbage did not pay up; Alleyn further confirmed the identity of the company in residence as the Admiral's men by naming James Tunstall as one of the players who heard Burbage a week later speaking defiantly about appeals to any lords to resolve disputes.[9] It is therefore possible to assert with some confidence that *The Jew of Malta* was in performance at the Theatre at some point during its maiden run.

In addition, *The Jew of Malta* was most likely performed on the road. In 1589–90 the Admiral's men gave performances in East Anglia, the Southeast, Midlands, Southwest and West Midlands.[10] Tying these performances to a specific date, and thus ordering them into touring itineraries, is difficult. Provincial records tend to enter payments annually, as from Michaelmas to Michaelmas; consequently, a record listed in a mass entry for 1589–90 may be narrowed only by surrounding entries with more precise dates, as illustrated by those for the Admiral's men in Ipswich, which fall between the end of October and 17 February 1589–90.[11] However, payments at four towns in 1590 are specifically dated: Rye, 23 June; New Romney, 26 June; Marlborough, 25 July; and Gloucester, 17 September.[12] From these, it is possible to envision a southeastern tour to Rye and New Romney in early summer that might have included Maidstone, Folkestone and Lydd.[13] Gloucester is in the Western Midlands. The Admiral's men apparently turned west when they concluded the southeastern circuit in mid-summer; they could easily have stopped at Oxford and Bristol on their way to Gloucester, then headed north to Coventry.[14] By November, according to Alleyn's testimony in the Brayne-Burbage lawsuit, the Admiral's men were in London at the Theatre.

Contrary to the venerable scholarly assumption that provincial performances were given on the village green on portable stages (Jonson's 'boards and barrel heads' [III.iv.173]),[15] research associated with the Toronto-based project, Records of Early English Drama (REED), proves that indoor halls were a far more common venue. In Folkestone and Maidstone in 1590, that hall was the Town Hall; at Oxford, Bristol and Coventry, the Guildhall was. The *Patrons and Performances Web Site*, sponsored by REED, provides an illustration of the interior of the Guildhall at Coventry, St. Mary's (Figure 1), and a drawing of the exterior of the Bristol Guildhall (Figure 2). One other venue outside of London where the Admiral's men might have played is the residence of their patron in Effingham.[16] No documents confirm such performances, but REED records generally support the appearances of companies at the residences of their patrons. Effingham, like Hampton Court, was in Surrey and thus relatively convenient both to excursions from London and to tours beginning in Maidstone then swinging southeast to the high road that led through Canterbury to the coastal towns of Folkestone, New Romney and Lydd.

The claim above that *The Jew of Malta* was most likely performed on the road would have been considered fanciful by scholars a generation ago; it is considered so in some quarters still. Narratives of theatre history in the nineteenth century are dominated by scorn for provincial performances in terms of texts, quality of players and comprehension by the audience. The opinion became fact as the New Bibliographers of the twentieth century offered explanations for differences between some quartos of Shakespeare's plays and folio versions.[17] Those explanations, which depend upon belief that texts performed in the provinces had simple staging requirements or were stripped down versions of their London originals, would seem to rule out *The Jew of Malta*. Arguing precisely that in his company history of the Admiral's men, Andrew Gurr disqualifies it for touring because of the 'heavy demands for staging its finale, when Barabbas [sic] is made to fall down from the upper stage into the hellish cauldron'; he adds that Barabas's 'visible carpentry [. . .] precludes eventful staging', as does the call for a cauldron.[18] Leslie Thomson argues the opposite. In a survey of staging features of extant texts associated with adult commercial companies in the period, 1586–94, Thomson turns the conjunction of plain staging with touring on its head, suggesting that 'a company could have brought with it some plays with simple staging requirements for those venues where only basic facilities were available, [but] almost certainly a company would also have brought some plays that included characters appearing above, revealed by a drawn curtain, or rising from a trap'.[19] She provides tables that aptly demonstrate how circumscribed a company's choices would have been if it had taken only its plays that required 'a bare floor, a few props, and some costumes' (p. 533).[20] Making the obvious point that companies wanted to take on the road the plays popular in London and therefore most anticipated by provincial audiences, she considers how more complex staging might have been done (pp. 531, 535 passim).

Everyone who discusses touring concedes that there is almost no data on touring repertories, yet Thomson's premise that the extant texts suggest what *might* have been performed rather than demonstrate the ineligibility of specific plays for tours is liberating. It multiplies not only the venues where *The Jew of Malta* might have played but the repertorial competition it might have engaged as townspeople and VIPs in the Kentish hamlet of Lydd (for example) enjoyed performances in 1589–91 not only from the Admiral's men but also player-organizations of the earl of Essex, earl of Sussex, earl of Worcester, Lord Beauchamp and the Queen, including her Children of the Chapel. Of the adult companies, only the Queen's men and Admiral's men have documented appearances in London *c*. 1590. It is therefore quite possible that playgoers in the provinces could have seen more variety in company talent and repertorial offerings than did Londoners.

Both on the road and at a London venue in 1590, the Admiral's men had an impressive set of scripts to offer audiences. Probably since 1587, they had had *The Spanish Tragedy* by Thomas Kyd and Marlowe's *Tamburlaine the Great*, undeniably instant block-busters. Theatre historians cannot say whether either was still in production several years later. The run of *Tamburlaine* might have been extended when its second part was introduced, *c*. 1588; if so, the pairing for performance served as precedent for the Admiral's men of 1594, who kept the first part in active reper-tory at the Rose to accompany *Tamburlaine II* (Foakes, pp. 26–33). According to current scholarly consensus, the Admiral's men also had Marlowe's *Doctor Faustus*.[21] As with the two-part *Tamburlaine*, we do not know how long the maiden run of *Doctor Faustus* continued, but presumably *The Jew of Malta* followed its elder Marlovian siblings on stage, even if they were retired before it made its debut. According to Lukas Erne, Kyd is now considered the likely author both of *Soliman and Perseda*, the Ur-*Hamlet* and a contributor to 'Don Horatio'.[22] Regarding company ownership and repertories, one of many questions is whether by 1587 Kyd had shifted his allegiance from the Queen's men, for whom he wrote in 1583–5, to the Admiral's men, as marked by that com-pany's probable acquisition of *The Spanish Tragedy*. If so, *Soliman and Perseda* as well as the two lost plays were probably among the Admiral's holdings in 1589. Lucas Erne dates *Soliman and Perseda* 'in 1588 or 1589', pointedly relying on Marlowe's apparent use of Kyd's version of the siege of Rhodes rather than that in his-torical accounts (pp. 159–60). Erne implies that 'Don Horatio' was written in close proximity to its second part, *The Spanish Tragedy* (p. 20). He dates the lost 'Hamlet' at the same time, '*c.* 1588/9', relying primarily on the allusion to the play by Thomas Nashe in his preface to Robert Greene's *Menaphon*, which was registered at Stationers' Hall on 23 August 1589 and published in that year (p. 147). Two dramatists also connected to the Admiral's men are Thomas Lodge and George Peele. Lodge's play, *The Wounds of Civil War*, carried a title-page advertisement of the Admiral's men at its printing in 1594 (S. R. 24 May 1594). Peele's play, *The Battle of Alcazar*, also advertised ownership by the Admiral's men at its printing in 1594. Scholars generally have given both plays an earlier date based on a perceived imitation of Marlowe's *Tamburlaine*. Typical is E. K. Chambers, who chose *c.* 1588 for Lodge's play and *c.* 1589 for Peele's (3, p. 410). By that chronology, both plays very likely belonged to the Admiral's repertory when *The Jew of Malta* was new.

Compared to the wealth of commentary on the influence of Marlowe's *Tamburlaine* plays, scholars have little to say about the artistic influence of *The Jew of Malta*. However, marketing is broader than authorial influence. Plays exploited popular motifs in their repertorial fellows as well as in the rival offerings of other companies. In 1589 the Admiral's men apparently had no additional plays with a Jew as character, but *The Jew of Malta* participated in other networks of commercial competition within the repertory. One is the tragedy of revenge, the formula Kyd developed in *The Spanish Tragedy*. According to Fredson Bowers, Marlowe's play is the anti-Kydian revenge in that the revenger is a villain, the 'revenge ends [. . .] in the second scene of the third act', and 'no real counter-revenge' develops.[23] The character of villainous revenger, which disqualifies Marlowe's play as a Kydian clone, identifies it with a second and older network of competition built upon the character of the Vice. By the 1580s, and largely through Marlowe's genius, the Vice from moral plays of the 1560s and 1570s became (in Bowers's terms) 'a unifying hero' who is driven by 'a criminal passion' (pp. 108, 107). The third network is the foreign history play. As scholars have long recognized, the setting in Malta, the external threats from Turks and Spaniards, and the slave market are superficial characteristics of plays set in the Mediterranean, yet their superficiality does not undercut their stage value in terms of transgressive stereotypes in exotic costumes.

These motifs – revenge, criminal passion and cultural other-ness – are evident in several holdings assigned to the Admiral's men in 1589, and their presence suggests a commercial engage-ment with *The Jew of Malta*. The lost 'Hamlet' presumably imi-tated the revenge formula of *The Spanish Tragedy*, an inference based on its authorship as well as the remembrance of Thomas Lodge that its ghost 'cried so miserally at ye Theator like an oister wife, *Hamlet, reuenge*'.[24] *Soliman and Perseda* also has the trappings of conventional revenge; yet, as Erne argues, its 'striking clash of comic and tragic elements' marks it as a 'radical and experimental play' (p. 197). Erne, who links *Soliman and Perseda* specifically to *The Jew of Malta* in Marlowe's use of Kyd's details on the siege of Rhodes, links it further by exploring the blustering character of Basilisco. Though comic in his vaunting and misplaced love, Basilisco is both dangerous and poignant as a tool of revenge in the hands of Perseda (pp. 197–9). The foreign locations of the play in Rhodes and Constantinople give it the appearance of historicity, as Malta provides for Marlowe, but nothing historical happens. When Soliman has the lovers Erastus and Perseda in his grasp, his criminal passion takes over the play to their mutual destruc-tion.[25] *The Wounds of Civil War*, being set in Rome, does not share the setting of the eastern Mediterranean; and the bloody-minded Scilla has more Tamburlaine in his character than Barabas. Nonetheless, Scilla shares a criminal passion that drives him from one military atrocity to another. Similarly, *The Battle of Alcazar* has more in common with the *Tamburlaine* plays (including the need for a chariot), but the play opens with a dumb show of assas-sinations by the criminally passionate Moor, Muly Mahamet. At the command of extra-narrative characters, he becomes the tar-get of revenge: Nemesis, 'with bloudie whip in hand/ Thunders for vengeance on this Negro moore' (II. 309–10), and, besting the oyster-wife-voiced ghost in 'Hamlet', three ghosts in *The Battle of Alcazar* cry 'Vindicta' (l. 316).[26]

Barabas had no apparent Jewish counterpart in the repertory of the Admiral's men, but across company lines the Queen's men had at least *Selimus* with the poisoner, Abraham. In addition, *Selimus* exploited the commercially successful motifs of revenge, criminal passion and foreign history that situate *The Jew of Malta* within the repertory of the Admiral's men. Selimus bursts upon the stage with a 151-line tirade in which he announces his willingness to kill anyone for a crown, although Bajazet (his father) lives and he (Selimus) is third in line. Much of the speech expresses his contempt for God: 'I count it sacriledge, for to be holy' (ii.245).[27] He plans to 'arme [his] heart with irreligion' (ii.304); he sees laws, family loyalty and religion as 'bug-beares to keepe the world in feare' (ii.336). Daniel Vitkus observes that in this speech Selimus would have provided 'electrifying moments for the audience, who gasped to hear such fearless defiance of divine law'.[28] But Selimus is not the only Machiavel in the play. Acomat, the middle brother, sees opportunity in the chaos caused by Selimus's rebellion; he begins a murderous rampage that includes the on-stage torture of his father's messenger, Aga, whose eyes are plucked out, hands cut off and still-living body returned to Bajazet in a scene both grotesque and comic (xvi). Selimus then enlists Abraham, 'a cunning Iew,/ Professing phisicke', to kill his father (xxviii.1684–5).[29] In a bizarre three-way poisoning, Abraham drinks a toast to Bajazet, to whom he passes the poisoned cup, and the mutilated messenger drinks as well. In *The Queen's Men and their Plays* Scott McMillin and Sally-Beth MacLean call *Selimus* 'the most complex of the anti-Marlowe plays' in the repertory of the Queen's men (p. 158), but that judgement does not preclude its participating mutually in transgressive motifs that brought commercial success to *The Jew of Malta*.

The Queen's men might have had a second play with a memorable character of a Jew: *The Three Ladies of London*, which was published in 1584 without an advertisement of company affiliation. Two circumstances suggest that *Three Ladies of London* had a stage life with the Queen's men post-1588: its author, Robert Wilson, joined the Queen's men at its formation in 1583, perhaps with this and others of his scripts in hand; and, Wilson's sequel, *The Three Lords and Three Ladies of London*, was played by the Queen's men to celebrate victory over Spain and its warships. If *The Three Ladies of London* was revived to accompany its sequel, audiences in 1589 could have been recently reminded of the mercantile sub-plot that concerns Gerontus, a Jewish usurer and a Turk. In a play full of avaricious characters – for example, Lady Lucre and Usury – yet another one defined by money and goods might not have stood out, but Gerontus develops against type. Initially he sounds like Barabas in the opening soliloquy about 'infinite riches in a little room' (I.i.37).[30] Bragging to Mercadorus, an Italian merchant, Gerontus catalogues his wares, which include not only 'musk, amber, sweet powders, fine odours, pleasant perfumes, and many such toys' but also 'diamonds, rubies, emeralds, sapphires, smaradines, opals, onacles, jacinths, agates, turquoise, and almost of all kind of precious stones' (ix.31, 33).[31] He has already loaned Mercadorus 2,000 ducats for a term of three months, and the merchant soon defaults. In a trial scene set in a Turkish court, Mercadorus threatens to turn Turk in order to escape legal judgement. Gerontus is shocked that the man would 'forsake [his] faith so lightly' (xii.15). In an attempt to stop the conversion, Gerontus forgives the debt, and the merchant rewards such charity by glibly renouncing Islam. The Judge, disgusted, delivers the verdict that 'Jews seek to excel in Christianity, and Christians in Jewishness' (xiv.49). Hindsight suggests that Shakespeare exploited this scene in more particular ways than did Marlowe; but for playgoers in the intensely xenophobic post-Armada years, Wilson's Gerontus and Marlowe's Barabas would have projected a similar fascination as cultural aliens.

It is impossible to know precisely how the Admiral's men determined the commercial value of *The Jew of Malta* during its maiden run without records of company playlists and revenue. And these playlists would name items now lost. An example is 'Heliogabalus', to which Robert Greene referred in self-serving invective in an address to his readers in *Perimedes the Blacke-Smith* (1588 [S. R. 29 March]). Railing against criticism of his tragic drama, Greene accused 'two Gentlemen Poets', whose own work he characterized as 'daring God out of heauen with that Atheist **Tamburlan**, or blaspheming with the mad preest of the sonne'.[32] A logical identification of 'the mad preest of the sonne' is the play 'Heliogabalus', which was entered in the Stationers' Register on 19 June 1594 but not printed, in so far as is known.[33] 'Heliogabalus' would have featured the emperor Varius Avitus Bassianus, 218–22 CE, who was known for his worship of the Syrian god, Elagabalus. His misbehaviour, flagrant even by Roman standards, is relevant to *The Jew of Malta* in providing playgoers yet more context for Barabas's criminal passion and irreverence towards Christians. 'Heliogabalus' comes down to scholars of early modern English drama tied to the *Tamburlaine* pair (Greene's allusion), as do many of the plays offered here as repertorial context for *The Jew of Malta*. But there is room in 1589 for more than one play by Marlowe. Exotic settings, the illusory authority of history, the facile justification of revenge for wilful murder, and the allure of the cultural alien mark the special genius of *The Jew of Malta* but also define its place in a flourishing theatrical environment.

1592–4 and Companies at the Rose Playhouse

By February 1592 Lord Strange's men were performing *The Jew of Malta* at the Rose playhouse, which would be its primary London venue until the opening of the Fortune in 1600. A question about its new situation is how it changed hands from the Admiral's men to the company of Lord Strange. The answer may also explain why it is available to other companies at the Rose in 1594 before it returns to the Admiral's men in May of that year. Theatre historians know too little about the migration of plays. We know various texts did move, but particulars of movement are unclear.[34] The hypothesis with the strongest evidence is that players carried scripts as they left one troupe to join another. In the case of *The Jew of Malta* the prime agent has to be Edward Alleyn.[35] Alleyn had performed the role of Barabas when the play was new; he bought theatrical properties from Richard Jones in January 1589; he was performing with Lord Strange's men by 1592, even though he retained his status as servant of the Lord Admiral; he married into Philip Henslowe's family in October 1592 and thus into the playhouse business at the Rose; he was a member of the Admiral's men in May 1594; and he sold that company nine scripts from 22 August 1601 to 2 October 1602.[36] A second question is repertorial and commercial: how does the treatment of *The Jew of Malta* in revival suggest an emerging marketing strategy in the playhouse industry, 1592–4? The answer lies in the playlists entered by Henslowe at the Rose in the *Diary*. Henslowe began the playlists on 19 February 1592 with performances by Lord Strange's men, and by that time the company had probably been in residence for some months. Sally-Beth MacLean points out that Strange's players 'do not show up in provincial accounts on a regular basis between 1589 [. . .] and late June 1592'.[37] She deduces from this evidence that they were 'setting their sights on achieving commercial success in London and at court' (p. 46). Such a perception of future business in itself implies that the company was developing a new marketing strategy tailored to a particular stage in a fixed location with frequently returning playgoers, and theatre historians have explained the number and diversity of plays in their repertory as evidence of that strategy. Also, there are hints that the company saw commercial advantage in a calculated scheduling of offerings. For example, on four occasions in 1592, Strange's men scheduled 'Don Horatio' in tandem with *The Spanish Tragedy*,[38] yet 'Don Horatio' was not continued into the winter season of 1592–3 with its mate. These instances might be merely coincidence in lengthy runs for each play, but there are moments in the scheduling of *The Jew of Malta* when Strange's men could have reaped a benefit from intentional scheduling however unwittingly. One is the pairing with the now-lost 'Machiavel', an apparently old play whose title suggests a focus either on the Italian spin-doctor himself or a protégé.[39] Strange's men introduced 'Machiavel' on 2 March 1592; at its subsequent performances of 3 April and 29 May, it preceded

The Jew of Malta in the schedule (4 April, 30 May). Another is the pairing with 'Muly Mollocco', also apparently an old play and possibly lost.[40] 'Muly Mollocco' enjoyed many more performances independent of a pairing with *The Jew of Malta* than did 'Machiavel', but in one instance it directly preceded Marlowe's play (17 April) and on 31 May it completed a three-play sequence with 'Machiavel' (29th) and *The Jew of Malta* (30th). At least two other plays shared cultural motifs with Marlowe's but not a special relationship in scheduling. One, 'Titus and Vespasian', was a dramatization of the destruction of the Jews at Jerusalem by the emperor Titus and his son Vespasian.[41] A second, *Orlando Furioso*, was a play like Marlowe's in its foreign settings and quasi-historical characters in matching sets of ethnic costumes.

Lawrence Manley, who characterizes Strange's men as an 'innovative and politically daring company', points out a number of its holdings that require pyrotechnics: 'Fire, fireworks, the threat of fire, and above all the threat and the actual simulation of burning people alive are astonishingly prominent in the company's repertory'.[42] Manley includes plays with magic or devils such as *John of Bordeaux* and *A Knack to Know a Knave*.[43] *A Looking Glass for London and England* by Lodge and Greene has Old Testament fireworks: the queen of Ninevah, Remilia, is burned black by a lightning bolt; Priests of the Sun enter '*carrying fire in their hands*' (IV iii.1539); and '*A hand from out a cloud threateneth a burning sword*' (IV.iii.1556).[44] Though Joan of Arc is burned offstage, *Henry VI* by Shakespeare provides the promise of fire. A lost play, 'Bendo and Richardo', shared both a property and stagecraft with *The Jew of Malta*. The story is in William Painter's *Palace of Pleasure*: Bendo, 'a Florentine architect, builds a treasure-house for the duke of Venice [. . .] [with] a secret passageway through which he crawls nightly to steal from the duke' (Manley, p. 119). The duke discovers Bendo's treachery and sets a trap consisting of a cauldron of boiling pitch into which the thief falls. As Manley points out, Barabas also dies a '"hot death"' onstage (p. 119).

Strange's men went on tour in mid-summer 1592, and in the subsequent 18 months the stage history of *The Jew of Malta* reflects the normal uncertainties of early modern theatrical commerce. Henslowe recorded a return to the Rose for Strange's men from 29 December 1592 to 1 February 1593, at which time they continued *The Jew of Malta* during the run with some previous repertorial mates including 'Muly Mollocco' and 'Titus and Vespasian'. Then the company went on tour again. When Marlowe's play next appeared at the Rose, it was on 4 February 1594 as the next-to-last performance by the earl of Sussex's men, in a run that had begun five weeks earlier on 29 December 1593. Theatre historians have puzzled over the appearance of Sussex's men at Henslowe's playhouse, which was in some sense by now also Alleyn's playhouse. McMillin offers a plausible two-part explanation: (1) that the organization specified by Henslowe as Sussex's men was an ad hoc assembly of players from companies disrupted by playhouse closures in London and changes in patronage; and (2) that the organization, however briefly, included Alleyn (pp. 251–2). A result of these circumstances that explains also the appearance of Marlowe's play with the briefly partnered Sussex's and Queen's companies through Easter Week 1594 (1–8 April) is that *The Jew of Malta* had become in effect a 'house' play in which Alleyn performed regardless of the company in residence. The appeal of this account is that Sussex's men would not have been obligated to assign Alleyn a part in their ten old plays carried over from touring in 1593, nor would Sussex and Queen's similarly have had to adjust casting for their four offerings. In May the Admiral's men were reconstituted, and they gave three performances beginning with *The Jew of Malta* on the 14th. The play would remain in the Admiral's repertory through 1601 when it was revived to celebrate the company's new Fortune playhouse and the post-retirement return of its star player, Edward Alleyn.

The competition across company lines for *The Jew of Malta* in its early years at the Rose may be deduced from the repertories of Sussex's men, Queen's men and Pembroke's men. Like Strange's men at the Rose, these three companies might well have performed at public venues in London in 1592–3, but that activity cannot now be documented. However, all three did perform at court and go on tour. Sussex's men, for example, appeared at court on 2 January 1592; they were touring in 1592–3. Although provincial records do not name the plays performed on the road, Sussex's men turned up at the Rose on 29 December 1593 with a 'full-throttle calendar' of offerings.[45] A logical explanation is that they had been performing these works recently in the provinces. Of this repertory, all except *George a Greene* are lost; only 'Huon of Bordeaux' and 'Abraham and Lot' suggest by their titles any motifs of foreign and biblical history in common with Marlowe's play. The play most potentially competitive with *The Jew of Malta* was *Titus Andronicus*, which Sussex's men introduced 'ne' on 23 January 1594. For the ten days when both were in production, they recaptured the multi-layered repertorial connections of revenge, criminally passionate characters and exotic settings that Marlowe's play had enjoyed in the Admiral's holdings with *The Spanish Tragedy*, *The Wounds of Civil War* and *The Battle of Alcazar*. In June that competition was emphasized twice in sequential scheduling at the playhouse in Newington (4–5 and 12–13 June); shortly thereafter, when *Titus Andronicus* moved to the repertory of the Chamberlain's men, the competition would continue across company lines.

The Queen's men were also touring in 1592–3, and they were the only company called to perform at court in 1593–4 (6 Jan). By Easter Monday 1594, they were at the Rose through 8 April, performing jointly with Sussex's men. The Queen's men apparently contributed Robert Greene's *Friar Bacon and Friar Bungay* to the offerings (1, 3 April) and the anonymous *King Leir* (6, 8 April), but due perhaps to the brevity of the run at the Rose there is no sign here of plays registered with these two at Stationers' Hall on 14 May 1594: 'The Famous History of John of Gaunt', *David and Bethsabe*, and 'A Pastoral Pleasant Comedie of Robin Hood and Little John'.[46] The most interesting of these in terms of *The Jew of Malta* is the lost play on John of Gaunt. Its subtitle indicates a focus on the Conquest of Spain and the marriage of his daughters to the kings of Castile and Portugal and thus with the Mediterranean political landscape of *The Spanish Tragedy* and *The Battle of Alcazar*. Missing from the Rose lineup also is

Selimus, which had competed with Marlowe's play previously. It was published in 1594 without registration at Stationers' Hall. *The Jew of Malta* experienced the reverse situation: it was registered at Stationers' Hall on 17 May but not printed, in so far as is known.[47]

In 1592–3 Pembroke's men produced Marlowe's new play, *Edward II*, and thereby provided a dimension of repertorial competition that *The Jew of Malta* had not previously experienced. In content, *Edward II* had no special commercial *frisson* with *The Jew of Malta*, but the very fact of plays by the same dramatist in competition across company lines is worth notice. Coincidentally, Pembroke's men and Strange's men divided the court dates at Christmas, 1592–3; Pembroke's performed on 26 December and 6 January, Strange's men on 27 and 31 December, and 1 January. For some theatre historians, the appearance of Pembroke's men at court has signalled a fresh configuration of the company, which perhaps took up residence at James Burbage's Theatre and perhaps added Richard Burbage to their fellowship.[48] By 1594 Pembroke's company had broken up, but a reconstituted organization was touring again by 1595 and in London by 1597.[49] Their repertory in 1592–3 in addition to *Edward II* included *The Taming of A Shrew* and the quarto versions of Shakespeare's *2 Henry VI* and *3 Henry VI*. Because Pembroke's acquired plays written by Marlowe and Shakespeare, scholars have been tempted to assign to them every play known to exist in 1592–3 but not found either in Henslowe's *Diary* or the holdings of the Queen's men. Karl Wentersdorf, for example, suggests *Soliman and Perseda* and *Doctor Faustus* as possible Pembroke's offerings.[50]

An allusion in *Satiromastix* by Thomas Dekker implies that Pembroke's men had once had *The Spanish Tragedy* or its clone. In banter with Horace (the parody of Ben Jonson), Tucca, the blowhard man-about-town, jokes that Horace had formerly played the part of Hieronimo badly: 'I ha seene thy shoulders lapt in a Plaiers old cast Cloake, like a Slie knaue as thou art: and when thou ranst mad for the death of Horatio: thou borrowedst a gowne of *Roscius* the stager' (i.ii.354–6).[51] If Wentersdorf's guess and Dekker's jibe reflect commercial realities, Pembroke's men competed in 1593 not only with Marlovian siblings of *The Jew of Malta* but also with some mates from the repertory of the Admiral's men.

1594 and the Lord Admiral's Players

After the company reorganizations of May 1594, *The Jew of Malta* stayed with the Admiral's men at its various venues in London and on tour until some time after its revival in 1601 at the Fortune playhouse. In June 1594, before concern over the plague in London had subsided, the Admiral's men joined the also-newly constituted players of Henry Carey, Lord Chamberlain, for a ten-day run at the playhouse in Newington, about a mile to the south of London Bridge. Henslowe documents the joint performances with the heading, 'In the name of god Amen begininge at newington my Lord Admeralle men & my Lorde chamberlen men As ffolowethe 1594' (Foakes, p. 21). What 'ffolowethe' in repertorial terms is a preview of the competition that extended for years within the offerings of the Admiral's men and across company lines to the Chamberlain's men as well as other London companies. Andrew Gurr labels this period in London as the start of a duopoly established by two powerful privy councillors who allocated players, plays and playhouses to their companies, allegedly marginalizing other theatrical enterprises to the extent that playgoers' opportunities were 'restricted to one of the only two venues and companies open daily in the 1590s' (*Shakespeare's Opposites*, p. 2).[52] But that claim hinders an assessment of *The Jew of Malta* as a commercial property. Further, it is a claim dependent on an absence of evidence. If the offerings at the outdoor Swan (1595) and Boar's Head (1598) playhouses were better known, as well as those at the indoor children's venues of Paul's (1599) and Blackfriars (1600), there might appear connections between Marlowe's play and ones now unassigned to dates and companies. In addition, emerging scholarship on lost plays – constrained as it also is by absent evidence – nonetheless hints at repertorial competition heretofore invisible. The Admiral's men and Chamberlain's men played at Newington for ten days.

Although many details of the joint venture are unknown,[53] the repertorial lineup indicates two old connections and a new one. *The Jew of Malta* was reunited with two plays from its previous runs: 'Hamlet' (*c.* 1589) and *Titus Andronicus* (1594). The reunion was temporary because these plays became the properties of the Chamberlain's men (or so scholars assume). The new connection is with 'Hester and Ahasuerus', presumably also brought to Newington by the Chamberlain's men. The play was scheduled on 3 June as the opening show of the Newington run, followed immediately by *The Jew of* Malta on 4 June. Elizabethan playgoers knew the story from the Old Testament: Ahasuerus takes a bride, Hester, who is accompanied to court by her elder family member, Mardocheus. At Mardocheus's request, Hester conceals their identity as Jews. Haman, Ahasuerus's ambitious chieftain, envies Mardocheus's standing with the king; he persuades Ahasuerus to sign an edict for the slaughter of the Jews. Revealing her kinship, Hester contests that decision, and Ahasuerus rescinds it. Haman is hanged on the gallows he had constructed for Mardocheus, and Mardocheus is rewarded with the position of second-in-command to Ahasuerus.

Though 'Hester and Ahasuerus' is lost, several sources suggest how the story might have been retold and thus how the play might have competed with Marlowe's play in the marketplace. One such source is the earlier drama, *Godly Queen Hester* (Q1561); another, the popular perception of Hester as a strong, patriotic and virtuous wife. *Godly Queen Hester* (Q1561) is a late moral play with a double thrust: wise counsel and concern for the defenseless. The political theme focuses on Aman. The Vice characters – Pride, Adulation and Ambition – give Aman their attributes, knowing he will consequently destroy himself. Under their influence, Aman concocts the plan to have Assuerus massacre the Jews and thus remove Mardocheus, who is an impediment to Aman's advancement. Previously, Assuerus had chosen Hester from a bevy of eligible virgins for her beauty, wisdom and tender heart. She risks incurring the king's displeasure when she petitions him to lift the edict: her boldness challenges his domestic and political authority, her declaration that she is 'of that nation' challenges the cultural integrity of his household and lineage.[54] Assuerus responds with wisdom and compassion. Shocked by the danger to Hester and infuriated by Aman's deception, he revokes the decree. It is this image of Hester as the champion of common people and defender of the faith that colours many references to her in tracts, sermons and civic festivals. An example is Queen Elizabeth herself who, in a prayer, asks God to 'persist . . . in giving [her] strength so that [she], like another Deborah, like another Judith, like another Esther, may free Thy people of Israel from the hands of thy enemies'.[55] Mardocheus is also praised as the embodiment of royal advisor who, in the words of John Alymer, must 'bringe the ship of the common welth, the Church of Christe, and the Quenes realm, to a quiet port'.[56] Alymer, who was consecrated Bishop of London in 1576, further defended Mardocheus for his humble station, observing that 'sometime vnder a homelye coate, lieth hidden muche treasure, and pure gold is founde among muche drosse' (O3).

Another factor in the commercial theatrical moment of June 1594 is the execution of Roderigo Lopez. Seeking a reason for yet another revival of *The Jew of Malta*, scholars have called attention to a putatively false servant of the crown in Lopez, a Portuguese physician, who had moved to London in 1559 and developed a successful medical practice with aristocratic and royal clientele. On 28 February 1594 Lopez was arraigned on the crime of poisoning the queen; he was hanged, drawn and quartered at Tyburn on 7 June 1594. Stephen Greenblatt comments at length on the mocking response of the crowd to Lopez's scaffold declarations of innocence, Christian faith and patriotism.[57] However, the presence of 'Hester and Ahasuerus' in Henslowe's playlist for Newington suggests that a deeper and more complex cultural interplay was being exploited on London stages than the attitudes towards Jews invited by Marlowe's play. In the story of the lost play, Hester is a paragon; Mardocheus is the good servant; the preservation of Jewry is a noble and merciful act. Side by side at Newington, and thereafter from the Rose in Southwark to the

Theatre in Shoreditch, the continuing performances of 'Hester and Ahasuerus' and *The Jew of Malta* dramatized a pernicious contradiction in Elizabethan attitudes towards biblical and contemporary Jews. That contradiction is expressed in simple terms in a moral discourse on the story of Hester that was published in England in 1584: the author praises the Old Testament Hester but calls 'The Iewes of our time . . . the kindred of Aman'.[58]

When the Admiral's men returned to the Rose on 15 June, they continued *The Jew of Malta* for nine performances through 9 December 1594; the play was revived again for eight performances from 9 January to 21 June 1596.[59] Nothing about its scheduling in 1594 or 1596 suggests an attempt to market the play more aggressively in conjunction with ones sharing motifs. Indeed, as Holger Syme points out, by June 1594 the play 'was already a little stale, and it took over a year before it regained marketable appeal' (p. 509). Nothing about new acquisitions in 1594–5 or in 1595–6 suggests that themes in Marlowe's play influenced their purchase. Yet a modest case may be made for a claim that the Admiral's men continued to direct commercial energy towards plays with tangential connections to *The Jew of Malta* through the dramatization of outsized historical personages in exotic locations. The new plays in this group in 1594–5 include 'Galiaso', the second part of 'Godfrey of Bulloigne', the two-part 'Caesar and Pompey', and the two-part 'Hercules'.[60] An old play in this category was 'Mahomet', which could be a revival of George Peele's 'The Turkish Mahomet and Hiren the Fair Greek'.[61]

In April and May 1596, Marlowe's play shared the subject of Jewry but not adjacent scheduling with the short-lived new play, 'Julian the Apostate'. However in that spring *The Jew of Malta* had both content and scheduling in common with George Chapman's *Blind Beggar of Alexandria*, the repertorial blockbuster of the season for the Admiral's men. The main character in Chapman's play is the nobleman, Cleanthus; a fugitive, Cleanthus assumes serial disguises throughout the play. At least two identities recuperate Marlovian characters: Cleanthus himself, 'a shepheardes sonne' raised by merit like Tamburlaine to power; and Leon, a 'botle nosd' usurer (ll. 117, 1180).[62] Twice in the 13-performance run of *The Blind Beggar of Alexandria* (at its second and fourth performances), the Admiral's men scheduled *The Jew of Malta* in its wake (16–17 February, 13–14 May), and in the later case Henslowe's receipts rose slightly for Marlowe's play in a general decline through the run from 56s. to 13s. From a commercial point of view, the pairing of Marlowe's play with its partial parody begins the transformation of *The Jew of Malta* into theatrical nostalgia, which it will become more fully in the revivals of 1601 and 1632. Stale in 1594–5, as Syme points out, it is reinvigorated somewhat in 1596 by its parodic companion, *The Blind Beggar of Alexandria*. However, another story of theatrical marketing was soon to take the stage at another playhouse with the arrival of *The Merchant of Venice*.

Scholars discuss the repertorial competition of the Admiral's men from 1594 to 1603 largely in terms of Shakespeare and the Chamberlain's men. The Shakespearean bias in studies of early modern drama encourages such a focus, and other options are limited by a lack of evidence. Although the Swan playhouse opened in the summer of 1595, there are no records of the companies and plays on offer in its early days. If the reconstituted Queen's men were at the Swan in 1595,[63] they probably played some of their inherited repertory, but only the printings of *The Famous Victories of Henry V* (1598) and *Clyomon and Clamydes* (1599) suggest what those might have been. When Pembroke's men arrived at the Swan in February 1597, they aborted a longer residence by playing the notorious 'Isle of Dogs', now lost. After the breakup of Pembroke's men, players from that company joined the Admiral's men, apparently bringing playbooks with them; all now are lost, and their titles do not suggest any special connection with *The Jew of Malta*.[64]

Even for the Chamberlain's men no records permit the kind of daily assessment of theatrical activity for 1594–6 that Henslowe's records invite for the Admiral's men. As discussed above, the joint run of the two companies provides four titles offered at Newington that probably remained in the possession of the Chamberlain's men: 'Hester and Ahasuerus', 'Hamlet', *Titus Andronicus* and *The*

Taming of a Shrew. One of the four ('Hamlet') had had a long commercial history with *The Jew of Malta* already; two ('Hester', *Tit.*)
had had a recent one. *Romeo and Juliet* developed such a history in
1594, the putative date of its debut. An allusion by John Marston
to a silly playgoer whose playscript-riddled speech included
'pure *Juliat* and *Romeo*' reinforces the currency and popularity
of that play through 1594–6 when Marlowe's was in revival.[65]
Playgoers at the Theatre would have seen Shakespeare's appropriation of Marlowe's balcony scene, marked further by his theft
of Marlowe's line to create 'But stay, what star shines yonder in
the east?' (II.i.41).[66] A keen ear attending *A Midsummer Night's
Dream* might also have heard echoes of Barabas's 'Die, life: fly,
soul; tongue, curse thy fill, and die!' (V.v.88) in Pyramus's death
speech as Bottom strikes familiar chords: 'Thus I die, [. . .]/
Now am I fled;/ My soul is in the sky./ Tongue, lose thy light/
[. . .]/ Now die, die, die, die, die' (V.i.300–6). However, the fullest
expression of commercial energy in the Chamberlain's repertory
was Shakespeare's *Merchant of Venice*.[67] That dynamic is being
re-examined and illuminated by Ian McAdam in this volume; it
is therefore appropriate here only to point out that Shakespeare's
play extended a commercial engagement with *The Jew of Malta*
that had been going on in the theatrical marketplace since 1589.
Shakespeare's plays, as they themselves were revived onstage and
printed for sale in bookstalls around St. Paul's, participated in the
currency of that engagement.

The year 1600–1, when purchases in Henslowe's *Diary* of 'div-
ers thing*es*' and 'more thing*es*' for *The Jew of Malta* imply its last
known revival by the Admiral's men, was momentous for the company (Foakes, p. 170). In late summer of 1600, the players moved
to the newly built Fortune playhouse in Golding Lane, Middlesex.
By May of 1601, plans were underway for a massive number of
revivals to celebrate the return of Edward Alleyn from a retirement of three years. Paul Menzer, considering this transition to a
new playhouse with an old repertory, suggests that the Admiral's
company 'was writing itself into theatre history, forging [. . .] a
corporate history that privileged continuity over change, nostalgia

over novelty, and theatrical revivalism over theatrical innovation'.[68] Second in the lineup of payments for revivals was Chapman's *Blind Beggar of Alexandria* and third was Marlowe's *Jew of Malta*. In the 18 months that followed, the Admiral's men would pay for apparel, properties, new additions, and in many cases the scripts themselves for a dozen or so 'dramatic warhorses unstabled upon [Alleyn's] return' to advertise that the former star was once again 'at the reins' (p. 184). The significance of this moment in theatre history for *The Jew of Malta* is that it officially became an artefact of the Admiral's golden past and its dramatist their 'in-house ever-writer' (p. 187). The Prologues accompanying its revival in 1631–2 by Queen Henrietta's men – modesty tropes notwithstanding – make that point unapologetically (see below).

And yet, moribund as it might have been by some measures in May 1601, *The Jew of Malta* re-entered a repertory for the Admiral's men that included fresh descendants of its initial commercial context. Admiral's plays from 1596–8 had provided a spin-off from *The Battle of Alcazar* ('Stewtley', 11 December 1596), the history of a criminally passionate Old Testament king ('Nebuchadnezzar', 19 December 1596), and a revival of *The Spanish Tragedy* ('Joronymo', 7 January 1597). In 1598 the company acquired *A Woman Will Have Her Will, or Englishmen for my Money* (S. R. 3 August 1601, Q1616). Lloyd Kermode points out that the 'pivotal character is a Portuguese merchant and usurer [. . .] [whose] oral eloquence and sense of superiority are reminiscent of Marlowe's Jew of Malta, Barabas' (p. 42). According to Kermode, dramatist William Haughton appropriated 'a damnable character type' in order to refashion it into 'the accepting father of comedy' (p. 44). In 1599–1601 there was a revival of interest in the revenge plays generally across the playhouse world. The Children of Paul's inaugurated their return to the playhouse at Paul's in 1599 with the two-part revenge by John Marston, *Antonio and Melida* and *Antonio's Revenge*. Shakespeare wrote his version of *Hamlet*. And the Admiral's men paid Ben Jonson twice for additions to *The Spanish Tragedy* (25 September 1601, 22 June 1602). In this environment the company also made two payments for at least one new revenge play, *The Tragedy of Hoffman, or The Revenge for a Father*, by Henry Chettle (7 July, 29 December 1602). Lukas Erne sees a direct recall of *The Jew of Malta* in the name of the brothers in *Hoffman*, Lodowick and Mathias (p. 39). Indirectly, therefore, Marlowe's play remained a viable property.[69]

Post-1601 and Queen Henrietta Maria's Players

Evidence of further stage life for *The Jew of Malta* in the seventeenth century is contained in two documents. One is its registration at Stationers' Hall on 20 November 1632, antecedent to the printing of the play in 1633. The other is the title page of the printing, which, combined with paratexts included in the quarto, reveals significant information about the play's twilight years. The title page not only gives the play a title ('*The Famous* TRAGEDY OF THE RICH IEVV OF *MALTA*') but also advertises its performance before the king and queen at Whitehall by 'her Majesties Servants at the *Cock-pit*'. These documents probably signal the permanent retirement of Marlowe's play at the end of a 46-year performance history.

Much of this title-page information is a surprise. *The Jew of Malta* is not known previously to have been presented at court, although its company owners had ample opportunity to do so. The predictable company in 1633 to have Marlowe's play in stock is a descendent of the Admiral's men, who became Prince Henry's men in 1603/4. Following the prince's death in 1612, the company acquired the patronage of the Elector Palatine and became Palsgrave's (or the King of Bohemia's) men. Palsgrave's men were in residence at the Fortune when a midnight fire on 9 December 1621 destroyed the theatre including its store of apparel and playbooks. With the support of Edward Alleyn, the playhouse was rebuilt. It remained in business past 1642, but Palsgrave's men did not. Overcome by financial losses stemming also from the suspension of playing in 1625 due to plague, the players dispersed, a significant number moving to the newly formed King and Queen of Bohemia's company, which was itself defunct by 1631. Apparently,

though, *The Jew of Malta* moved by another track to Queen
Henrietta's men or their predecessor-companies. The simplest
explanation of how this migration occurred is another instance of
the process in 1592, that is, in the possession of a player. This time,
the player is Christopher Beeston, who had shown an entrepre-
neurial disposition at least since his membership in Queen Anne's
men and their residence at the Red Bull playhouse in 1607. Having
had the Cockpit playhouse built in 1616–17, Beeston was manag-
ing Queen Henrietta's company there by 1633. Another possibility
is also a player, Richard Perkins, who was Alleyn's apprentice in
1596; he joined various companies subsequently, one of which was
Worcester's/Queen Anne's men. Perkins, as the paratexts reveal,
took the part of Barabas for Queen Henrietta's men. The naming
of the Cockpit (*alias* Phoenix) is a change in predictable venues, if
not exactly a surprise. Performances at the Cockpit locate the play,
which heretofore had had a history on the outdoor stages of public
playhouses, on the stage of a private, indoor theatre.[70]

   Though it is impossible to know when *The Jew of Malta*
migrated to its final company destination, the impression collectively of the 1633 paratexts is that its acquisition was recent.
Thomas Heywood, himself a veteran of Worcester's/Queen Anne's
men, provided a dedicatory epistle to accompany *The Jew of Malta*
into print, as well as Prologues and Epilogues for Whitehall and
London performances. The two Prologues in particular call attention to the age of *The Jew of Malta* and impose a rhetorical spin on
its revival that has significance for the play as an active, influential
member of Queen Henrietta's current repertory. As Jeremy Lopez
argues, 'The Prologue Spoken at Court' assures the audience that
the play will be performed 'exactly as it has always been'; its choice
'is because it is a classic, and the mark of its classical status is that
it is resistant to the ravages of time, to the stylistic and thematic
erosions one might expect to be effected by changes in fashion,
personnel, venue, and historical perspective'.[71] Queen Henrietta's
men had many new plays at their disposal in 1632–3; playlists in
Alfred Harbage's *Annals* yield at least seven items by dramatists
as diverse as John Ford (1), Ben Jonson (1), Thomas Nabbes (1),

James Shirley (3) and John Tatham (1). Yet they also had a stock of old plays; in addition to *The Jew of Malta*, they acquired over time Francis Beaumont's *Knight of the Burning Pestle*, Chettle's *Hoffman*, Dekker's *The Honest Whore*, Heywood's *If You Know Not Me, You Know Nobody*, Thomas Middleton's *A Mad World, My Masters* and John Webster's *The White Devil*. Lopez interprets this mix of old plays with new as 'cultivating a highly contemporary repertory [but also] marketing, in counterpoint, a brand of theatrical nostalgia' (p. 172). The value of *The Jew of Malta* on the stage in 1632–3 was therefore as institutional memory, recollecting Alleyn through Richard Perkins's impersonation of Alleyn, as Alleyn had impersonated himself in the 1601 revival at the Fortune. Its commercial currency in terms of the offerings at the Globe and Blackfriars, where the King's men re-enacted the classics of Shakespeare as well as *The Maid's Tragedy*, *Volpone* and *The Merry Devil of Edmonton* as late as 1638–9, was not as an influence on drama yet to be written but as one of the greatest hits from the golden age of professional drama.

To label the revival of *The Jew of Malta* in 1632–3 an exercise in theatrical nostalgia is not also to consider the play diminished thereby. To the contrary, its performances at Whitehall and the Cockpit elevate it to elite venues it might not previously have enjoyed. It consequently participates in a scholarly debate about theatrical repertories in the post-Elizabethan era based on a binary division of 'citizen' *versus* 'elite' audiences. Andrew Gurr expresses the traditional view in a comparison of Prince Henry's/Palsgrave's men with the King's company: 'by the end of their long life the Admiral's company catered chiefly for the mass of "citizen" playgoers at the cheaper outdoor playhouses, whereas their opposites, the King's Men, fed and chiefly lived off the richer playgoers at the indoor Blackfriars' ('*Shakespeare's Opposites*', p. 4). Gurr further claims that the Admiral's stock from 1587–90 was forever 'the beating heart of the company's repertory', necessarily implying that companies keeping such old plays alive through revival fell increasingly behind the commercial curve ('*Shakespeare's Opposites*', p. 171). Paul Menzer characterizes the revivalism of 1601–2 quite differently. He considers the return of more than a dozen old plays to the stage at the new Fortune tantamount to an 'instant history for the company' and the 'canonization' of its playwrights (pp. 190, 191). *The Jew of Malta* might well have enjoyed the longest stage life of Marlowe's plays. After a youth in public playhouses, it graced upscale venues in old age. As Thomas Heywood put it, in 1632–3 – as in 1589–96 and 1601–2 – *The Jew of Malta* was and had remained 'second unto none'.[72]

Figure 1 *St. Mary's Guildhall, Coventry.*
Source: Andrew Paterson.

Figure 2 *Bristol Guildhall.*
Source: REED: Patrons and Performances Website.

FIVE

New Directions: *The Jew of Malta* and *The Merchant of Venice*: A Reconsideration of Influence

IAN MCADAM

In any consideration of the artistic influence of Christopher Marlowe on William Shakespeare, the pairing of *The Jew of Malta* and *The Merchant of Venice* represents an obvious example but also constitutes one of the more problematic and contentious cases. In spite of their radical generic differences – one a tragedy of sorts, or a 'savage farce' if we prefer to follow T. S. Eliot,[1] and the other a romantic comedy of sorts, but darkly contextualized with religious and racial prejudice – I will argue for a close affinity between these two plays, perhaps the most controversial texts produced by each of the playwrights. The controversy appears rooted in the political/economic and the psychological/theological levels of meaning in the two plays, and an examination of these aspects reveals Shakespeare taking important cues from Marlowe. The unbridled materialism of Malta and Venice, and of Christian as well as Jew, leads to an exposure of Christian hypocrisy; the Catholic context of the parallel Christian communities ostensibly offers an ideological buffer for a predominantly Protestant theatre audience in London, but in both plays English mercantilism and 'spiritual' self-righteousness is implicated indirectly. Such aggressive and secular concerns throw light on the pressures of masculine self-fashioning in the face of waning theological scruples, and anxiety about masculine control also contributes to the establishment of subtle but significant homoerotic subtexts in Marlowe as well as Shakespeare.

While I thus imply important thematic connections between these plays, it will be helpful to first recognize and contextualize their obvious differences. This essay admittedly challenges, in one sense, a critical position I am in other ways fundamentally in agreement with. Robert Logan, in a definitive assessment of Marlowe's influence on Shakespeare, has asserted that 'Shakespeare shows himself primarily interested in the theatrical and literary techniques of Marlowe that made him a successful commercial playwright, and not in Marlowe, the Cambridge intellectual reflecting and moralizing on serious issues'.[2] This assertion of, essentially, continuities of dramatic style over content is consistent with the apparent differences between *The Jew* and *The Merchant*, which, while treating similar sociopolitical contexts, seem comparable primarily in that they both contain a Jewish anti-hero, in the former as protagonist and in the latter as antagonist. With respect to this parallel treatment of Jewishness, readers are apt to embrace the distinctions drawn by Julia Reinhard Lupton:

> It is the fate of Marlowe's Jew of Malta to find himself forever lurking a few steps behind Shakespeare's Shylock. Barabas is Shylock's evil twin and nasty precursor – a rougher, meaner, and more starkly stereotypical stage Jew whose exorbitant antics bring into relief that glimmer of humanity that partly illuminates Shakespeare's achievement.[3]

The comparison would seem to give Shakespeare the (artistic and moral) advantage for having created a more psychologically realistic character less dependent on anti-Semitic stereotypes. What reader can fail to compare the sense of outraged humanity and injured dignity in Shylock's famous 'Hath not a Jew' speech (III.i.50–69) with Barabas, in his false nose,[4] gleefully regaling Ithamore with a history of his personal atrocities: 'As for myself, I walk abroad o'nights,/ And kill sick people groaning under walls[. . .]' (II.iii.179–80).[5] And yet in some paradoxical sense – the first of several surprising inversions or contradictions we will note in this discussion – Shakespeare has produced, potentially, a more disturbingly anti-Semitic play. Simon Shepherd, for one, confidently pronounces *The Jew of Malta* 'a play about racism, not a racist play', and suggests in contrast that, politically, '*Merchant* is a naïve, if not nasty, play, with its eventually OK Arianism [presumably Aryanism] resident in Belmont, its suggestion that there is always a Belmont above the grubby world of commerce, its silence over the links of personal and political and its sentimentalising of wealth'.[6] While I find *The Merchant* an enormously complicated and subtle, not naïve, play, its ability to disconcert and disturb is undeniable. Moreover, Shakespeare, but not Marlowe, is historically open to the accusation that, in writing his work, he was consciously taking advantage – as an irresistible 'commercial' opportunity – of the swell of anti-Semitic feelings in London after the execution in 1594 of the Queen's physician Roderigo Lopez, a converted Jew found guilty of attempting to poison her.

Marlowe's portrayal of Barabas itself has been cited as a 'source' for Shakespeare's anti-Semitic depiction of a 'villainous' Shylock,[7] and it is not my intention to summarize or delineate the (unending, especially in the case of Shakespeare) debate concerning either playwright's personal or private attitudes towards Jews. In general, I would suggest that the protagonist/antagonist distinction I have identified above probably goes far in explaining why the stereotypes and prejudices explored in both texts have been received as more disturbing or troubling in Shakespeare. In Marlowe we are clearly encouraged to identify with Barabas; as Thomas Cartelli claims,

> Marlowe offers a free-form approach to theatrical representation which encourages the audience's unqualified engagement with the fantasies of power, play, and moral abandon he cultivates. [. . .] The insistently shifting ground of the play works in concert with Marlowe's demystifying approach to the rhetoric of secular and religious authority to disarm the audience of its ties to defined structures of reception and belief.[8]

Just as clearly, in Shakespeare 'we' – or perhaps more accurately, for historical reasons, the Elizabethan spectators – are invited to sympathize with the Christian opponents of Shylock. But Shakespeare's subtlety is in some sense insidious, not simply because his satire is in effect largely directed at Christian hypocrisy, as in Marlowe. The generic constraints of Shakespeare's romantic comedy, especially in terms of the resolution of its plot, do incline even many contemporary readers, such as Logan, to insist on what I regard as an excessive idealization of the Christian characters. Nevertheless, Shakespeare engages in a demystification of (at least) religious authority which ultimately resembles, and I contend was influenced by, Marlowe's own artistic strategies. Through plot configurations that are apparently the complete inversion of each other – a tragedy that modulates into a black comedy, and a comedy that raises its own antagonist to a tragic level and ends with a decidedly compromised romantic vision – both plays map out opposing trajectories that are, in the final analysis, anchored in similar ideological and psychological concerns.

The ideological concerns are notably materialistic in both plays. While the advent of new historicism has steadily intensified our interest in the economic and material motives that underlie human social interaction – as expressed, directly or indirectly, in early modern drama – this Marxist critical bias has led to increasingly sophisticated and complex readings of the politico-economic and legal contexts of Shakespeare's *The Merchant of Venice* in particular.[9] With the assiduous historicization of Shakespeare has come the recognition that Marlowe's own attention to nascent capitalist urges in *The Jew of Malta* cannot be ignored as a significant influence.[10] In an important discussion treating the appeal of capitalism in Marlowe, Daniel Vitkus observes that 'Barabas is in many ways a strikingly modern figure. He embodies a new force that was reshaping English society – emergent capitalism in its international manifestation.'[11] Again we discover a paradox or contradiction: the cruder character, the stereotype descended from the Vice figure of the interludes and moralities, is actually more 'modern' than Shakespeare's more psychologically realistic figure.

Vitkus's claim here is consistent with Walter Cohen's observation that 'Both the characterization and the outcome of *The Merchant of Venice* mark Antonio as the harbinger of modern capitalism. [. . .] Shylock, by contrast, is a figure from the past: marginal, diabolical, irrational, archaic, medieval' (p. 771). To clarify this contradiction we might consider Cohen's claim that *The Merchant* carefully contrasts 'usurers and merchants' (p. 768) – evident in the contrast between Antonio and Shylock. Marlowe, it must be emphasized, portrays Barabas as a merchant, not a usurer. It is true that Ferneze's remark to Barabas, 'Shamest thou not thus to justify thyself,/ As if we knew not thy profession' (I.ii.122–3), may allude to activities as usurer as well as merchant, and it is also true that Barabas has claimed to practise usury in the past:

> Then after that I was an usurer,
> And with extorting, cozening, forfeiting,
> And tricks belonging unto brokery,
> I filled the jails with bankrupts in a year. (II.iii.195–8)

But this claim belongs to the list of outrageous crimes, related to Ithamore, that most critics, including Vitkus, assume to be fictions in a 'bombastic and ironical' confession (p. 61). Barabas's role as *merchant* crucially conveys both the 'exhilarating power' and 'the transgressive thrill' that 'internationalized capitalism brought to bear on the culture of London'. Vitkus does observe that during the later sixteenth century the meaning of 'usury' changed to accommodate 'any of a variety of new ways of making money without producing a needed commodity or offering a legitimate service', but still distinguishes Barabas as a 'new, capitalist speculator' as opposed to 'the old, medieval moneylender' (pp. 62, 64).

The heroic dimension of Barabas's (initial) economic aspirations are interestingly contextualized by one of the most exciting new readings of Marlowe, Patrick Cheney's *Marlowe's Republican Authorship*. Cheney notes that Marlowe's translation of the pro-republican Roman poet, *Lucan's First Book*, 'forms a keystone to Marlowe's canon of poems and plays', but notes that 'Marlowe's republican authorship [. . .] is strange and unique; it shows not a patriotic political program but an afflicted imaginative expression, at once obsessed with and tormented by the republican fantasy of freedom, and thus inextricably bound by its binary opposite, the servitude of empire'.[12] Cheney acknowledges few critical precursors to his thesis, but does note an earlier essay by William Blissett, who sees the playwright's 'Lucanian characterology' as supplemented by his '"wealth of geographical and ethnological detail", [and] his "rationalism" or contempt for orthodox supernaturalism'.[13] Cheney thus fascinatingly politicizes the oft-observed personal assertiveness and secular iconoclasm of Marlowe's protagonists. The application to *The Jew of Malta* is particularly interesting in that it complicates a reading of the Prologue by Machevill. Machiavelli has often been seen as supportive of monarchical ideology through his assertions in *The Prince*, but was in fact more personally invested in the republican values conveyed in *The Discourses*.[14] While Malta in Marlowe's play is subject to imperializing pressure from both Spain and Turkey, it is in essence a kind of 'Christian republic'. Cheney's reading clarifies the curious reference whereby Barabas in his initial soliloquy links the 'Samnites' with 'the men of Uz' (I.i.4), the latter inevitably recalling the opening of the book of Job:

> Marlowe's conjunction [. . .] may be less meaningless if we recall the Lucanian republican genealogy: the Samnites are a [. . .] defeated republic who admirably fought the tyranny of Rome, only to fall into slavery when they were defeated, as Machiavelli recurrently records [. . .]. Clearly, Marlowe attempts to link the classical example of oppression with the biblical one, so that Barabas can criticize both and offset his own commercial freedom. (p. 127)

The 'biblical' example of oppression here is presumably God's testing of Job, underlining the theologically radical nature of Marlowe's portrayal of Barabas as an anti-Job figure. Interestingly,

Shakespeare also sets his play in a republic, the Venetian state, as if intentionally testing the waters of Marlovian subversion, both political and theological.[15] We might predictably conclude that the more conservative Shakespeare arrives at a more conservative vision of social order; indeed, Cohen observes that the 'concluding tripartite unity of Antonio, Bassanio, and Portia enacts [an] interclass harmony between aristocratic landed wealth and mercantile capital [. . .]. A belief that some such relationship provided much of the social foundation of the English monarchy accounts for Shakespeare's essentially corporatist defense of absolutism in the 1590's' (p. 772). Nevertheless Marlowe's radicalism troubles the waters of Shakespeare's social vision more thoroughly than such an assessment would suggest.

To explore further the seeds of subversion, let us first return to the question of the 'transgressive thrill' that Barabas offers his Elizabethan audience. Vitkus argues that

> Marlowe's Barabas is not a radically alien figure, not simply 'the Jew.' He is a character who [. . .] exemplifies the activities and attitudes of the ambitious Christian merchants of Elizabethan England, men who pursued profit ruthlessly.

Significantly Malta lies at the 'crossroads' of the Mediterranean, 'where Christian and Muslim powers overlapped' (p. 63). According to a historian of early modern Jewry, 'Jews also benefited from the renewed religious bifurcation of the Mediterranean into warring Christian and Muslim worlds. [. . .] this division gave at least some advantage to the religiously "neutral" Jews who could pass between the two worlds with relative ease.'[16] Thus Barabas's subversive appeal arises not only from his untrammeled material aspirations but his lack of culturally specific religious scruples. He emerges as something of an avaricious Everyman. As Emily Bartels has observed, 'Although [Barabas] attempts to define himself in terms of Judaic doctrines and heritage, his terms are as unconvincing as they are unsustained.'[17] As Stephen

Greenblatt has noted, Barabas's proverb-laden speech is not 'the exotic language of the Jews but the product of the whole society, indeed, its most familiar and ordinary face.' In fact, Greenblatt subsequently touches upon the perennial sore spot in criticism of the play when he adds, 'the effect of [these proverbs'] recurrent use by Barabas is to render him more and more typical, to *de-individualize* him. [. . .] Most dramatic characters – Shylock is the appropriate example – accumulate identity in the course of their play; Barabas loses it.'[18]

But of course what Greenblatt observes here may already intimate that Marlowe, playing his usual artistic game, has established limits to the 'transgressive thrill' offered by Barabas. That is, although Barabas and Shylock are radically different characters, the playwrights have, as Logan argues, created intentional ambiguity in the way these characters are dramatically perceived by their respective audiences. In Barabas's case, the 'exhilarating power' evoked by his fantasies of wealth and power struck a chord with Elizabethan audiences since 'England was [. . .] beginning to experience a new economic and cultural openness' and this 'process of socioeconomic transformation [. . .] particularly affected London'[19] – but other political developments in London created resentment towards the capital's increasing cosmopolitanism. The Dutch Church Libel of 1593, postdating *The Jew of Malta* by only about three years, reveals deep animosity towards the growing number of foreign workers, displaced by religious persecution on the continent and attracted to London's mercantile opportunities. The xenophobic poem attached to the wall of the Dutch churchyard is addressed to 'Ye strangers [that] doe inhabite in this lande', and warns,

> Your Machiavellian Marchant spoyles the state,
> Your vsery doth leave vs all for deade
> Your Artifex, & craftesman works our fate,
> And like the Jewes, you eate us vp as bread.[20]

That the poem is notoriously signed '*per*. Tamberlaine' mysteriously associates it with Marlowe. Possibly the libeller assumed that the subversive potential of Marlowe's dramas could be co-opted to attack the Elizabethan government's 'supposed cosseting of "Flemings and Strangers" resident in London'.[21] The 'moral abandon' that Cartelli suggests Barabas encourages in his audience would likely, on some level, be qualified by popular, or lower-class, envy of the increasing wealth of the merchant class, foreign or indeed English. The image of Jews consuming the poor like bread evokes, I suggest, a Eucharistic motif and thus implicitly signals the lack of Christian charity evident in the dealings of the wealthy classes.

Admittedly, the anti-Christian brutality of Barabas's later machinations – the poisoning of an entire convent of nuns, the murder of Friar Jacomo and the framing of Friar Barnadine (those 'two religious caterpillars' [IV.i.21]) – plays up to anti-Catholic sentiments in predominantly Protestant London. As Lupton observes, Malta was part of the Spanish dominions but 'was under the direct rule by the Knights of St John [. . .] a militant Catholic order with its roots in the Crusades' (p. 145). Many critics assume the historical background of Marlowe's play is the Turkish siege of Malta in 1565, but since Marlowe does not represent events with any historical accuracy, and since the Jews had been expelled from Malta and other Spanish dominions in 1492, the playwright may even wish to vaguely evoke a pre-Reformation setting for the play. Any perception of the ruthless opportunism and religious hypocrisy of Ferneze's government could therefore be attributed to a 'Catholic' despotism, Machiavellianism and materialism. Nevertheless, the play's relentless evocation of the materialism of *general humanity* – whether Christian, Muslim and Jew – can hardly be ignored, as this oft-quoted passage emblematizes:

> *Fern.* Welcome, great basso [. . .]
> What wind drives you thus into Malta road?
> *Bash.* The wind that bloweth all the world besides,
> Desire for gold. (III.v.1–4)

Since fear of Turkish enslavement ran high in early modern Christendom – and in fact slaving raids by Muslims were surprisingly extensive, even in Western Europe[22] – there is some Marlovian irony in having the Christian *Spanish* appear in the play as the major traders in the slave market, when Del Bosco enters at II.ii with his cargo of Grecian, Turkish and Moorish slaves. Del Bosco's business interests are one of the main reasons he persuades Ferneze to defy the Turks' demand for tribute, even while Del Bosco ironically objects the Knights of Malta should not 'buy [their league] basely [. . .] for sums of gold' (29). Since Christians are willing to barter in human flesh as readily as 'these barbarous misbelieving Turks' (46), and since, as noted earlier, the initial appeal of Barabas's mercantile aspirations chimes with English merchants' own dreams of economic expansion, Marlowe in effect erodes the satirical buffer that supposedly distinguishes between Catholic and Protestant Christians. Vitkus's concluding emphasis on a moral principle is therefore hardly surprising: '*The Jew of Malta* represents Jews, Turks, and Roman Catholic Christians in the Mediterranean context, but its critique of greed and religious hypocrisy also points back home to "Jewish" or "Turkish" merchants and policy-makers in Protestant England who put profit before religious principles' (p. 71).

Shakespeare in *The Merchant of Venice* focuses more narrowly, in a cultural sense, on a Jewish-Christian binary, although Morocco's wooing of (the racially discriminating) Portia may constitute a deliberate attempt to echo Marlowe's Muslim contexts.[23] Marlowe likely influenced Shakespeare's exploration of a mercantile willingness to barter in human flesh – through Shylock's references to slavery in defense of his bond with Antonio.[24] Marlowe almost certainly influenced Shakespeare's satirical presentation of an Italian Catholic community in Belmont and Venice whose insistence on, or tacit assumption of, a more 'spiritual' status, in contrast to the supposedly more materialistic Jews, is subtly eroded during the course of the play. Such 'erosion' is painfully evident when Bassanio makes the proper spiritual or 'Christian' choice of the leaden casket – not 'judging by appearances', by external, material reality – through a speech that ironically underlines his own racism: 'The world is still deceived with ornament [. . . which is] but the guilèd shore/ To a most dangerous sea, the beauteous scarf/ Veiling an Indian beauty' (III.ii.74–99). But the effect of Marlovian subversion, especially with respect to the nature of the 'religious principles' in question, goes further than simply an exposure of hypocritical Christian self-righteousness.

Cheney's emphasis on the republican thrust of Marlowe's writings, especially the concomitant 'contempt for orthodox supernaturalism', is significant in that this theory supports not only the striving for greater individual liberty in the playwright's opus, but also a concern for proper 'manly' assertiveness and independence. In *The Irony of Identity* I argued that, while Marlowe's plays are subversive, 'what they tend to subvert are ideologies and belief systems – primarily religious ones – that interfere with the project of achieving "manliness" or personal cohesiveness'.[25] What is remarkable about this project in Marlowe is that it always *fails*. Cheney may anticipate the tenuous nature of the political agenda in his own recognition that the Marlovian 'republican fantasy of freedom' is 'tormented' and 'bound by its binary opposite, the servitude of empire', but in general I see more irony in Marlowe than Cheney does. The very concept Cheney invokes to explain the grandiose expression of the republican aspirations – the sublime – seems more productive of ironic deflation than what Cheney calls 'an eternizing poetics of the sublime as a phoenix arising from the ashes of defeat' (p. 20). Cheney considers Barabas's famous opening soliloquy – 'Bags of fiery opals, sapphires, amethysts' – and asserts, '*This* is what Jonson saw as Marlowe's great achievement, his ability to locate the sublime in the beauty of the material'. Barabas is obsessed not just with the 'great price' of his possessions but their 'political currency', their ability to 'ransom great kings from captivity': 'This paradoxical project – *freeing kings* – speaks directly to the commerce between monarchical and republican values in Marlowe's play' (p. 132). Yet ransoming great kings from captivity may in fact suggest a parody or inversion of Christian doctrine: a 'great king' who ransoms humankind from captivity to sin. Ironically, in this 'eternizing poetics of the sublime' celebrating republican liberty, Marlowe implicitly poses the questions: can one serve both God and Mammon, and (even more ironically) what qualities of self-assertiveness must one cultivate if one chooses clearly to serve the *latter*? G. K. Hunter has suggested that the famous line, 'Infinite riches in a little room' (I.i.37) blasphemously echoes rhetorical formulae traditionally used to describe the womb of the pregnant Virgin Mary.[26] This image coincides with other references in the play which associate Barabas with maternal status or female procreative function.[27] I would therefore hazard the generalization that the 'sublime' in Marlowe, in the form of 'the republican fantasy of freedom', very often carries implications of narcissism and self-delusion.

In fact *The Jew of Malta* evokes a profound ambiguity of mercantile aspirations as both an expression of manly liberty and narcissistic indulgence. An examination of this apparent contradiction is crucial not only to an understanding of Marlowe's play, but to a consideration of how the themes of manliness, competition and personal control are developed through the division, in *The Merchant of Venice*, of the character of a Jewish merchant into the pairing of a Christian merchant and a Jewish usurer that Shakespeare presents – partly of course under the influence of his source in Giovanni Fiorentino's *Il pecorone*.[28] Considering the cultural and mercantile ambition and energy that Barabas personifies at the beginning of *The Jew of Malta*, it is interesting to note how commentators have intuited his ineffectuality; thus Cartelli: 'The audience, which has been led to expect a recognizably Machiavellian intriguer, seems to get [. . .] a relative innocent in his stead' (p. 168). Barabas observes pointedly that the Jews do not seek *political* power per se: 'crowns come either by succession,/ Or urged by force; and nothing violent,/ Oft have I heard tell, can be permanent' (I.i.130–2). Of course his foolish and fatal decision to trust Ferneze at the end, after Calymath has created him Governor of Malta, stems from the same reluctance to accept the *responsibility* of rule. Barabas's great mercantile status thus seems on one level to be reduced to a hoarding of wealth that Constance Kuriyama sees as regressive substitute for phallic aggression – the protagonist's (and Marlowe's) 'more subtle and "civilized," and at the same time, psychogenetically more primitive, modes of defining and regulating power relationships'.[29] It is significant, however, that Barabas remains haunted by thoughts of more 'phallic' masculinity, for in his superb soliloquy at the beginning of act II, he laments, 'And of my former riches rest no more/ But bare remembrance; like a soldier's scar,/ That has no further comfort for his maim' (II.i.9–11). The 'tragic' sentiments of the play seem underwritten by nostalgia – or longing – for more manly encounters, although the metaphor here suggests passivity, not aggression.

The apparently 'effeminizing' aspects of the merchant role in early modern society may be confirmed by the relationship that Debora Shuger has drawn between Renaissance passion narratives and anxiety about urbanization and the excesses of capitalism. Works such as Nashe's *Christ Tears over Jerusalem* (1593) and Thomas Deloney's *Canaans Calamitie, Jerusalems Misery* (1618) emphasize the effeminacy of the Jews by stressing 'the "daintinesse and delicasie" of Jerusalem before the sack', the Roman annihilation of 70 C.E. *A Larum for London* (1602) depicts the parallel fall of Antwerp to the Hapsburg army. Antwerp's citizens are vulnerable because, like the Jews, they have become 'us'd to soft effeminate silkes,/ And their nice mindes set all on dalliance;/ Which makes them fat for slaughter, fit for spoile'. Obviously, then, both Jerusalem and Antwerp – 'delicate she-cit[ies]' which succumb to the violation of 'male savagery' – serve as a warning to London, by implying 'a conceptual link between economic prosperity and the decomposition of manhood into effeminacy or brutality'.[30]

Conversely, however, Bruce Smith in *Shakespeare and Masculinity* suggests the exact opposite about mercantile manliness by including the 'Merchant Prince' as one of five ideals of masculinity in the early modern period. The merchant is a kind of prince since, through the 'good government' of his 'little commonwealth', he provides generously for his family and social subordinates.[31] Moreover, Walter Lim clinches his entire argument about 'spiritual commercialism' in Shakespeare by borrowing Paul Stevens's assertion of the idealization of global capitalism as a 'manifestation of [the] circulation of grace':

> In *The Merchant*, the Jewish usurer is portrayed [negatively] not only because of his adherence to the legalistic letter of the law [. . .] but also because he is not open to the taking of risks requisite for profit making in capital ventures. 'Shylock,' as Paul Stevens notes, 'is most virulently satirized for *not* being a capitalist, that is, for not being an adventuring, risk-taking, truly globalizing capitalist.'[32]

Yet this logic would simply equate the mercantile heroism of Barabas and Antonio, and erase the connections between the two Jewish anti-heroes of *The Jew* and *The Merchant*. Clearly a more careful contextualization of Jewishness, nascent capitalism and manliness is required in order to elucidate the peculiarities of Marlowe's influence on Shakespeare.

Shakespeare is, I think, deeply sensitive to Marlowe's portrayal of a merchant capitalist – initially almost magically immune to loss – who degenerates rapidly through narcissistic manipulation, which reveals a refusal to 'engage with the risk of an injury'.[33] Shakespeare offers instead a merchant capitalist whose greatest 'risk of an injury', forestalled, displaces repressed erotic desire. As we have observed, Barabas's grandiose mercantile venture is subtly exposed as a narcissistic, even anal, hoarding of wealth – and anality also figures in Barabas's clearest act of aggression, surreptitiously leading 500 of Calymath's troops through the 'common channels' or sewers of the city (V.i.89) in order to surprise and conquer the Knights of Malta. In contrast, the titular merchant of Shakespeare's play is revealed at the outset as indeed a great risk-taker, and possibly melancholy or anxious over these very threats to his professional and personal security:

> Your mind is tossing on the ocean,
> . . . .

> Believe me, sir, had I such venture forth,
> The better part of my affections would
> Be with my hopes abroad.
> . . . .
> Should I go to church
> And see the holy edifice of stone
> And not bethink me straight of dangerous rocks
> Which, touching but my gentle vessel's side,
> Would scatter all her spices on the stream,
> Enrobe the roaring waters with my silks,
> And, in a word, but even now worth this,
> And now worth nothing? (I.i.8–36)

However, Antonio denies Salarino and Solanio's 'material' explanations for his melancholy. Significantly, their language – 'The better part of my affections' – intriguingly suggests the displacement or sublimation of spiritual or erotic energy into mercantile concerns. The image of church walls as dangerous reefs suggests the transformation of (traditional) religious consolation into (modern) secular anxiety, with the unexpectedly gentle verb 'touch' – as a catalyst for a kind of orgasmic dispersal – again subtly intimating erotic desire. Antonio consequently objects most vehemently to the more direct suggestion, 'Why, then you are in love' (46).

   Any suggestion here that Antonio 'doth protest too much' raises the most notorious crux of the text, the possibility of the merchant's *unconscious* homoerotic desire for his friend Bassanio: 'In sooth I know not why I am so sad'. To cut a very controversial Gordian knot of critical debate, I will admit my mystification when Harry Berger, who accepts Lawrence Hyman's assertion that 'the main action of the play is centered on the struggle between Portia and Antonio for Bassanio's love', commends Hyman's argument 'for its careful avoidance of the temptation to convert the powerful *mono*sexual attachment of Antonio for Bassanio into a *homo*sexual attachment'.[34] While most scholars of early modern culture now carefully avoid the anachronistic term 'homosexual', preferring (the in fact no less anachronistic) 'homoerotic' – albeit a term which does not identify a distinct personality type – the insistence on 'monosexual' seems simply a rhetorical elision of an erotic longing whose social or psychic reality cannot be, for whatever reason, addressed. James O'Rourke argues that *The Merchant* even rather directly addresses its Elizabethan audience's anxiety about sodomitical desire; when Antonio offers to Bassanio that 'my person [. . .] lies[s] all unlocked to your occasions' (I.i.138–9), the 'suggestiveness of Antonio's metaphor is reinforced by English stereotypes of the sexual behavior of Italians'.[35] The most persuasive treatment of the sexual themes of Shakespeare's play to date remains Steve Patterson's argument that Antonio's 'passionate love falls into an early modern tradition of homoerotic friendship, or amity'. Since that tradition was losing its ideological currency in the later Renaissance, the play 'dramatizes the travails of the ideal friend in a society that is re-evaluating its definitions of love and its virtues – a shift so disruptive that Antonio as amorous lover seems sadly outmoded, himself a kind of anachronism'.[36] We arrive at yet another striking contradiction: the play's progressive capitalist is in fact deeply compelled by erotic longings that can only find expression through virtually obsolete social traditions.

Both merchant figures, I would argue, appear compelled by unconscious homoerotic desires – that is, 'spiritual' or emotional needs that are barely masked by their committed (if ultimately tenuous and surprisingly fragile) economic aggression. Both Antonio and Barabas apparently resist the overt possibility of the expression of sexual love, Antonio rhetorically, 'Fie, fie' (I.i.46), and Barabas maniacally through a wholesale destruction of anyone with erotic desires who crosses his path: the lecherous Friars, Ithamore, Bellamira (plus pimp), Mathias, Lodowick and even his daughter Abigail. As I observe in *The Irony of Identity*, Barabas easily 'transfers his need for a second self from Abigail to Ithamore', with whom he becomes far more intimate 'than we would expect from a Machiavellian manipulator of men'. Near the end he demonstrates the same compulsion to confide in, to share intimacy with, another man; with Ferneze, as with Ithamore, 'he becomes positively effusive': 'Governor, I enlarge thee; live with me [and be

my love?]' (V.ii.91). Admittedly, in both cases, Barabas has asides
that imply continuing manipulation and a denial of the affection
he has shown, yet he remains unconscious of his own emotional
poverty. Overall his career 'consists of a series of unstable "counterfeit professions" that lead him to a precarious pinnacle, where
he is destroyed by a negative and fatal "unseen hypocrisy": his
own lack of awareness of a dark and complex mixture of accumu-
lated insecurities, fears, and longings, which [fail to] be released
or worked through in more human, natural ways'.[37] Antonio is
not destroyed but *saved* from destroying himself, as his attempt
at masochistic self-sacrifice through the bond of flesh is defeated
by Portia's legal machinations in court. Nevertheless both merchants fail in the masculine control of their destiny. Barabas cooks
to death in an emblematic hell.[38] Antonio, through his own admission a 'tainted wether of the flock' – publicly declaring, as Janet
Adelman suggests, that he is 'unmanned by his desire'[39] – has his
life saved through Portia's legal manoeuvres and, surprisingly, his
mercantile status restored through her God-like knowledge of the
contents of sealed letters indicating that all his ships, miraculously,
have come in.

What further delineates, and significantly links, this failure
of masculinity are the theological implications of the mercantile
careers. Marlowe remains a 'God-haunted atheist',[40] although the
biblical ironies of the text – the counting-house as the womb of
the pregnant Virgin Mary, the cauldron as emblematic hell, and so
on – do not appear to reinforce 'typological norms'.[41] They suggest rather a destruction of humanist aspiration through implod-
ing self-cohesion – as does Antonio's repressed erotic agenda, his
passive-aggressive manipulation of Bassanio through his supposed
imitation of Christ, laying down his life for his friend. Antonio's
main motive, in a bizarrely Eucharistic sense, is to ensure the
permanent or 'eternal' nature of Bassanio's mourning or memo-
rialization: 'You cannot better be employed, Bassanio,/ Than to
live still and write mine epitaph' (IV.i.116–17). For Marlowe,
Barabas's failure of manliness might evoke cultural associations
of Jewishness and effeminacy. While James Shapiro observes

that it was Freud who first directly argued that '[c]ircumcision is unconsciously equated with castration',[42] the critic also traces the evolution of readings of *The Merchant* suggesting that Shylock, with the cut to Antonio's body, initially wishes (unconsciously) to culturally turn the tables by castrating his nemesis. Such 'turning of tables' is anticipated in Marlowe: Wilbur Sanders notes 'the medieval libel of *foeter judaicus*' – alleged menstruation in Jewish males – and argues that Marlowe 'maliciously re-applies it'[43] when Barabas taunts Lodowick that the Jew must purge himself after conversing with Gentiles (II.iii.44–8). Shakespeare apparently continues the interrogation of the link between Jewishness and emasculation by having his Christian merchant suffer symbolic castration (as a 'tainted wether'), and his Jewish usurer uphold an aggressive masculinity.

One recent critic who explores the obsession in Western culture with Jewishness and masculinity, Matthew Biberman, traces images of both the 'Jew-Devil' and 'Jew-Sissy' in the early modern period, with the Jew-Devil carrying a sense of hyper-masculine assertiveness. Biberman offers the questionable reading of Marlowe's Barabas as an unqualified embodiment of the Jew-Devil, ignoring the potentially effeminized nature of the merchant role noted above; in this reading the presumably effeminate aspects of Barabas's 'maternal' roles become rather hyper-masculine appropriations of the maternal, reflecting Jewish antagonism to 'Christianity and femininity, especially procreative, maternal femininity'. Biberman chooses instead to emphasize Shylock's reduction of agency and power relative to Barabas, identifying in Shakespeare the emergence of the Jew-Sissy: 'By dramatizing this transformation, Shakespeare appropriates Marlowe's Devil and domesticates him, with the clear intent of dispelling the horrific and terrifying power of the Jew-Devil.'[44] While I understand the 'domestication' of Shylock, I would argue that Biberman gets his assignment of masculine and effeminate Jew in Marlowe and Shakespeare exactly wrong. If Greenblatt is right to assert that Shylock 'accumulates identity' in the course of the play, it is a distinctly *masculine*, fiercely independent one.

Venetian Christians may comically attempt to symbolically castrate Shylock – 'Why, all the boys in Venice follow him,/ Crying, "His [significantly *two*] stones [testicles], his daughter, and his ducats!"' (II.viii.23–4) – but they fear his emasculating power: '[Antonio] shall pay for this' (26). As Shapiro notes, 'exorbitant moneylending was often referred to as "biting" usury, and the elision of Jews as economic exploiters and literal devourers of Christian flesh was easily made',[45] as it was in the Dutch Church Libel. Shakespeare very much associates Shylock with a sense of phallic aggression, especially as he whets his knife in court.

Even within his 'domesticated' world, Shylock bears a more manly presence than Barabas. He clearly still loves his deceased wife: 'It was my turquoise [that Jessica has stolen and exchanged]. I had it of Leah when I was a bachelor. I would not have given it for a wilderness of monkeys' (III.i.113–6). Barabas never mentions his; only 'fornication' with an anonymous wench, now dead, in another country (IV.i.43–5). The plainest verbal echo between the two plays, to which Logan calls attention (pp. 117–19), may draw a parallel between shocking – or comical – (Jewish) materialism, but still suggests a crucial moral contrast. With almost incestuous intensity, Barabas is in raptures when Abigail restores to him his hidden cache of wealth: 'Oh my girl,/ My gold, my fortune, my felicity [. . .] O girl, O gold, O beauty, O my bliss!' (II.i.47–54). Shakespeare consciously echoes this line in Shylock's fury over Jessica's elopement and theft: 'My daughter! O my ducats! O my daughter!/ Fled with a Christian! O my Christian ducats!/ Justice! The law! My ducats and my daughter!' (II.viii.15–17). Yet the fact that Solanio in fact relates this outburst raises the possibility of exaggeration and misrepresentation, in a way that possibly preserves some of Shylock's dignity in the comparison. At any rate, the equation of ducats and daughters in Shylock's case may be rationalized by the deep feelings of anger, violation and betrayal he feels towards both Jessica and the Christians who have assisted her. The joy Barabas feels does less to qualify, morally, his materialism; he habitually, and narcissistically, sees people as extensions of his object world, to be possessed or destroyed as his machinations, and his precarious sense of self, determine.

Shylock's notable self-possession and radical independence are crucially linked, ideologically and psychologically, to his faith in, and insistence on, 'the law': 'What judgement shall I dread, doing no wrong?' (IV.i.88). It is true he has little sense of forgiveness and no concept of 'grace', which is why he fails to foresee the (ironic) re-application of grace and 'conversion' in the Christians' annihilation of his social and religious status at the end of the courtroom scene. But by directly introducing a debate between Jewish law and Christian grace in his play, Shakespeare is responding to the supposedly 'gracious' aspect of mercantile dominance that Marlowe is parodying in his play. Barabas's gloating in 'the blessings promised to the Jews' and 'old Abram's happiness' (I.i.104–5) in a very real sense reflects the mercantile aspirations of the 'chosen' elect, the Protestant merchants of Elizabethan England. Shakespeare suggests, ironically, that his non-merchant Jew, his more individualized or 'Jewish' Jew, is really the more masculine.

Shylock, the old-fashioned usurer anti-capitalist, tragically fails – but in a sense his *masculinity* does not, as he relies on his own (however flawed) moral and professional integrity.[46] Antonio's capitalist triumph is ambiguous at best, since it consists in effect of Portia's defeat of his own masochistic impulses and unconscious desires – those deep emotional needs that true 'manliness' (in patriarchal cultures) more ruthlessly represses. Marlowe's republican project in *The Jew of Malta* is curiously dissipated through the resurgence of such needs within the psyche of the hero-villain. Antonio's theological/emotional and social dependencies may be related to Walter Cohen's assertion of 'Shakespeare's essentially corporatist defense of absolutism in the 1590's' that we have already observed. It is almost irresistible to compare Antonio's passion for the penurious but presumably aristocratic Bassanio[47] with the Sonnet speaker's (equally frustrated) passion for the beautiful young man. Of course republican tendencies have been detected in Shakespeare as well, although his works may suggest he was either more circumspect, or more conflicted, regarding these issues.[48] It is not my intention, however, to restate a literary cliché by simply implying a contrast between a radical Marlowe and a more conservative Shakespeare. With his interest in viable masculine self-fashioning and enhanced personal agency, Shakespeare was influenced – psychologically and politically – by Marlowe's ironic deconstruction of certain doctrines of (especially Reformed) Christianity: in particular the individual's radical dependency on God's grace and the supersession of the 'law' on which Shylock's whole sense of masculine control and identity remains contingent. While this influence likely originates in the earlier Marlowe of *Tamburlaine* and *Faustus*, Shakespeare's revision of *The Jew of Malta* in *The Merchant of Venice* indicates his continuing, possibly intensifying, response to Marlovian theological subversions. Further exploration of ideological developments in both playwrights' careers might consider whether Shakespeare was not more subtly, but ultimately even more aggressively, committed to this particular cultural interrogation.

SIX

New Directions: *The Jew of Malta* as Print Commodity in 1594

KIRK MELNIKOFF

On 17 May 1594, the London booksellers Nicholas Ling and Thomas Millington registered their intention to publish what would have been the first edition of *The Jew of Malta*.[1] As is well known, at least in the 'little room' of Marlowe studies, no such Elizabethan publication now exists. Our earliest print edition remains instead a ten-sheet quarto published by Nicholas Vavasour in 1633.[2] Whether Ling and Millington followed through on their ambition remains today a minor mystery that likely will never be solved. It may indeed be, as C. F. Tucker Brooke surmised in his *The Works of Christopher Marlowe* (1910), that the pair did publish a 1594 edition but that this press run is no longer extant. Or it may be that Ling and Millington – after paying two pounds to acquire and authorize, six pence to license and four pence to enter the play – decided to cut their losses and pursue other projects.[3]

Subscribing for the most part to a scenario in which *The Jew of Malta* was not brought to press in the 1590s, editors and scholars alike have been quick to accept Ling and Millington's initial eagerness to venture upon a play by Marlowe even as they have thrown up their hands at the booksellers' apparent failure to seal the deal.[4] The extent to which Ling and Millington may have been inspired, however, by a widespread contemporary fervour for all things Marlowe in choosing to enter '*The famouse tragedie of the Riche Jewe of Malta*' in the Stationers' Register – 'Marlowe' as recent sensational news, as print commodity, as professional theatre wunderkind – is certainly open to debate.[5] This is not to say that Marlowe's 1593 demise was unnoticed. Richard Baines and

Thomas Kyd, of course, offered their own testimonials in its immediate aftermath. But unlike the extensive print-market flurry that
quickly followed Robert Greene's 1592 death, Marlowe's demise at
the hands of Ingram Frizer sparked only a trickle of isolated print
pamphlet epitaphs.[6] Nominal too was the value of a 'Marlowe'
brand in London's 1594 print market. John Wolfe's twin August
1593 Stationers' Register entries both cite Marlowe – the Lucan
translation described as being 'Englished by CHRISTOPHER
MARLOW'; and *Hero and Leander* 'an amorous poem devised by
CHRISTOPHER MARLOW' (Arber 2, p. 636) – but neither the
1590 or 1593 *Tamburlaine* octavo includes Marlowe's name even
while their publisher Richard Jones alludes to 'the eloquence of
the Author that writ them' in his dedicatory epistle (sig. A2v).[7] And
though both Thomas Woodcock's 1594 *Dido* and William Jones's
1594 *Edward II* do name Marlowe as author, these title-page references are counterbalanced by loud allusions to the professional
stage and by tags touting Marlowe as a gentleman.[8] That 'Marlowe'
had become a ubiquitous name in the professional theatre of the
early 1590s – so much so that Ling and Millington would have
jumped at the opportunity to print one of his plays – is equally
questionable. For all our confidence in Marlowe's revolutionizing
influence over the professional stage, we have precious little evidence that Marlowe's name was widely known in the late 1580s or
even that a 'Marlowe' brand was recognized commodity among
theatre professionals before his death.[9]

Less debatable it would seem is *The Jew of Malta*'s almost unri-
valled success in the early 1590s professional theatre. If Ling and
Millington were not in a position to be inspired by 'Marlowe',
they at the very least would have been able to recognize the commercial value of a contemporary theatrical mega-hit.[10] As is clear
from the limited purview of Henslowe's *Diary*, between 1592 and
1594 *The Jew of Malta* was a frequent offering at the Rose, and its
average take was – with the exception of *1 Tamburlaine* – not just
higher than what we now know to be Marlowe's other plays but also
higher than most other plays written before 1594. These figures –
along with similar evidence for *1 Tamburlaine*, *The Massacre at*

Paris and *Doctor Faustus* – have led commentators such as Andrew Gurr to pronounce confidently that Marlowe's dramas 'were and remained for decades the [Admiral's] company's favorite plays'.[11] But as Holger Syme has recently suggested in drawing attention to the preponderance of now-lost plays in repertories at the Rose, the plays that we today know constituted the core of Marlowe's dramatic canon were not necessarily the theatrical blockbusters that many have insisted upon, nor were they in fact the dominant offerings in the Admiral's Men's repertory. 'The [Rose's] most successful "old" play ("Long Meg of Westminster")', observes Syme, 'was not by Marlowe. While his plays did better on average than most plays written before 1594, those only accounted for a fraction of a repertory that was dominated, both in terms of what was staged and in terms of revenue, by newer work'.[12]

But even if we admit that *The Jew of Malta* was at least *one* of the Rose's more popular offerings in the early 1590s, it does not necessarily follow that Ling and Millington would have been eager to risk a substantial sum in bringing the play to press based on the promise of theatrical popularity alone. Success on the professional stage was never an absolute guarantee of success on the bookstalls of St. Paul's. For every multi-edition bestseller like *The Spanish Tragedy*, in other words, there were a number of single-edition disappointments like *A Knack to Know a Knave*.[13] Moreover, as Peter Blayney has argued, professional plays were generally not the 'best selling money-spinners' that scholars have long wished them to have been, especially when compared to other kinds of printed books. The financial risk associated with printing professional plays was particularly high before the mid-1590s when few professional plays were brought to press, and fewer still garnered substantial profits in reaching multiple editions.[14]

What all of this suggests is that Ling and Millington's decision to finance an edition of *The Jew of Malta* was in all probability the product of more factors than simply Marlowe's alleged public celebrity and/or the play's respectable recent runs at the Rose. As I will show, the venture needs to be understood in terms of these booksellers' prevailing publishing practices and print

specialties at the time.[15] Profit, of course, was certainly an important motivation for booksellers, but it is misleading to assume, as
Kirschbaum did, that 'Like the grocer and the goldsmith, [the sta-
tioners] were mainly interested in money. They were thoroughly
wideawake business men who were out for a quick penny'.[16] Profit,
Kirschbaum failed to realize in offering his important corrective
to Pollard's mythology of piracy and skullduggery, was measur-
able by more than simply 'thus much coin'; it was also for these
men the product of their effectively seeding the print market
with their niche products, of developing a reliable community of
patrons and buyers, of successfully speculating upon their products' meanings, and – in some cases – of contributing to England's
developing religious and cultural spheres.[17] For Ling, successful
publishing meant investing in texts that furthered a particular
political vision or helped realize a vernacular literary canon. And
for Millington – the partner in *The Jew of Malta* project who I
believe was its driving force – it meant choosing texts that effectively took advantage of recent happenings in the London public
sphere or that appealed to buyers interested in the very real threat
of civil conflict at home and the reality of it abroad.

Publishing at Ling's Shop at the West Door of Paul's

The joint entry of *The Jew of Malta* in 1594 would prove to be
Ling and Millington's only collaborative project. Ling himself, the more established stationer of the two, had worked as a
bookseller and publisher in London since 1580 out of a number
of different shops.[18] As Gerald Johnson has traced, collaborative
publishing was the norm for this London stationer throughout his
career. He routinely shared the burden of bringing copies to press
between 1580 and 1607, often relying upon other stationers such
as John Busby and Cuthbert Burby to procure copies. Over three
decades, Ling was involved in the publication of 66 titles, many of
which were literary by the likes of Thomas Lodge, Thomas Nashe,
Robert Greene and especially Michael Drayton. In the mid-1590s,

around the time *The Jew of Malta* was entered in the Stationers' Register, Ling's publishing endeavours took two significant turns. Beginning in 1595 with *A Mirror for English Soldiers*, Ling would not only finance nine different books of *sententiae* or wise sayings, but he also would also go on to involve himself with the compilation of four distinct editions of the substantial sententiae collection *Politeuphuia Wit's Commonwealth* (1597, 1598[2], 1608). As Zachary Lesser and Peter Stallybrass have recently argued, this change in focus was part of a larger effort led by the grocer Sir John Bodenham to create a new canon of contemporary English literature based upon its 'commonplaceability'.[19] Ling's interest in *The Jew of Malta* might have been connected to his work with this circle. At the same time as he was dedicating much of his energy to sententiae volumes, Ling also was financing a number of titles with explicit political themes having to with republican political thought, titles such as *Cornelia* (1594), *The Legend of Humphrey Duke of Gloucester* (1600) and *A Commonwealth of Good Counsel* (1607).[20]

If Ling meant to turn to *The Jew of Malta* as a potential resource for vernacular sententiae, his intention apparently never came to be realized in print. Even while pithy sayings from a number of Ling's 1590s vernacular publications appear in sententiae collections such as *Politeuphuia*, *England's Parnassus* (1600), and *Bel-vedére* (1600), lines from *The Jew of Malta* are not likewise appended.[21] And this clearly was not a comment upon the quality of Marlowe's work. *Bel-vedére* both includes '*Christopher Marlow*' in its opening list of 'Moderne and extant Poets' (sig.A5v) and prints over 40 passages from *Hero and Leander* along with 7 from *Edward II*; similarly, *England's Parnassus* includes dozens of passages from *Hero and Leander*, each with an attribution to Marlowe.[22] *England's Parnassus* is especially provocative because a large number of its sententiae are taken from recently printed offerings of the professional stage, from plays like *Friar Bacon and Friar Bungay* (1594), from *James the Fourth* (1598) and from Marlowe's own *The Massacre at Paris*. Dramatic verse, in other words, was definitely not a bar to canonicity for Ling and the Bodenham circle.

Ling's turn to *The Jew of Malta* might as well have been connected to his burgeoning interest in texts with republican political themes.[23] As has been well outlined by Pocock, Skinner and others, much of Machiavelli's work has strong republican political valences.[24] This can be seen most clearly in *The Discourses on Livy*, a work that the London printer John Wolfe published (with a false imprint) in the Italian in 1584. As Patrick Cheney has recently traced, Marlowe's play frequently invokes ideas from this republican treatise, particularly its political binary of Monarchy versus Republic as well as its idealizing of the dynamic of liberty and commerce.

Given the looming posture of 'Macheuill' as melodramatic villain at the beginning of the play, however, it is also possible that Ling was inspired by a strand of contemporary political discourse – republican in its extended probing of the grounds and extent of monarchic power – that saw Machiavelli as the symbol *par excellence* of corrupted leadership, the apolitical machinations of his followers the grounds of recent monarchic tyranny. This discourse emerged in a series of pamphlets after the Huguenot Massacre in 1572, perhaps most vividly in the widely circulated Latin tract *Vindiciae Contra Tyrannos* (1579).[25] There, in its preface, 'Cono Superantius' argues that the 'perfect image of the governance of kingdoms, [was once] a legitimate, chaste, blameless matron without any excessive adornment; in its place these Machiavellians do not hesitate to present us with an illegitimate, painted, lewd, and wanton harlot'.[26] Barabas, of course, looks very much the insidious knave, especially after he trades in his business acumen for Machiavellian policy after being abused by Ferneze in the play's first scene (Cheney, p. 136). In one of its final patently ironic moments, the play shows Barabas being destroyed by Ferneze even as he is conjured up in the Malta governor's own Barabas-like amoral policy. Learning of Barabas's plot against him and his soldiers, Calamath exclaims, 'Oh monstrous treason!' To whom Ferneze replies with all the twisted 'ends justifies the means' logic of Barabas, 'A Iewes curtesie: / For he that did by treason worke our fall, / By treason hath deliuered thee to vs' (sig.K2v). Like Superantius's Machiavellians, Barabas ultimately debases all authority, seemingly possessing Ferneze with the spirit of a double-dealing harlot. In 1594, Ling may have been in a position to recognize this.

Publishing Practices at Millington's Shop under St. Peter's Church in Cornhill

Millington had only finished his apprenticeship in the stationers' trade a little less than three years before his one-time collaboration with veteran Ling.[27] He seems to have initially secured his own bookshop 'under Saint Peters Church in Cornhill' in the spring of 1594, from which he sold a number of news pamphlets wholesale and close to a half dozen professional plays. Millington's ten years of publishing also included more than two dozen ballads along with work by the famed balladeer Thomas Deloney.[28] With some small company fines and what was thought to have been his trade in bad quartos, these broadsheets led to his low repute among New Bibliographers such as Alfred W. Pollard and W. W. Greg. In 1603, Millington's last publications were a series of pamphlets having to do with events surrounding the transfer of monarchal power in England, with the death of Elizabeth and the coronation of James I.[29]

Even as a maturing Ling was moving to sententiae, to political themes, and to an emergent literary canon in order to carve out his share of an ever expanding body of book-buying readers, the newly minted Millington turned to the tintinnabulum of current events as fodder for his speculative endeavours. It is within the context of this particular publishing strategy that Millington's own involvement with *The Jew of Malta* in 1594 can be more fully understood. Again and again during his ten years of publishing, Millington would move quickly to capitalize upon contemporary happenings, in most cases using a spurt of ballad publication to prepare the ground for more substantial, more costly pamphlets on the same topic. This was certainly his strategy in late August, 1594. At that time, he, Thomas Gosson, and John Danter jointly entered in the Stationers' Register both a ballad – '*BE[E]CHE his ghoste. complayninge on ye wofull murder committed on him and THOMAS WINCHESTER his servaunt*' (Arber 2, p. 658) – and a pamphlet – '*A true discourse of a most cruell and barbarous murther committed by one THOMAS MERREY, on the persons of ROBERTE BEECHE and THOMAS WINCHESTER his servaunt*' (Arber 2, p. 658). Both works recounted the recent grisly murder of the London chandler Robert Beech and his boy Thomas Winchester by his neighbour, the food and beer vendor Thomas Merry.[30] Over the next two weeks, Millington would match Danter's '*a lamentable ballad describing the wofull murder of ROBERT BEECHE*' (Arber 2, p. 659) and Gosson's '*the lamentable ende of THOMAS MERRYE and RACHELL his Sister*' (Arber 2, p. 659) with two further ballads of his own, a lamentation by Merry (entered with Gosson) and a lamentation by Merry's sister Rachel (Arber 2, p. 659). Together, these cheap print publications flooded London's bookstalls in the late summer of 1594, Millington simultaneously sharing risk, manufacturing buzz, and securing his investments in sponsoring as many as four titles in a total stationer output of seven.

This strategy also clearly undergirded Millington's publication of a series of titles having to do with recent events in the French Wars of Religion.[31] These ballads and pamphlets appeared between late October 1594 and mid-January 1595, one set pertaining to Sir John Norris's victories in Britanny and the other to an assassination attempt upon the French King by the Jesuit scholar Jean Chastel. Like he did two months earlier with the Merry murders, Millington seeded London's bookstalls with a ballad, this time '*A Triumphant newe successe which our Englishe men had in Britanye*' (Arber 2, p. 664). Three weeks later, he entered the two-sheet eyewitness account *Newes from Brest. A diurnal of al that Sir Iohn Norreis hath doone since his last ariuall in Britaine* (1594). Expanding upon what was apparently the ballad's general overview of recent English successes in Northwest France, this pamphlet describes in great detail Norris's victory against the Spanish at the fort of Crozon, and it provides two lists of English elite either 'Hurte', 'Slaine' or 'Burned with pouder' at the siege (sig.B1).[32] It ends by praising 'the greate resolution' (sig.B3v) of the Spanish commander in defending Crozon. Two weeks later in early December, likely around the time of the printing of *News from Brest*, Edward White – the co-publisher with Millington of *Titus Andronicus* – entered another ballad exploiting the occasion, '*A sorrowfull songe made vppon ye valiant Souldiour Sir MARTIN FROBISHER who was slayne neere Brest*' (Arber 2, p. 666). The same 'Mariner' Frobisher is singled out in *News from Brest* as having 'aquitted [himselfe] wonderfull brauely: and [. . .] exceeding forwarde in all attemptes' on the fort (sig.B2v).

While Millington's contributions to the international news market were undoubtedly still being absorbed by the English reading public, in late December 1594, a young French Jesuit scholar by the name of Jean Chastel narrowly failed in an assassination attempt upon Henry IV and within a week was subsequently executed. Millington wasted little time in response. Less than a week after Chastel's knife had barely missed the French king's throat, Millington entered one ballad and one 'booke' in the Stationers' Register on 27 December (Arber 2, p. 668). While the ballad described Chastel's treasonous attempt, the book – *The Decree of the Court of Parliament against John Chastel* – recounted the verdict of his subsequent trial, a ruling which not only called for Chastel to be tortured, then drawn and quartered, but also directed that 'all priestes & schollers of the colledge of *Cleremont*, or all other that entitle themselues of the same society [be exiled], as corrupters of youth, disturbers of common quietnes and enemies to the king and the estate. [. . .] All goods mooueable and immoueable [. . .] to bee employed upon deeds of charity' (sig. A4–A4v).[33] A week after this in early January, likely before the 1595 *Decree* had been printed and distributed, Millington financed another ballad, this one describing Chastel's execution (Arber 2, p. 668). Before the month would end, two more pamphlets having to do with these developments in France emerged. Taking advantage of Millington's print-market bustle, the St. Paul's bookseller Edward Aggas financed his own translation of Alexander

Pontaymeri's *A State Discourse upon the Late Hurt of the French King*.[34] And Millington himself would put his own final stamp on the news flurry that he had created by publishing *The Copie of a Letter Sent by the French King to the People of Artoys and Henault* (1595). This pamphlet includes Henry IV's declaration of 'open warre' against the king of Spain, an action in part precipitated by what Henry describes as the Spanish king 'caus[ing] attemptes to be made of taking awaie his Maiesties life, by trecheries and villainous detestable meanes: as appeared not many daies past: and worse had it happened, to the greate woe of *France*, had not God the true protector of kings, wonderfullie turned aside that horrible stroke, offered by the hand of a Frenchman [. . .] but driuen to that art by a spirit most voide of humanitie and indeed Spaniardlike, euen againste the kings sacred maiestie' (sig.B3v).

After a spate of sporadic ballad, pamphlet and reprint publishing between 1595 and 1602, Millington would ultimately return at the end of his short bookselling career to his early selling strategy in 1603. In May of that year, following a tsunami of titles exploiting the coming coronation of James I, Millington moved to finance texts dedicated both to the new king and to the memory of its recently departed queen.[35] He entered the first of these *The True Narration of the Entertainment of his Royal Majesty, from the Time of his Departure from Edinburgh til his Receiving at London* in the Stationers' Register with Cuthbert Burby two days after James's 'mobbed' entry into London on the 7th of May.[36] Unfinished copy in that the printed pamphlet would record James's activities up until the 13th of May, *The True Narration* was meant quickly to capitalize upon the exciting spectacle of a new monarch living in London. Weeks earlier, Millington was also making preparations to bring out another more substantial title having to do with the succession, Henry Chettle's *England's Mourning Garment*, a work that both panegyrizes Elizabeth and celebrates James.[37] Once printed, this would be Millington's most successful title, it reaching a second edition by the end of the year. Millington seems also to have been planning to offer two companion pieces to *The True Narration*: a pamphlet description of Elizabeth's funeral procession and a new edition of the 1559 pamphlet *The Royal Passage of her Majesty from the Tower of London, to her Palace of White-hall*.[38] The former was never printed and the latter was apparently delayed by Millington's own demise.[39] Together, these four projects speak to what was Millington's dependence – early and late in his bookselling career – upon contemporary happenings as staple for his publishing endeavours.

In May 1594, the London to-do that appears to have had much to do with Millington's investment in *The Jew of Malta* was the reopening of London's professional theatres in late 1593 after being closed for almost a year due to a particularly virulent outbreak of the plague.[40] Fifteen years ago, Peter Blayney suggested that this reopening led the playing companies to attempt to revive their unstable industry by offering up unprecedented numbers of their valuable playtexts for sale in St. Paul's Churchyard.[41] Theatre marketing thus would explain what has been called a 'boomlet' of play publication in 1594 and 1595 when *The Jew of Malta* and more than 2-dozen professional plays were entered in the Stationers' Register and 14 professional plays came to press.[42] Printed editions of plays like *Friar Bacon and Friar Bungay* (1594) and *A Knack to Know a Knave* (1594) amounted to advertisements, announcing to the world that the Queen's Men and the Admiral's Men respectively were again open for business in early 1594. In this formulation, since professional plays were as of yet still risky print commodities and the professional stage was on shaky footing, Millington's investment in *The Jew of Malta* would appear to have been part of a wide-scale marketing event, one possibly undergirded by some working arrangement with the players.

Evidence, however, suggests that the professional theatre may not have been so unstable in late 1593, even that the resumption of playing in the London professional theatres at this time was in fact greeted with immediate and widespread enthusiasm.[43] As Carol Chillington Rutter has pointed out, receipts at the Rose between late December 1593 and early February 1594 were 'exceptional' (p. 79), with Sussex's Men's *The Jew of Malta* and *Titus Andronicus* bringing particularly high returns.[44] The February 1593 minutes of the Privy Council seem to support this assessment, worrying in the face of another possible outbreak of the plague that 'certein infourmation is given that the very great multitudes of all sorts of people do daylie frequent & resort to common playes lately again set vp in & about London'.[45] The first half of 1594 was apparently so successful for the professional playing companies that the 'profiteer . . . land-pirate' (Rutter, p. 85) Francis Langley was inspired to begin preparations for the construction of yet another outdoor playhouse at Bankside, what in 1595 would be the Swan.[46] Millington's interest in *The Jew of Malta*, then, very well could have been inspired by the general excitement surrounding the reopening of London' professional theatres. He might have been the beneficiary of a playing-company-driven advertising event in having an opportunity to obtain a copy of the play, but his apparent willingness to risk capital in investing in *The Jew of Malta* may also have been at least partially driven by popular commotion that drew him that same year to the shocking murder of Thomas Merry and to the sensational events across the Channel. Millington and Ling's entry in the Stationers' Register, after all, was not simply for 'the Riche Jewe of Malta'; it was in fact for '*The* famous *tragedie of the Riche Jewe of Malta*' (my emphasis), a formulation possibly alluding not just to the play's centrality as a repertory offering from early 1592 but also to its recent success in the Rose's reopening efforts after December 1593.[47]

Whether facilitated by an advertising campaign or inspired by a popular swell surrounding the reopening of the Theatre, the Curtain and the Rose, Millington's 1594 turn to *The Jew of Malta* and the cultural arena of the professional theatres was not entirely a shot in the dark. His venture seems also to have been the product of a recently hatched publishing strategy propagated by the aforementioned printer and bookseller John Danter. While Ling had yet to finance a professional play in 1594, Millington had by that time involved himself with the publication of two professional plays: *The Most Lamentable Roman Tragedy of Titus Andronicus* and *The First Part of the Contention betwixt the Two Famous Houses of York and Lancaster*. Sometime around February

(Arber 2, p. 644), Millington entered into an arrangement involving the former play with Danter and the bookseller Edward White.[48] Danter entered *Titus* in the Stationers' Register in early February (Arber 2, p. 644). He then printed the play with White and Millington handling wholesale distribution at White's shop 'at the little North doore of Paules at the signe of the Gunne'.[49] As an offshoot of this project, Danter also brought out 'the ballad thereof' (Arber 2, p. 644) of *Titus*, an extended broadside that in 30 four-line stanzas tells the story of the Roman general's fall from Titus's own perspective ('You noble minds and famous martiall wights, / That in defence of natiue countrey fights: / Giue eare to me that ten yeares fought for Rome. / Yet reapt disgrace when I returned home') (sig.E8v).[50] Fourteen months earlier in December 1592, Danter had entered another ballad recounting a professional play, this '*the honors ach[i]eved in Ffraunce and Spaine by iiii prentises of London*' (Arber 2, p. 623) based upon Thomas Heywood's play *The Four Prentices of London*. Together, these two ballads constitute the range of what would be Danter's oft-repeated efforts in 1594 to make a profit from London's professional stage by publishing broadside offshoots which retold the stories of its repertory and which sometimes also ushered the coming of professional playbooks into print. This strategy helps explain Danter's 1594 entries of the ballads '*GODFREY of Bulloigne with the Conquest of Jerusalem*' (Arber 2, p. 654); '*the lyfe and Deathe of HELIOGABILUS*' (Arber 2, p. 654); '*BELLIN DUNS Confession*' (Arber 2, p. 656); '*a knacke howe to knowe an honest man from a knaue*' (Arber 2, p. 664), and '*the storye of TAMBURLAYNE the greate*' (Arber 2, p. 664).[51] More significantly for my purposes, the stratagem also explains Ling and Millington's entering *The Jew of Malta* immediately after Danter himself had entered the now-lost ballad '*the murtherous life and terrible death of the riche Jew of Malta*' (Arber 2, p. 649) in the Stationers' Register the day before. Such synchronicity suggests not simply the probability of a working arrangement between the three stationers (akin to the *Titus* publishing scheme), but also a real likelihood that the printed playbook of *The Jew of Malta* was originally part of a project to take advantage of the play's concurrent performances at the Rose.

Publishing Specialties at Millington's Shop under St. Peter's Church in Cornhill

Millington's publishing practices along with his connection with Danter offer an explanation for Millington's interest in *The Jew of Malta* in May, 1594. What appears to be his early specialization in titles having to do with civil conflict provides another. Characterized as 'the hungry 1590s' by historians, the last decade of the sixteenth century saw exceptional economic and social strain as a result of a stultifying combination of bad harvests and heavy taxation. Together, these factors contributed in the mid-decade to a 'perceived crisis' having to do with what seemed to many to be unprecedented spikes in vagrancy, inflation and – in frequent apprentice riots in the first half of the decade – civil disorder.[52] To an elite chorus calling for a tightening of the machinery of social regulation was also a medley of voices in the pamphlet material of 1593 and 1594 invoking civil unrest as both cause and a potential consequence of the city's worst plague within memory.[53] Writing in the summer of 1593 of London's plague, Thomas Nashe, in his long list of England's sins in *Christ's Tears over Jerusalem* (1594), includes 'Contention' as one: '*London*, beware of Contention, thou art counted the nursing-mother of Contention. No Sect or Scism but thou affordest Disciples to. If thou beest too greedie of innouation and contention, the sword of inuasion and ciuill debate, shall leaue thy house desolate unto thee' (sig.S1–S1v). Millington's early publications exploit these fears as much as they fan their flames.

As has often been pointed out, Millington was one of Shakespeare's first publishers. Not only was he involved with the 1594 publication of *Titus Andronicus*, but within a year he also published the first edition of *The First Part of the Contention betwixt the Two Famous Houses of York and Lancaster* (1594) and the first edition of *The True Tragedy of Richard Duke of York and the Death*

*of Good King Henry the Sixth, with the Whole Contention between
the Two Houses Lancaster and York* (1595).[54] Up until the last few
decades, the latter texts were routinely identified as bad quartos,
the heirs of Pollard parsing over them in a seemingly unending
search for signs of memorial reconstruction. At best imagined to
be a grub-street man looking to make a quick shilling, at worst a
piratical leach consciously preying on the genius of Shakespeare,
Millington came to be defined by what were considered to be his
low-brow publishing (i.e. ballads) and by his Stationers' Company
indiscretions, both seen as the inevitable pursuits of an untrust-
worthy and desperate man. Ignored in these bibliographic mem-
oirs of Millington's greed and skullduggery, however, was the
obvious. This being that Millington's earliest publishing gambits
involving professional plays all share an obvious theme: the tragedy of civil war.

That Shakespeare's extended rumination upon the kingship of
Henry VI is primarily concerned with the workings, grounds and
consequences of civil war would have been impossible to overlook.
Beyond the obvious narrative arcs of the respective plays, civil
conflict is announced in both titles' foregrounding of the word
Contention, even more so in the extended purview of the earlier
play's full title with its references to Cade's rebellion, to Suffolke's
and Winchester's machinations, and to the Duke of York's play
for the crown: 'The First part of the Contention betwixt the two
famous Houses of Yorke and Lancaster, with the death of the
good Duke Humphrey: And the banishment and death of the
Dukes of *Suffolke,* and the Tragicall end of the proud Cardinall of
Winchester, with the notable Rebellion of *Jacke Cade: And the Duke
of Yorkes first claime unto the Crowne.*' It is also made manifest in
the characters' frequent chorus-like complaints where the consequences of civil strife are reiterated. '[T]hese daies are dangerous,'
laments Duke Humphrey the night before his murder, 'And would
my death might end these miseries, / And staie their moodes for
good King Henries sake, / But I am made the Prologue to their
plaie, / And thousands more must follow after me' (sig.D4v). In
the later play, looking over a son tragically killed by his own father,

King Henry bemoans the fatal consequences of the War of the Roses for the country's 'lambs': 'Wo aboue wo, griefe more then common griefe, / Whilst Lyons warre and battaile for their dens, / Poore lambs do feele the rigor of their wraths: / The red rose and the white are on his face, / The fatall colours of our striuing houses, / Whither one rose, and let the other flourish, / For if you striue, ten thousand liues must perish' (sig.C3).

Titus, too, sounds of civil war, initially as a looming possibility between the patrician followers of Saturninus and the 'louing friends' of Bassianus. Even after the two agree to stand down after their initial tense confrontation and '[p]leade [their] deserts in peace and humblenes' (sig.A3v), Marcus's endorsement of Titus for the Emperie sparks an aggressive and ominous response from Saturninus: 'Romaines doe me right, / *Patricians* draw your swords and sheath them not, / Till *Saturninus* be Romes Emperour' (sig.B2v). Titus's support of Saturninus is clearly the only bolster protecting Rome from outright civil conflict. Acts later, after Saturninus and Titus lie dead and Lucius's army is gathered at the gates of Rome, the play represents the tense final scene as the 'scattered' product of internecine conflict. Addressing the gathered crowd, Marcus laments, 'You sad facde men, people and sons of Rome / By vprores seuerd as a flight of fowle, / Scatterd by winds and high tempestuous gusts, / Oh let me teach you to knit againe, / This scattered corne into one mutuall sheaffe, / These broken limbs againe into one bodie' (sig.K3).

On the face of it, Millington's investment in *The Jew of Malta* was an exception in his early specialization in professional plays having to do with civil war. Unlike Shakespeare's Rome or his fifteenth-century England, Marlowe's Malta is not evenly divided against itself, nor does it face a civil uprising on the order of Cade's. Instead, Ferneze's governorship is never contested, his directives – be they to pay the Turks or to resist the Turks – are barely questioned. What the play does contain, however, are strands of a contemporary anti-monarchal discourse that was in the late sixteenth century often accused of sowing the seeds of civil discontent. Elements of this discourse pervade more than one of Barabas's claims, especially his comment to the audience at the end of the play, 'why, is not this / A kingly kinde of trade to purchase Townes / By treachery, and sell'em by deceit? / Now tell me, worldlings, vnderneath the summe, / If greater falshood euer has bin done' (sig.K1v). Barabas's worldly cynicism about the 'trade' of kingship echoes tracts like John Ponet's *A Short Treatise of Political Power* (1556) and especially François Hotman's *Francogallia* (1573) and the aforementioned *Vindiciae Contra Tyrannos* (1579), pamphlets written in the wake of the Huguenot massacre in 1572.[55] *The Jew of Malta* specifically alludes to mid-sixteenth-century arguments about popular sovereignty that saw political authority as ultimately resting with the citizenry and not with their kings. George Buchanan's *De Jure Regni apud Scoots* (1579) was one of the most widely circulated of these tracts, and his ideas were picked up and cited in the resistance theories of the French Catholic League put forward after Henry III's assassination of the Guise.[56] It is these radical political ideas of popular authority that underpin Machevill's pragmatic contention at the beginning of *The Jew of Malta*, suggesting as it does that monarchic authority was originally wrested from the people just as Caesar attempted to wrest imperial authority from the Roman Republic. 'Many will talke,' he says, 'of Title to a Crowne. / What right had *Cesar* to the Empire? / Might first made Kings, and Lawes were then most sure / When like *Drancus* they were writ in blood' (sig.B1).[57]

In his early publishing ventures, Millington was drawn not simply to fictional representations of civil conflict. As we have seen, at the end of 1594, he gravitated as well towards the seemingly never-ending civil unrest in France, towards news having to do with the new French king's efforts to quash the remnants of the Spanish-supported Catholic League.[58] In two months – from early November 1594 to early January 1595 – he would finance three ballads and three pamphlets recounting recent developments across the Channel. These publications culminated with *The Copy of a Letter Sent by the French King to the People of Artoys and Henault* (1595), a two-text pamphlet ending with an extended proclamation of open war against the Spanish king. In rationalizing the

proclamation, Henry IV makes it clear that much of the damage
promulgated by the Spanish in France began with its fomenting
of internal religious strife between Catholics: '[I]n the yeare one
thousand fiue hundred fourescore and fiue: for the Frenchmen
then enioying, wholie and quietlie, Religion, Justice, the kings
great fauour, and generall rest, [. . .] the k. of *Spaine* euen then
under false forged shewes went about to fill all the Realme with
fire, bloodshed, and extreame desolation, arming the Catholickes
one against another; yea and againste as Catholicke a king as euer
raigned' (sig.B2v).

This summary of violent events across the Channel just prior
to the assassination of Henry III in 1589 – 'fire, bloodshed, and
extreame desolation' – echoes a string of allusions to France's
recent political turmoil in *The Jew of Malta*, the most obvious of
these positioned at the start of the Prologue.[59] There, the play opens
with the soul of 'Macheuill', newly arrived from France after the
assassination of the infamous architect of the St. Bartholomew's
Day massacre Henri de Lorraine, third Duke of Guise. 'Albeit the
world thinke *Macheuill* is dead', muses Machevill as chorus, 'Yet
was his soule but flowne beyond the *Alpes*, / And now the *Guize*
is dead, is come from *France* / To view this Land, and frolicke
with his friends' (sig.B1). As Machevill's 'Tragedy of a Iew' (sig.
B1v) progresses, it continues to represent France as the epitome of
political machinations and political instability. Taking account of
his vast wealth in the following scene and intimating that such success is a function of ineffectual governmental oversight, Barabas
ultimately calls to mind a list of Jewish traders like himself, pointing out that France holds the highest number of his malignant
brethren: 'There's *Kirriah Iairim*, the great Iew of *Greece*, / *Obed*
in *Bairseth*, *Nones* in *Portugall*, / My selfe in *Malta*, some in *Italy*,
/ Many in *France*, and wealthy euery one' (sig.B3). France also,
at least for Millington and his sixteenth-century English readers,
would have come quickly to mind – given its recent violent history – when Barabas concludes in the same speech that 'Crownes
come either by succession / Or vrg'd by force; and nothing violent, / Oft haue I heard tell, can be permanent' (sig.B3v). Later,

Barabas again alludes to France and its past political intrigues when he confides to Ithamore that he once was 'an Engineere, / And in the warres 'twixt *France* and *Germanie*, / Vnder pretence of helping *Charles* the fifth, / Slew friend and enemy with my stratagems' (sig.E2).[60]

Barabas's bravado in the slave market is not simply Vice-like, isolated bluster; it matches what is his decidedly soldier-like perspective in first coming to terms with loss and later in enacting his revenge. Over-determined in its effects, Barabas's perspective plays to Elizabethan anxieties about the vagrant soldier even as it conjures up a discourse of French siege warfare most immediately available in news pamphlets like *The True Report of the Service in Britanny* (1591), *A True Relation of the French King his Good Success* (1592), and later in Millington's *News from Brest*.[61] Responding to the second Jew's advice that he 'be patient' in the face of his losses, Barabas ominously replies, '[G]iue him liberty at least to mourne, / That in a field amidst his enemies, / Doth see his souldiers slaine, himselfe disarm'd, / And knowes no meanes of his recouerie: / [. . .] Great iniuries are not so soone forgot' (sig.C3). Later, he again imagines his experience of loss in military terms. '[O]f my former riches rests no more,' he tells the audience at the beginning of Act two, 'But bare remembrance; like a souldiers skarre, / That has no further comfort for his maime' (sig.D2).[62] At the end of the drama, Barabas once again plays the soldier, channeling his vocational expertise as a military 'Engineere' in order to plan not just the underground assault by Calymath's soldiers (sig.I2) but his pièce de résistance the exploding monastery. Of the latter, Barabas boasts to Ferneze, 'vnderneath / In seuerall places are field-pieces pitch'd, / Bombards, whole Barrels full of Gunpowder, / That on the sudden shall disseuer it, / And batter all the stones about their eares, / Whence none can possibly escape aliue' (sig.K1v).

Together, the practices and specialties of Ling and Millington offer new contexts for understanding what was apparently intended to be the earliest booking of *The Jew of Malta*. Granted, what I have outlined here are not the titillating habits of Pollard's thieves hell-bent on skullduggery, nor the pragmatic procedures of Kirschbaums's 'wideawake business men . . . out for a quick penny'. What I've mapped instead are the compound vocational trajectories of two of the play's earliest readers, conjoined apparently for a few fateful months around a theatrical event and a rich, multi-faceted object. For now, the eager pronouncement that the play was '*Written by* CHRISTOPHER MARLO' still falls to Vavasour.

SEVEN

New Directions: The Nose Plays: Ovid in *The Jew of Malta*

M. L. STAPLETON

his visage (or vizard) like the artificiall Jewe of *Maltaes* nose.

(William Rowley, *The Search for Money*, 1609)

Ouiddius Naso was the man. And why in deed *Naso*, but for smelling out the odifererous flowers of fancy? the ierkes of inuention[;] imitarie is nothing.

(*Love's Labour's Lost*, 1598)

These two passages, published a decade apart, one famous and the other hopelessly obscure, may validate Patrick Cheney's observation that an 'Ovidian gene' helped generate the appendage that Edward Alleyn wore to identify himself as Barabas. They also explain in some ways how it 'plays', to borrow an eminently useful phrase from the Steven Soderberg film *Ocean's Thirteen* (2007).[1] Rowley's satirical image of the moneylender suggests that London audiences would have remembered such a proboscis (far from lithe, as that epithet goes), evocative of Ithamore's phrase to describe his master, a 'bottle-nosed knave' (*The Jew of Malta*, III.3.10).[2] And Shakespeare's Holofernes the Pedant, in his typical fashion of getting things exactly wrong – 'imitarie', or *imitatio*, as Elizabethan schoolboys were made to understand the concept, could not be more essential to *inventio* – identifies how sixteenth-century readers knew the great Roman poet by both metonymy (the Nose) and synecdoche (that part representing the whole). He was truly 'the man' himself, smelling things out, poetically speaking, in this most elemental sense for his monumental compositions: *iamque opus exegi*. I propose to draw these elements together under a related concept known to the principals across a millennium and a half, *aemulatio*, a type of authorial competition with eminent predecessors.[3] More specifically, in his humorous amorality, Barabas embodies the Ovidian persona with whom his creator was the most intimately acquainted, the glib, delusional and self-aggrandizing young lover in the *Amores* whose hundreds of lines he translated into English as the *Elegies*. The ancient author's role in *The Jew of Malta* is one way in which the nose 'plays', besides its service as a prop for the protagonist's stereotypical ethnicity. In this case, 'imitarie' was everything for Marlowe, as critics too innumerable to count, armed with this very passage from *Love's Labour's Lost*, observe that it was for Shakespeare.

Those who write about Marlowe's Ovidianism have traditionally confined their analysis to the discursive and descriptive passages in *Hero and Leander* that emulate the *Metamorphoses*. Some work variations on Cheney's storied thesis, that the corpus reveals a truly 'counterfeit profession', a disguised intention to conduct a literary career as a counter-Vergilian, counter-Spenserian poet and playwright, such as Georgia Brown, who holds that this conception of Ovid demands that he be 'reinterpreted' as a 'catalyst for cultural change in the 1590's' beyond the political and into the private, erotic realm. With these exceptions, what has curiously received short shrift in criticism is the most pronounced intersection of the two authors, the *Amores* translation in its dual initial forms: the truncated *Certaine of Ovids Elegies* that the Bishops' Ban indexed and burned as part of its attack on satirical publications in 1599, and the relatively complete *All Ovids Elegies*. A small yet growing body of analytical and interpretive work exists about both texts, in contrast with preceding scholarship that concerns either bibliography or mistakes in rendering the Latin elegiacs accurately into idiomatic English couplets.[4] I contend, therefore, that those of us studying the subject have in some sense missed the point, and that in this underrated translation's recesses one may find the beginnings of Marlowe's conception of individual voice and rhetorical habits that his various tragic personae tend to exhibit, among them Barabas, and that this process demonstrates one way that he, to invoke Heather James's phrase, 'lavishes Ovidian sensuality and significance on his dramatic characters'.[5]

It is unsurprising that a young writer such as Marlowe Englished the *Amores* during the great vogue for sonnets and translations of Ovid in the 1580s and 90s, and that in both his rendition and the original it influenced his peers – Shakespeare, Drayton, Daniel – who practised the form and revered the great Naso, just as they tended to enjoy, as parallel texts, the Latin *Metamorphoses* and Arthur Golding's metaphrase of it into fourteeners. This set of neoteric elegies comprises the only extended set of meditative and love-oriented poems with a clear narrative framework from antiquity widely known to medieval and early modern readers. The resemblance to a sonnet sequence and the uncanny replication of some of its conventions (e.g. the detailed portrayal of the speaker's troubled mind and obsessive focus on one woman as addressee or subject, with the unabashed evocation of feeling) in *La vita nuova*, the *Rime sparse* and their many successors argue that it was foundational for such storied lyric productions.[6]

Yet Marlowe's translation, a multiplex variation on a sonnet sequence that also established him as an interpreter of one of the three Roman poets, along with Horace and Vergil, who so influenced Elizabethan writers, probably also served as his literal staging ground for the development of the soliloquy, which would reach its apogee in Faustus and Hamlet. His *Elegies* rendition preserves the familiar shifts and turns in voice, mood and feeling in the *Amores*, their imitation of a mind at work and in conflict with itself. In the process, he prepares himself for his creation of Gaveston, Mephistophiles and Dido. Ovid's speaker, who unconsciously epitomizes himself as the *desultor Amoris* (*Amores* I.3.15), or circus-rider of love jumping from mount to mount, reveals his character and motivations gradually in the larger pattern of the text and more subtly within individual elegies while in quest of his married mistress, Corinna. None of this seems to have been lost on the apprentice playwright and ersatz classicist, who realized this clownish Roman youth as a type of self-deluded gallant whom one might find in *Every Man in His Humour* or *Bartholomew Fair* some years later, just as *The Jew of Malta* may have served as an important precursor for Jonson's understanding of city comedy, as Sarah K. Scott explains.[7]

I

Barabas's Ovidian contours seem to have been recognized as early as the seventeenth century. Whoever wrote the Prologues and Epilogues printed as prefatory verse to the 1633 quarto, perhaps Thomas Heywood, praises Alleyn for his skill in evoking the very characteristics of Marlowe's antagonistic creation that happen to epitomize the dissembling persona that he cultivated in his *Elegies*. Even 40 years after his death, someone wished to foreground these dimensions of the protagonist and his play, which may have reflected contemporary reception: reading, playgoing and acting.[8] 'The Prologue Spoken at Court' naturally emphasizes Barabas's perfidy as well as the current production's assumed fidelity to the playwright's intentions by use of a simple adverb: 'you shall find him still, / In all his projects, a sound Machevill; / And that's his character'. Indeed, the 'character' of this Italian stage-devil remains the same, both continually and at the present time, like that of the *desultor* in both nature and duration. Accordingly, in 'The Prologue to the Stage, at the Cockpit', Alleyn, 'peerless' as an actor, was a veritable 'Proteus for shapes, and Roscius for a tongue, / So could he speak, so vary'. If Heywood indeed authored these lines, he would have been well aware of their Ovidian resonance, now linked to Barabas and Machevill to boot. As a translator of the *Ars amatoria* and probably also the *Remedia Amoris*, he surely knew that Proteus the changeable sea divinity was the signature god of the *auctor*, appearing repeatedly in his works as an emblem of the masterfully deceptive lover.[9] Similarly, the Cockpit Epilogue begins with another image associating Alleyn with the ever-variegating Ovid: 'In graving, with Pygmalion to contend / [. . .] Must be disgrace: our actor did not so, / He only aimed to go, but not

out go'. Along with Daedalus, the maker of mazes with their analogues to complex narratives that would later be called romances,
Pygmalion is another type of the *artifex* from the *Metamorphoses*,
in this case of truly anamorphic artistry in matters devoted to love.
So, in a subtle way, the Barabas that seventeenth-century audiences experienced, including Charles and Henrietta Maria, may
have possessed a lineage that at least some playgoers recognized
as deviously Ovidian. Even the apparently innocuous concluding
couplet of the Court Epilogue evades responsibility for the ensu-
ing play by attributing its words to a speaker who is a construction, as opposed to the author himself: 'if aught here offend your
ear or sight, / We only act and speak what others write'.[10] This is
precisely how Ovid distinguishes his personal character from his
literary productions in the *Tristia* and defends himself, a practice
he began in the concluding elegy of the *Amores* as he disavows the
preceding material, which Marlowe renders, 'Nor am I by such
wanton toys defamed' (*Elegies* III.14.4).[11] He could be speaking
Machevill's Prologue in which this incarnation of Old Nick relates
himself to Barabas: 'Grace him as he deserves, / And let him not
be entertained the worse / Because he favours me' (*The Jew of
Malta*, Prologue.33–5).

Twentieth-century critics who sought to justify what they
believed to be a radical change in tone in the play after the first
two acts never considered that Marlowe's early work in translation
gave him invaluable experience with a text so complex in its mood
and feeling as the *Amores*. T. S. Eliot, Una Ellis-Fermor, Muriel C.
Bradbrook and Paul H. Kocher explored and debated the notion
of the farcical or sought to establish the unity of *The Jew of Malta*
in the wake of this generic assumption. How could a dramatic
tale that seems to begin as revenge tragedy devolve into a travesty of this form, replete with glibly imagined elements such as
the poisoning of nuns, filicide and falling into a trap of one's own
design?[12] My answer is, simply put: read Ovid. The intertwining
of savagery and humour in the *Metamorphoses* creates many such
tonal shifts. Are readers supposed to empathize with a divine rap-
ist and discount the terror of his victim, who then involuntarily

transforms into a tree that is sacred to him? Or a daughter whose lust for her father is expressed in a soliloquy that arouses more than mild amusement, as well as pity and terror? Similarly, the *Amores* that Marlowe renders as the *Elegies* features what could be described as wild mood swings, a kind of poetical bipolarity. For example, angry derision of the eunuch, Bagoas, who guards his master's door from prospective cuckolders such as the lover (II.3) precedes another in which this speaker admits his general perfidy (II.4), followed by an anti-feminist screed that criticizes Corinna by suspecting her of the same infidelity (II.5), which is in turn followed by a poem devoted to a dead parrot (II.6). And the elegy in which the speaker laments his impotence and even addresses his recalcitrant member as the offending party (III.6), replete with clashing tonal movements, is itself a veritable paradigm of this technique. Barabas's behaviour and actions are similarly, and usefully, disjunctive.

Marlowe's lover in the *Elegies* embodies some more recent thematic interpretations of Barabas and his milieu that explain or ameliorate his stereotypical ethnicity by contending that he serves as surrogate for the Elizabethan debate about Machiavellianism, embodies his play's self-conscious theatricality or represents social anxieties about outsiders in English culture. The deceitful youth's fatuous claim to Corinna that he lives a 'spotless life' and that 'her I love, change never' (*Elegies* I.3.13, 15) corresponds in part to Howard S. Babb's thesis that *The Jew of Malta* explores and critiques 'policy', the political parallel to the rogue male ethos that Ovid presents. This figure also anticipates the composite Barabas (Machevill, anti-Semitic devil, morality Vice) that David Bevington and N. W. Bawcutt excavate in their dramaturgical archaeology, since the youth's interrelated adultery and misogyny – for example, 'a wench is a perpetual evil' (II.5.4) – comprising an attack on marriage, invites and promulgates in microcosm such societal disorder as an 'underhanded, scheming, anti-Christian villain' may leave in his wake, as Catherine Minshull theorizes in her related study. William Hamlin's contention that Barabas is self-deluded about the amorality he seems to champion also describes the shifts and evasions of the boastful *Elegies* persona who suggests that he still hopes for the very fidelity in a woman that his own behaviour would appear to discourage: 'I have been wanton, therefore am perplexed, / And with mistrust of the like measure vexed' (I.4.45–6). In this figure who expresses his alienation as a poet in a culture that values 'a rich chuff' over verse, the making of which included 'Wit was sometimes more precious than gold' (III.7.9, 3), Marlowe anticipates the outsider perspective of his play's protagonist that James Shapiro interprets as coded social anxiety about the Strangers, the Dutch and Flemish immigrants who flooded the London labour market in the late sixteenth century, or that corresponds to the perpetually alone Barabas whom Ian McAdam argues is a representation of the playwright's personal angst about his sexuality and what is 'sodomitical'.[13] In these several ways, then, Marlowe's Ovidianism serves as adjunct to three centuries of analysis and reception of what is arguably his most controversial work, and can help expand and enhance our understanding of its critical traditions.

II

What specific ligatures can be detected between play, character, poem and speaker? Marlowe underscores Barabas's *Amores*-Ovidian lineage with his modulations in rhetorical patterns and his unbridled delight in deceiving all those around him as he executes his comic revenge. Several of the translated *Elegies* could serve as examples of this developmental stage in the playwright's conception of dissimulative dramatic speech. The translation of *Amores* II.4, labelled *Quod amet mulieres, Cuiuscunque formae sint* [That he loves women, no matter what their looks may be] seems particularly suggestive of the origins of his Maltese protagonist and his ilk, though at first glance their similarity is not apparent.[14] After many instances of what might be called inadvertent autoincrimination, the lover surprises us with an unlikely admission of his own louche character at the midpoint of the work. Although this is knowledge that his audience has possessed for some time,

he now expresses an awareness of his 'vices being many', prepared
to reveal himself as fully as he thinks he is able: 'Here I display
my lewd and loose behaviour' (*Elegies* II.4.2, 4). He chases women
for no reason at all: 'If she be learned, then for her skill I crave
her, / If not, because she's simple I would have her' (II.4.17–18).
Barabas shows a similarly bemused understanding of his own perfidy, although he would never describe it as Vice. There is another
factor to consider here, as well. Just as the young lover justifies
some of his deeds against womankind by blaming their allegedly
deceitful nature, his dramatic successor faults the culture that
oppresses him, albeit not without reason, which accounts in some
respects for this notorious set of precepts for Ithamore's benefit:

> be thou void of these affections,
> Compassion, love, vain hope, and heartless fear;
> Be moved at nothing, see thou pity none,
> But to thyself smile when the Christians moan. (*The Jew of
> Malta*, II.3.173–6)

This obsessive villainy becomes a kind of mindless compulsion,
similar to the youth in the *Elegies* and his amoral skirt-chasing. 'I
loathe, yet after that I loathe, I run' and 'I cannot rule myself, but
where love please' (II.4.5, 7) correspond to Barabas's increasingly
unhinged hatred and mindless greed, which both fuel the momen-
tum that leads him to the scaffold by which he tumbles into the
boiling cauldron. The bravura passage that features the frenetic
duet with Abigail in which he assures her that his cursing of her
for taking her vows is mere dissembling, replete with asides about
where to find the riches that Ferneze and his minons have not
already requisitioned (*The Jew of Malta*, I.2.355–65), proves pro-
phetic and ironic, given her subsequent demise and his consistent
amorality: 'Seducèd daughter (*Aside to her*) Go, forget not' (359).
Running after what one loathes in the manner of the Ovidian youth
is the nonpareil of perversity, a tendency that Marlowe illustrates
by linking such disparate elements in the same line. The daughter's fate suggests that her father lies to her here as well, though

she obeys him and does not forget, paragon of filial duty as she is, unaware that he has in a sense seduced her and cares for nothing but money. For both Barabas and the lover, malevolence and a lack of self-control strengthen and even sustain one another. The two of them also demonstrate an awareness of, and curious respect for, conventional morality by their happy violation of it. They 'deeply can dissemble' (*Elegies*, II.4.16). Similarly, Abigail hears from her father:

> as good dissemble that thou newer mean'st
> As first mean truth, and then dissemble it;
> A counterfeit profession is better
> Than unseen hypocrisy. (*The Jew of Malta*, I.2.292–5)

In the ocean of generally warped logic that is *The Jew of Malta*, this makes sense. It is better to be forthright about one's own corruption – even to embrace it – than attempting to fool oneself and others that one is not innately depraved. As Ithamore later warns Bellamira about his master, 'The meaning has a meaning' (IV.4.91), unaware, naturally, that this phrase epitomizes her blandishments to him as well as Barabas's exquisite dissembling. In the same spirit, *Elegies* II.4 concludes with an epithet that describes its speaker perfectly: 'Nay what is she that any Roman loves / But my ambitious ranging mind approves' (47–8). Not only does it recall Harry Levin's venerable conception of the overreacher for Marlowe's dramatic protagonists and include the lover in their notorious company, but it is how his usurer would describe himself if he were given to such interiority and self-reflection as his amorous predecessor, to his credit, demonstrates.[15]

At times, in spite of their apparent disparity, *The Jew of Malta* and the *Elegies* echo within each other's foundational chambers, though the erotic element does not seem as pronounced in the play as it does in Marlowe's other works. Yet there are moments. When Lodowick objects to a certain pair of wandering eyes, 'Good Barabas, glance not at our holy nuns', the drolly ironic reply, considering its underlying psychopathic intent, resonates in the amorous fashion as well: 'No, but I do it through a burning zeal' (*The Jew of Malta*, II.3.87–8). Barabas thinks of the novices not only as revenge fodder but as sexual beings and looks at them this way so obviously that even this exceedingly doltish and unobservant scion of a governor notices. The little referential forays into fornication continue, Ithamore memorably gulled by Bellamira, and culminate in Barabas's famous declaration about the dead wench in another country – one that the young Eliot so cherished that he used it as the epigraph for the allusively titled 'Portrait of a Lady' in his first poetical collection (1917).[16] Mathias's risible appraisal of Abigail sounds like something the *desultor Amoris* would say if he lived in medieval or early modern England and his Corinna were the object of desire in a work informed by Ovidian *fin' Amors*:

> Tut, she were fitter for a tale of love
> Than to be tirèd out with orisons:
> And better would she far become a bed,
> Embracèd in a friendly lover's arms,
> Then rise at midnight to a solemn mass. (*The Jew of Malta*, I.2.369–73)

Predictable puns abound ('fit', 'tale', 'tirèd out', 'rise') that can be found almost anywhere in the *Elegies*, and it is not difficult to detect a palimpsest of fabliau with an *Amores* heritage. This novice, in the libertine's estimation, would indeed be put to better use as what we would call a sexual object, just as his ancient counterpart remarks about all women, young and old: 'Nowhere can they be taught but in the bed' (*Elegies*, II.5.61). Conversely, though the young swain of the *Elegies* agonizes continually over his married lady and her friends and learns, the hard way, how truly unimportant he is to them, he frets almost as much about matters fiduciary. One elegy, the very poem that follows the anguished complaint about his untimely flaccidity in the lists with Corinna (III.6 and III.7), is all about money and sounds like something Barabas might utter if he spoke in couplets and possessed a social conscience:

Gold from the earth instead of fruits we pluck,
Soldiers by blood to be enriched have luck.
Courts shut the poor out; wealth gives estimation,
Thence grows the judge and knight of reputation. (*Elegies*,
III.7. 53–6)

The speaker only launches into this apparent jeremiad against those who would oppress the downtrodden for the sake of seeming to generalize beyond his own selfish concerns, which always come first. He mentions 'Soldiers' because Corinna took one of this newly moneyed class for her latest lover as a replacement for him, perhaps because of his bedroom dysfunction. He invokes 'the poor' because, as the poem explains at length, poets such as himself tend not to be rewarded with gold for their considerable efforts. This Sulmonian parvenu in his gate-crashing of patrician Roman society could surely relate to Barabas's fifth observation in his opening soliloquy: 'The needy groom that never fingered groat, / Would make a miracle of thus much coin' (*The Jew of Malta*, I.1.12–13). Both Marlovian overreachers end up alone, to some extent because of both money and sex, and tumble into boiling cauldrons of their own making. Though one's demise is literal and the other's merely figurative, it is hard to say which one of them suffers more, or longer.

III

Though *The Jew of Malta* allegedly bifurcates itself between the tragic and the farcical after Act II, a careful reading suggests that the Barabas who establishes his character and motives in the play's first scene never really changes except to become even more himself, which the rest of the text bears out. I contend that Marlowe's evocation of the part of his protagonist's literary ancestry rooted in the classical past remains similarly consistent. An apparent enjoyment of wrongdoing that masks a deep sense of alienation, a conflict that necessitates a duplicity so indelible that even his amorality is not quite as pronounced as he boasts, also describes the

Ovidian lover in the *Elegies*. Their rapaciousness, one for women and one for money, is of a piece. That both figures as a result of these characteristics tend to make statements that redound ironically upon them would appear almost predictable. Let us see how Marlowe's translation helps connect, if not exactly reconcile, the two halves of his play.

Barabas's comic relish of his own misdeeds constitutes another Ovidian feature of his dramatic personality that the 1633 quarto emphasizes by the many asides included in the text, some quite nuanced, providing direction to any actor, perhaps a feature preserved from Marlowe's own time for the audiences at the Cockpit and at court.[17] The character pitches most of these stagey side-comments at the audience for what he seems to think is its benefit so that it can commiserate or even collude with him, as Shakespeare's Richard Crookback and Iago will later. Since virtually each of the *Elegies* functions as an extended aside or a soliloquy, the playwright had manifold opportunities to meditate on how this principle might work as he translated. Barabas enjoys sounding patriotic in a recognizably hyperbolic way: 'Why let 'em come, so they come not to war; / Or let 'em war, so we be conquerours. / (*Aside*) Nay, let 'em combat, conquer, and kill all, / So they spare me, my daughter, and my wealth' (*The Jew of Malta*, I.1.149–52). Sometimes, he lets us know with just one word that he not only lies but enjoys the way that mendacity subtly accomplished benefits him: 'If anything shall there concern our state / Assure yourselves I'll look unto (*aside*) myself' (I.1.171–2). The faithless lover of the *Elegies*, in what constitutes a somewhat gigantic aside, seems greatly pleased with himself as he reveals that his declaration to Corinna at the beginning of our time with him is simply balderdash: 'Accept him that will love with spotless truth' (*Elegies*, I.3.6). He is not merely amoral but self-consciously and joyously immoral:

> Let one wench cloy me with sweet love's delight:
> If one can do't, if not, two every night.
> Though I am slender, I have store of pith:

Nor want I strength, but weight to press her with.
Pleasure adds fuel to my lustful fire:
I pay them home with that they most desire. (II.10.21–6)

The moneylender's corrosive cynicism about the culture that tol-
erates him in spite of its hatred of and distrust for him has its analogue in the lover's similar, almost despairing misogyny. Whatever
Roman women or the good citizens of Malta 'most desire', both
of Marlowe's speakers plan to provide it in ways that their victims
could not possibly have foretold. That this tendency in Barabas
only accelerates as he accomplishes his schemes, chuckling bit-
terly away, also has its analogue in the *Elegies*. To choose lines or
passages from the second half of the play to illustrate the point
is not a difficult prospect, only deciding which would be most
appropriate. 'How sweet the bells ring now the nuns are dead'
(*The Jew of Malta*, IV.1.2) seems best, since it adds pleasure to his
Ovidian lustful fire, in this case, for his revenge. The message is:
admire me.

This enthusiastic enjoyment of wrongdoing for its own sake
arises from a sense of alienation from surroundings and culture
that both Barabas and the Ovidian lover use to justify more perfidy.
Why should the Maltese not be victimized by their own greed?
'Who hateth me but for my happiness? / Or who is honoured now
but for his wealth?' (*The Jew of Malta*, I.1.111–12). Since this
phrase occurs in the moneylender's first speech, it appears to function, like so much else in this soliloquy, as an expression of theme.
The young man in the *Elegies* expresses a similarly bitter sense
of distance from the society that rejects him, but for the opposite
reason from the protagonist he precedes. He has no money: 'See
a rich chuff whose wounds great wealth inferred / For bloodshed
knighted, before me preferred' (*Elegies*, III.7.9–10). This is how he
rationalizes his faithlessness to Corinna, which he tells her plainly:
'Ask'st why I change? Because thou crav'st reward: / This cause
hath thee from pleasing me debarred' (I.10.11–12). Why should
he be faithful to someone who is concerned only with 'reward', or
capital? Surely she should be grateful that one of such a promising

poetical bent wishes to make love to her. At the same time, as honest with himself about his own dishonesty as Barabas is, the youth knows that the women he pursues will lie to him, as well: 'But me let crafty damsels words deceive: / Great joys by hope I inly shall conceive' (II.9.43–4). Such cynicism would have been a useful tonic for Ithamore with Bellamira. The lover could probably not express his estrangement and isolation any more clearly than 'Nothing I love, that at all times avails me' (II.19.8). Barabas loves nothing also, which sustains him. He despises his fellow members of his own ethnic group as they bend to the Christians: 'See the simplicity of these base slaves, / Who for the villains have no wit themselves' (*The Jew of Malta*, I.2.218–19). That his enemies have tried to obliterate him is no cause for despair or suicide: 'No, I will liue; nor loath I this my life'; 'I'll rouse my senses, and awake myself' (I.2.267, 271). The speech that has offended so many readers and theatregoers, beginning 'We Jews can fawn like spaniels when we please' (II.3.20–9), is meant to express precisely such self-reliance as a result of the profound alienation, surely a survival instinct, that its speaker feels. As he fantasizes how his enemies might 'starve upon a stall', he relishes the idea of desecrating the 'offering-basin' that his own congregation would pass around in a humanitarian gesture: 'Even for charity I may spit into't'. There is no sense of *caritas* for the speaker of the *Elegies*, either.

This conflict for the young lover and Barabas – sociocultural estrangement in turbulent tandem with bravado *cum* braggadocio – forms a paradigm of duality that determines their dominant characteristic absolutely, duplicity. Why should the moneylender not ask two questions such as these in his first scene? 'now how stands the wind? / Into what corner peers my halcyon's bill?' (*The Jew of Malta*, I.1.38–9). Neither seems entirely rhetorical. His mention of the 'bill' may be yet another example of how the nose (or the Nose) plays, and his utterance evokes a lack of free will as well as its operation. He may spy into any corner he likes, yet the wind determines his direction of inquiry as he fulfils his role as halcyon, the calm associated with the mythical bird another drolly ironic authorial touch, a misnomer for one of such volatility.[18]

This speaker would call down confusion on one and all, ascertaining first that his interests are protected:

> How ere the world go, I'll make sure for one,
> And seek in time to intercept the worst,
> Warily guarding that which I have got.
> *Ego mihimet sum semper proximus.*
> Why let 'em enter, let 'em take the towne. (I.1.185–9)

Even more than everyone else, he is indeed always nearest to himself, a phrase that the playwright happily borrows from Terence and that in turn Jonson will use many years later to similarly felicitous effect.[19] If Geffrey Whitney had taken this as an apothegm from which to create a full-fledged emblem in his great work of that name, published the year before *Tamburlaine* was probably performed, the engraving might have looked something like Ovid's *desultor Amoris*, whose aggressive duality, which the precocious Marlowe expertly preserves in his translation, foretells Barabas's dissembling and amoral bifurcation.[20] Virtually every elegy contains some instance of similar duplicity, happily and brazenly rationalized, but two examples deserve special mention. In one poem early in the first book, the youth, addressing Corinna, proposes to dally with her in front of her unsuspecting husband, using secret signs such as surreptitious foot contact and writing cryptic messages on the table in wine. Should she ignore him or attend to her *vir* in a way that violates the lover's sense of entitlement, he warns, 'If thou giv'st kisses, I shall all disclose, / Say they are mine, and hands on thee impose' (*Elegies*, I.4.39–40). Similarly, in the next book of the *Elegies*, he denies that he is sleeping with her maid and hairdresser, Cypassis: 'Myself unguilty of this crime I know' (II.7.28). Yet no sooner is this last line of that poem delivered that the next elegy immediately establishes that this denial is a lie, since he threatens the *ancilla* with the same exposure with which he attempted to intimidate her mistress: 'If thou deni'st, fool, I'll our deeds express, / And as a traitor mine own fault confess' (II.8.25–6). He will betray those women who do not give themselves to him exclusively to those who can do them the most harm. He too is always nearest to himself – close enough, it seems, so that he is unaware of his own repellent nature. Similarly, the twofaced Barabas does not always seem to be aware that some of his most important utterances in the rest of the play are often inherently depraved in their dualism, such as his imperative to the uncomprehending Abigail about Lodowick: 'Dissemble, swear, protest, vow to love him' (*The Jew of Malta*, II.3.234); his directive to himself on that same swain and Ithamore: 'like a cunning spirit feign some lie, / Till I have set 'em both at enmity' (388–9); and his admission to the audience, worthy of the Machevill of the play's Prologue, about seeming to follow both the Turks and the Maltese: 'Thus loving neither, will I live with both, / Making a profit of my policy; / And he from whom my most advantage comes, / Shall be my friend' (V.2.111–14). One could not get much nearer to oneself, a horrifying perspective in this case, equivalent to his description of Lodowick: 'the slave looks like a hog's cheek new singed' (II.3.42–3).

Both characters, poetical and dramatic, cherish their amorality that arises from their duplicity, puffed up with something like pride at its efficacy. Yet each betrays a conventionally moral sensibility. Barabas berates his thieving Christian neighbours for the immorality that underlies what he considers to be the tenets of a misguided, intolerant religion: 'bring you Scripture to confirm your wrongs? / Preach me not out of my possessions. / Some Jews are wicked, as all Christians are' (*The Jew of Malta*, I.2.114–16). The imperative that begins the second line mimetically alliterates with the final noun and underscores what their reasons for sermonizing truly are. He prepares us for this specific charge by his generalization in the previous scene's opening soliloquy: 'I can see no fruits in all their faith, / But malice, falsehood, and excessive pride'. The mention of these stock vices, straight from Central Casting, at least for a morality play, implies that he knows perfectly well what such sins are, and that since his enemies have committed them, he is conscious that a state of grace exists for those who have not. Another implication of this statement is that he himself has lived, or has attempted to live, in such a state. In the same vein, 'Happily some hapless man hath conscience, / And for his conscience lives in beggary' (*The Jew of Malta*, I.115–16, 118–19), clearly shows an understanding of what conscience is. In deriding the pious ascetics as fools, the sheer heat and emotion of his statement may signify that he has a touch of guilt for the less fortunate who do not know the joys of counting infinite riches in a little room. He has possessed, at least at one time, a sense of *fas* and *nefas*. He can distinguish between degrees of offence in ways that are not entirely advantageous to him. Covetousness (his honestly sinful impetus for acquiring his fortune) shrinks away from outright larceny (the monstrously hypocritical Maltese appropriation of his wealth): 'take not from me then, / For that is theft; and if you rob me thus, / I must be forced to steal and compass more' (I.2.128–30). The young lover of the *Elegies* engages in similar logical contortions strangely dependent on an innate moral sense, even as his true motive is to obscure his own faithlessness. Annoyed with Corinna's 'rash accusing' and 'vaine belief' that he wants to fornicate with her hairdresser (which he does, wishes on the way proving effects), he says, impatiently, 'Would I were culpable of some offence, / They that deserve pain, bear't with patience' (*Elegies*, II.7.13, 11–12). He understands – and respects – the general concept of 'offence' well enough to articulate an idea of guilt, that one can 'deserve pain' and endure it according to a pseudo-Protestant ideal. This special knowledge, the idea of culpability, also leads him to assert his incapability to commit a crime such as adultery, as he assures the very husband he intends to cuckold in spite of his alertness to this unthinkable possibility: 'Nor canst by watching keep her mind from sin. / All being shut out, th'adulterer is within' (*Elegies*, III.4.7–8). It is as if the amorous Ovidian gallant and Barabas lament that they live in a world in which such corruption compels them to be as they are, and to do as they may. As Marlowe's moneylender retorts to Ferneze's assertion that he has had 'nought but right', anticipating Bassanio's later retort to Shylock: 'Your extreme right does me exceeding wrong' (*The Jew of Malta*, II.2.155–6). 'It's no sin to deceive a Christian' (II.3.314) indeed, at least one such as this.[21]

Yet neither figure could be considered a moralist in his own right and thereby a proto-Jonsonian satiric scourge who serves as authorial surrogate. Both are too sociopathic for this, and besides, their statements that resemble normative prescriptions redound most ironically against them, perhaps the deepest bond they share. Much of what they say could be used as evidence to convict them in ways that even they could understand. The lover explains that women's incorrigibility means, 'Nowhere can they be taught but in the bed' (*Elegies*, II.5.61), though his lack of success in this area suggests that his erotic pedagogy has failed both them and him, and that he lacks the proper knowledge to engage in teaching or fornicating because of his own utter imperviousness to learning from experience or observation. He boasts in each book of the *Elegies* of his success with the woman most frequently named therein, but then Ovid-Marlowe immediately discredits him. 'Conquered Corinna in my bosom lays' (II.12.2) results, it seems, in a pregnancy so untimely and unwanted that 'rashly her womb's burthen she casts out' (II.13.1), an immediate self-inflicted abortion. Later, the speaker's insolent assertion to her husband, 'stolen pleasure is sweet play' (III.4.31), finds its counterpoint in his own inability to perform and enjoy either, 'Yet could I not cast anchor where I meant' (III.6.6). His final comeuppance is to discover himself in the same position as the man he has so enjoyed cuckolding, put aside for another, asking Corinna as the scorned husband must have, 'canst thou him in thy white arms embrace?' (III.7.11). Yes, she can.

If this young lover could have starred in his very own theatrical entertainment, he might have sounded just as Barabas does, whose statements Marlowe just as relentlessly undermines. He says to himself: 'search this secret out. / Summon thy senses, call thy wits together: / These silly men mistake the matter clean' (*The Jew of Malta*, I.1.176–8). Yet he too is silly, and his mistakes guarantee he will be clean found out. Though he professes his love for Abigail, his classical analogy meant to express this affection foretells her fate, almost risibly: 'one sole daughter, whom I hold as dear / As

Agamemnon did his Iphigen' (I.1.136–7). It can at least be said of
the Greek epic hero that he was able to justify this terrible sacrifice
as an act unwillingly undertaken for the common good, and then
had the decency to perish at the hands of his own adulterous wife
as she accomplished her revenge. None of these extenuating factors can be applied to Barabas. '*Enter with a hammer above, very
busy*' (V.5.sd); Marlowe's hilarious stage direction that precedes
his protagonist's great downfall proves to be symbolic as well as
literal, with its image of his feverish and enthusiastic construction
of his own ruin even as he believes he builds a snare for someone
else. His statement to the carpenters a few lines later, continuing
the metaphor of building, is truly its own trap door that leads to
an extremity of heat pinching him with intolerable pangs: 'Leave
nothing loose, all levelled to my mind. / Why now I see that you
have art indeed' (V.5.3–4).

Art, indeed. Marlowe employs the term, analogous to the
ars of the *magister* – skill, craft and guile – over 50 times in the
canon, including the *Elegies*, embodied by the approving description of Pygmalion in the *Metamorphoses*, 'ars adeo latet arte sua'
(X.252) [so did his art conceal his art], which in turn epitomizes
the technique of both poets.[22] Therefore, one part of Brown's
thesis about Ovid as catalyst for change in Elizabethan literary
culture cited at the outset, that writers such as Shakespeare and
Lodge 'repeatedly invoked' Ovid 'to provide the classical sanc-
tion for self-proclaimed modernity', is not true of Marlowe.[23] He
did not need to refer explicitly to his classical predecessor since
he was reanimating him instead in the theatre and on the page,
and sometimes, as in our present example, in both places at once,
demonstrating how completely Naso was the Man. For instance,
the passage from *The Jew of Malta* that so amused the youthful
Eliot has a certain Ovidian resonance:

> *Bernadine*: Thou has committed –
> *Barabas*. Fornication?
> But that was in another country:
> And besides, the wench is dead. (IV.1.43–5)

This demonstrates the same verbal facility that the *desultor Amoris* frequently shows, as well as the tendency that Ovid himself reveals in the voice of his exile poetry to make excuses for his past behaviour, as one whose sins are very much in the past. Yet Barabas's comment to Ithamore might as well have been made to the speaker in the *Elegies*: 'make account of me / As of thy fellow; we are villains both' (II.3.218–20). And in a complementary fashion, the Elizabethan circus-rider of love could have returned the compliment to his canonical brother boiling away in a pot in Malta. The Nose plays for both.

EIGHT

A Survey of Resources

SARAH K. SCOTT

The Jew of Malta has been enjoying an increase in scholarly attention in recent years that shows it to be worthy of study in and of itself. In the distant past, Marlowe's play was relegated by students and teachers of Elizabethan drama, as well as by scholars, to the status of supplemental material in order to illuminate *The Merchant of Venice*, since Marlowe's drama seems concerned with similar issues of racial and religious discrimination. Yet critics have long been analysing it for its own merits, especially in the last half-century. To be sure, *The Jew of Malta* provides a complex treatment of subjects that include religion and politics, Machiavellian policy and issues of genre and dramatic technique. Moreover, questions that this play may have invited its original audience to entertain persist in altered forms in the present day. Do we, for instance, blindly follow a cynical 'golden rule' similar to that which governs Malta? Do those with the gold make the rules in our societies? If so, why? Issues of meaning abound in Marlowe's text as well, such as whether the playwright can be understood to be exposing religious hypocrisy in order to reform the play's morally depraved Malta (a thinly veiled London), or whether he simply intended to represent reality as he understood it – that 'evils are apt to happen every day', as Barabas avers (I.2.225). Scholars and students of the drama additionally find themselves asking whether it expresses anti-Semitic, anti-Christian or anti-religious points of view. The following discussion presents an array of scholarship that includes editions, critical essays, critical companions and media-based resources to encourage meaningful and productive classroom examination of Marlowe's provocative play.

The proliferation of editions of the Marlowe canon that began after World War I continues to the present, and among these are several single text versions of *The Jew of Malta* designed for study at the college-level, the best of which are edited by Bawcutt, Bevington, Lynch, Martin and Siemon, the last the most preferred. *The Jew of Malta* exists in only one early modern version, the 1633 quarto published by John Beale for Nicholas Vavasour, the last of Marlowe's works to be published for the first time, 40 years following his death. Scholars attest to its popularity by citing its performance record in Philip Henslowe's diary, 29 times between 1592 and 1596, with Edward Alleyn performing the role of Barabas. This early stage history, combined with its first appearance in the Stationers' Register in 1594 and the claims by Gerard Langbaine that the 'play was in much esteem', indicate the play was well received.[1] Its textual difficulties seem relatively minor compared to the scholarly controversy surrounding the first two printings of *Doctor Faustus*.

Perhaps the most important topic to address initially when teaching the play is Marlowe's treatment of Jewishness in the figure of Barabas. Most scholarship on the subject analyses early modern conceptions of his religion and ethnicity, which are often difficult for students to comprehend. G. K. Hunter's exhaustive 'The Theology of Marlowe's *The Jew of Malta*' (1964) examines a series of ironic contrasts that show Barabas, who shares the name of the murderer set free in place of Christ, to be a parody of Job. Barabas's immense material assets reveal a dearth of spiritual fulfilment, which Marlowe contrasts with conceptions of the divine wealth that both the merchant and the Maltese sorely lack. In this interpretation, Hunter contends that Marlowe is better able to reveal Christian hypocrisy. Alan C. Dessen, in 'The Elizabethan Stage Jew and Christian Example: Gerontus, Barabas, and Shylock' (1974), presents a theatre historian's approach to understanding the construction of Jewishness on the Elizabethan stage, especially in the context of the morality play tradition, in order to differentiate post-Holocaust perspectives from those of the sixteenth century. This dramatic tradition frequently employed the stereotype of Jews as morally depraved and avaricious as a caveat against the materialism that was perceived to threaten Christian stability. *The Merchant of Venice* and Robert Wilson's *The Three Ladies of London* resemble Marlowe's play in this respect, suggesting that the greatest dangers to the social fabric are not foreign but domestic, those that truly threaten from within, such as Christian pretensions to moral superiority. The essay 'Marlowe, Marx, and Anti-Semitism' (1978) by Stephen J. Greenblatt uses Marx's 'On the Jewish Question' as a means to understand *The Jew of Malta* by contrasting the authors' representations of anti-Semitic ideology. Marlowe and Marx depict stereotypes of Jewish figures engaged in activities seemingly foreign to their communities but that in actuality are integral to them. Greenblatt's study of Marlowe and Marx's extensive use of the aphorism illustrates subtle but essential differences in the two writers' points of view. Peter Berek's 'The Jew as Renaissance Man' (1998) provides a thorough historical account of the *Marranos*, or *conversos*, Iberian Jews who claimed conversion to Christianity but who remained true to Judaism, to reveal the difficult position of Jews dwelling in sixteenth-century England. Berek argues that Marlowe used the Christian conception of the *converso* to create a protagonist whose condition was recognized as ambiguous, ethically problematic, and who was therefore inherently evil. He concludes that this presentation persisted and therefore fed theatrical stereotypes, such as the usurer. For those seeking a general overview of Jewish peoples in early modern England, James Shapiro's *Shakespeare and the Jews* (1996) is the most valuable resource of its kind. Chapter 2, 'Myths, Histories, Consequences', investigates events such as the Expulsion of the Jews by Edward I in 1290, the 1656 Readmission during the Commonwealth and the years in between by analysing historical and mythological accounts to reveal subtle and overt shifts in English conceptions of national identity. His findings show that medieval and early modern historical interpretations of Judaism and its people reflected cultural anxieties about expanding foreign populations to reveal complicated social, political, legal and religious tensions. Shapiro also examines the fascination with dramatic representations of Jewishness in contemporary literary studies. He criticizes scholarship that relies uncritically on the biased work of earlier historical and literary studies or that is skewed by a scholar's cultural milieu and personal perspective.

Another topic central to discussions of *The Jew of Malta* is that of Machiavellian political policy. For example, scholars continue to study the relationship between Machiavelli's theories about the role of religion in the art of statecraft and the pronouncement by Marlowe's Machevill character in the play's Prologue that religion is pure pretense, a 'childish toy' (Prologue 40). In the past, commentators cited Innocent Gentillet's *Anti-Machiavel* (1576) as Marlowe's probable source because it severely misrepresents Machiavelli as a proponent of atheism and the epitome of greed. N. W. Bawcutt's 'Machiavelli and Marlowe's *The Jew of Malta*' (1970) first argued against such conventional thinking by demonstrating that Marlowe and his contemporaries had access to *The Prince*, the *Discourses* and many sixteenth-century commentaries that represent the political philosopher's concepts more accurately. Bawcutt contends that these materials were in such wide circulation that it does not matter whether Marlowe had access to specific texts. Instead, it is more accurate to assert that his character Machevill represents the period's cynical, self-centred attitude commonly associated with the author of *The Prince*. In 'Marlowe's "Sound Machevill"' (1982), Catherine Minshull finds that although the playwright designs Barabas as a stereotypical sixteenth-century villain, it is Ferneze who instead most embodies Machiavellian scheming and self-centredness. Marlowe thus employs Barabas for ironic effect in order to expose the Maltese governor's duplicity, manipulate the expectations of his audience at the Rose, and satirize the hypocrisy of English politicians who truly embodied the Italian author's pronouncements on statecraft as they understood them. Minshull additionally asserts that Marlowe's portrayal of Barabas as Machiavellian caricature ironically promulgated the stereotype, for audience members unfamiliar with his writings would have been unable to understand the satire. Thomas Cartelli's 'Machiavel's Ghost', in *Marlowe, Shakespeare, and the Economy of Theatrical Experience* (1991), argues that the flexibility of the play's structure manipulates audience expectations so as to reveal the dramatic function of the Machevill. A series of shifting perspectives that vacillate between traditional Christianity and soulless materialism, which the 'ghost' Machevill initiates and Barabas fulfils, produces a coherent moral message that exposes the dangers of deception.

The genre of *The Jew of Malta* continues to be a much-discussed issue in criticism. The quarto title calls the play a 'tragedy', but the performance record and scholarship has challenged that conception, such as Edmund Kean's theatrical revival in 1818 and T. S. Eliot's description of the play as a 'tragic farce' 100 years later. David Bevington's '*The Jew of Malta*' in *From Mankind to Marlowe* (1962), argues that the play's story is essentially secular and grafted onto moral drama, although elements of tragedy from the morality tradition clearly inform the design. Therefore, Barabas is far more than a type of the Vice. He is a complex human figure who fits imperfectly into the formula of homiletic drama as he seeks revenge in a world governed by *cupiditas*, rather than *caritas*. Erich Segal's 'Marlowe's *Schadenfreude*: Barabas as Comic Hero' (1972) reads the play as pure black comedy. To him, the playwright directs audiences to distance themselves from the central character so as to delight in the misfortunes of others, thereby entertaining them in the vein of English 'savage farce' in Eliot's sense, analogues of which persist in classical and early modern literature. Barabas, Segal maintains, is the consummate 'other' who repeatedly invites audiences to delight in his diabolical machinations for the sake of illicit laughter. Clare Harraway's 'A Production of Kinds: Genre, *The Jew of Malta* and the Promise of Repetition' in *Re-citing Marlowe: Approaches to the Drama* (2000) argues that the play's alleged genre confusion results from critics' misinterpretation of authorial intent. She claims that Marlowe consciously set out to problematize conventional dramatic classifications. A 'farce of genres' thus displaces expectations of tragedy, and Marlowe succeeds in his intent to delight audiences with the resulting parodic, paradoxical effects. Another approach to understanding the play's genre is to consider it an early form of city comedy. In '*The Jew of Malta* and the Development of City Comedy: "The Mean Passage of a History"', I argue that Barabas's exaggerated behaviour and semi-farcical plot reflect this dramatic form, which developed out of the native English dramatic tradition to become prominent on the stage in the early decades of the seventeenth century. The essay proposes a reading that attempts to reflect theatregoers' views of the period and takes into account the performance history of the text, its reception and the oft-employed device of the aside for humorous effect.

Studies of the play's performance history and metadramatic qualities offer perspectives on these issues of genre as well as those of dramatic interpretation that provide insights into its reception. James L. Smith's '*The Jew of Malta* in the Theatre' (1968) traces the play's production history from the sixteenth century to the twentieth to reveal that the most successful performances are those that have recognized its darkly comic qualities. Smith accounts for the failure of Kean's Drury Lane adaptation to its interpretation of Marlowe's play as tragedy, a reflection of conventional thinking in contemporary textual scholarship. The subsequent stagings that demonstrated the greatest success according to critics were those recognizing the drama as farce. The most notable of these are the 1964 productions of Peter Cheeseman (Victoria Theatre) and Clifford Williams (Royal Shakespeare Theatre). '"So neatly plotted, and so well perform'd": Villain as Playwright in Marlowe's *The Jew of Malta*' (1992) by Sara Munson Deats and Lisa S. Starks argues that the play's theatricality reveals it to be a willing participant in the antitheatrical debates of the early modern period as well as an important influence on the tragedies and satiric comedies that follow. Barabas's obsession with playmaking in a series of episodes reveals him to be a quintessential dramaturge and actor through whom Marlowe expresses the delights and dangers of his dramatic art as well as his ambivalence towards the medium. Stephanie Moss's 'Edmund Kean, Anti-Semitism, and *The Jew of Malta*' (2008) investigates this short-lived 1818 production to discover the reason for its limited run. The production modified the text in order to present Barabas in a sentimental way, as a tragic figure deserving of pathos. However, Moss demonstrates in her analysis of the negative reviews of Kean's version that this very strategy produced the opposite effect, unconsciously promulgating stereotypes that inadvertently reinforced the audience's native anti-Semitism.

Despite the absence of pedagogically oriented essays dedicated to *The Jew of Malta*, two excellent guidebooks provide essential information about the playwright and his works for classroom discussion. Stevie Simkin's *A Preface to Marlowe* (2000) is divided into two parts. 'The Writer and His Setting' relates the facts known about Marlowe's life to early modern religion, politics and society, and discusses the importance of the theatre and the business of playgoing in England. 'Critical Survey' explores the themes, cultural contexts and sources of his works. The chapter 'Unhallowed Deeds: *The Jew of Malta*' provides an overview related to the notion of cultural difference, especially religion, race and ethnicity. Simkin discusses the tensions between early modern conceptions of Jewishness and those of the present day; the dual portrayal of Barabas as victim and villain; the play's genre complications (part tragedy, part black comedy); its relationship to *The Merchant of Venice*; the function of the Machevill; the play's metadramatic qualities; and contemporary performances that explore religious and ethnic questions.

The second guidebook, *The Cambridge Companion to Christopher Marlowe* (2004), edited by Patrick Cheney, addresses *The Jew of Malta* in four separate essays. Cheney's 'Introduction: Marlowe in the twenty-first century' details the play's critical heritage, accounting for its reception; David Riggs's 'Marlowe's life' concerns his early years, education and relationship with the secret service, which he associates with the figure of Barabas; and Garrett A. Sullivan, Jr.'s 'Geography and identity in Marlowe' explores the relationship between these entities in the play. Julia Reinhard Lupton's '*The Jew of Malta*', the only essay that focuses entirely on the work in question, specifically analyses its treatment of Judaism as related to the concept of fellowship in its social, religious and economic forms. She details the history of Malta in the early modern period and its Spanish, Turkish, Papal and Maltese political tensions, and the problematic position of Jews in that milieu.

Despite the increased reliance upon the internet in the twenty-first century, online resources for *The Jew of Malta* are relatively few compared to those of Marlowe's celebrated contemporary born in the same year. Yet one senses that many more sites will appear in the months and years to come. Still to be constructed, for instance, is a site that allows for exploration into such primary texts as the Dutch Church Libel, the Baines note and the Book of Job, and that complement it, such as Montaigne's 'On Presumption', Henslowe's diary of Rose playhouse accounts, and antitheatrical writings. Opportunities for textual studies abound in the burgeoning field of digital humanities research. Marlowe's works have yet to be included in the Metadata Offer New Knowledge (MONK) Project (http://monkproject.org) or in Martin Muller's WordHoard (http://wordhoard.northwestern. edu/userman/index.html), both of which encourage sophisticated investigations into verbal and linguistic texture.

When using internet resources for the study of Marlowe, care must be taken to avoid those pages that present false claims or that misdirect impressionable students to material that encourages ahistorical thinking and poor scholarship. Several internet resources provide profitable avenues to enrich classroom pedagogy. Project Gutenberg supplies full access to Alexander Dyce's 1850 *Works* (available also in Google Books) in multiple formats, including HTML and Plain Text, as well as through an Online Reader format. Although the edition is somewhat outdated, it is still useful for basic reading purposes, and possesses important historical value. The play can even be made accessible on mobile phones by scanning Gutenberg's QR Code (Quick Response Code). Another helpful site is the Perseus Digital Library (Gregory R. Crane, Editor-in-Chief), which offers online access to Marlowe's poetic and dramatic works. Links throughout the edition of *The Jew of Malta* reflect some collation of the Quarto. *Luminarium: Anthology of English Literature*, created by Anniina Jokinen, features several student-friendly pages that introduce the poet and playwright. These include a bibliography, a listing of popular quotations and a collection of scholarly and student essays that examine a range of issues related to the play. Links to two online versions of *The Jew of Malta*, those of the Perseus Project and A. H. Bullen's 1884 edition, accessible through Google Books, are listed. An additional online resource is the Marlowe Society of America (MSA) website (www.marlowesmightyline.org) edited by M. L. Stapleton. The site supplies current news and information on Marlowe studies; a performance archive with links to images, videoclips and reviews; and access to back issues of the *Marlowe Society of America Newsletter*, which features book and performance reviews and an annual listing of recent publications in the areas of Marlowe biography, scholarship and criticism.

The Grandfather Films adaptation of *The Jew of Malta*, scheduled for release in 2012, will be the first video production of the play to be made available to the public. Directed by Douglas Morse and to be distributed by Films for the Humanities, it follows closely the 1633 quarto with few textual cuts or transpositions, thus proving a fine addition to the classroom approaches that combine text and performance. Morse's production, which presents Marlowe's drama as dark satire, will be a valuable contribution to the play's performance history and critical tradition, acting as a record of an early-twenty-first-century interpretation that can be compared to those of the 1960s, the Edmund Kean revival in the early nineteenth century and the Cockpit production of 1633, thus illuminating, where possible, not only a director's reading of Marlowe's work but the cultural consciousness of the audience watching it. The film will enhance performance studies, which have gained prominence in the mid-twentieth century, primarily as natural development out of academic interest in the early dramatists and the work of William Hazlitt and Leigh Hunt. It will serve as a useful tool for critical issues such as Christian hypocrisy, father–daughter relationships, anti-Semitism and controversies about the play's structure, such as the alleged tonal inconsistencies between the first two and last three acts of the play.

The following annotated bibliography of books, journal articles, essays in edited collections and media resources documents
the extensive critical tradition of *The Jew of Malta*.

Complete works

Bowers, Fredson, ed., *The Complete Works of Christopher Marlowe*, 2 vols, revised
  edn (Cambridge: Cambridge University Press, 1981). Volume 1 provides an
  old-spelling text of the play with fulsome critical apparatus, historical colla-
  tion and notes.
Brooke, C. F. Tucker, ed., *The Works of Christopher Marlowe* (Oxford: Clarendon
  Press, 1910). A one-volume, old-spelling edition with critical apparatus.
Burnett, Mark Thornton, ed., *Christopher Marlowe: The Complete Plays*.
  (London: J. M. Dent, 1999). An annotated modern-spelling Everyman edition
  with chronology, introduction and discussion of critical trends. The partner to
  Burnett's *Complete Poems* (2000).
Romany, Frank and Lindsey, Robert, eds, *Christopher Marlowe: The Complete
  Plays* (New York: Penguin, 2003). A modern-spelling edition with introduc-
  tion, notes and glossary, and commentary, as well as scene summaries and
  documents, including the Baines Note and the Collier Leaf. Serves as a complement to Stephen Orgel's 2007 edition of Marlowe's complete poetry.

Single text editions

Bawcutt, N. W. ed., *The Jew of Malta*, Revels Plays Edition (Manchester:
  Manchester University Press, 1978). A lavishly annotated modern-spelling
  edition of the play with substantial introduction including text and stage his-
  tory, sources, thematic issues.
Bennett, H. S., ed., '*The Jew of Malta*' and '*The Massacre at Paris*', vol. 3,
  The Works and Life of Christopher Marlowe, gen. ed. R. H. Case (London:
  Methuen, 1931). A modern-spelling edition with introduction, notes, com-
  mentary, textual history.
Bevington, David, ed., *The Jew of Malta*, Revels Student Editions (Manchester:
  Manchester University Press, 1997). A well-annotated student edition that
  includes general introduction to the play and description of recent critical
  trends.
The Famous / TRAGEDY / OF/ THE RICH JEW/ OF *MALTA*. / AS IT WAS
  PLAYD / BEFORE THE KING AND /QUEENE, IN HIS MAJESTIES /
  Theatre at *White-Hall*, by her Majesties / Servants at the *Cock-pit*. / *Written
  by* Christopher Marlo. / [Device] / Printed by *I*[ohn]. *B*[eale]. for *Nicholas
  Vavasour*, and are to be sold / at his Shop in the Inner-Temple, neere the /
  Church. 1633. STC 17412.
Gill, Roma, ed., *The Jew of Malta*, vol. 4, *The Complete Works of Christopher
  Marlowe*, gen. ed. Roma Gill (Oxford: Clarendon, 1995). An old-spelling

critical edition providing a 30-page commentary, detailed textual apparatus and bibliography. A scholarly edition.

Lynch, Stephen J., ed., *'The Jew of Malta' with Related Texts* (Indianapolis: Hackett, 2009). A modern-spelling student edition with source material from Machiavelli, Gentillet and Bacon. Introduction features biography as well as discussion of ethnic and religious contexts and treatment of themes, such as avarice versus free-market capitalism, Barabas as playwright and Catholicism and Christianity. Inclusion of a map of the Mediterranean world *c.* 1565 is especially useful for undergraduate classrooms.

Martin, Matthew, ed., *The Jew of Malta* (Peterborough, Ontario: Broadview Press, 2011). An annotated modern-spelling student edition with a wealth of source material from the period that covers the topics of Jewishness in England, European-Ottoman relations, Machiavellianism and Marlowe's reputation.

Ribner, Irving, ed., *'The Jew of Malta': Text and Major Criticism* (New York: Odyssey, 1970). Modern-spelling text with explanatory notes and scholarly commentary. Essays: *'The Jew of Malta'*, F. P. Wilson; *'The Jew of Malta* as Tragic Farce', M. M. Mahood; *'The Jew of Malta'*, J. B. Steane; 'Policy in Marlowe's *The Jew of Malta'*, H. S. Babb; 'Barabas the Jew: Incarnation of Evil', Douglas Cole; 'Innocent Barabas', Alfred Harbage; 'The Traditional Structure of *The Jew of Malta'*, D. M. Bevington; 'The Theology of Marlowe's *The Jew of Malta'*, G. K. Hunter; 'How Bad Is the Text of *The Jew of Malta?'*, J. C. Maxwell.

Siemon, James R., ed., *The Jew of Malta*, New Mermaids Series, 3rd edn (London: A & C Black, 2009). The preferred single scholarly edition, thoughtfully and thoroughly annotated. Detailed introduction addresses topical concerns. Also offers facsimile and transcript of the Dutch Church Libel.

Van Fossen, Richard, ed., *The Jew of Malta*, Regents Renaissance Drama Series (Lincoln: University of Nebraska Press, 1991). A modern-spelling edition with chronology and introduction that addresses publishing history, sources and influences and themes.

Concordances

Crawford, Charles, *The Marlowe Concordance*, 3 vols (Louvain: Uystpruyst, 1911–13). An index based upon Alexander Dyce's *The Works of Christopher Marlowe* (London: Edward Moxon, 1858). First two volumes available through internet Archive.

Fehrenbach, Robert J. et al., ed., *A Concordance to the Plays, Poems, and Translations of Christopher Marlowe* (Ithaca: Cornell University Press, 1983). An index based upon Bowers's *Complete Works, supra.* Extremely detailed and comprehensive. The standard work.

Ule, Louis, ed., *A Concordance to the Works of Christopher Marlowe.* The Elizabethan Concordance Series (Hildesheim: Georg Olms Verlag, 1979). An index based upon Brooke's *The Works of Christopher Marlowe, supra.*

Selected Textual Scholarship and Criticism
(Essays and Book Chapters)

Babb, Howard S., 'Policy in Marlowe's *The Jew of Malta*', *English Literary History*, 24 (1957), pp. 85–94. Argues against those who find the play tonally inconsistent by examining the numerous puns on 'policy'. Reprinted in Ribner, '*The Jew of Malta': Text and Major Criticism, supra*.

Bartels, Emily, 'Capitalizing on the Jew: The Third Term in *The Jew of Malta*', in *Spectacles of Strangeness: Imperialism, Alienation, and Marlowe* (Philadelphia: University of Pennsylvania Press, 1993), pp. 82–108. Argues that the play complicates and ultimately dismantles distinctions of self/other advanced by New Historicism to reveal that locating the true subject of discrimination is more complicated than audiences generally believe at the outset. Presents conceptions of Jews in the writings of Holinshed, Stow, and Stubbes, and discusses the powerful significance of Malta as setting. Reprinted in *Christopher Marlowe*, ed. Richard Wilson (London: Longman, 1999). See also Emily Bartels, 'Malta: *The Jew of Malta*, and the Fictions of Difference', *English Literary Renaissance*, 20 (1990), pp. 1–16.

Bawcutt, N. W., 'Machiavelli and Marlowe's *The Jew of Malta*', *Renaissance Drama*, n.s. 3 (1970), pp. 3–49. A comprehensive analysis of sixteenth-century contemporary European conceptions of Machiavelli, with specific comparison to Marlowe's Machevill.

Berek, Peter, 'The Jew as Renaissance Man', *Renaissance Quarterly*, 51 (1998), pp. 128–62. Marlowe (and shortly thereafter Shakespeare) is responsible for creating the greedy, self-absorbed figure of the stage Jew that still lingers in present-day Western culture. This caricature is vastly different than the English *marranos* of the 1590s. A comprehensive history of Jewish peoples in early modern England and Europe that includes a detailed discussion of Dr Roderigo Lopez, physician to Queen Elizabeth I.

Bevington, David M., '*The Jew of Malta*', in *From* Mankind *to Marlowe: Growth of Structure in the Popular Drama of the Tudor Period* (Cambridge: Harvard University Press, 1962), pp. 218–33. A study of the play as secular narrative with a homiletic, moral structure yielding a profoundly ambivalent effect. Barabas is a lifelike, secular Vice figure, descended from similar abstractions in *The Longer Thou Livest* and Worldly Man in *Enough Is as Good as a Feast*. Reprinted in Ribner's *Marlowe: A Collection of Critical Essays, supra*, and in Clifford Leech, ed., *Marlowe: A Collection of Critical Essays* (Englewood Cliffs: Prentice-Hall, 1964).

Bowers, Rick, 'Wresting with Comic Villainy: Barabas and Other "Heels" in *The Jew of Malta*', in *Radical Comedy in Early Modern England: Contexts, Cultures, Performances* (Aldershot: Ashgate, 2008), pp. 23–35. Argues the excessive theatricality of the play's characters is analogous to the comedic and enjoyable spectacle of professional wrestling.

Bradbrook, M. C., '*The Jew of Malta* and *Edward II*', in *Marlowe: A Collection of Critical Essays*, ed. Clifford Leech (Englewood Cliffs: Prentice-Hall, 1964), pp. 120–7. Compares structural parallels in *The Jew of Malta* and *Edward II* to demonstrate their similarities. Perceives a shift in tone from the first two acts to the rest of the play. Adapted from Bradbrook, 'Christopher Marlowe', in *Themes and Conventions of Elizabethan Tragedy* (Cambridge: Cambridge University Press, 1935), pp. 137–64.

Cartelli, Thomas, 'Machiavel's Ghost', in *Marlowe, Shakespeare, and the Economy of Theatrical Experience* (Philadelphia: University of Pennsylvania Press, 1991), pp. 161–80. Marlowe creates a highly theatrical experience for his audience by presenting a series of competing interpretations of events. The play's theme of hypocrisy is instigated by the Machiavel and sustained by the actions of Barabas.

Cheney, Patrick, 'Machiavelli and the Play of Policy in *The Jew of Malta*', in *Marlowe's Counterfeit Profession: Ovid, Spenser, Counter-Nationhood* (Toronto: University of Toronto Press, 1997), pp. 136–56. A study of Marlowe's debt to Ovid and Spenser. Compares Barabas to Mammon and analyses the playwright's staging of metadiscourse.

Cole, Douglas, 'Incarnations of Evil: Barabas the Jew and the Duke of Guise', in *Suffering and Evil in the Plays of Christopher Marlowe* (Princeton: Princeton University Press, 1962), pp. 123–58. Barabas is a spectacle of evil because he fulfils three villainous types in early modern drama: stage Jew, Machevill and Vice. Compares Barabas's actions to those of the Guise, finding the former obsessed with means and the latter the ends. Selections reprinted as 'Barabas the Jew: Incarnation of Evil' in Ribner, *supra*.

Cunningham, Karen, 'Renaissance Execution and Marlovian Elocution: The Drama of Death', *PMLA*, 105 (1990), pp. 209–22. Marlowe uses public violence and executions in his plays as a means to analyse the justice of those performed by the state. The playwright employs the aside and the spectacle of Barabas's false death as a means to examine government policies.

Deats, Sara Munson and Starks, Lisa S., '"So neatly plotted, and so well perform'd": Villain as Playwright in Marlowe's *The Jew of Malta*', *Theatre Journal*, 44 (1992), pp. 375–89. A new historicist approach that argues Marlowe's play is a calculated response to antitheatrical debates. Barabas is a consummate actor and dramaturge, and Marlowe's surrogate.

Dessen, Alan C., 'The Elizabethan Stage Jew and Christian Example: Gerontus, Barabas, and Shylock', *Modern Language Quarterly*, 35 (1974), pp. 231–45. A comparative analysis of the theatrical function of the stage Jew in *The Three Ladies of London*, *The Jew of Malta* and *The Merchant of Venice*. Marlowe's play is 'sardonic', and the abrasive treatment of Christian hypocrisy tempers the play's anti-Semitism.

Eliot, T. S., 'Marlowe', in *Selected Essays: New Edition* (New York: Harcourt, Brace, and World, 1950), pp. 100–6. A discussion of Marlowe's works in general and the first analysis of the play as both farce and tragedy.

Engle, Lars, 'Oedipal Marlowe, Mimetic Middleton', *Modern Philology*, 105 (2008), pp. 417–36. Compares the two playwrights' representations of agency, finding that Marlowe expresses repressive desires and Middleton imitative ones.

Freer, Coburn, 'Lies and Lying in *The Jew of Malta*', in '*A Poet and a Filthy Play-maker*': *New Essays on Christopher Marlowe*, ed. Kenneth Freidenreich, Roma Gill and Constance B. Kuriyama (New York: AMS Press, 1988), pp. 143–65. An examination of the doctrine of 'policy' as dominant metaphor.

Friedenreich, Kenneth, '*The Jew of Malta* and the Critics: A Paradigm for Marlowe Studies', *Papers on Language and Literature*, 13 (1977), pp. 318–35. Provides a history of critical traditions from the beginning of the twentieth century to the 1970s. Concludes that performance study may be the best method for determining the play's genre.

Friedman, Alan Warren, 'The Shackling of Accidents in Marlowe's *The Jew of Malta*', *Texas Studies in Literature and Language*, 8 (1965), pp. 155–67. Argues against the common criticism that the play lacks dramatic unity. Reasons that Acts 3, 4 and 5 function as extended metaphors of Barabas's disordered condition, signalled, for instance, by his shift to prose.

Grantley, Darryll, '"What meanes this shew?": Theatricalism, Camp and Subversion in *Doctor Faustus* and *The Jew of Malta*', in *Christopher Marlowe and English Renaissance Culture*, ed. Darryll Grantley and Peter Roberts (Aldershot: Scolar Press, 1996), pp. 224–38. Marlowe employs an exaggerated, theatrical style to comment subversively on forms of Elizabethan orthodoxy. This is especially the case with Barabas's machinations, all of which exhibit theatricality in device and effect.

Greenblatt, Stephen, 'Marlowe, Marx, Anti-Semitism', *Critical Inquiry*, 5 (1978), pp. 291–307. Uses Marx's 'On the Jewish Question' to analyse Marlowe's play. Marlowe and Marx employ the figure of the Jew as a powerful symbol, but to different ends. Reprinted in *Christopher Marlowe*, ed. Richard Wilson (London: Longman, 1999), pp. 140–58.

Hamlin, William, 'Misbelief, False Profession, and *The Jew of Malta*', in *Placing the Plays of Christopher Marlowe: Fresh Cultural Contexts*, ed. Sara M. Deats and Robert A. Logan (Burlington, VT: Ashgate Publishing, 2008), pp. 125–34. Barabas exhibits a deep sense of transcultural morality, although he does not recognize it. This encourages the audience to perceive his vulnerability, thereby eliciting its sympathy.

Harbage, Alfred, 'Innocent Barabas', *Tulane Drama Review*, 8.4 (1964), pp. 47–58. Contrary to received critical opinion, neither Marlowe nor his creation Barabas was evil. Barabas is insufficiently corrupt, even innocent of wrongdoing, compared to his heirs. Reprinted in Ribner, *supra*.

Harraway, Clare, 'A Production of Kinds: Genre, *The Jew of Malta* and the Promise of Repetition', in *Re-citing Marlowe: Approaches to the Drama* (Aldershot: Ashgate, 2000), 168–204. Marlowe consciously constructed the play to transgress classifications of genre.

Hirsch, Brett D., 'Counterfeit Professions: Jewish Daughters and the Drama of Failed Conversion in Marlowe's *The Jew of Malta* and Shakespeare's *The Merchant of Venice*', *Early Modern Literary Studies*, Special Issue 19 (2009), [n.p.]. Early moderns often viewed conversions from Judaism to Christianity as insincere, which the Abigail and Jessica episodes in the two plays reflect.

Holmer, Joan Ozark, 'Jewish Daughters: The Question of Philo-Semitism in Elizabethan Drama', in *The Merchant of Venice: New Critical Essays*, ed. John W. Mahon and Ellen Macleod Mahon (London: Routledge, 2002) pp. 107–43. An insightful comparison of Marlowe's Abigail and Shakespeare's Jessica that demonstrates qualities of philo-Semitism in the two plays.

Hunter, G. K., 'The Theology of Marlowe's *The Jew of Malta*', *Journal of the Warburg and Courtauld Institutes*, 27 (1964), pp. 211–40. Examines the play's ironic structure by arguing that its presentation of Jews is early modern and theological, and does not reflect present-day racial and ethnic conceptions. Provides a detailed discussion of Barabas as parody of Job and Jewish usurer, which contributes to the drama's broad satire of self-interested politicians and merchants.

Ide, Arata, '*The Jew of Malta* and the Diabolic Power of Theatrics in the 1580's', *Studies in English Literature*, 46 (2006), pp. 257–79. A study of Barabas's theatrical tableaux in the contexts of the antitheatrical movement and anti-Catholic English polemics. Malta represents England, and Barabas reflects xenophobia towards the Jesuits and the Spaniards.

Kermode, Lloyd Edward, 'Marlowe's Second City: The Jew as Critic at the Rose', *Studies in English Literature*, 35 (1995), pp. 215–29. South Bank theatres functioned as alternate cites to London, and Barabas is the marginal figure who challenges dominant early modern ideologies relating to strangers.

Kitch, Aaron, 'Shylock's Sacred Nation', *Shakespeare Quarterly*, 59 (2008), pp. 131–55. Provides extensive historical context of Jews in Europe and their perceived emergence as a monolithic trading nation to elucidate their conception in *The Jew of Malta* and *The Merchant of Venice*. Marlowe presents Barabas as Levantine in order to examine the relationship between commerce, religion and the state, as well as the assimilation of Jews into commercial centres. Shylock employs his status to the end of citizens' economic rights, but Portia refutes these rights in the name of Christian universalism. Revised and reprinted as 'Shylock's "Sacred Nation": Commerce, Statehood, and the Figure of the Jew in Marlowe's *Jew of Malta* and Shakespeare's *Merchant of Venice*', in *Political Economy and the States of Literature in Early Modern England* (Surrey: Ashgate, 2009), pp. 105–28.

Kocher, Paul H., 'English Legal History in Marlowe's *Jew of Malta*', *Huntington Library Quarterly*, 26 (1963), pp. 155–63. Marlowe must have been aware of the event that led to the creation of statute 22 Henry VIII, cap. 9 that declared poisoning an act of high treason, punishable by death by boiling in water, when he conceived the poisoning of the nuns and the death of Barabas episodes. This probable influence strongly supports the idea of the play as savage farce.

Lenker, Lagretta Tallent, 'The Hopeless Daughter of a Hapless Jew: Father and Daughter in Marlowe's *The Jew of Malta*', in *Placing the Plays of Christopher Marlowe: Fresh Cultural Contexts*, ed. Sara Munson Deats and Robert A. Logan (Aldershot: Ashgate, 2008), pp. 63–73. Analyses sixteenth-century concepts of the father–daughter relationship to illuminate Marlowe's conception of Barabas's comic cruelty and Abigail's agency.

Lesser, Zachary, 'Marlowe's Jew Goes to Church: Nicholas Vavasour and the Creation of Laudian Drama', in *Renaissance Drama and the Politics of Publication: Readings in the English Book Trade* (Cambridge: Cambridge University Press, 2004), pp. 81–114. Nicholas Vavasour probably publishes the play in 1633 because it complimented his avowedly pro-Laudian publications, especially those that recommend abolishing the Stranger churches. As a political device, the text would then have participated in the ending of early Stuart society and the beginning of the Civil War.

Logan, Robert A., '"For a Tricksy Word / Defy the Matter": The Influence of *The Jew of Malta* on *The Merchant of Venice*', in *Shakespeare's Marlowe: The Influence of Christopher Marlowe on Shakespeare's Artistry* (Aldershot: Ashgate, 2007), pp. 117–41. The similarities between the two works reflect Shakespeare's desire to capitalize on the sensational Lopez trial and the revival of *The Jew of Malta* in 1594. The use of Marlowe's play in *Merchant* suggests 'the comradeship among dramatists', especially the shared desire to promote both 'business sense' and 'aesthetic concerns'.

Lunney, Ruth, 'Framing the Action', in *Marlowe and the Popular Tradition: Innovation in the English Drama Before 1595* (Manchester: Manchester University Press, 2002), pp. 93–123. Discusses Marlowe's experiments with the moral play and its framing rhetoric of contradiction in *The Jew of Malta* by comparing it to *The Tide Tarrieth No Man*, *The Three Ladies of London* and other dramas.

Lupton, Julia Reinhard, 'Deformations of Fellowship in Marlowe's *Jew of* Malta', in *Citizen-Saints: Shakespeare and Political Theology* (Chicago: University of Chicago Press, 2005), pp. 51–72. A thorough investigation into Pauline motifs in the play that reveals deep differences between conceptions of the *civic* and the *civil*. Barabas participates in the *civil* yet ultimately betrays these values, which causes his removal from Malta. Discusses perceived relationships between Islam and Judaism, as well as representations of Jews in the Elizabethan theatre and the city of London.

—, '*The Jew of Malta*', in *The Cambridge Companion to Christopher Marlowe*, ed. Patrick Cheney (Cambridge: Cambridge University Press, 2004), pp. 144–57. Examines the complexities of social, economic and religious forms of fellowship and early modern European perspectives of Judaism to contextualize Malta's Jewish community as well as the play's representation of Islam.

Mahood, M. M., 'Marlowe's Heroes', in *Poetry and Humanism* (London: Jonathan Cape, 1950), pp. 54–86. Asserts Marlowe's plays are emblems of Renaissance humanism. Finds *The Jew of Malta* to be a ludicrous, tragical farce focused on the world of empty mercantilism with both Christians and Jews serving as villains. Selections reprinted as '*The Jew of Malta* as Tragic Farce' in Ribner, *supra*.

Maxwell, J. C., 'How Bad Is the Text of *The Jew of Malta?*', *Modern Language Review*, 84 (1953), pp. 435–8. Examines theories of textual corruption and editorial emendation in previous studies of the 1633 quarto, using bibliographical analysis to conclude that the play's faulty transmission was the result of bad printing rather than changes in manuscript.

Melnikoff, Kirk, '"[I]ygging Vaines" and "Riming Mother Wits": Marlowe, Clowns and the Early Frameworks of Dramatic Authorship', *Early Modern Literary Studies*, Special Issue 16 (2007), [n. p.]. Analyses the clowning tradition and comic episodes in *Doctor Faustus* and *The Jew of Malta*, finding the humour of the latter develops into farce. Focuses primarily on the dramatic function of Ithamore.

Minshull, Catherine, 'Marlowe's "Sound Machevill"', *Renaissance Drama*, n.s. 13 (1982), pp. 35–53. Marlowe likely had first-hand knowledge of the writings of Machiavelli, which he uses to ironic effect. The satirical function of Barabas reveals Ferneze to be the true Machiavellian, although the audience's prejudice against Jews discouraged them from seeing the Christian as most deceitful figure.

Moss, Stephanie, 'Edmund Kean, Anti-Semitism, and *The Jew of Malta*', in *Placing the Plays of Christopher Marlowe: Fresh Cultural Contexts*, ed. Sara Munson Deats and Robert A. Logan (Aldershot: Ashgate, 2008), pp. 43–59. A discussion of the contemporary reception of Edmund Kean's 1818 revival that closed after eleven performances, perhaps due to the audience's conflict between an acknowledged belief in egalitarianism and an unspoken anti-Semitism.

Nakayama, Randall, '"I Know She Is a Courtesan by Her Attire": Clothing and Identity in *The Jew of Malta*', in *Marlowe's Empery: Expanding His Critical Contexts*, ed. Sara Munson Deats and Robert A. Logan (Newark: University of Delaware Press, 2002), pp. 150–63. Examines the role of clothing in the play, especially that which would have likely been worn by Bellamira, and its relation to early modern sumptuary laws. Considers as well Barabas's stage nose and the use of costume in *Edward II*.

Palmer, Daryl W., 'Merchants and Miscegenation: *The Three Ladies of London*, *The Jew of Malta*, and *The Merchant of Venice*', in *Race, Ethnicity, and Power in the Renaissance*, ed. Joyce Green MacDonald (Cranbury, NJ: Fairleigh Dickinson University Press, 1997), pp. 36–66. Studies early modern merchant texts and the ways dramatists employ them to represent forms of miscegenation and hospitality. Racial issues in Marlowe's play demonstrate the destructiveness of commerce.

Parker, John, 'Barabas and Charles I', in *Placing the Plays of Christopher Marlowe: Fresh Cultural Contexts*, ed. Sara Munson Deats and Robert A. Logan (Aldershot: Ashgate, 2008), pp. 167–81. Argues the Caroline revival of the play was intended to criticize Charles I's Catholic sympathies.

Proser, Matthew N., 'Malta's Jew: Policy "Cunningly Performed"', in *The Gift of Fire: Aggression and the Plays of Christopher Marlowe* (New York: Peter Lang, 1995), pp. 111–38. Discusses the play within the framework of Marlowe's evolving artistry as it relates to the playwright's attention to dramatic structure and the theme of policy.

Ribner, Irving, 'Marlowe and Shakespeare', *Shakespeare Quarterly*, 15.2 (1964), pp. 41–53. A study of the relationship between the two playwrights that finds Marlowe's influence on Shakespeare much more evident in their historical dramas than in *The Jew of Malta* and *The Merchant of Venice*, for they share little but stereotypical Elizabethan conceptions of Jews in Barabas and Shylock. Selections reprinted in Ribner, *supra*.

Rocklin, Edward, 'Marlowe as Experimental Dramatist: The Role of Audience in *The Jew of Malta*', in '*A Poet and a Filthy Play-maker': New Essays on Christopher Marlowe*, ed. Kenneth Freidenreich, Roma Gill and Constance B. Kuriyama (New York: AMS Press, 1988), pp. 129–42. Marlowe's talent for innovation contributed significantly to the development of a new dramaturgy emerging out of the morality play tradition. The experimental techniques that he used to construct Machevill and Barabas prove critical to the creation of later villains, such as Richard III, Iago and Edmund.

Rosen, Alan, 'Into the Ghetto: Representing Jewish Space in Elizabethan England', *JTD: Journal of Theatre and Drama*, 7–8 (2001–2), pp. 95–104. A study of the topographical and dramatical image of the ghetto in Stow's *Survey of London*, Marlowe's *The Jew of Malta* and Shakespeare's *The Merchant of Venice*. Discusses policies of expulsion and integration by comparing Stow's description of London's Jewish quarter with the playwrights' representations of Jewish houses.

Rothstein, Eric, 'Structure as Meaning in *The Jew of Malta*', *Journal of English and Germanic Philology*, 65 (1966), pp. 260–73. A thorough examination of the play's plotlines as skilfully constructed moral farce, with explanation of religious allusion and symbolism elucidating thematic parallels.

Rutter, Tom, '*The Jew of Malta* and *The Massacre at Paris*', in *The Cambridge Introduction to Christopher Marlowe* (Cambridge: Cambridge University Press, 2012), pp. 61–78. Provides a general discussion of the Vice figure and race, religion and nationality in the two plays, as well as a comparison of the soliloquy and aside. Volume is part of the Cambridge Introductions to Literature Series.

Sales, Roger, 'The Stage, the Scaffold and the Spectators: The Struggle for Power in Marlowe's *Jew of Malta*', in *Christopher Marlowe and English Renaissance Culture*, ed. Darryll Grantley and Peter Roberts (Aldershot: Scolar Press, 1996), pp. 119–28. Studies the choreography of power on the two stages of scaffold and theatre by comparing the public executions of John Stubbes and the Babington conspirators to that of Barabas.

Sanders, Wilbur, 'Dramatist as Realist: "The Jew of Malta"', in *The Dramatist and the Received Idea: Studies in the Plays of Marlowe and Shakespeare* (Cambridge: Cambridge University Press, 1968), pp. 38–60. Argues against Charles Lamb's assertion that the playwright has produced an anti-Semitic drama. Instead the play presents brutality as realism that degenerates into a form of self-indulgence. Reprinted in Harold Bloom, *Modern Critical Views Christopher Marlowe* (New York: Chelsea House, 1986).

Scott, Sarah K., '*The Jew of Malta* and the Development of City Comedy: "The Mean Passage of a History"', in *Christopher Marlowe the Craftsman: Lives, Stage, and Page*, ed. Sarah K. Scott and M. L. Stapleton (Aldershot: Ashgate, 2010), pp. 91–108. Argues that Marlowe's play is a precursor to the city comedy genre of the Jacobean period and that it influenced the work of Jonson.

Segal, Eric, 'Marlowe's *Schadenfreude*: Barabas as Comic Hero', in *Veins of Humor*, ed. Harry Levin (Cambridge, MA: Harvard University Press, 1972), pp. 69–91. A historical account of the causes of humour resulting from a combination of harm and pleasure. Emphasizes Barabas as Odysseus's heir and antithesis of Elizabethan orthodoxy. Reprinted in Harold Bloom, *Modern Critical Views: Christopher Marlowe* (New York: Chelsea House, 1986).

Shapiro, James, 'Myths, Histories, Consequences', in *Shakespeare and the Jews* (New York: Columbia University Press, 1996), pp. 43–88. A comprehensive, general discussion of the Jewish peoples in early modern England and their portrayal by English and Continental writers.

Shepard, Alan, 'Paying Tribute in Occupied Malta: From Chivalry to Commerce', in *Marlowe's Soldiers: Rhetorics of Masculinity in the Age of the Armada* (Aldershot: Ashgate, 2002), pp. 113–39. The play is a tragicomedy dramatizing the early modern rivalry of merchant and knight, commerce and war, as they vie with one another to influence London's evolving civic identity.

Simkin, Stevie, 'Unhallowed Deeds: *The Jew of Malta*', in *A Preface to Marlowe* (Harlow, Eng.: Longman, 2000), pp. 133–67. A thorough introduction to the play and its cultural contexts within a guide dedicated entirely to the study of the life and work of the poet and playwright. The chapter discusses a range of subjects including Jews in European history; the villainy, victimization and dissembling of Barabas; and the portrayal of ethnicity and the play-in-performance.

Simmons, J. L., 'Elizabethan Stage Practice and Marlowe's *The Jew of Malta*', *Renaissance Drama*, n.s. 4 (1971), pp. 93–104. Examines a crux in staging Act 5, the moment Barabas's body is to be cast over Malta's walls, conjecturing that the actor was rolled onto the yard.

Smith, James L., '*The Jew of Malta* in the Theatre', in *Christopher Marlowe: Critical Commentaries*, ed. Brian Morris (New York: Hill and Wang, 1968), pp. 3–23. Surveys the play's performance history from 1591 to 1966, variously interpreted by its directors as sentimental tragedy, farce, satire and *pantomime noir.*

Stapleton, M. L., 'Christopher Marlowe', in *Oxford Bibliographies Online: British and Irish Literature,* ed. Andrew Hadfield (New York: Oxford University Press, 2012). Online bibliography with annotated entries for editions and critical studies of the Marlowe canon for both collected and individual works. There are also sections devoted to theatre history, earlier texts and studies, edited collections, reception, textual criticism, and journals, concordances and other supplemental resources.

Steane, J. B., '*The Jew of Malta*', in *Marlowe: A Critical Study* (London: Cambridge University Press, 1970), pp. 166–203. Discusses the play's themes, structure, humour and style while contrasting them with Marlowe's other plays and those of Jonson, Milton, Nashe, Orwell and Shakespeare, especially as they present figures resembling Barabas as comic villain.

Tambling, Jeremy, 'Abigail's Party: "The Difference of Things" in *The Jew of Malta*', in *In Another Country: Feminist Perspectives on Renaissance Drama*, ed. Dorothea Kehler and Susan Baker (Metuchen, NJ: Scarecrow Press, 1991), pp. 95–12. A study of Abigail as female Other and victim.

Thurn, David, 'Economic and Ideological Exchange in *The Jew of Malta*', *Theatre Journal,* 46 (1994), pp. 157–70. Presents an alternative to the containment model of Greenblatt (*supra*) through a theory of exchange drawn from economics to account for the thematic relationship between culture and capital. Marlowe places Barabas at the centre of this discourse to demonstrate the absurdity of his actions, symbolic of the free market and its constraints. Reprinted in Oz, Avraham, ed., *Marlowe*, New Casebooks Series (Basingstoke: Palgrave, 2003).

Tromly, Fred B., 'Playing with Avarice: *The Jew of Malta*', in *Playing with Desire: Christopher Marlowe and the Art of Tantalization* (Toronto: University of Toronto Press, 1998), pp. 92–7. Argues that Barabas represents Tantalian covetousness, but that the Christians do so more significantly, and that those audience members who demand moral and theatrical stereotypes from their playwrights exhibit an avariciousness of their own. Discussion integrates Marlowe's translation of Ovid's *Amores*, the *Elegies*, and *Tamburlaine*.

Vitkus, Daniel, 'Turks and Jews in *The Jew of Malta*', in *Early Modern English Drama: A Critical Companion*, ed. Garrett A. Sullivan, Jr., Patrick Cheney and Andrew Hadfield (Oxford: Oxford University Press, 2006), pp. 61–72. An introductory essay that contextualizes the play within the contexts of Anglo-Mediterranean trade, relationships between Jews and Muslims, the 1565 Turkish invasion of Malta, the Maltese slave trade and English xenophobia.

Webb, David, '"Pageants Truly Played": Self-Dramatization and Naturalistic Character in *The Jew of Malta*', *Renaissance Forum: An Electronic Journal of Early Modern Literary and Historical Studies,* 5.1 (2000). A thorough discussion of the ways Marlowe creates self-dramatization in his characters, which generates character interiority leading to naturalism. The technique contributes to the themes of religion and political power.

Wilson, F. P., '*The Jew of Malta* [and] *Doctor Faustus*', in *Marlowe and the Early Shakespeare* (Oxford: Clarendon Press, 1954 [corrected edn from 1953]), pp. 57–85. A study of the playwright's poetical decorum and influence, especially on Jonson. Finds the first two acts of *The Jew of Malta* to be works of genius, arguing the absence of virtuosity in the final three acts proves authorship other than Marlowe. Believes the playwright could not have read the writings of Machiavelli. Selection reprinted as '*The Jew of Malta*' in Ribner, *supra*.

Internet Resources

Christopher Marlowe (1564–93). www.luminarium.org/renlit/marlowe.htm. Features links to essays and articles, biographical background and images.

Christopher Marlowe. www.theatrehistory.com/british/marlowe001.html. Provides biographical background and some helpful links to Marlowe studies.

The Complete Works of Christopher Marlowe: An Electronic Edition. www.perseus. tufts.edu/hopper/searchresults?q=marlowe. A searchable edition of the play, as well as Marlowe's other works, provided by the Perseus Digital Library.

Elizabethan and Jacobean Drama. www2.warwick.ac.uk/fac/arts/ren/elizabethan_jacobean _drama/christopher_marlowe/christopher_marlowe/stage_history/professional/. A catalogue of professional productions that includes photographs.

The Marlowe Concordance, 3 vols (Louvain: Uystpruyst, 1911–13). An index composed by Charles Crawford for Alexander Dyce's *The Works of Christopher Marlowe* (London: Edward Moxon, 1858). Available through internet Archive, www.archive.org/search.php?query=marlowe%20concordance.

The Jew of Malta. Project Gutenberg www.gutenberg.org. Provides access to the play in several electronic formats. Uses Alexander Dyce's edition, first appearing in *The Works of Christopher Marlowe*, printed initially in 1858 (London: Edward Moxon).

Marlowe Society of America. www.marlowesmightyline.org/. A non-profit organization devoted to the life, works and time of Christopher Marlowe. Publishes the *Marlowe Society of America Newsletter*, which contains book reviews and scholarly news related to Marlowe, other playwrights of the period and staging history. The website features archival resources pages, including catalogues of editions and performance records.

Video Recordings

The Jew of Malta. Directed by Douglas Morse. www.jewofmalta.com/. Distributed by Films for the Humanities and Sciences, 2012. The only full-length film adaptation of the play. Cast: Ben Curns (Machevill), Seth Duerr (Barabas), Derek Smith (Ferneze), Ben Steinfeld (Ithamore), Barzin Akhavan (Selim-Calymath), Fajer Al-Kaisi (Callapine), Katherine Heaney (Abigail), Geoffrey Murphy (Lodovick), Ian Antal (Mathias), Uma Incrocci (Katherine), Mario Quesada (Del Bosco), Ian Gould (Friar Jacomo), Paul Klementowicz (Friar Bernadine), Elizabeth Ruelas (Bellamira), Alvin Keith (Pilia-Borza), Suzan Perry (Abbess), Glenn Wein (Temainte), Allan Greenberg (First Jew), Paul L. Coffey (First Officer), Ben Beckley (First Knight), Thomas Jeffery (Second Knight), Rob Gaines (Messenger).

NOTES

Introduction

1 For a detailed discussion of 'the increase in scholarship and criticism', see Robert A. Logan, 'Marlowe Scholarship and Criticism: The Current Scene', in Christopher Marlowe the Craftsman: Lives, Stage, and Page, ed. Sarah K. Scott and M. L. Stapleton (Burlington, VT: Ashgate, 2010), pp. 15–22.

2 Henslowe's Diary, ed. R. A. Foakes, 2nd edn (Cambridge, Eng.: Cambridge University Press, 2002). For a detailed discussion of the date, stage history, sources, the play and the text, see the Introduction to N. W. Bawcutt's edition of The Jew of Malta: Christopher Marlowe (Manchester, Eng.: Manchester University Press, 1978), pp. 1–57. For the most thorough, up-to-date coverage of the play in the more encompassing context of theatre history, see in the present volume Roslyn L. Knutson's 'The Jew of Malta in Repertory'. For additional information about the sources, see Christopher Marlowe: The Plays and their Sources, ed. Vivien Thomas and William Tydeman (London, Eng.: Routledge, 1994), pp. 293–337.

3 Bawcutt, ed., p. 1.

4 Ibid., pp. 1–2. Henslowe stopped keeping detailed records of individual plays in November of 1597. Even so, Bawcutt is able to account for the impact of the play not only in the final decade of the sixteenth century but also in the first decade of the seventeenth century (p. 2).

5 See Holger Schott Syme, 'The Meaning of Success: Stories of 1594 and Its Aftermath', Shakespeare Quarterly, vol. 61, no. 4 (Winter, 2010), pp. 490–525, who shows how none of Marlowe's plays, for all their initial popularity, made the list in Henslowe's Diary of the 12 top-grossing productions.

6 The Blind Beggar of Alexandria and A Knack to Know an Honest Man. See Syme, pp. 504–8.

7 See Bawcutt, pp. 2–3, for dramatic and non-dramatic evidence of the influence of the play in England and Germany from the late sixteenth through the eighteenth centuries.

8 See Peter Berek, 'Tamburlaine's Weak Sons: Imitation as Interpretation before 1593', Renaissance Drama, n.s. 13 (1982), pp. 55–82.

9 Some scholars believe that Doctor Faustus came later, but there is little evidence either way. The belief that it came earlier appears to grow out of a sense of stylistic advances in The Jew of Malta.

10 Bawcutt, ed., pp. 44–7.

11 For a photo of the title page, see Bawcutt, ed., p. 2, and for a copy of Heywood's Dedicatory Epistle, Prologues and Epilogues, see Christopher Marlowe: The Complete Plays, ed. Mark Thornton Burnett (London, Eng.: J. M. Dent, 1999), pp. 459–61. All quotations from the play will be taken from this edition with act, scene and line numbers given in the text.

12 There is no hard and fast evidence that Heywood wrote the Prologues and Epilogues but scholars have considered it likely, given Heywood's statements in his dedicatory epistle about his involvement with productions of the play at court and at the Cockpit.

13 John Parker in 'Barabas and Charles I' in Placing the Plays of Christopher Marlowe: Fresh Cultural Contexts, ed. Sara Munson Deats and Robert A. Logan (Aldershot, Eng.: Ashgate, 2008), pp. 167–81, argues that the revival of The Jew of Malta 'was an attempt . . . to use explicitly dated material as a means of contesting publicly – yet somehow invisibly, too – the increasingly Catholic appearance of Charles's regime' (p. 168).

14 For a more complete account of potential sources from a wide variety of backgrounds, see Bawcutt, ed., pp. 4–16 and Thomas and Tydeman, eds, pp. 295–307. See also the introductions of Stephen J. Lynch, ed., The Jew of Malta with Related Texts (Indianapolis, IN: Hackett Publishing Company, Inc., 2009), pp. viii–xliv, and James R. Siemon, ed., Christopher Marlowe: The Jew of Malta (London, Eng.: A & C Black, 2009), pp. vii–xxxii. All of these editors suggest in their introductions that Marlowe may have been vaguely familiar with the history of Joseph Nassi, a wealthy and influential Jewish financier, and all but Lynch mention an even less likely source, David Passi.

15 Thomas and Tydeman, eds, pp. 299–300, consider four possibilities and print excerpts from them, pp. 313–28.

16 James Shapiro, Shakespeare and the Jews (New York, NY: Columbia University Press, 1996), p. 36.

17 Ibid., p. 100.

18 Perhaps spelled this way to create a visual pun: make evil? Although Machevill mentions his name twice in the Prologue (ll.1 and 7), I am not as certain that this is an Elizabethan auditory pun as Lynch, ed. maintains in note 11 of his Introduction (p. xxv); Machevill first has to establish for the audience that he is Machiavelli. Lynch does not mention in support of his argument that in the Prologue to Charles and Henrietta, Heywood rhymes 'still' (l.7) with 'Machevill' (l.8). In the Prologue, Heywood highlights Barabas's connection with Machiavelli as a way of stimulating his royal audience's interest, indicating that they already know of the connection (ll.5–11). That he sees Barabas as a 'sound Machevill' (l.8) is mystifying; as I go on to argue, Barabas bears little relation to the true Machiavelli. Heywood either seems not to know this or not to care. See also the comments on Machevill as a pun and on Barabas as a Machiavellian figure in Tom Rutter's The Cambridge Introduction to

Christopher Marlowe (Cambridge, Eng.: Cambridge University Press, 2012), p. 61.

19 For discussions of Marlowe and Machiavelli, see Bawcutt, ed., pp. 11–15; David Bevington, David, gen. ed., English Renaissance Drama (New York, NY: W. W. Norton & Company, 2002), pp. 287–8; Burnett, ed., pp. 628–9; Catherine Minshull, 'Marlowe's "Sound Machevill"', Renaissance Drama, n.s. 13 (1982), pp. 35–53; and Patrick Cheney, Marlowe's Republican Authorship: Lucan, Liberty, and the Sublime (Basingstoke, Eng.: Palgrave, 2009), pp. 27–8, chapters 3 and 4, and pp. 122–39 for discussion of Machiavelli and The Jew of Malta. Several scholars believe that Marlowe may have read a popular anti-Machiavellian polemic such as Innocent Gentillet's Discourse upon the Means of Well Governing and Maintaining in Good Peace a Kingdom or Other Principality . . . Against Nicholas Machiavel the Florentine (1576). In addition to Bawcutt, ed., pp. 11–16, see Stephen J. Lynch, ed., pp. xxiii–xxviii and Siemon, ed., p. xxviii who believe that Marlowe may have been influenced by Gentillet's treatise which unsparingly condemns Machiavelli.

20 Henslowe mentions a lost play called 'matchavell' that was performed three times (March, April and May of 1592) and may have presented the figure of Machiavelli on stage. The first listed performance was less than a week after the first listed performance of The Jew of Malta. See Foakes, ed., pp. 16–18.

21 See Bawcutt, ed., p. 62, n. 3.

22 See Cheney, pp. 129–30 for a more detailed explanation.

23 Presumably, the Turks would fall under the same strictures as the Catholics and Jews, but Marlowe seems less interested in whipping them than he does in taking to task the other two groups. Of course, his primary target among the Jews is Barabas.

24 See, for example, the essay by Alfred Harbage, 'Innocent Barabas', Tulane Drama Review, 8 (1964), pp. 47–58. With wit and eminent common sense, Harbage calls Eliot on the murkiness and erroneousness of his statements.

25 T. S. Eliot, 'Christopher Marlowe', Selected Essays (New York: Harcourt, Brace, 1932), p. 123.

26 I realize that twenty-first-century sympathies towards such injustice are easier to come by than sixteenth-century English sympathies. However, although a sixteenth-century audience might well have been less disturbed by the Christians' demands on the Jews, Marlowe does not exonerate their behaviour here or elsewhere in the play.

27 For a discussion of the complications of Marlowe's manipulation of his audience's response, see Edward L. Rocklin, 'Marlowe as Experimental Dramatist: The Role of the Audience in The Jew of Malta', in 'A Poet & a Filthy Play-maker': New Essays on Christopher Marlowe, ed. Kenneth Friedenreich, Roma Gill and Constance B. Kuriyama (New York: AMS Press, 1988), pp. 129–42.

28   An example of an inconsistency is Barabas's attitude towards his daughter
     which shifts from her being at the centre of his world (1.1.151–2) to mur-
     dering her without compunction; an example of ambivalence is Ithamore's
     complete about-face in his attitude towards Barabas, from favoured loyal
     co-conspirator to blackmailer; and an example of ambiguity is the uncer-
     tainty of Barabas's motives for his actions throughout the play but especially
     at the end when he relinquishes his power to Ferneze.

29   I have already discussed at some length Marlowe's characterization of
     Barabas in Shakespeare's Marlowe: The Influence of Christopher Marlowe
     on Shakespeare's Artistry (Aldershot: Ashgate, 2007), pp. 119 and 130–5.
     Therefore, the following remarks may overlap with the earlier ones.

1: The Critical Backstory

1   Prologue, lines 30, 33. The edition cited throughout is Mark Thornton
    Burnett, ed., *Christopher Marlowe: The Complete Plays* (London: J. M. Dent,
    1999).

2   See, for example, John Bakeless, *The Tragicall History of Christopher Marlowe*,
    vol. 1 (Cambridge: Harvard University Press, 1942, rept. Westport, CT:
    Greenwood Press, 1970), p. 329, and Roma Gill, ed., *The Complete Works of
    Christopher Marlowe*, vol. 4: *The Jew of Malta* (Oxford: Oxford University
    Press, 1995), p. xvi.

3   N. W. Bawcutt, ed., *The Jew of Malta* (Manchester: Manchester University
    Press, 1978), pp. 1–2. Frederick S. Boas, for example, concludes that the
    expenditures represent a revival: *Christopher Marlowe: A Biographical and
    Critical Study* (1940; Oxford: Clarendon Press, 1960), p. 129.

4   S. P. Cerasano, 'Edward Alleyn, the New Model Actor, and the Rise of
    Celebrity in the 1590s', *Medieval and Renaissance Drama in England*, 18
    (2005), pp. 47–58.

5   See Bawcutt, p. 38; Gill, p. xvi; and Fredson Bowers, ed., *The Complete Works
    of Christopher Marlowe*, vol. 1 (Cambridge: Cambridge University Press,
    1973), p. 255.

6   Ibid.

7   C. F. Tucker Brooke, ed., *The Works of Christopher Marlowe* (Oxford: Oxford
    University Press, 1910), p. 231.

8   Una Ellis-Fermor, *Christopher Marlowe* (London: Methuen, 1927), pp. 95, 97.

9   F. P. Wilson, *Marlowe and the Early Shakespeare* (Oxford: Clarendon Press,
    1953), p. 65; Irving Ribner, 'Marlowe's "Tragicke Glasse"', in *Essays on
    Shakespeare and Elizabethan Drama in Honor of Hardin Craig*, ed. Richard
    Hosley (Columbia: University of Missouri Press, 1962), pp. 91–114 (p. 101);
    and Irving Ribner, ed., *The Complete Plays of Christopher Marlowe* (New
    York: Odyssey, 1963), p. xxxi.

10 Leo Kirschbaum, 'Some Light on *The Jew of Malta*', *Modern Language Quarterly*, 7 (1946), pp. 53–6 (p. 56).

11 J. C. Maxwell, 'How Bad is the Text of *The Jew of Malta?*', *Modern Language Review*, 48 (1953), pp. 435–8.

12 George Coffin Taylor, 'Marlowe's "Now"', in *Elizabethan Studies and Other Essays in Honor of George F. Reynolds*, University of Colorado Studies, Series B, Studies in the Humanities, vol. 2, no. 4 (Boulder: University of Colorado Press, 1945), pp. 93–100.

13 Robert Ford Welsh, 'Evidence of Heywood Spellings in *The Jew of Malta*', *Renaissance Papers* (1963), pp. 3–9.

14 D. J. Lake, 'Three Seventeenth-Century Revisions: *Thomas of Woodstock*, *The Jew of Malta*, and *Faustus B*', *Notes and Queries*, 30 (1983), pp. 133–43.

15 Bowers, p. 256; Leo Kirschbaum, ed., *The Plays of Christopher Marlowe* (Cleveland: World Publishing, 1962), p. 464; Richard W. Van Fossen, ed., *The Jew of Malta* (Lincoln: University of Nebraska Press, 1964), p. xxvii; and Bawcutt, *Jew*, p. 40.

16 John Parker, 'Barabas and Charles I', in *Placing the Plays of Christopher Marlowe: Fresh Cultural Contexts*, ed. Sara Munson Deats and Robert A. Logan (Aldershot: Ashgate, 2008), pp. 167–81; and Zachary Lesser, 'Marlowe's *Jew* Goes to Church: Nicholas Vavasour and the Creation of Laudian Drama', in *Renaissance Drama and the Politics of Publication: Readings in the English Book Trade* (Cambridge: Cambridge University Press, 2004), pp. 81–114.

17 Vivien Thomas and William Tydeman, eds, *Christopher Marlowe: The Plays and their Sources* (London: Routledge, 1994).

18 Lisa Hopkins, '"Malta of Gold": Marlowe, *The Jew of Malta*, and the Siege of 1565', *(Re)Soundings*, 1.2 (1997); reprinted http://shura.shu.ac.uk/1294/ [no pagination].

19 Leon Kellner, 'Die Quelle von Marlowe's *Jew of Malta*', *Englische Studien*, 10 (1887), pp. 80–111; Ethel Seaton, 'Fresh Sources for Marlowe', *Review of English Studies*, 5 (1929), pp. 385–401.

20 Randall Martin, 'Anne Dowriche's *The French History*, Christopher Marlowe, and Machiavellian Agency', *Studies in English Literature*, 39 (1999), pp. 69–87 (p. 75).

21 Thomas P. Harrison, 'Further Background for *The Jew of Malta* and *The Massacre at Paris*', *Philological Quarterly*, 27 (1948), pp. 52–6.

22 Michael G. Brennan, 'Christopher Marlowe's *The Jew of Malta* and Two Newsletter Accounts of the Siege of Malta', *Notes and Queries*, 40 (1993), pp. 157–60.

23 H. D. Purcell, 'Whetstone's *English Myrror* and Marlowe's *Jew of Malta*', *Notes and Queries*, 13 (1966), pp. 288–90.

24 Paul H. Kocher, 'English Legal History in Marlowe's *Jew of Malta*', *Huntington Library Quarterly*, 26 (1963), pp. 155–63.

25   James H. Sims, *Dramatic Uses of Biblical Allusions in Marlowe and Shakespeare*,
     University of Florida Monographs, Humanities, no. 24 (Gainesville:
     University of Florida Press, 1966).

26   R. M. Cornelius, *Christopher Marlowe's Use of the Bible*, American University
     Studies 4: *English Language and Literature*, 23 (New York: Peter Lang, 1984),
     pp. 190–214.

27   Sara M. Deats, 'Biblical Parody in Marlowe's *The Jew of Malta*: A
     Re-Examination', *Christianity and Literature*, 37.2 (1988), pp. 27–48
     (pp. 27–8).

28   Martha Tuck Rozett, *The Doctrine of Election and the Emergence of Elizabethan
     Tragedy* (Princeton: Princeton University Press, 1984), p. 208.

29   Catherine Brown Tkacz, '*The Jew of Malta* and the Pit', *South Atlantic
     Review*, 53.2 (1988), pp. 47–57.

30   Ruth L. Hanusa, 'Killing the Daughter: Judges' Jephthah and *The Jew of
     Malta*'s Barabas', *Notes and Queries*, 46 (1999), pp. 199–200.

31   Edward Meyer, *Machiavelli and the Elizabethan Drama*, Litterarhistorische
     Forschungan, no. 1 (Weimar: Emil Felber, 1897).

32   Bennett, H. S., ed., *The Jew of Malta and The Massacre at Paris, The Life
     and Works of Christopher Marlowe*, gen. ed. R. H. Case (1931; reprinted New
     York: Gordian Press, 1956), p. 14.

33   Mario Praz, 'Machiavelli and the Elizabethans', *Proceedings of the British
     Academy*, 14 (1928), pp. 49–97; and Felix Rabb, *The English Face of
     Machiavelli: A Changing Interpretation, 1500–1700* (London: Routledge and
     Kegan Paul, 1964).

34   Irving Ribner, 'Marlowe and Machiavelli', *Comparative Drama*, 16 (1954),
     pp. 348–56 (p. 350).

35   N. W. Bawcutt, 'Machiavelli and Marlowe's *The Jew of Malta*', *Renaissance
     Drama*, 3 (1970), pp. 3–49 (p. 14).

36   Paul H. Kocher, *Christopher Marlowe: A Study of His Thought, Learning and
     Character* (New York: Russell and Russell, 1946), pp. 196–200.

37   Antonio D'Andrea, 'Studies in Machiavelli and His Reputation in the
     Sixteenth Century, I: Marlowe's Prologue to *The Jew of Malta*', *Medieval
     and Renaissance Studies*, 5 (1961), pp. 214–48 (pp. 238–9).

38   Howard S. Babb, 'Policy in Marlowe's *The Jew of Malta*', *ELH*, 24 (1957),
     pp. 85–94 (p. 86).

39   Catherine Minshull, 'Marlowe's "Sound Machevill"', *Renaissance Drama*, 13
     (1982), pp. 35–53 (pp. 42, 53).

40   Luc Borot, 'Machiavellian Diplomacy and Dramatic Developments in
     Marlowe's *Jew of Malta*', *Cahiers Elisabéthains*, 33 (1988), pp. 1–11 (p. 10).

41   Carol F. Heffernan, '*The Jew of Malta*: Barabas's "Fine Madness"', *Dutch
     Quarterly Review of Anglo-American Letters*, 8 (1978), pp. 94–107 (p. 97).

42   Bob Hodge, 'Marlowe, Marx, and Machiavelli: Reading into the Past', in
     Literature, Language and Society in England, 1580–1680, ed. David Aers, Bob
     Hodge and Gunther Kress (Totowa, NJ: Barnes and Noble, 1981), pp. 1–22
     (p. 8).

43 James Shapiro, *Shakespeare and the Jews* (New York: Columbia University Press, 1996), pp. 46–55.

44 Wilbur Sanders, *The Dramatist and the Received Idea: Studies in the Plays of Marlowe and Shakespeare* (Cambridge: Cambridge University Press, 1968), p. 341.

45 Peter Berek, 'The Jew as Renaissance Man', *Renaissance Quarterly*, 51 (1998), pp. 128–62 (p. 130).

46 Berek, pp. 153–9. See also Bakeless, pp. 367–75 and Bawcutt, *Jew of Malta*, p. 2.

47 James L. Smith, '*The Jew of Malta in the Theatre*', in *Christopher Marlowe*, ed. Brian Morris (London: Ernest Benn, 1968), pp. 1–23 (p. 7).

48 Thomas Dabbs, *Reforming Marlowe: The Nineteenth-Century Canonization of a Renaissance Dramatist* (Lewisburg: Bucknell University Press, 1991), p. 40.

49 Stevie Simkin, '"A Scattered Nation": *The Jew of Malta* in the Warsaw Ghetto', *On-Stage Studies,* 21 (1998), pp. 31–51 (p. 34). See also Carolyn D. Williams, 'Interview Given by Stevie Simkin, Director of Marlowe's *Jew of Malta*, to Carolyn D. Williams', *Cahiers Elisabéthains*, 55 (1999), pp. 65–73.

50 Douglas Cole, *Suffering and Evil in the Plays of Christopher Marlowe* (Princeton: Princeton University Press, 1962), p. 132.

51 G. K. Hunter, 'The Theology of Marlowe's *The Jew of Malta*', *The Journal of the Warburg and Courtauld Institutes*, 27 (1964), pp. 211–40 (p. 215).

52 Alan C. Dessen, 'The Elizabethan Stage Jew and Christian Example: Gerontus, Barabas, and Shylock', *Modern Language Quarterly*, 35 (1974), pp. 231–45 (p. 244).

53 Jean-Marie Maguin, '*The Jew of Malta*: Marlowe's Ideological Stance and the Play-World's Ethos', *Cahiers Elisabéthains*, 27 (1985) pp. 17–26 (p. 24).

54 Charles E. Peavy, '*The Jew of Malta* – Anti-Semitic or Anti-Catholic', *McNeese Review*, 2 (1959–60), pp. 57–60.

55 Thomas Cartelli, 'Shakespeare's *Merchant*, Marlowe's *Jew*: The Problem of Cultural Difference', *Shakespeare Studies*, 20 (1988), pp. 255–60 (p. 255).

56 Stephen Greenblatt, *Renaissance Self-Fashioning: From More to Shakespeare* (Chicago: University of Chicago Press, 1980), p. 203.

57 Jerry Philips, 'Cannibalism qua Capitalism: The Metaphorics of Accumulation in Marx, Conrad, Shakespeare, and Marlowe', in *Cannibalism and the Colonial World*, ed. Francis Barker, Peter Hulme and Margaret Iversen (Cambridge: Cambridge University Press, 1998), pp. 183–203, 273–6 (p. 183).

58 David H. Thurn, 'Economic and Ideological Exchange in Marlowe's *Jew of Malta*', *Theatre Journal*, 46.2 (1994), pp. 157–70 (p. 158).

59 Daryl W. Palmer, 'Merchants and Miscegenation: *The Three Ladies of London, The Jew of Malta*, and *The Merchant of Venice*', in *Race, Ethnicity, and Power in the Renaissance*, ed. Joyce Green MacDonald (London: Associated University Presses, 1997), pp. 36–66 (p. 36).

60 Lloyd Edward Kermode, '"Marlowe's Second City": The Jew as Critic at the Rose in 1592', *Studies in English Literature*, 35.2 (1995), pp. 215–29 (pp. 215–16).

61 William Poel, 'Shakespeare's Jew and Marlowe's Christians', *The Westminster Review*, January, 1909, reprinted in *Shakespeare in the Theatre* (London and Toronto: Sidgwick and Jackson, 1913, reprinted by Project Gutenberg, 2011, <www.gutenberg.org>), p. 79.

62 Irving Ribner, 'Marlowe and Shakespeare', *Shakespeare Quarterly*, 15.2 (1964), pp. 41–53 (p. 45).

63 Arthur Humphreys, '*The Jew of Malta* and *The Merchant of Venice*: Two Readings of Life', *Huntington Library Quarterly*, 50 (1987), pp. 279–93 (p. 289).

64 Michael J. Echerou, 'Shylock and the "Conditional Imagination": A Reinterpretation', *Shakespeare Quarterly*, 22 (1971), pp. 3–15 (p. 9).

65 Margaret Hotine, 'The Politics of Anti-Semitism: *The Jew of Malta* and *The Merchant of Venice*', *Notes and Queries*, 38.1 (1991), pp. 35–8 (p. 38).

66 Maurice Charney, 'Jessica's Turquoise Ring and Abigail's Poisoned Porridge: Shakespeare and Marlowe as Rivals and Imitators', *Renaissance Drama*, 10 (1979), pp. 33–44 (p. 44).

67 James Shapiro, *Rival Playwrights: Marlowe, Jonson, Shakespeare* (New York: Columbia University Press, 1991), p. 108.

68 John T. Shawcross, 'Signs of the Times: Christopher Marlowe's Decline in the Seventeenth Century', in *'A Poet and a Filthy Play-maker': New Essays on Christopher Marlowe*, ed. Kenneth Friedenreich, Roma Gill and Constance B. Kuriyama (New York: AMS, 1988), pp. 63–71 (p. 64).

69 Brooke includes the scene in his appendix to *Doctor Faustus*, (pp. 198–202).

70 See Dabbs, p. 28. Extracts from Beard, Wood, Baines and Ritson are reprinted in Millar MacLure, *Marlowe: The Critical Heritage, 1588–1896* (London: Routledge and Kegan Paul, 1979), pp. 41–2, 54, 36–8 and 65–6, respectively.

71 Extracts are reprinted in MacLure, pp. 68–70, 77–81.

72 J. A. Symonds, *Shakespeare's Predecessors in the English Drama*, 1884. The passage is reprinted in MacLure, p. 122.

73 Irving Ribner, 'Marlowe and the Critics', *Tulane Drama Review*, 8.4 (1964), pp. 211–24 (p. 216).

74 Harry Levin, 'Marlowe Today', *Tulane Drama Review*, 8.4 (1964), pp. 22–31, reprinted as 'Reconsidering Marlowe', in *Shakespeare and the Revolution of the Times: Perspectives and Commentaries* (New York: Oxford University Press, 1976), pp. 261–73.

75 Dabbs; Kenneth; Kenneth Friedendreich, *Christopher Marlowe: An Annotated Bibliography of Criticism since 1950* (Metuchan, NJ: The Scarecrow Press, 1979), pp. 1–17.

76 Harry Levin, *The Overreacher: A Study of Christopher Marlowe* (Cambridge: Harvard University Press, 1952), p. 23.

77 The quotation is from Greenblatt, p. 220. For Ian McAdam's acknowledgement that 'my iconoclastic, psychological readings place me in the romantic camp', see *The Irony of Identity: Self and Imagination in the Drama of Christopher Marlowe* (Newark: University of Delaware Press, 1999), p. 244.

78 T. S. Eliot, 'Notes on the Blank Verse of Christopher Marlowe', in *The Sacred Wood* (London: Methuen, 1920); repr. as 'Marlowe', in *Selected Essays*, New Edition (New York: Harcourt, Brace, and World, 1950), p. 105.

79 See Kenneth Friedenreich's survey '*The Jew of Malta* and the Critics', *Papers on Language and Literature*, 13 (1977), pp. 318–35 (p. 319).

80 Bennett, p. 17; and M. C. Bradbrook, *Themes and Conventions of Elizabethan Tragedy* (Cambridge: Cambridge University Press, 1952), p. 156.

81 Friedenreich, '*The Jew of Malta* and the Critics', p. 323.

82 M. M. Mahood, *Poetry and Humanism* (1950; repr. Port Washington, NY: Kennikat Press, 1967), p. 74; Levin, *The Overreacher*, pp. 75 and 79; Erich Segal, 'Marlowe's *Schadenfreude*: Barabas as Comic Hero', in *Veins of Humor*, ed. Harry Levin (Cambridge: Harvard University Press, 1972), pp. 69–91 (p. 80).

83 Friedenreich, *Christopher Marlowe*, identifies nearly 600 pieces of Marlowe criticism between 1950 and 1979. The rate of production accelerated, and Bruce E. Brandt lists 542 works in the next decade: *Christopher Marlowe in the Eighties: An Annotated Bibliography of Marlowe Criticism from 1978 through 1989* (West Cornwall, CT: Locust Hill Press, 1992).

84 Bernard Spivack, *Shakespeare and the Allegory of Evil: The History of a Metaphor in Relation to His Major Villains* (New York: Columbia University Press, 1958), p. 352.

85 Cole; David; David Bevington, *From Mankind to Marlowe: Growth of Structure in the Popular Drama of Tudor England* (Cambridge: Harvard University Press, 1962).

86 Robert C. Jones, *Engagement with Knavery: Point of View in* Richard II, The Jew of Malta, Volpone, *and* The Revenger's Tragedy (Durham: Duke University Press, 1986), p. 63.

87 Nan Cooke Carpenter, 'Infinite Riches: A Note on Marlovian Unity', *Notes and Queries*, 196 (1951), pp. 50–2; Alan W. Friedman, 'The Shackling of Accidents in Marlowe's *Jew of Malta*', *Texas Studies in Literature and Language*, 8 (1966), pp. 155–67 (p. 156); and Don Beecher, '*The Jew of Malta* and the Ritual of the Inverted Moral Order', *Cahiers Elisabéthains*, no. 12 (1977), pp. 45–58 (p. 55).

88 J. W. Flosdorf, 'The *Odi et Amo* Theme in *The Jew of Malta*', *Notes and Queries*, 7 (1960), pp. 10–14; Ribner, *Collected Plays*, p. xxxii; Bruce E. Brandt, *Christopher Marlowe and the Metaphysical Problem Play* (Salzburg: Universität Salzburg, Institut für Anglistik und Amerikanistik, 1985), p. 143.

89 John P. Cutts, *The Left Hand of God: A Critical Interpretation of the Plays of Christopher Marlowe* (Haddonfield, NJ: Haddonfield House, 1973), p. 151.

90 Dale G. Priest, 'Knave or Fool? Ithamore as Dramatic Paradigm in *The Jew of Malta*', *Explorations in Renaissance Culture*, 8–9 (1992–3), pp. 85–96 (p. 94).

91 Constance Brown Kuriyama, *Hammer or Anvil: Psychological Patterns in Christopher Marlowe's Plays* (New Brunswick, NJ: Rutgers University Press, 1980), p. 149.

92   Matthew N. Proser, *The Gift of Fire: Aggression and the Plays of Christopher Marlowe* (New York: Peter Lang, 1995), p. 133.

93   Eric Rothstein, 'Structure as Meaning in *The Jew of Malta*', *The Journal of English and Germanic Philology*, 65 (1966), pp. 260–73 (p. 272).

94   W. L. Godshalk, *The Marlovian World Picture* (The Hague: Mouton, 1974), p. 222.

95   Charles G. Masinton, *Christopher Marlowe's Tragic Vision: A Study in Damnation* (Athens: Ohio University Press, 1972), pp. 4, 85.

96   Judith Weil, *Christopher Marlowe: Merlin's Prophet* (Cambridge: Cambridge University Press, 1977), p. 2.

97   Simon Shepherd, *Marlowe and the Politics of Elizabethan Theatre* (New York: St Martin's Press, 1986), p. 208.

98   Emily C. Bartels, *Spectacles of Strangeness: Imperialism, Alienation and Marlowe* (Philadelphia: University of Philadelphia Press, 1993), p. xv.

99   Roger Sales, 'The Stage, the Scaffold and the Spectators: The Struggles for Power in Marlowe's *Jew of Malta*', in *Christopher Marlowe and English Renaissance Culture*, ed. Darryll Grantley and Peter Roberts (1996; Aldershot: Ashgate, 1999), pp. 119–28 (p. 119).

100 Thomas Cartelli, *Marlowe, Shakespeare, and the Economy of Theatrical Experience* (Philadelphia: University of Pennsylvania Press, 1991), p. 163.

101 Darryll Grantley, '"What means this shew?": Theatricalism, Camp and Subversion in Doctor Faustus and The Jew of Malta', in *Christopher Marlowe and English Renaissance Culture*, ed. Darryll Grantley and Peter Roberts (1996; Aldershot: Ashgate, 1999), pp. 224–38 (p. 225).

102 Clare Harraway, *Re-Citing Marlowe: Approaches to the Drama* (Aldershot: Ashgate, 2000), p. 168.

103 Fred B. Tromly, *Playing with Desire: Christopher Marlowe and the Art of Tantalization* (Toronto: University of Toronto Press, 1998), p. 93.

104 Barbara J. Baines, 'Sexual Polarity in the Plays of Christopher Marlowe', *Ball State University Forum*, 23.3 (1982), pp. 3–17 (4).

105 Jeremy Tambling, 'Abigail's Party: "The Difference of Things" in *The Jew of Malta*', in *In Another Country*, ed. Dorothea Kehler and Susan Baker (Metuchen, NJ and London: The Scarecrow Press, 1991) pp. 95–112 (pp. 96–7).

106 Ren Draya, 'Silenced Women: Abigail in Marlowe's *The Jew of Malta*', *Publications of the Missouri Philological Association*, 24 (1999), pp. 11–19 (18).

2: The Performance History

1   N. W. Bawcutt, Introduction to *The Jew of Malta*, ed. Bawcutt (Manchester: University Press, 1978), p. 1.

2   Philip Henslowe, *Henslowe's Diary*, ed. R. A. Foakes and R. T. Richert (Cambridge University Press, 1961), pp. 16–47.

3   H. S. Bennett, Introduction to *The Jew of Malta* and *The Massacre at Paris*, ed. Bennett (New York: Gordian Press, 1966), p. 2.

4   Bawcutt, p. 2; see also John Bakeless, *The Tragicall History of Christopher Marlowe*, vol. 1 (Hamden, CT: Archon Books, 1964), pp. 367–75.

5   *The Jew of Malta* in *Complete Plays of Christopher Marlowe*, ed. Mark Thornton Burnett (London: J. M. Dent, 1999), pp. 459–60.

6   John Parker, 'Barabas and Charles I', in *Placing the Plays of Christopher Marlowe: Fresh Critical Contexts*, ed. Sara Munson Deats and Robert A. Logan (Aldershot: Ashgate, 2008), p. 168.

7   The *Times*, 25 April 1818; *The Literary Gazette: A Weekly Journal of Literature and Science*, 2 (1818), p. 286, excoriated the play in language very similar to that of the *Times*, denouncing the drama as a 'tissue of extravagance and horror'.

8   *The European Magazine and London Review*, 73 (1818), p. 429.

9   James L. Smith, '*The Jew of Malta* in the Theatre', in *Christopher Marlowe: Mermaid Critical Commentaries*, ed. Brian Morris (New York: Hill and Wang, 1968), p. 56. I have gained much valuable information for my review of Kean's production from Smith's article, pp. 4–11, as well as from the following: Rima Hakim, *Marlowe on the English Stage 1588–1988: A Stage History of Three Marlowe Plays*, Dr Faustus, Edward II, *and* The Jew of Malta (Dissertation: University of Leeds, 1990), pp. 105–15; Stephanie Moss, 'Edward Kean, Anti-Semitism, and *The Jew of Malta*', in *Placing the Plays of Christopher Marlowe*, pp. 43–59.

10 See *Marlowe's Celebrated Tragedy of the Jew of Malta: in Five Acts*, by Christopher Marlowe, Samson Penley (London: Richard White, Sherwood, Neeley and Jones, and T. Earle, 1818).

11 *Blackwood's Magazine*, 3 (1818), p. 210; for exponents of this view, see Sara Munson Deats and Lisa Starks, '"So neatly plotted and so well perform'd": Villain as Playwright in Marlowe's *The Jew of Malta*', *Theatre Journal*, 44 (1992), p. 381.

12 Hakim provides a detailed account of all the additions and omissions in Penley's script in *Marlowe and the English Stage*, pp. 107–15.

13 For this traditional reading, see Bennett, p. 19; see also C. F. Tucker Brooke, ed., *The Works of Christopher Marlowe* (Oxford: Clarendon Press, 1910), p. 232.

14 The *Times*, 25 April 1818; *Blackwood's Magazine*, p. 310; *The European Magazine and London Review*, 73 (1818), p. 430.

15 *The New Monthly Magazine*, 9 (1818), p. 430.

16 *The Literary Gazette: A Weekly Journal of Literature and Science*, 2 (1919), p. 286.

17 For an insightful speculation on the reasons for the play's failure, see Moss, pp. 43–99.

18 I am much indebted to the following sources for information on twentieth-century productions of the play: Smith, pp. 11–23; Hakim, pp. 204–43; Lois Potter, 'Marlowe in Theatre and Film', in *A Cambridge Companion to*

Christopher Marlowe, ed. Patrick Cheney (Cambridge: Cambridge University Press, 2004), pp. 262–81.

19   Eliot (*Selected Essays* [New York: Harcourt, Brace and World, Inc., 1950], pp. 104–5) famously characterized the tone of Marlowe's play as follows:

> If one takes *The Jew of Malta* not as a tragedy . . . but as a farce, the concluding act becomes intelligible. . . . I say farce, but with the enfeebled humour of our times the word is a misnomer: It is the farce of the old English humour, the terribly serious, even savage comic humour, that humour which spent its last breath in the decadent genius of Dickens.

20   *Blackwood's Magazine*, 212 (December, 1922), p. 833.
21   Francis Birrell, The *New Statesman*, 11 November 1922.
22   *Blackwoods Magazine*, p. 834.
23   The *Daily News*, 7 November 1922.
24   The *Times*, 7 November 1922.
25   The *Manchester Guardian*, 7 November 1922.
26   Frank Free, *The Curtain*, 1:12 (December 1922), p. 41.
27   *The Curtain*, p. 141.
28   The *New Statesman*.
29   The *Times*.
30   The *Times*.
31   Programme notes to the Reading production, cited Smith, p. 13. Irving Ribner, 'Marlowe and Machiavelli', *Comparative Literature*, 6 (1954), pp. 352–3, and Catharine Minshull, 'Marlowe's "Sound Machevill"', *Renaissance Drama*, n.s. 13 (1982), pp. 40–8, both discuss Barabas's violation of several important Machiavellian precepts, while arguing that Ferneze is the true Machiavel of the play.
32   The *Times*, 14 May 1954. This was the only review of the production that I could locate.
33   The *Times*, 19 February 1964; *Stage and Television Today*, 27 February 1964.
34   The *Times*.
35   The *Times*. See also the discussion by Hakim, pp. 213–14, particularly the decision to dress Barabas as the stereotypic Jew.
36   Peter Roberts, *Plays and Players*, May 1964.
37   Programme notes to the Victoria Theatre production, cited by Smith, pp. 14, 20.
38   Roberts, *Plays and Players*.
39   The *Times*, 16 March 1964; see also Benedict Nightingale, the *Guardian*, 11 March 1964.
40   Nightingale, the *Guardian*.
41   The *Times*, 2 October 1964.
42   The *Queen*, 21 October 1964, cited by Smith, p. 18.
43   Leonard, *Plays and Players*, December 1964.

44 The *Daily Mail,* 2 October 1964.

45 See interview with Clifford Williams by Hakim, pp. 217–18.

46 Leonard, *Plays and Players;* the *Times.*

47 The *Times.*

48 Interview with Clifford William in *Plays and Players,* May 1965, pp. 10–11.

49 Hakim, p. 219.

50 The *Daily Telegraph,* 15 April 1965.

51 Harold Hobson, the *Sunday Times,* 18 April 1965; see also, *Stage and Television Today,* 15 April 1965.

52 The *Liverpool Daily Post,* 15 April 1965.

53 Landstone, 'Contrasting View of a Jew', The *Jewish Chronicle,* 23 April 1965.

54 Robert Speaight, 'Shakespeare in Britain', *Shakespeare Quarterly* 16:4 (Autumn, 1965), p. 317.

55 *The Times,* 15 April 1965.

56 Speaight, p. 317.

57 *Clyde Farnsworth, New York Times,* 17 April 1965.

58 The *Times,* 17 April 1965.

59 For two insightful comparisons of the two productions, see Peter Roberts, *Plays and Players,* June 1965, p. 43, and Harold Hobson, the *Sunday Times.*

60 David Nathan, 'Shakespeare Shown Up by Marlowe', the *Sun,* 17 April 1965.

61 For a fuller discussion of the ARC production, see my review in *Marlowe Society of American Newsletter (MSAN)* 5.1 (1985), pp. 6–7.

62 Wardle, the *Times,* 15 July 1987. The term 'functional ambiguity' derives from Annabel Patterson, who posits that the censorship laws of the period constrained early modern playwrights to obscure subversive material in their texts beneath deliberate ambiguity and to craft plays that they intended to be experienced differently by diverse audiences; see *Censorship and Interpretation: The Conditions of Writing and Reading in Early Modern England* (Madison: University of Wisconsin Press, 1984), pp. 17–18.

63 Mark Thornton Burnett, *MSAN,* 7.2 (1987), p. 7.

64 Jeremy Kingston, the *Times,* 25 March 1988.

65 Burnett, p. 7.

66 During the intermission of the 1987 production, I polled several members of the audience, primarily American tourists who had never read *The Jew,* concerning their opinion of Barabas. Supporting the judgement of the reviewers, they all professed to be on his side. When I pointed out that he was a murderer and a schemer, they unanimously objected that he was no worse than the rest of the Malta crowd. One spectator added, 'And, unlike the others, he is honest – at least to us'.

67 Kingston, the *Times,* 1988.

68 Machiavelli insists that the Prince should always *seem* 'pitiful, faithful, mild, religious, and of integrity', although 'there is no necessity for the Prince to be imbued with these above qualities'. Indeed, 'having these qualities and always

regulating himself by them, they are hurtful; but seeming to have them, they are advantageous'; see *The Prince*, in *Three Renaissance Classics*, ed. Burton A. Milligan (New York: Charles Scribner's Sons, 1953), pp. 65–7.

69   Burnett, p. 7.

70   Peter Kemp, the *Independent*, 25 March 1988.

71   The *Observer*, 19 July 1987, p. 25.

72   David Nathan, the *Jewish Chronicle*, 1 April 1988, cited Potter, p. 270.

73   Nicholas de Jongh, the *Evening Standard*, 6 October 1999.

74   Michael Billington, the *Guardian*, 7 October 1999.

75   Matt Wood, *Variety*, 7 November 1999.

76   The *Evening Standard*, 6 October 1999.

77   Kate Kellaway, the *New Statesman*, 18 October 1999.

78   Laurie Maguire, *MSAN* 19.2 (1999), p. 6.

79   Terry Grimley, the *Birmingham Post*, 11 August 1999.

80   Daniel Johnson, the *Daily Telegraph*, 5 October 1999.

81   Peter J. Smith, *Cashiers Elisabethains*, 57 (April, 2000), p. 128.

82   Henry Traeger, *MSAN*, 29.1 (2000), p. 3.

83   Doug DeVita, 'Oy! The Jew of Malta', www.oobr.com/top/volSix/eleven/1113jew.html. Web. 19 July 2011.

84   Walter Goodman's commentary in the *New York Times*, 23 March 1987 was the only review of this production that I was able to locate.

85   This information was derived from the article by Stevie Simkin, 'A Scattered Nation: *The Jew of Malta* in the Warsaw Ghetto', *On-Stage Studies*, 21 (1998), pp. 31–51.

86   See Carolyn D. Williams's interview of Simkin in *Cashiers Elisabéthains*, 55 (1999), p. 72.

87   D. J. R. Bruckner's review was the only treatment of this production that I was able to find.

88   Edmund Gould, '*The Jew of Malta:* A Physical Nightmare', www.edinburghguide.com/festival/2005/fringe/review_theatre.php?page=j. Web.12 July 2011.

89   Rachel Lynn Brody, 'The British Theatre Guide', The Edinburgh Fringe, www.britishtheatreguide.into/othersources. Web 20 July 2011.

90   Potter, p. 271.

91   The review by Michael Billington, 'The Theatre of the Repressed', the *Guardian*, 19 January 2002, was the only treatment of this provocative production that I was able to discover.

92   Michael L. Basile, '*The Merchant of Venice* and *The Jew of Malta*', *Shakespeare Bulletin*, 25.3 (2007), pp. 111–15.

93   Perhaps because they were presented in different theatres with different casts and directors, the paired 1987 productions were rarely compared.

94   For insightful comparisons of the two plays, see Michael Basile, pp. 111–15; Irene Dash, 'The Theatre for New Audience's *Merchant of Venice* and *The*

Jew of Malta', Shakespeare Newsletter (Winter 2006–7), pp. 103–18; Maryann Feola, 'Barabas Goes to Broadway', *MSAN,* 17.1 (2007), pp. 1, 3; Charles Isherwood, *New York Times,* 5 February 2007.

95 Isherwood; for the cartoonish nature of the characters in the production, see also Elyse Sommer, 'A Curtain Up Review: *The Jew of Malta',* www.com/jewofmalta.html. Web. 15 July 2011.

96 Isherwood. Other reviewers praising Arnie Burton's Ithamore include Dash, 118; Feola, 3; Victor Gluck, 'Elizabeth Duo: *The Merchant of Venice* and *The Jew of Malta',* www.theaterscene.net/ts%5Carticles.nsf. Web. 15 July 2011. In production after production over the decades, reviewers have singled out the actor playing Ithamore for particular praise, making me aware for the first time what a singular opportunity the character of Ithamore offers for an actor.

97 Seth Duerr, *York Shakespeare Company,* N.p.n.d.Web. 20 July 2011.

98 Hussen Ibish, 'The "Jew" and the "Merchant" at the JCC of Manhattan', *Irishblog.* www.irishblog.com/blog.hibish/2009/12/15/jew_and_merchant-jcc_manhatten. Web. 20 July 2011.

99 Chris Harum, *'The Merchant of Venice/The Jew of* Malta', nytheater.com review. New York Theatre Experience. 2011. Web. 20 July 2011.

3: The State of the Art: Current Critical Research

1 The publication of Stephen Greenblatt's 'Marlowe, Marx, and Anti-Semitism', *Critical Inquiry,* 5.2 (1978), pp. 291–307 seems to mark a particular turning point, with discussion of the play sparsely distributed before it and appearing on close to an annual basis since. For a full account of the play's critical heritage see Bruce E. Brandt's chapter in this volume.

2 See Andrew Hiscock, *The Uses of This World: Thinking Space in Shakespeare, Marlowe, Cary and Jonson* (Cardiff: University of Wales Press, 2004) pp. 52–82; Julia Reinhard Lupton, *'The Jew of Malta',* in Patrick Cheney, ed., *The Cambridge Companion to Christopher Marlowe* (Cambridge: Cambridge University Press, 2004), pp. 144–57 and Julia Reinhard Lupton, *Citizen-Saints: Shakespeare and Political Theology* (Chicago: University of Chicago Press, 2005), pp. 49–72. William Hamlin also discusses the space created by Barabas's detachment from systems of belief in 'Misbelief, False Profession and *The Jew of Malta',* in S. M. Deats and R. A. Logan, eds, *Placing the Plays of Christopher Marlowe: Fresh Cultural Contexts* (Aldershot: Ashgate, 2008), pp. 125–34.

3 See Richard Wilson, 'Another Country: Marlowe and the Go-Between', in W. von Koppenfels, ed., *Renaissance Go-Betweens: Cultural Exchange in Early Modern Europe* (Berlin: de Gruyter, 2005), pp. 207–39, and Daniel Vitkus, *Turning Turk: English Theater and the Multicultural Mediterranean, 1570–1630* (New York: Palgrave Macmillan, 2003), pp. 163–98.

4 See, for example, Daniel Vitkus, 'Turks and Jews in *The Jew of Malta*', in Andrew Hadfield, ed., *Early Modern English Drama: A Critical Companion* (Oxford: Oxford University Press, 2006), pp. 61–72, and Shawn Smith, 'A Society of One: Reading the *Jew of Malta* through Serres's Theory of Exchange', *Exemplaria*, 15.2 (2003), pp. 419–50.

5 T. S. Eliot, 'Christopher Marlowe', in *Elizabethan Dramatists* (London: Faber & Faber, 1963), p. 63.

6 See Anna Beskins, 'From Jew to Nun: Abigail in Marlowe's *The Jew of Malta*', *Explicator*, 65.3 (2007), pp. 117–30; Lagretta Tallent Lenker, 'The Hopeless Daughter of a Hapless Jew: Father and Daughter in Marlowe's *The Jew of Malta*', in Deats and Logan, eds, *Placing the Plays of Christopher Marlowe*, pp. 63–73; Ruth Lunney, *Marlowe and the Popular Tradition: Innovation in the English Drama before 1595* (Manchester: Manchester University Press, 2002), pp. 93–123, and Sarah K. Scott, '*The Jew of Malta* and the Development of City Comedy: "The Mean Passage of a History"', in Sarah K. Scott and M. L. Stapleton, eds, *Christopher Marlowe the Craftsman: Lives, Stage, and Page* (Aldershot: Ashgate, 2010), pp. 91–108.

7 Harraway, *Re-Citing Marlowe: Approaches to the Drama* (Aldershot: Ashgate, 2000), pp. 168–205.

8 In highlighting Marlowe's medieval inheritance, Lunney builds on work carried out in David Bevington's classic study *From Mankind to Marlowe: Growth of Structure in the Popular Drama of Tudor England* (Cambridge, MA: Harvard University Press, 1962). Further compelling work in this area has been carried out by John Parker, in his *The Aesthetics of Antichrist: From Christian Drama to Christopher Marlowe* (Ithaca, NY: Cornell University Press, 2007), and Kirk Melnikoff's '"[I]ygging Vaines" and "Riming Mother Wits": Marlowe, Clowns and the Early Frameworks of Dramatic Authorship', *Early Modern Literary Studies*, Special Issue 16 (2007) n.p. While continuity and influence between Marlowe's and Shakespeare's work has often been noted, Scott's characterization of the play as an early city comedy would seem to present less well-trodden ground; further readings of the play alongside early city comedies might well bear fruit.

9 Catherine Minshull, 'Marlowe's Sound Machevill', *Renaissance Drama*, 13 (1982), pp. 35–53.

10 Patrick Cheney, *Marlowe's Republican Authorship: Lucan, Liberty, and the Sublime* (Basingstoke: Palgrave, 2009), pp. 121–39.

11 See Zachary Lesser, 'Marlowe's Jew Goes to Church: Nicholas Vavasour and the Creation of Laudian Drama', in his *Renaissance Drama and the Politics of Publication: Readings in the English Book Trade* (Cambridge: Cambridge University Press, 2004), pp. 81–114; John Parker, 'Barabas and Charles I', in Deats and Logan, eds, *Placing the Plays of Christopher Marlowe*, pp. 167–81; and Lucy Munro, 'Marlowe on the Caroline Stage', *Shakespeare Bulletin*, 27.1 (2009), pp. 39–50.

12 *The Jew of Malta* continues to crop up in essays which concern themselves
    more fully with *The Merchant of Venice*, although the value-laden compara-
    tive approach seems now to be a thing of the past. Recent examples include
    Aaron Kitch's 'Shylock's Sacred Nation', *Shakespeare Quarterly*, 59.2 (2008),
    pp. 131–5; Joan Fitzpatrick's 'Early Modern Dietaries and the Jews: *The
    Merchant of Venice* and *The Jew of Malta*', in R. Fotheringham, C. Jansohn
    and R. S. White, eds, *Shakespeare's World / World Shakespeares* (Neward, DE:
    University of Delaware Press, 2008) and Lara Bovilsky's 'Exemplary Jews
    and the Logic of Gentility', in her *Barbarous Play: Race on the Renaissance
    Stage* (Minneapolis, MN: University of Minnesota Press, 2008).

13 See Robert A. Logan, *Shakespeare's Marlowe: The Influence of Christopher
    Marlowe on Shakespeare's Artistry* (Aldershot: Ashgate, 2007). See also Deats
    and Logan, *Placing the Plays of Christopher Marlowe*, which contains a sec-
    tion entitled 'Marlowe and Shakespeare'.

14 Beard's account can be found in Jean de Chassanion, *The Theatre of Gods
    Iudgements [. . .] Translated out of French, and Avgmented by More than Three
    Hundred Examples, by Th. Beard* (London, 1597), STC/376:12.

15 See Lisa Hopkins, *Christopher Marlowe: A Literary Life* (Basingstoke:
    Palgrave, 2000); Constance B. Kuriyama, *Christopher Marlowe: A Renaissance
    Life* (Ithaca, NY: Cornell University Press, 2002); David Riggs, *The World
    of Christopher Marlowe* (London: Faber & Faber, 2004); Park Honan,
    Christopher Marlowe: Poet and Spy (Oxford: Oxford University Press, 2005)
    and T. Kozuka and J. R. Mulryne, eds, *Shakespeare, Marlowe, Jonson: New
    Directions in Biography* (Aldershot: Ashgate, 2006). Other related work
    includes Lisa Hopkins's *A Christopher Marlowe Chronology* (Basingstoke:
    Palgrave, 2005) and Roy Kendall's *Christopher Marlowe and Richard Baines:
    Journeys through the Elizabethan Underground* (Madison, NJ: Feirleigh
    Dickinson University Press, 2003).

16 See J. A. Downie's 'Marlowe: Facts and Fictions' in J. A. Downie and
    J. T. Parnell, eds, *Constructing Christopher Marlowe* (Cambridge: Cambridge
    University Press, 2000), pp. 13–29, and 'Reviewing What We Think We Know
    about Christopher Marlowe, Again', in Scott and Stapleton, eds, *Christopher
    Marlowe the Craftsman*, pp. 33–46. See also Lukas Erne, 'Biography,
    Mythography, and Criticism: The Life and Works of Christopher Marlowe',
    Modern Philology, 103.1 (2005), pp. 28–50.

17 The introduction to Clare Harraway's *Re-Citing Marlowe* outlines her ratio-
    nale for eschewing biographical readings, the dust jacket of Ruth Lunney's
    Marlowe and the Popular Tradition proclaims 'Spy, troublemaker, homosex-
    ual, atheist, University wit? Not in this study', and Sara Munson Deats and
    Robert Logan state in the introduction to their collection *Placing the Plays of
    Christopher Marlowe* that the essays therein 'will focus not upon Marlowe, the
    man, but Marlowe, the playwright' (p. 1).

18 C. Marlowe, *The Jew of Malta*, ed. J. R. Siemon (London: Methuen, 2009).

4: New Directions: *The Jew of Malta* in Repertory

1 R. A. Foakes, ed., *Henslowe's Diary*, 2nd edn (Cambridge: Cambridge University Press, 2002), p. 16. For the manuscript image, see Henslowe-Alleyn Digitisation Project (www.henslowe-alleyn.org.uk/images/MSS-7/007r. html).

2 The date of composition and the initial company ownership of *The Jew of Malta* are uncertain but not in scholarly dispute. On the date, see the Introduction for details. In this essay, I treat the date of 1589–90 as fact and, for convenience, use 1589 as shorthand for that period of months when Marlowe composed the play and its company readied it for performance. On company ownership, the choice of the Admiral's men is based on their previous acquisition of the two-part *Tamburlaine the Great* and Edward Alleyn's allegiance to the company patron; I follow that logic here. However, the lines are blurred between the companies of the Lord Admiral and Lord Strange, 1589–92; it is therefore possible that from the start *The Jew of Malta* was owned by Strange's men.

3 W. W. Greg, *A Bibliography of the English Printed Drama to the Restoration*, 4 vols (London Bibliographic Society, 1970), 2, p. 624 (item 475).

4 Constance B. Kuriyama, *Christopher Marlowe: A Renaissance Life* (Ithaca, NY: Cornell University Press, 2002), p. xvi. For documents pertaining to the Bradley incident, see pp. 203–6.

5 David Mateer, 'New Sightings of Christopher Marlowe in London', *Early Theatre*, 11.2 (2008), pp. 13–39. The suits are *James Whetley v. Christopher Marlo*, which concerns the acquisition of a horse and tackle on 10 August 1587 that Marlowe had not returned when it was due a year later; and *Edward Elvyn v. Christopher Marley*, which concerns a loan of £10 on 11 April 1588 that Marlowe had not repaid by the time Elvyn filed suit at the beginning of Michaelmas Term (9 October 1588).

6 Several documents testify to the presence of the Admiral's men in London, 1587–9. One is from the correspondence of Sir Francis Walsingham on 25 January 1587; another from the London lord mayor on 6 November 1589 (E. K. Chambers, *The Elizabethan Stage*, 4 vols [Oxford: Clarendon Press, 1923], 4, pp. 303, 305). Still another is a letter from Philip Gawdy to his father dated 16 November 1587. It describes an accident that resulted in audience casualties when one of 'My L. Admyrall his men and players' mishandled a loaded caliver in the midst of a performance at an unspecified London theatrical venue (2, p. 135).

7 The best source for a condensed yet detailed history of early modern English playing venues is the headnotes by Herbert Berry in the section, 'Playhouses, 1560–1660', in *English Professional Theatre, 1530–1660*, ed. Glynne Wickham, Herbert Berry and William Ingram (Cambridge: Cambridge University Press, 2000). In addition, for London inns, see the forthcoming monograph by David Kathman, anticipated in essays such as 'Inn-yard Playhouses', in

The Oxford Handbook of Early Modern Theatre, ed. Richard Dutton (Oxford: Oxford University Press, 2009), pp. 153–67. For venues in the provinces, see the *Patrons and Performances Web Site* (http://link.library.utoronto.ca/reed/) and *The Queen's Men and their Plays* by Scott McMillin and Sally-Beth MacLean (Cambridge: Cambridge University Press, 1998), esp. pp. 67–83.

8   Berry condenses the details of the suit, which precipitated further suits, in Wickham, New York: AMS Press, 1987, pp. 330–1. Scholars disagree about the date of the shouting match between Alleyn and the Burbages. Berry says 'November 1590', and that is good enough for me *Shakespeare's Playhouses*. With Illustrations by C. Walter Hodges (New York: AMS Press, 1987).

9   Wickham, item 287 (d), pp. 362–3. William Ingram provides a thumbnail biography of Tunstall and his professional associations in *The Business of Playing: The Beginnings of the Adult Professional Theater in Elizabethan London* (Ithaca, NY: Cornell University Press, 1992), pp. 25–9. For biographical information on the Alleyn brothers, see S. P. Cerasano, 'Edward Alleyn's Early Years: His Life and Family', *Notes and Queries*, 232.2 (1987), p. 239. For players in general, see Edwin Nungezer, *A Dictionary of Actors* (1929, rpt. New York: Greenwood Press, 1968).

10 I rely here on the REED-sponsored *Performances and Patrons Web Site* unless otherwise noted (http://link.library.utoronto.ca/reed/). For further context on touring, the REED volumes are available in libraries and online (www.reed.utoronto.ca/index.html). The relevant volumes cited here are *Kent* (vol. 2, ed. James M. Gibson [Toronto, 2002]), *Oxford* (vol. 1, ed. John R. Elliott and Alan H. Nelson [University]; Alexandra Johnston and Diana Wyatt [City] [Toronto, 2004]), *Coventry* (ed. R. W. Ingram, Toronto, 1981), *Sussex* (ed. Cameron Louis [Toronto, 2000]), *Bristol* (ed. Mark C. Pilkinton [Toronto, 1997]), and *Cumberland/Westmorland/Gloucestershire* (ed. Audrey Douglas and Peter Greenfield [Toronto, 1986]). For tour routes specifically, see Sally-Beth MacLean, 'Tour Routes: "Provincial Wanderings" or Traditional Circuits?', *Medieval and Renaissance Drama in England*, 6 (1993), pp. 1–14.

11 *Malone Society Collections II*.3 (1931; rpt. New York: AMS Press, 1985), p. 276.

12 The Marlborough record is in John Tucker Murray, *English Dramatic Companies 1558–1642*, 2 vols (Boston and New York: Houghton Mifflin, 1910), 1, p. 142.

13 The records for Maidstone span 1 November 1589 to 1 November 1590; thus the performance for which the Admiral's men were paid 10s. could have taken place in some proximity to the performances in June at Rye and New Romney. Likewise, records for Folkestone (8 September 1589–8 September 1590) and Lydd (22 July 1589–22 July 1590) accommodate payments for activity in the month of June 1590.

14 The records for Oxford span 29 September 1589–29 September 1590; thus the performance for which the Admiral's men were paid 6s. 8d. could have taken place in some proximity to the performance at Gloucester on

17 September. The Bristol payment was made sometime between 9 and 15 August 1590, pinpointing rather neatly a performance there before the one at Gloucester. Records for Oxford (29 September 1589–29 September 1590) and Coventry (1 November 1589–31 October 1590) accommodate payments for activity before and after the September performance at Gloucester. There is also an item for Winchester '[b]efore Feb., '91' that might fit with the westward turn from New Romney (Murray, I, p. 142).

15 Ben Jonson, *Poetaster*, ed. Tom Cain (Manchester: Manchester University Press, 1995).

16 The Lord Admiral had other residences including a Chelsea manor house and lodgings at Arundel House in the Strand.

17 The critical history linking 'bad' quartos with touring is complicated. To follow its development through the lens of revisionist arguments, see Paul Werstine, 'Narratives About Printed Shakespeare Texts: "Foul Papers" and "Bad" Quartos', *Shakespeare Quarterly*, 41 (1990), pp. 65–86; Laurie Maguire, *Shakespearean Suspect Texts* (Cambridge: Cambridge University Press, 1996); Barbara D. Palmer, 'Early Modern Mobility: Players, Payments, and Patrons', *Shakespeare Quarterly*, 56 (2005), pp. 260–305; and Peter Greenfield, 'Touring', in *The Oxford Handbook of Early Modern Theatre*, ed. Richard Dutton (Oxford: Oxford University Press, 2009), pp. 292–306.

18 Andrew Gurr, *Shakespeare's Opposites: The Admiral's Company 1594–1625* (Cambridge: Cambridge University Press, 2009), p. 75. Gurr is thinking specifically of 1594 and following, but his supposition of the ineligibility of Marlowe's play – if valid – would have applied in 1590 also.

19 Leslie Thomson, 'Staging on the Road, 1586–1594', *Shakespeare Quarterly*, 61 (2010), pp. 526–50, esp. 533.

20 According to Thomson's tables, 69 per cent of the extant plays from 1586–94 would have been eliminated from a touring repertory if plays with simple staging were the only ones performable on the road.

21 Sara Munson Deats, ed., *Doctor Faustus: A Critical Guide* (London and New York: Continuum, 2010), p. 1. On the date of *Doctor Faustus*, see 'The Critical Backstory' by Bruce E. Brandt (Deats, pp. 21–2). For early venues, see 'The Performance History' by David Bevington (Deats, pp. 41–2).

22 Lucas Erne, *Beyond* The Spanish Tragedy (Manchester: Manchester University Press, 2001), pp. 20, 150 and 168. Erne does not discuss company affiliations of *The Spanish Tragedy* except to rule out the Queen's men (p. 163). Lost plays are indicated here by quotation marks; extant plays are indicated by italics.

23 Fredson Bowers, *Elizabethan Revenge Tragedy* (Princeton: Princeton University Press, 1940), pp. 104–9, esp. pp. 105, 106. Bowers nonetheless details the 'obvious debt' Marlowe's play owes to *The Spanish Tragedy* (p. 108). Erne, who calls *The Jew of Malta* 'Marlowe's most Kydian play' (pp. 221–2), demonstrates that debt further (p. 58).

24 Thomas Lodge, *Wits Miserie, and the Worlds Madnesse* (1596), p. 56.

25 Samuel Chew points out that Soliman has moments of 'courtesy and mag-
    nanimity', even 'sentimentality', but he devolves into 'the conventional
    oriental despot gorged with the blood of his victims' (*The Crescent and the
    Rose* [Oxford: Oxford University Press, 1937], p. 497). Perseda herself is a
    revenger to be reckoned with; to punish Soliman, she paints the lips he wants
    to kiss with poison (*The Works of Thomas Kyd*, ed. Frederick Boas [Oxford:
    Clarendon Press, 1901], V.iv.117–18).

26 George Peele, *The Battle of Alcazar*. Malone Society Reprints (1907). *The
    Battle of Alcazar* and *The Jew of Malta* share another theatrical motif: the
    dead body as a property. In Marlowe's play, the corpse is Friar Barnadine; in
    Peele's it is Abdelmelec, who is displayed in a chair to his troops as incentive
    to continue fighting.

27 *The Tragical Reign of Selimus*. Malone Society Reprints (1908).

28 Daniel Vitkis, ed., *Three Turk Plays from Early Modern England* (New York:
    Columbia University Press, 2000), p. 22.

29 In a gesture worthy of Barabas, Abraham offers Selimus a sip: 'wold your
    grace would once but tast of them/ I could as willingly affoord them you'
    (xviii.1727–8). The stage direction indicates that Abraham, like Barabas,
    'Speakes aside'.

30 Mark Thornton Burnett, ed., *Christopher Marlowe: The Complete Plays*
    (London: J. M. Dent, 1999).

31 Lloyd Edward Kermode, ed., *Three Renaissance Usury Plays* (Manchester:
    Manchester University Press, 2009).

32 Robert Greene, *Perimedes the Blacke-Smith*, 1588, p. A3.

33 See 'Heliogabalus' in the *Lost Plays Database*.

34 Only a handful of plays can be tracked from one company to another by
    Henslowe's lists: for example, *Jeronimo* [*The Spanish Tragedy*], the two parts
    of 'Tamar Cham', 'The Fair Maid of Italy' and *Titus Andronicus*.

35 For Alleyn's early acquisition of plays, see the letter from Richard Jones
    (player), which specifies 'playinge apparel Playe bookes Jinstrumentes and
    other commodities [. . .] solde, to the same Edwarde Allen' (W. W. Greg, ed.,
    Henslowe Papers [London: A. H. Bullen, 1907], p. 31). Scott McMillin makes
    a case for Alleyn's acquisition of *JM* in 'The Ownership of *The Jew of Malta*,
    Friar Bacon, and *The Ranger's Comedy*', *English Language Notes*, 9 (1972),
    pp. 249–52, esp. 251.

36 *The Jew of Malta* was not one of the texts Alleyn sold, but *The Massacre at
    Paris* was. Henslowe's *Diary* documents Alleyn's sale of playbooks (Foakes,
    pp. 180, 181, 184, 187, 204 and 205). For details on Alleyn's professional life,
    see Susan Cerasano, 'Edward Alleyn, the New Model Actor, and the Rise of
    the Celebrity in the 1590s', *Medieval and Renaissance Drama in England*, 18
    (2005), pp. 47–58.

37 Sally Beth MacLean, 'Adult Playing Companies, 1583–1593', in Dutton,
    pp. 39–55, esp. p. 46.

38   Those dates were 13–14 and 30–31 March; 22–24 April (no play is listed for the 23rd); and 21–22 May.

39   Even though there is scholarly scepticism about the meaning of Henslowe's mark, 'ne', I take its absence (as with 'Machiavel') to indicate a play with a previous stage history; I take its presence to indicate a play being marketed as new. Foakes discusses several options for 'ne' (pp. xxxiv–xxxv).

40   Often considered *The Battle of Alcazar* by another name, 'Muly Mollocco' is treated here as a discrete play (see its entry in the *Lost Plays Database*).

41   'Titus and Vespasian' was formerly misidentified as *Titus Andronicus* (see its entry in the *Lost Plays Database*).

42   Lawrence Manley, 'Playing with Fire: Immolation in the Repertory of Strange's Men', *Early Theatre*, 4 (2001), pp. 115–29, esp. 116. Manley acknowledges that some of the plays he cites did not originate in the holdings of Strange's men (p. 124).

43   Manley accepts the argument that the 'Friar Bacon' in the holdings of Strange's men was *John of Bordeaux*, not Robert Greene's *Friar Bacon and Friar Bungay* (for that argument, see McMillin, 'Ownership', p. 251).

44   *The Plays & Poems of Robert Greene*, ed. J. Churton Collins, 2 vols (Oxford: Clarendon Press, 1905), p. 1.

45   Roslyn L. Knutson, 'What's So Special about 1594?', *Shakespeare Quarterly*, 61 (2010), pp. 449–67, esp. p. 462.

46   On assignment of plays to the Queen's men, see McMillin and MacLean, pp. 88–93. For lost plays, see the *Lost Plays Database*.

47   A ballad entitled 'the murtherous life and terrible death of the riche Jew of Malta' was registered at Stationers' Hall on 16 May 1594 (Chambers 3, p. 424).

48   Gurr, *The Shakespearian Playing Companies* (Oxford: Clarendon Press, 1996), pp. 267–70. There are two theories of origin for Pembroke's men in 1592–3. The one favoured by Chambers is that Pembroke's were an off-shoot of Strange's men, who had grown too large (2, p. 129). The one favoured by Gurr is that Pembroke's were independently formed at the initiative of James Burbage, who 'moved to set up a new company led by his son under a new patron' (p. 267).

49   Chambers, 2, pp. 128–32. The authority for the break-up of Pembroke's men in late summer 1593 is the letter dated 28 September 1593 from Philip Henslowe to Edward Alleyn, in which Henslowe says that Pembroke's men 'are all at home' and had been for five or six weeks because they could 'not saue ther carges <w>ᵗʰ trauell' (Foakes, p. 280).

50   Karl P. Wentersdorf, 'The Repertory and Size of Pembroke's Company', *Theatre Annual*, 33 (1977), pp. 71–85.

51   Fredson Bowers, ed., *The Dramatic Works of Thomas Dekker*, 4 vols (Cambridge: Cambridge University Press, 1953), p. 1. Presumably the jest refers to Pembroke's touring repertory prior to February 1597, at which time they came to London and took up residence at the Swan playhouse. Jonson

and Nashe were writing for them in July when their play, 'The Isle of Dogs', ran afoul of authorities.

52 The privy council members were the Lord Admiral and the Lord Chamberlain; the playhouses were the Rose and Theatre (later, the Fortune and Globe). Gurr developed his argument for a duopoly in 'Three Reluctant Patrons and Early Shakespeare', *Shakespeare Quarterly*, 44 (1993), pp. 159–82. In subsequent scholarship including collective histories of companies (*Shakespearian Playing Companies*), a specific history of the Chamberlain's/King's (*The Shakespeare Company, 1594–1642* [Cambridge: Cambridge University Press, 2004]), and a specific history of the Admiral's (*Shakespeare's Opposites*), he has refined and embellished that claim. Among dissenting opinions are those by Knutson in 'What's So Special' and Holger Schott Syme, 'The Meaning of Success: Stories of 1594 and Its Aftermath; *Shakespeare Quarterly*, 61 (2010), pp. 490–525.

53 It is not clear whether the companies were blended or playing on alternate days. Seeing the small sums paid Henslowe, some scholars draw the conclusion that the run was poorly attended; however, no one knows the financial arrangement made by Henslowe and the companies in the lease of the Newington playhouse that produced these receipts.

54 *A New Interlude [. . .] of Godly Queen Hester*, ed. John S. Farmer, *Six Anonymous Plays* (Second Series), Early English Drama Society, 1906, p. 279.

55 Leah S. Marcus, Janet Mueller and Mary Beth Rose. *Elizabeth I: Collected Works* (Chicago: University of Chicago Press, 2000), p. 157.

56 John Alymer, *An Harborovve For Faithfvll and Trevve Svbiectes, agaynst the late blowne Blaste, concerninge the Gouernment of VVemen. wherin be confuted all such reasons as a straunger of late made in that behalf, with a briefe exhortation to Obedience* (1559), O3.

57 Stephen Greenblatt, *Will in the World: How Shakespeare Became Shakespeare* (New York: Norton, 2004), pp. 273–8.

58 Johannes Brenz, trans. John Stockwood. *A right godly and learned discourse vpon the book of Ester Most necessary for this time and age, to enstruct all noble men, and such as God hath aduanced vnto high places about princes* (1584), p. 690.

59 It is a curiosity and no more that three performances in 1594 (23, 30 June, 20 October) and one in 1596 (18 January) fall on a Sunday, a day when theatre historians of Greg's generation were sure that no performances took place.

60 'Galiaso' is a possibility if it was the story of the guileful Italian oligarch, Gian Galeazzo Visconti, who was named the first Duke of Milan in 1395 (see the entry in the *Lost Plays Database*).

61 See the entries in the *Lost Plays Database* for 'Mahomet' and 'The Turkish Mahomet and Hiren the Fair Greek'.

62 George Chapman, *The Blind Beggar of Alexandria*, Malone Society Reprints (1928).

63 William Ingram makes such a guess possible by finding lodgings of players
    with the Queen's men in the neighbourhood of the Swan (*A London Life in
    the Brazen Age: Francis Langley, 1548–1602* [Cambridge: Harvard University
    Press, 1978], pp. 115–20).

64 For a list of Pembroke's migrating repertory, see W. W. Greg, ed., *Henslowe's
    Diary*, 2 vols (London: A. H. Bullen, 1904–8), 2, pp. 186–7; and the *Lost
    Plays Database*.

65 John Marston, 'Satire X', *The Scourge of Villanie*, 1598 (S. R. 8 September);
    'Satire X' is 'Satire XI' in the 1599 printing.

66 G. B. Evans, gen. ed., *The Riverside Shakespeare*, 2nd edn (Boston and New
    York: Houghton Mifflin, 1997).

67 There apparently was also a play called 'The Jew of Venice', supposedly
    by Thomas Dekker. The title is recorded in the Stationers' Register on
    9 September 1653 in the possession of Humphrey Moseley. Although much
    conjecture has been generated by scholars on its relationship to Shakespeare's
    (and inferentially Marlowe's) play, G. E. Bentley states bluntly that 'there
    is no reason to connect *The Jew of Venice* which Moseley owned in 1653
    with any other play at all' (*The Jacobean and Caroline Stage*, 7 vols [Oxford:
    Clarendon Press, 1941–68] 3, p. 252).

68 Paul Menzer, 'Shades of Marlowe', *Marlowe Studies: An Annual*, 1 (2011),
    pp. 181–92, esp. p. 182.

69 Depending on playgoers' theatrical experience and memory, various aspects
    of *A Larum for London* (Chamberlain's men, *c.* 1599) might also have recalled
    Marlowe's plays. Sancto Danila, the chief invading Spanish warrior, boasts in
    mighty lines throughout. In one sequence, having accosted an old man whose
    daughter has taken refuge in a nunnery, Danila at first claims this 'Iewell' as
    his 'loue', then murders her and her father because there is not a place in
    Antwerp to keep her safe from other marauders until he can return to ravish
    her (Malone Society Reprints [New York: AMS Press, 1985], ll. 945, 1050,
    1075–80).

70 See Bentley for details on Prince Henry's/Palgrave's men (1, pp. 134–57),
    Queen Henrietta's men (1, 218–59), Beeston (2, 363–70), Perkins (2, 525–8)
    and the Cockpit/Phoenix (6, 47–77).

71 Jeremy Lopez, 'Alleyn Resurrected', *Marlowe Studies: An Annual*, 1 (2011),
    pp. 167–80, esp. pp. 173, 174.

72 'The Prologue Spoken at Court', l. 4.

5: New Directions: *The Jew of Malta* and *The Merchant of Venice*: A Reconsideration of Influence

1 More accurately, a 'farce of the old English humour, [a] terribly serious, even
   savage comic humour' (T. S. Eliot, 'Christopher Marlowe', *Selected Essays*
   [New York: Harcourt, Brace & World, 1964], p. 105).

2 Robert Logan, *Shakespeare's Marlowe: The Influence of Christopher Marlowe on Shakespeare's Artistry* (Aldershot: Ashgate, 2007), p. 120.

3 Julia Reinhard Lupton, 'The Jew of Malta', in *Cambridge Companion to Christopher Marlowe*, ed. Patrick Cheney (Cambridge: Cambridge University Press, 2004), p. 144.

4 This aspect of Barabas's costume reflects not simply an anti-Semitic stereotype but underlines his descent from the Vice figure, with its demonic associations, in the Tudor interludes. See N. W. Bawcutt, ed., introduction to *The Jew of Malta* (Manchester: Manchester University Press, 1978), pp. 2, 10, 52 n.46. Also III.iii.10 n.

5 All quotations of *The Merchant of Venice* are from Jay Halio, ed. (Oxford: Oxford University Press, 1993). All quotations of *The Jew of Malta* are from *Christopher Marlowe: The Complete Plays*, ed. Mark Thornton Burnett (London: J. M. Dent, 1999).

6 Simon Shepherd, *Marlowe and the Politics of Elizabethan Theatre* (Brighton: Harvester Press, 1986), pp. xi, 173.

7 See, for example, Jay Halio's introduction to the Oxford edition of *The Merchant of Venice*, p. 7.

8 Thomas Cartelli, *Marlowe, Shakespeare, and the Economy of Theatrical Experience* (Philadelphia: University of Pennsylvania Press, 1991), p. 163.

9 The seminal discussion for the veritable explosion of later discussions of the socio-economic contexts of Shakespeare's play is Walter Cohen's '*The Merchant of Venice* and the Possibilities of Historical Criticism', *ELH*, 49 (1982), pp. 765–89.

10 In a recent article, for example, Walter Lim asserts that 'Shakespeare's dramatization of economic activities prompts a comparison with Christopher Marlowe's [. . .] *The Jew of Malta* [. . .]. The relationship between the Jew and Maltese society obtains its meanings in relation to the distinctive ethos of an exuberant internationalized commercialism' ('Surety and Spiritual Commercialism in *The Merchant of Venice*', *SEL* 50.2 [2010], pp. 355–81 [p. 358]).

11 Daniel Vitkus, 'Turks and Jews in *The Jew of Malta*', in *Early Modern English Drama: A Critical Companion*, ed. Garrett Sullivan, Patrick Cheney and Andrew Hadfield (New York: Oxford University Press, 2006), p. 62.

12 Patrick Cheney, *Marlowe's Republican Authorship: Lucan, Liberty, and the Sublime* (Basingstoke: Palgrave, 2009), pp. 9, 22.

13 Ibid., p. 9, citing William Blissett, 'Lucan's Caesar and the Elizabethan Villain', *Studies in Philology*, 53 (1956), pp. 553–75 (p. 566).

14 See Cheney, p. 27, citing Quentin Skinner, *The Foundations of Modern Political Thought* (Cambridge: Cambridge University Press, 1978), 1, pp. 153–68.

15 Andrew Hadfield, in *Shakespeare and Republicanism* (Cambridge: Cambridge University Press, 2005), observes that 'Venice was seen by many English authors as the most desirable state in Europe [. . .] notable for its wealth, relative tolerance of strangers [. . .], and a sophisticated, complex but clear

constitution that brought out the best in its citizens' (p. 214). Although Shakespeare's assignation to Venice of a ruling Duke might appear a reflection of 'aristocratic' rule, three of the six elected Signori in Venice in fact 'had greater powers than the Duke, enabling them to control and limit his actions' (p. 40). Hadfield also admits that the Venetian authorities in *Othello* 'make every effort to deal with racial prejudice – in marked contrast to Shakespeare's earlier representation of Venice in *The Merchant of Venice*' (p. 215).

16 Bernard Dov Cooperman, 'Venetian Policy Towards Levantine Jews in Its Broader Italian Context', *Gli Ebrei e Venezia* (Milano: Edizioni di Comunita, 1987), pp. 68–69; quoted in Vitkus, 'Turks and Jews', p. 67.

17 Emily Bartels, *Spectacles of Strangeness: Imperialism, Alienation, and Marlowe* (Philadelphia: University of Pennsylvania Press, 1993), p. 97.

18 Stephen Greenblatt, *Renaissance Self-Fashioning: From More to Shakespeare* (Chicago: University of Chicago Press, 1980), p. 208.

19 Vitkus, 'Turks and Jews', p. 63.

20 Quoted in Arthur Freeman, 'Marlowe, Kyd, and the Dutch Church Libel', *ELR*, 3 (1973), pp. 44–52 (pp. 50–1).

21 Ibid., 45.

22 Diarmaid MacCulloch gives a rather surprising description of the persistence of Muslim slave traders: 'Even when the activities of the Ottoman fleet were curbed after the battle of Lepanto in 1571 [. . .], north African corsairs systematically raided the Mediterranean coasts of Europe to acquire slave labour; in fact they ranged as far as Ireland and even Iceland, kidnapping men, women, and children. Modern historians . . . produce reliable estimates that Islamic raiders enslaved around a million western Christian Europeans between 1530 and 1640' (*The Reformation* [New York: Penguin, 2005], p. 57).

23 See Gustav Ungerer, 'Portia and the Prince of Morocco', *Shakespeare Studies*, 31 (2003), pp. 89–126, for an eye-opening account of English relations with Moroccan Muslims, and their 'Jewish middlemen'.

24 I question Cohen's idealization of Christian behaviour in *The Merchant*. He argues, 'by the end of Act IV, [Shylock's] analogies are strictly irrelevant to most of the Christian characters in the play. They have either given up the practices that Shylock attributes to them, or they have never been guilty of them at all: certainly we meet no Christian slaveholders' ('Possibilities of Historical Criticism', p. 774). Antonio indicates he has every intention of continuing his abusive behaviour towards Shylock (I.iii.126–7). The fact that we *see* no Christian slaveholders certainly does not preclude their existence, since slavery was practised not only in Venice but through much of Europe.

25 Ian McAdam, *The Irony of Identity: Self and Imagination in the Drama of Christopher Marlowe* (Newark: University of Delaware Press, 1999), p. 24.

26 G. K. Hunter, 'The Theology of Marlowe's *The Jew of Malta*', *Journal of the Warburg and Courtauld Institutes*, 27 (1964), pp. 211–40 (pp. 221–5).

27 See McAdam, *Irony of Identity*, pp. 153–4.

28 The actual story in *Il pecorone* from which Shakespeare borrows part of his plot is helpfully summarized by Jay Halio in his introduction to the Oxford edition, pp. 14–16.

29 Constance Kuriyama, *Hammer or Anvil: Psychological Patterns in Christopher Marlowe's Plays* (New Brunswick: Rutgers University Press, 1980), p. 141.

30 Debora Kuller Shuger, *The Renaissance Bible* (Berkeley: University of California Press, 1994), pp. 124–6.

31 Bruce R. Smith, *Shakespeare and Masculinity* (Oxford: Oxford University Press, 2000), p. 51.

32 Walter Lim, 'Surety and Spiritual Commercialism in *The Merchant of Venice*', p. 377, quoting Paul Stevens, 'How Milton's Nationalism Works: Globalization and the Possibilities of Positive Nationalism', in *Early Modern Nationalism and Milton's England*, ed. David Loewenstein and Paul Stevens (Toronto: University of Toronto Press, 2008), p. 280.

33 Part of Peter S. Donaldson's description of the pre-Oedipal patterns of behaviour in Marlowe's protagonists ('Conflict and Coherence: Narcissism and Tragic Structure in Marlowe', in *Narcissism and the Text: Studies in Literature and the Psychology of Self*, ed. Lynne Layton and Barbara Ann Schapiro [New York: New York University Press, 1986], p. 46).

34 Harry Berger, 'Marriage and Mercifixion in *The Merchant of Venice*: The Casket Scene Revisited', in *Making Trifles of Terrors*, ed. Peter Erickson (Stanford: Stanford University Press, 1997), p. 3; quoting Lawrence Hyman, 'The Rival Lovers in *The Merchant of Venice*', *Shakespeare Quarterly*, 21 (1970), pp. 109–16 (p. 109).

35 James O'Rourke, 'Racism and Homophobia in *The Merchant of Venice*', *ELH*, 70 (2003), pp. 375–97 (p. 377).

36 Steve Patterson, 'The Bankruptcy of Homoerotic Amity in Shakespeare's *Merchant of Venice*', *Shakespeare Quarterly*, 50 (1999), pp. 9–32 (pp. 10, 14).

37 McAdam, *The Irony of Identity*, pp. 171–3.

38 On the cauldron as 'a traditional image of hell', see Hunter, 'The Theology of *The Jew of Malta*', pp. 233–5.

39 Janet Adelman, *Blood Relations: Christian and Jew in* The Merchant of Venice (Chicago: University of Chicago Press, 2008), p. 121.

40 Hunter, 'Theology of Marlowe's *Jew of Malta*', p. 240.

41 See Sara Munson Deats, 'Biblical Parody in Marlowe's *The Jew of Malta*: A Re-Examination', *Christianity and Literature*, 37 (1988), pp. 27–48, and my response, *Irony of Identity*, pp. 146–73.

42 James Shapiro, 'Shakespeare and the Jews', in *New Casebooks: The Merchant of Venice*, ed. Martin Coyle (New York: St. Martin's Press, 1998), p. 81.

43 Wilbur Sanders, *The Dramatist and the Received Idea: Studies in the Plays of Marlowe and Shakespeare* (Cambridge: Cambridge University Press, 1968), p. 42.

44 Matthew Biberman, *Masculinity, Anti-Semitism and Early Modern English Literature* (Aldershot: Ashgate, 2004), pp. 25–7, 33.

45   Shapiro, *Shakespeare and the Jews* (New York: Columbia University Press, 1996), p. 110.

46   Shapiro in *Shakespeare and the Jews* notes that Shakespeare's father was 'twice accused of violating usury laws', and in only one case fined (p. 256, n. 35). Suzanne Penuel, 'Castrating the Creditor in *The Merchant of Venice*', *SEL*, 44 (2004), pp. 255–75, suggests 'the play's association of usury with fatherhood' (p. 272, n. 11), which would encourage Shakespeare's masculine identification with Shylock.

47   Walter Lim considers the ambiguity of Bassanio's class status, 'Surety and Spiritual Commercialism', p. 363 and n. 21.

48   See, for example, Andrew Hadfield's *Shakespeare and Republicanism*, which perhaps raises as many questions as it answers, especially with respect to the development of Shakespeare's republican thought over the span of his career.

6: New Directions: *The Jew of Malta* as Print Commodity in 1594

1   I owe a large debt to Roslyn L. Knutson for reading a late draft of this chapter. Except in those cases where they are derived from a specific edition, all titles have been modernized for spelling and punctuation. For Ling and Millington's Stationers' Register entry, see Edward Arber, ed., *A Transcript of the Registers of the Company of Stationers of London 1554–1640*, vol. 2 (London: privately printed, 1875–94), p. 650.

2   Most recent editors (e.g. Van Fossen [1964], Bawcutt [1978] and Siemon [1994]) have concluded that the 1633 edition was derived from authorial foul papers. For an account of Vavasour's motives in bringing *The Jew of Malta* to press in 1633, see Zachary Lesser, *Renaissance Drama and the Politics of Publication* (Cambridge: Cambridge University Press, 2004), pp. 81–114.

3   Such a decision was not at all unusual; a number of titles entered in the Stationers' Register were apparently never published. My figures for the costs associated with acquisition, authority, license and entry come from Peter W. M. Blayney, 'The Publication of Playbooks', in *A New History of Early English Drama*, ed. John D. Cox and David Scott Kastan (New York: Columbia University Press, 1997), pp. 394–405.

4   For such editorial responses, see, for example, C. F. Tucker Brooke, ed., *The Works of Christopher Marlowe* (Oxford: Clarendon Press, 1910), p. 231 and H. S. Bennett, ed., *The Jew of Malta and The Massacre at Paris* (New York: Gordian Press, 1931), pp. 3–4. Some editors of the play have also suggested that Ling and Millington's entry might have been a 'blocking entry'. N. W. Bawcutt, in a note in his 1978 edition, surmises that 'possibly Ling and Millington were about to publish a "bad quarto" of the play but were

somehow prevented from doing so' (p. 55, n. 104). For a strong refutation of Pollard's theory of 'blocking entries', see Blayney.

5 For 'Marlowe's sensational exit from the world and stage' as an explanation for Ling and Millington's *The Jew of Malta* entry and for the publication of *Tamburlaine* (1593), *Dido* (1594), and *Edward II* (1594), see Richard Proudfoot, 'Marlowe and the Editors', in *The Cambridge Companion to Christopher Marlowe*, ed. J. A. Downie and J. T. Parnell (Cambridge: Cambridge University Press, 2000), pp. 41–54; and Lukas Erne, *Shakespeare as Literary Dramatist* (Cambridge: Cambridge University Press, 2003), pp. 46–7. For Marlowe's contemporary acclaim as professional playwright, see John Bakeless, *The Tragicall History of Christopher Marlowe*, 2 vols (Cambridge: Harvard University Press, 1942); David Riggs, *The World of Christopher Marlowe* (New York: Macmillan, 2004), pp. 221–2; and Park Honan, *Christopher Marlowe: Poet & Spy* (Oxford: Oxford University Press, 2005), pp. 286, 361.

6 Robert Greene died in early September 1592. Before 18 months had passed, 3 separate accounts of Greene's final hours would appear in St. Paul's churchyard; Greene would also be eulogized in a collection of sonnets by Richard Barnfield and conjured as a wandering ghost in separate pamphlets by Henry Chettle and Barnabe Rich. For the wide range of response to Greene's death, see Kirk Melnikoff, ed., *Robert Greene* (Aldershot: Ashgate, 2011). For transcripts of the Baine and Kyd responses to Marlowe's death, see Constance B. Kuriyama, *Christopher Marlowe: A Renaissance Life* (Ithaca: Cornell University Press, 2002), pp. 219–31. For print epitaphs within two years of Marlowe's death, see George Peele, *The Honour of the Garter* (London, 1593), sig.A4v; and Thomas Nashe, *Christs Teares Over Ierusalem* (London, 1594), sig.**1.

7 Marlowe's translation of Lucan was not published until 1600; *Hero and Leander*'s first print edition appeared in 1598.

8 The first edition of *The Massacre at Paris* cites 'Christopher Marlow' on the title page, but its imprint has no date. Carter Hailey, in 'The Publication Date of Marlowe's Massacre at Paris, with a Note on the Collier Leaf', *Marlowe Studies*, 1 (2011), pp. 25–40, has recently argued for a 1596 publication date based on paper stock evidence.

9 For a similarly sceptical take on the 'Marlowe' brand in the early 1590s, see J. A. Downie, 'Reviewing What We Think We Know about Christopher Marlowe, Again', *Christopher Marlowe the Craftsman: Lives, Stage, and Page*, ed. Sarah K. Scott and M. L. Stapleton (Aldershot: Ashgate, 2010), pp. 33–46.

10 For an example of this assumption, see H. S. Bennett, ed., *The Jew of Malta and The Massacre at Paris* (London, 1931), p. 4.

11 Andrew Gurr, 'The Great Divide of 1594', in *Words That Count: Essays on Early Modern Authorship in Honor of MacDonald P. Jackson*, ed. Brian Boyd (Newark: University of Delaware Press, 2004), p. 45. See also Tom Rutter,

'Marlovian Echoes in the Admiral's Men Repertory: *Alcazar, Stukeley, Patient Grissil'*, *Shakespeare Bulletin*, 27 (2009), pp. 27–38, esp. p. 28.

12 Holger Schott Syme, 'The Meaning of Success: Stories of 1594 and its Aftermath', *Shakespeare Quarterly*, 61.4 (2010), p. 505. I am indebted to Syme's article for much of this paragraph.

13 *The Spanish Tragedy* was first published by Edward White in 1592, with new editions following in 1594 and 1599. *A Knack to Know a Knave* was published by Richard Jones in 1594; it was never reprinted. Both plays appear to have been successful on the professional stage.

14 Professional plays were first published in significant numbers in 1594. Lesser and Farmer have called this a 'boomlet'. See Blayney; and Alan Farmer and Zachary Lesser, 'The Popularity of Playbooks Revisited', *Shakespeare Quarterly*, 56 (2005), pp. 1–32.

15 For specialization as an important facet of early modern publishing, see Lesser.

16 Leo Kirschbaum, *Shakespeare and the Stationers* (Columbus: Ohio State University Press, 1955), p. 25.

17 See Marta Straznicky's introduction in *Shakespeare's Stationers* (Philadelphia: University of Pennsylvania Press, 2012), forthcoming.

18 For an overview of Ling's life and career, see Gerald D. Johnson, 'Nicholas Ling, Publisher 1580–1607', *Studies in Bibliography*, 38 (1985), pp. 203–14.

19 Zachary Lesser and Peter Stallybrass, 'The First Literary *Hamlet* and the Commonplacing of Professional Plays', *Shakespeare Quarterly*, 59.4 (2008), pp. 371–420.

20 For republican elements in Ling's publications, see Kirk Melnikoff, 'Nicholas Ling's Republican *Hamlet* (1603)', in *Shakespeare's Stationers*, ed. Marta Straznicky (Philadelphia: University of Pennsylvania Press, 2012), forthcoming; Andrew Hadfield, *Shakespeare and Republicanism* (Cambridge: Cambridge University Press, 2005); and Curtis Perry, 'The Uneasy Republicanism of Thomas Kyd's *Cornelia'*, *Criticism*, 48.4 (2006), pp. 535–55.

21 These publications include *Greene's Never Too Late* (1590), *Cornelia* (1594), *Matilda* (1594), *Rosalynde* (1596) and *Skialetheia* (1598). See Lesser and Stallybrass, p. 386.

22 For *Bel-vedére* attributions, see Charles Crawford, 'Belvedere, or, The Garden of the Muses', *Englische Studien*, 43 (1910–11), pp. 198–228.

23 For republican resonances in *The Jew of Malta*, see Patrick Cheney, *Marlowe's Republican Authorship: Lucan, Liberty and the Sublime* (New York: Palgrave, 2009), pp. 122–39.

24 For *The Jew of Malta* in the context of sixteenth-century responses to Machiavelli, see N. W Bawcutt, 'Machiavelli and Marlowe's *The Jew of Malta'*, *Renaissance Drama*, 3 (1970), pp. 3–49.

25 In England, *Vindiciae Contra Tyrannos* would be reprinted (in French, Latin and English versions) numerous times by 1622. For a publication history of

the tract, see Anne McLaren, 'Rethinking Republicanism: "Vindiciae, contra tyrannos" in Context', *The Historical Journal*, 49.1 (2006), p. 24. For a helpful overview of these tracts, see William C. Carroll, ed., *Macbeth: Texts and Contexts* (New York: St. Martin's, 1999), pp. 231–6.

26 George Garnet, ed. and trans., *Vindiciae, Contra Tyrannos: or, Concerning the Legitimate Power of a Prince Over the People, and of the People Over a Prince* (Cambridge: Cambridge University Press, 1994), p. 8.

27 Millington's master was the bookseller Henry Carre. For accounts of Millington's life and career (including his minor company indiscretions), see R. B. McKerrow, ed., *A Dictionary of Printers and Booksellers in England Scotland, and Ireland, and of Foreign Printers of English Books 1557–1640* (London: The Bibliographical Society, 1968), pp. 193–4; and especially Kirschbaum, pp. 307–8.

28 Like most ballads entered in the Stationers' Register, Millington's ballads are almost entirely lost. Millington also was involved with Deloney's *Thomas of Reading* (Arber 3, p. 204) and *Jack of Newberry* (Arber 3, pp. 81, 84, 87).

29 The publication *The True Narration of the Entertainment of His Royal Majesty* (1603) contains a dedicatory epistle signed 'T.M.' which the editors of the ESTC have tentatively ascribed to Millington.

30 Neither the pamphlet nor any of the ballads recounting this murder are now extant. Our knowledge of this horrific crime comes from one of the two plots in Robert Yarington's *Two Lamentable Tragedies* (1601). See Roslyn L. Knutson, 'Toe to Toe Across Maid Lane: Repertorial Competition at the Rose and Globe, 1599–1600', in *Acts of Criticism: Performance Matters in Shakespeare and His Contemporaries*, ed. June Schlueter and Paul Nelsen (Madison and Teaneck: Fairleigh Dickinson University Press, 2005), pp. 21–37.

31 See J. H. M Salmon, *Society in Crisis: France in the Sixteenth Century* (New York: AMS, 1975); and Mack P. Holt, *The French Wars of Religion, 1562–1629* (Cambridge: Cambridge University Press, 1995).

32 For an overview of the English involvement in the French Wars of Religion, see Wallace T. MacCaffrey, *Elizabeth I: War and Politics, 1588–1603* (Princeton: Princeton University Press, 1992).

33 None of Millington's ballads having to do with this assassination attempt are now extant.

34 Aggas published and translated himself a significant number of pamphlets having to do with the French Wars of Religion.

35 In 1603, after her death, a dozen works were printed in London eulogizing Elizabeth. At the same time, more than a dozen works were printed in London celebrating James I, with these were two editions of James's *Daemonologie*, three editions of his *True Law of Free Monarchies* and as many as nine editions of *Basilikon Doron*. For the ubiquity of *Basilikon Doron* in print, see Johann P. Sommerville, ed., *King James VI and I: Political Writings* (Cambridge University Press, 1994), p. 268.

36   See Alan Stewart, *The Cradle King: A Life of James VI & I* (London: Chatto and Windus, 2003), pp. 167–9.
37   On 25 April 1603, Millington was directed not to publish *England's Mourning Garment* 'vnles he bring my Lord graces [of CANTERBURY] hand or my Lord of LONDONs hand, for Aucthoritie' (Arber 3, p. 35). Six week later, Matthew Law was fined 20 shillings for printing copies of *England's Mourning Garment* in violation of Millington's right to copy (Arber 2, p. 836).
38   On 28 April 1603, Millington was directed not to publish *The Proceeding at the Funeral of the High and Mighty Princess Elizabeth* until the text was authorized (Arber 3, p. 35).
39   Millington's widow Joan ended up publishing *The Royal Passage* in 1604. Thomas's shop is described as 'her shop' in the imprint.
40   The professional theatres seem to have been officially closed on 28 January 1593 as a consequence of a Privy Council order. Playing did not resume at the Rose until 27 December 1593. Playing was again interrupted by plague concerns for approximately two months by a Privy Council order on 3 February 1594. For the documents associated with these closures, see Carol Chillington Rutter, *Documents of the Rose Playhouse* (Manchester: Manchester University Press, 1999), pp. 66–80.
41   See Blayney, pp. 383–422. Blayney's argument has been well received and has been almost universally preferred over Pollard's early assessment that playing company financial difficulties were responsible for this flooding of the print market with play texts. Roslyn Lander Knutson, in *Playing Companies and Commerce in Shakespeare's Time* (Cambridge: Cambridge University Press, 2001), pp. 63–74, for example, essentially agrees with Blayney's assessment. The flood of professional plays onto the print market in 1594 has also been explained through the 'dissolutions and recombinations' (p. 279) of playing companies at that time. For arguments along these lines, see Evelyn May Albright, *Dramatic Publication in England, 1580–1640: A Study of Conditions of Conditions Affecting Content and Form of Drama* (New York: Heath, 1927), pp. 276–84; and Scott McMillin and Sally-Beth MacLean, *The Queen's Men and Their Plays* (Cambridge: Cambridge University Press, 1998), pp. 84–5.
42   For differing accounts of this peak period of play publication, see Blayney; and Farmer and Lesser 'The Popularity of Playbooks Revisited'.
43   For the many flaws in assuming that in 1593 'the playhouse world was teetering on the brink of collapse', See Roslyn L. Knutson, 'What's So Special about 1594?', *Shakespeare Quarterly*, 61.4 (2010), pp. 449–67.
44   *Titus Andronicus'* healthy receipts must also have been due to it being a new company offering.
45   E. K. Chambers, *The Elizabethan Stage*, vol. 4 (Oxford: Clarendon Press, 1923), pp. 314–15.
46   The Swan likely opened its doors in 1595. That Langley's preparations were well under way in 1594 is suggested by a letter from the Lord Mayor to Lord Burghley dated 3 November 1594 (Chambers 4.316–17). For an account

of Langley, see William Ingram, *A London Life in the Brazen Age: Francis Langley 1548–1602* (Cambridge: Harvard University Press, 1978).

47 *The Jew of Malta* was staged ten times at the Rose in 1592 (between February and June); in 1593, it was staged twice in January and once in February; and in the first half of 1594 between February and June, it was staged six times. See Neil Carson, *A Companion to Henslowe's Diary* (Cambridge: Cambridge University Press, 1988), pp. 85–8.

48 Before his career was over, Ling would publish the third edition of *Every Man out of His Humor* (1600); the first two editions of *Hamlet* (1603, 1604); and the third edition of *The Taming of a Shrew* (1607). Danter has long been associated by Pollard and others with the piratical printing of professional drama. For an admirably measured overview of Danter's stationer career, see Kirschbaum, pp. 296–9.

49 The particular arrangements between Danter, White and Millington in bringing *Titus* to press are unknown. Millington transferred his share in the play's right-to-copy to the draper-turned-bookseller Thomas Pavier in 1602 (Arber 3, p. 204). Edward White brought out a second edition of the play in 1611.

50 This 1594 ballad is no longer extant. With the title '*Titus Andronicus* complaint', it is reprinted, however, in Richard Johnson's *The Golden Garland of Princely Pleasures and Delicate Delights* (1620), sig.E8v–F3. Most scholars believe that this ballad was written after the play.

51 These ballads are based upon the plays *Godfrey of Boulogne* (lost), *Heliogabilus* (lost), *Bellindon* (lost), *A Knack to Know an Honest Man* and *Tamburlaine* respectively. For more information on the lost plays, see the *Lost Plays Database*, ed. Roslyn L. Knutson and David McInnis (Melbourne: University of Melbourne, 2009), Web. Henslowe's Diary's 1594 entries indicate that the last three of these ballads were based on what were at that time repertory mainstays of the Rose Playhouse. Moreover, *Tamburlaine* had recently reached a second edition in 1593. Danter's now-lost ballad '*The userer's rewarde*' (entered in the Stationers' Register on 19 June 1594 [Arber 2, p. 654]) might conceivably have been connected to *The Jew of Malta* as well. Apparently following Danter's lead, Thomas Gosson and Joseph Hunt entered the ballad '*the coolinge of curst KATE*' (Arber 2, p. 662) on 16 October 1594, five months after *The Taming of a Shrew* was entered into the Stationers' Register by Peter Short (Arber 2, p. 648).

52 For this perception of crisis, see Ian W. Archer, *The Pursuit of Stability: Social Relations in Elizabethan London* (Cambridge University Press, 1991).

53 Stow estimates that 10775 Londoners died from the plague between December 1592 and December 1593, this of a total population that was somewhere around 200,000 in 1600. See Paul Slack, *The Impact of Plague in Tudor and Stuart England* (New York: Routledge, 1985).

54 Half a decade later in 1600, Millington would also publish the first edition of *The Cronicle History of Henry the Fift* and the second editions of both *The*

First Part of the Contention and *The True Tragedie*. In 1602, Millington transferred his rights to copy *Titus* along with what is described as the '*The first* and *Second parte* of HENRY the VJ' to Thomas Pavier (Arber 3, p. 204).

55 *Vindiciae Contra Tyrannos* was for the first time partially translated into English in the 1588 pamphlet *A Shorte Apologie for Christian Souldiors*. This text was published by Millington's master Carre while Millington was still his apprentice.

56 In, for example, Jean Boucher's *De Justa Henrici Tertii Abdicatione* (1589) and William Reynold's *De Justa Reipublicae Christianae* (1590). See Salmon, *The French Wars* 130–2; and his 'Catholic Resistance Theory, Ultramontanism, and the Catholic Response, 1580–1620', in *The Cambridge History of Political Thought, 1450–1700*, ed. J. H. Burns (Cambridge University Press, 1991), p. 227.

57 This claim that monarchy first emerged through violence was argued by the French Huguenot Jean Bodin. See Cheney, pp. 126–31.

58 As James B. Wood has written in *The King's Army: Warfare, Soldiers, and Society during the Wars of Religion in France* (Cambridge University Press, 1995), '[By 1581], [c]ivil war had become the defining experience for the French people and would remain so until the end of the sixteenth century' (1).

59 For contemporary English interest in the French Wars of Religion as measured by English publications between 1560 and 1598, see J. H. M. Salmon, *The French Civil Wars in English Political Thought* (Oxford: Clarendon Press, 1959), pp. 171–80. Paul Kocher, in 'Contemporary Pamphlet Backgrounds for Marlowe's *The Massacre at Paris*', *Modern Language Quarterly*, 8 (1947), pp. 151–73, has argued that Marlowe himself was very familiar with contemporary discourse having to do with the French Wars of Religion. A number of the ideas of this discourse, like faith need not be kept with heretics and the impermanence of violent governments, can be found in *The Jew of Malta* (Bawcutt, 'Machiavelli', pp. 31–2).

60 This is an allusion to a series of past wars between the Holy Roman Emperor Charles the Fifth and Francis I, the French king (1519–58).

61 For the nature and costs of siege warfare in the French Wars of Religion, see Wood. For an example of contemporary anger at English involvement in these campaigns, see 'The Dutch Church Libel', in *The Jew of Malta*, ed. James R. Siemon (London: A & C Black, 1994), p. 118. For the Elizabethan constructions of the vagrant soldier newly returned from wars in France and the Low Countries, see Linda Woodbridge, *Vagrancy, Homelessness, and English Renaissance Literature* (Urbana: University Illinois Press, 2001).

62 For Barabas's soldier allusions as negative indices of Malta's destructive militarism, see Alan Shepherd, '"Thou art no soldier; thou art a merchant": The *Mentalité* of War in Malta', *Marlowe, History, and Sexuality: New Critical Essays on Christopher Marlowe*, ed. Paul Whitfield White (New York: AMS, 1998), pp. 118–19.

7: New Directions: The Nose Plays: Ovid in
The Jew of Malta

1   In the film, Linus Caldwell (Matt Damon), in his disguise as Lenny
    Pepperidge, adopts an enormous false nose as part of a larger stratagem
    to gull the deserving by their own greed, which is strangely analogous to
    Barabas's own methods. Linus uses the phrase in my foretitle in the form of
    a question to ensure the veracity of the device. For Cheney, see *Marlowe's
    Counterfeit Profession: Ovid, Spenser, Counter-Nationhood* (Toronto:
    University of Toronto Press, 1997), p. 141. To him, Barabas is 'a figure for
    the comedy of Ovidian tragedy', and in his opening soliloquy 'a highly suc-
    cessful Ovidian artist: the English Renaissance playwright-prince' (p. 142).
    For Rowley, see *A Search for Money, Or The Lamentable Complaint for the
    Losse of the Wandring Knight, Monsieur L'Argent* (London: Joseph Hunt,
    1609), p. 12. For Shakespeare, see *A Pleasant Conceited Comedie Called,
    Loues Labors Lost* (London: W.W. for Cuthbert Burby, 1598), sig. E2
    (IV.2.138–41).

2   Act, scene and line numbers from *The Jew of Malta* follow the notation in *The
    Complete Plays*, ed. Mark Thornton Burnett (London: J. M. Dent, 1999). For
    the two other references to Barabas's nose, see II.3.178 and IV.1.24.

3   For the standard work on the subject, see George W. Pigman III, 'Versions of
    Imitation in the Renaissance', *Renaissance Quarterly*, 33 (1980), pp. 1–32; and
    Thomas M. Greene, *The Light in Troy: Imitation and Discovery in Renaissance
    Poetry* (New Haven: Yale University Press, 1982).

4   For the critical tradition that faults the verbal inaccuracies in translation, see
    Roma Gill, 'Snakes Leape by Verse', in *Christopher Marlowe*, ed. Brian Morris
    (New York: Hill and Wang, 1968), pp. 133–50; and 'Marlowe and the Art of
    Translation', in '*A Poet and a Filthy Play-maker': New Essays on Christopher
    Marlowe*, ed. Kenneth Friedenreich, Roma Gill and Constance Kuriyama
    (New York: AMS Press, 1988), pp. 327–42. L. C. Martin's *Marlowe's Poems*
    (London: Methuen, 1931) painstakingly details the errors Marlowe makes.
    Millar MacLure is more generous: 'one who sets himself to translate Latin
    elegiacs into closed English pentameter couplets is not engaged in the diver-
    sion of an idle hour, and Marlowe carries it off with remarkable success'.
    See *The Poems: Christopher Marlowe* (London: Methuen, 1968), p. xxxii. For
    the actions of the Bishops in 1599, see Richard A. McCabe, 'Elizabethan
    Satire and the Bishops' Ban of 1599', *Yearbook of English Studies*, 11 (1981),
    pp. 188–93. For Brown, see *Redefining Elizabethan Literature* (Cambridge:
    Cambridge University Press, 2004), p. 36. Cheney pays great attention to
    the *Elegies* in an early section of *Counterfeit Profession* (pp. 25–68) but makes
    much different use of this text than I do.

5   See 'The Poet's Toys: Christopher Marlowe and the Liberties of Erotic
    Elegy', *Modern Language Review*, 67 (2006), pp. 103–27. I would also extend
    her intriguing argument to the rest of the opus, that the inherent sense in the

Elegies of poetical compositions as 'toyes' demonstrates its author's inheritance of the Ovidian concept of *ioca* (games, play), a subversive habit of mind (p. 124).

6   Gallus (whose works were lost), Propertius and Tibullus were also known, but not as widely disseminated as Ovid was. For the formative effect of the *Amores* on the concept of the sonnet sequence, see M. L. Stapleton, *Harmful Eloquence: Ovid's 'Amores' from Antiquity to Shakespeare* (Ann Arbor: University of Michigan Press, 1996), pp. 91, 116–19.

7   For Scott, see '*The Jew of Malta* and the Development of City Comedy: "The Mean Passage of a History"', in *Christopher Marlowe the Craftsman: Lives, Stage, and Page*, ed. Sarah K. Scott and M. L. Stapleton (Burlington, VT: Ashgate Publishing, 2010), pp. 91–108. For Marlowe's influence on Jonson, see, for example, T. S. Eliot, 'Ben Jonson', in *The Sacred Wood: Essays on Poetry and Criticism* (London: Methuen, 1920), pp. 95–111.

8   In the Epistle to Thomas Hammon that precedes the text of the play, Heywood implies that he wrote them: 'As I ushered it unto the Court, and presented it to the Cockpit, with these prologues and epilogues here inserted' (*Complete Plays*, ed. Burnett, p. 459).

9   For Proteus, see, for example, *Metamorphoses* 8.731, 11.221, 11.255, 13.918. For Heywood's translations of Ovid's erotic works, see *Thomas Heywood's 'Art of Love': The First Complete English Translation of Ovid's 'Ars Amatoria'*, ed. M. L. Stapleton (Ann Arbor: University of Michigan Press, 2000); and M. L. Stapleton, 'A *Remedy* for Heywood?' *Texas Studies in Literature and Language*, 43 (2001), pp. 74–115.

10 For all quotations from this supplementary matter from the play, see *Complete Plays*, ed. Burnett, pp. 459–61.

11 All references to Marlowe's translation are taken from *Christopher Marlowe: The Complete Poems*, ed. Mark Thornton Burnett (London: J. M. Dent, 2000). Numerous passages in the *Tristia* attempt to be self-exculpatory, for example, 'neque me nuptae didicerunt furta magistro, / quodque parum novit, nemo docere potest. / sic ego delicias et mollia carmina feci, / strinxerit ut nomen fabula nulla meum' (II.347–50) [no brides have learned deceptions through my teaching; nobody can teach that of which he knows too little. I have written trifles and tender verses but in such fashion that no scandal has ever touched my name]. Text and translation: *Tristia [and] Ex Ponto*, trans. Arthur Leslie Wheeler (Cambridge: Harvard University Press, 1924, rpt. 1985), pp. 80–1.

12 Respectively: Ellis-Fermor, *Christopher Marlowe* (London: Methuen, 1927), pp. 89–102; Eliot, 'Notes on the Blank Verse of Christopher Marlowe', in *The Sacred Wood*, pp. 86–94; Bradbrook, *Themes and Conventions of Elizabethan Tragedy* (Cambridge: Cambridge University Press, 1935), pp. 155–9; Kocher, *Christopher Marlowe: A Study of His Thought, Learning, and Character* (Chapel Hill: University of North Carolina Press, 1946), pp. 285–9. See also M. M. Mahood, *Poetry and Humanism* (London: Jonathan Cape, 1950), pp. 74–81;

and Nan C. Carpenter, 'Infinite Riches: A Note on Marlovian Unity', *Notes and Queries*, 194 (1951), pp. 50–2.

13 Babb claims that the play 'explores a single set of issues: religious hypocrisy and governmental expedience as they are informed by a pervasive lust for wealth'. See 'Policy in Marlowe's *The Jew of Malta*', *English Literary History*, 24 (1957), pp. 85–94 (p. 86). Respectively: Bawcutt, 'Machiavelli and Marlowe's *The Jew of Malta*', *Renaissance Drama*, new ser., 3 (1970), pp. 3–49; Bevington, *From Mankind to Marlowe: Growth of Structure in the Popular Drama of the Tudor Period* (Cambridge: Harvard University Press, 1962), pp. 222–3; Minshull, 'Marlowe's "Sound Machevill"', *Renaissance Drama* new ser., 13 (1982), pp. 35–53 (p. 53); Hamlin, 'Misbelief, False Profession, and *The Jew of Malta*', in *Placing the Plays of Christopher Marlowe: Fresh Cultural Contexts*, ed. Sara M. Deats and Robert A. Logan (Burlington, VT: Ashgate Publishing, 2008), pp. 125–34; McAdam, 'Carnal Identity in *The Jew of Malta*', *English Literary Renaissance*, 26 (1996), pp. 46–74; Shapiro, *Shakespeare and the Jews* (New York: Columbia University Press, 1996), p. 184. On the metatheatrics of the play, see Sara M. Deats and Lisa S. Starks, '"So neatly plotted, and so well perform'd": Villain as Playwright in Marlowe's *The Jew of Malta*', *Theatre Journal*, 44 (1992), pp. 375–89; Thomas Cartelli, 'Endless Play: The False Starts of Marlowe's *The Jew of Malta*', in *'A Poet and a Filthy Play-maker'*, ed. Friedenreich et al., pp. 117–28.

14 Another connection between *Elegies* II.4 and the play: one of Barabas's devices, when he approaches Ithamore and Bellamira to find out if they mean to betray him, '*Enter Barabas with a lute, disguised*' (*The Jew of Malta*, IV.4.34), may have taken its genesis from one of the lover's examples of women who arouse him: 'Or if one touch the lute with arte and cunning / Who would not love those hands for their swift running?' (*Elegies* II.4.27–8). Marlowe's protagonist touches the instrument with enough art and cunning to deceive his enemies. The lover disguises his love for the female lutanist, which is certainly feigned.

15 Levin thinks one should accept the play 'as an artistic whole, noting its ambiguities and tensions', and relates Barabas to other overreachers in Marlowe, similarly undone by their own schemes. See *The Overreacher: A Study of Christopher Marlowe* (Cambridge: Harvard University Press, 1952), p. 75.

16 See *Prufrock and Other Observations* (London: Complete Press, 1917), p. 17.

17 Virtually all the asides in the first printing of the play, the first quarto of 1633, are in the margins, in accordance with seventeenth-century printing house practice. For more analysis of these, see Scott, '*The Jew of Malta* and the Development of City Comedy', p. 100.

18 The conventional Latin motto for the halcyon (kingfisher) was 'Ex pace ubertas' [prosperity is the result of peace]. Andrea Alciati (also Alciato) provides the standard emblem in *Livret des Emblemes* (Paris: Chrestien Wechel, 1536), sig. C8ᵛ.

19   The original source of this information is Lane Cooper, review of *The Villain as Hero in Elizabethan Tragedy*, by Clarence Valentine Boyer, *Journal of English and Germanic Philology*, 15 (1916), pp. 443–51 (p. 451, n. 10). See also Morris P. Tilley, 'Proverbs and Proverbial Allusions in Marlowe', *Modern Language Notes*, 50 (1935), pp. 347–55 (p. 351). Both cite the same two passages from Jonson, *Cynthia's Revels* (IV.7.29): 'as everyone is nearest to himself'; and *Sejanus* (IV.2.9–10): 'the thoughts borne nearest / Unto ourselves, move swiftest still, and dearest'. Tilley later identifies the locus classicus in Terence, *Andria* (635) 4.1.11: 'heu, proximus sum egomet mihi' [alas, I am nearest to myself indeed]. See *A Dictionary of the Proverbs in England in the Sixteenth and Seventeenth Centuries* (Ann Arbor: University of Michigan Press, 1950), entry N57.

20   *A Choice of Emblemes and Other Devises* (Leiden: Christopher Plantyn, 1586). Whitney's emblem of the fox on ice, one who outsmarts himself, might be most apposite: 'Nullus dolus contra casum' [no craft against chance]; 'this foxe, on Ice: / Doth shewe, no subtill crafte will serue, / When Chaunce doth throwe the dice' (22). *2 Tamburlaine* has often been dated from the Philip Gawdy letter of 16 November 1587, about a terrible gun accident in what seems to have been a performance of that play. See E. K. Chambers, *The Elizabethan Stage*, 4 vols (Oxford: Oxford University Press, 1923), II:135.

21   'To do a great right, do a little wrong' (*The Merchant of Venice* IV.1.215).

22   See Charles Crawford, *The Marlowe Concordance*, 3 vols (Louvain: Uystpruyst, 1911–13), I: 70. Text and translation, *Metamorphoses*, trans. Frank Justus Miller, 2 vols (Cambridge: Harvard University Press, 1916), II, pp. 82–3.

23   *Redefining Elizabethan Literature*, 36.

8: A Survey of Resources

1   See *An Account of the English Dramatick Poets* (Oxford: Printed by L. L. for George West and Henry Clements, 1691), p. 343: 'This Play was in much esteem, in those days the Jew's Part being play'd by Mr. *Edward Allen*, that Ornament both to *Black-friars* Stage, and to his Profession'.

WORKS CITED AND SELECTED FURTHER READING

Adelman, Janet, *Blood Relations: Christian and Jew in* The Merchant of Venice (Chicago, IL: University of Chicago Press, 2008).

Albright, Evelyn May, *Dramatic Publication in England, 1580–1640: A Study of Conditions of Conditions Affecting Content and Form of Drama* (New York: Heath, 1927).

Alciati, Andrea, *Livret des Emblemes* (Paris: Chrestien Wechel, 1536).

Allen, Lea Knudsen, '"Not Every Man Has the Luck to Go to Corinth": Accruing Exotic Capital in *The Jew of Malta* and *Volpone*', in *Global Traffic: Discourses and Practices of Trade in English Literature and Culture from 1550 to 1700* (Basingstoke: Palgrave, 2008), pp. 95–114.

Altman, Joel B., *The Tudor Play of Mind: Rhetorical Inquiry and the Development of Elizabethan Drama* (Berkeley, CA: University of California Press, 1978).

Alymer, John, *An Harborovve For Faithfvll and Trevve Svbiectes, agaynst the late blowne Blaste, concerninge the Gouernment of VVemen. wherin be confuted all such reasons as a straunger of late made in that behalf, with a breife exhortation to Obedience* (1559).

Anonymous, *A Larum for London*. Malone Society Reprints (New York: AMS Press, 1985).

—, *The Tragical Reign of Selimus*. Malone Society Reprints (1908).

Arber, Edward, ed., *A Transcript of the Registers of the Company of Stationers of London 1554–1640*, 5 vols (London: privately printed, 1875–94).

Archer, Ian W., *The Pursuit of Stability: Social Relations in Elizabethan London* (Cambridge Eng.: Cambridge University Press, 1991).

Babb, Lawrence, 'Policy in Marlowe's *The Jew of Malta*', *English Literary History*, 24 (1957), pp. 85–94.

Baines, B. J., 'Sexual Polarity in the Plays of Christopher Marlowe', *Ball State University Forum*, 23.3 (1982), pp. 3–17.

Bakeless, John E., *The Tragicall History of Christopher Marlowe*, 2 vols (Cambridge, MA: Harvard University Press, 1942; Hamden, CT: Archon Books, 1964).

Barroll, Leeds, 'Mythologizing the Ottoman: *The Jew of Malta* and *The Battle of Alcazar*', in *Remapping the Mediterranean World in Early Modern English Writings*, ed. G. V. Stanivukovic (Basingstoke: Palgrave, 2007), pp. 117–30.

Bartels, Emily C., 'Malta, the Jew, and the Fictions of Difference: Colonialist Discourse in Marlowe's *The Jew of Malta*', *English Literary Renaissance*, 20 (1990), pp. 1–16.

—, *Spectacles of Strangeness: Imperialism, Alienation, and Marlowe* (Philadelphia, PA: University of Pennsylvania Press, 1993).

—, ed., *Critical Essays on Christopher Marlowe* (New York, NY: G. K. Hall, 1996).

Bawcutt, N. W., 'Machiavelli and Marlowe's *The Jew of Malta*', *Renaissance Drama*, n.s. 3 (1970), pp. 3–49.

—, ed., *The Jew of Malta* (Manchester, Eng.: Manchester University Press, 1978).

Beecher, D., '*The Jew of Malta* and the Ritual of the Inverted Moral Order', *Cahiers Elisabéthains*, no. 12 (1977), pp. 45–58.

Bel-vedére or The Garden of the Muses (London, 1600).

Bennett, H. S., 'Introduction', in *The Jew of Malta and The Massacre at Paris*, ed. H. S. Bennett (New York: Gordian Press, 1966), pp. 1–19.

Berek, Peter, 'The Jew as Renaissance Man', *Renaissance Quarterly*, 51 (1998), pp. 128–62.

—, '*Tamburlaine*'s Weak Sons: Imitation as Interpretation before 1593', *Renaissance Drama*, n.s. 13 (1982), pp. 55–82.

Berger, Harry, 'Marriage and Mercifixion in *The Merchant of Venice*: The Casket Scene Revisited', in *Making Trifles of Terrors*, ed. Peter Erickson (Stanford: Stanford University Press, 1997), pp. 1–9.

Bertram, Benjamin, *The Time is out of Joint: Skepticism in Shakespeare's England* (Newark: University of Delaware Press, 2004).

Beskins, Anna, 'From Jew to Nun: Abigail in Marlowe's *The Jew of Malta*', *Explicator*, 65.3 (2007), pp. 133–6.

Bevington, David, gen. ed., *English Renaissance Drama* (New York, NY: W. W. Norton & Company, 2002).

—, *From Mankind to Marlowe: Growth of Structure in the Popular Drama of Tudor England* (Cambridge, MA: Harvard University Press, 1962).

—, 'The Performance History', in *Doctor Faustus: A Critical Guide*, ed. Sara Munson Deats (London and New York: Continuum, 2010), pp. 41–71.

Biberman, Matthew, *Masculinity, Anti-Semitism and Early Modern English Literature* (Aldershot: Ashgate, 2004).

Blayney, Peter W. M., 'The Publication of Playbooks', in *A New History of Early English Drama*, ed. John D. Cox and David Scott Kastan (New York: Columbia University Press, 1997), pp. 394–405.

Blissett, William, 'Lucan's Caesar and the Elizabethan Villain', *Studies in Philology*, 53 (1956), pp. 553–75.

Boas, F. S., *Christopher Marlowe: A Biographical and Critical Study* (1940; Oxford: Clarendon Press, 1960).

Boehrer, Bruce, 'Disorder in the House of God: Disrupted Worship in Shakespeare and Others', *Comparative Drama*, 38.1 (2004), pp. 83–103.

Borot, Luc, 'Machiavellian Diplomacy and Dramatic Developments in Marlowe's *Jew of Malta*', *Cahiers Elisabéthains*, 33 (1988), pp. 1–11.

Bovilsky, Lara, *Barbarous Play: Race on the English Renaissance Stage* (Minneapolis, MN: University of Minnesota Press, 2008).

Bowers, Fredson, *Complete Works of Christopher Marlowe*, vol. 1 (Cambridge, Eng.: Cambridge University Press, 1981).

—, *Elizabethan Revenge Tragedy* (Princeton: Princeton University Press, 1940).

Bowers, Rick, 'Wresting with Comic Villainy: Barabas and Other "Heels" in *The Jew of Malta*', in *Radical Comedy in Early Modern England: Contexts, Cultures, Performances* (Aldershot: Ashgate, 2008), pp. 23–35.

Bradbrook, Muriel Claire, *Themes and Conventions of Elizabethan Tragedy* (Cambridge: Cambridge University Press, 1935).

Brandt, Bruce E., *Christopher Marlowe and the Metaphysical Problem Play* (Salzburg: Universität Salzburg, Institut für Anglistik und Amerikanistik, 1985).

—, *Christopher Marlowe in the Eighties: An Annotated Bibliography of Marlowe Criticism from 1978 through 1989* (West Cornwall, CT: Locust Hill Press, 1992).

—, 'The Critical Backstory', in *Doctor Faustus: A Critical Guide*, ed. Sara Munson Deats (London and New York: Continuum, 2010), pp. 17–40.

—, 'Marlowe Bibliography, 2000–2009', in *Marlowe Studies: An Annual*, vol. I, ed. Sarah K. Scott and M. L. Stapleton (Fort Wayne, IN: Indiana University-Purdue University, 2011).

Brennan, Michael G., 'Christopher Marlowe's *The Jew of Malta* and Two Newsletter Accounts of the Siege of Malta', *Notes and Queries*, 40 (1993), pp. 157–60.

Brenz, Johannes, trans. John Stockwood, *A right godly and learned discourse vpon the book of Ester Most necessary for this time and age, to enstruct all noble men, and such as God hath aduanced vnto high places about princes* (1584).

Brooke, C. F. Tucker, ed., *The Works of Christopher Marlowe* (Oxford: Clarendon Press, 1910).

Brown, Eric C., 'Violence, Ritual and the Execution of Time in Marlowe's *The Jew of Malta*', *Cahiers Elisabethains: Late Medieval and Renaissance Studies*, 58 (2000), pp. 15–29.

Brown, Georgia, *Redefining Elizabethan Literature* (Cambridge: Cambridge University Press, 2004).

Brown, John Russell, ed., *Marlowe: 'Tamburlaine the Great,' 'Edward II,' and 'The Jew of Malta': A Casebook* (London, Eng.: Macmillan, 1982).

Burnett, Mark Thornton, ed., *Christopher Marlowe: The Complete Plays* (London: J. M. Dent, 1999).

Carpenter, Nan C., 'Infinite Riches: A Note on Marlovian Unity', *Notes and Queries*, 194 (1951), pp. 50–2.

Carroll, William C., ed., *Macbeth: Texts and Contexts* (New York: St. Martin's, 1999).

Carson, Neil, *A Companion to Henslowe's Diary* (Cambridge: Cambridge University Press, 1988).

Cartelli, Thomas, 'Endless Play: The False Starts of Marlowe's *The Jew of Malta*', in *'A Poet and a Filthy Play-maker': New Essays on Christopher Marlowe*, ed. Kenneth Friedenreich, Roma Gill and Constance B. Kuriyama (New York: AMS Press, 1988), pp. 117–28.

—, *Marlowe, Shakespeare, and the Economy of Theatrical Experience* (Philadelphia: University of Pennsylvania Press, 1991).

—, 'Shakespeare's *Merchant*, Marlowe's *Jew*: The Problem of Cultural Difference', *Shakespeare Studies*, 20 (1988), pp. 255–60.

Cerasano, S. P., 'Edward Alleyn's Early Years: His Life and Family', *Notes and Queries*, 232.2 (1987), pp. 237–43.

—, 'Edward Alleyn, the New Model Actor, and the Rise of the Celebrity in the 1590s', *Medieval and Renaissance Drama in England*, 18 (2005), pp. 47–58.

Chambers, E. K., *The Elizabethan Stage*, 4 vols (Oxford: Oxford University Press, 1923).

Chapman, George, *The Blind Beggar of Alexandria*. Malone Society Reprints (1928).

Charney, Maurice, 'Jessica's Turquoise Ring and Abigail's Poisoned Porridge: Shakespeare and Marlowe as Rivals and Imitators', *Renaissance Drama*, 10 (1979), pp. 33–44.

Cheney, Patrick, *Marlowe's Counterfeit Profession: Ovid, Spenser, Counter-Nationhood* (Toronto, Canada: University of Toronto Press, 1997).

—, *Marlowe's Republican Authorship: Lucan, Liberty, and the Sublime* (Basingstoke: Palgrave, 2009).

—, ed., *The Cambridge Companion to Christopher Marlowe* (Cambridge, Eng.: Cambridge University Press, 2004).

Chew, Samuel, *The Crescent and the Rose* (Oxford: Oxford University Press, 1937).

Cohen, Walter, '*The Merchant of Venice* and the Possibilities of Historical Criticism', *English Literary History*, 49 (1982), pp. 765–89.

Cole, Douglas, *Christopher Marlowe and the Renaissance of Tragedy* (Westport, CT: Greenwood Press, 1995).

—, 'Incarnations of Evil: Barabas the Jew and the Duke of Guise', in *Suffering and Evil in the Plays of Christopher Marlowe* (Princeton: Princeton University Press, 1962), pp. 123–58.

Cooper, Lane, 'Review of *The Villain as Hero in Elizabethan Tragedy*, by Clarence Valentine Boyer', *Journal of English and Germanic Philology*, 15 (1916), pp. 443–51.

Cooperman, Bernard Dov, 'Venetian Policy Towards Levantine Jews in Its Broader Italian Context', *Gli Ebrei e Venezia* (Milano: Edizioni di Comunita, 1987).

Craik, R., 'The Lion in "Burbank" and Charles Lamb', *Yeats Eliot Review: A Journal of Criticism and Scholarship*, 16.4 (2000), pp. 31–2.

Crawford, Charles, 'Belvedere, or, The Garden of the Muses', *Englische Studien*, 43 (1910–11), 198–228.

—, *The Marlowe Concordance*, 3 vols (Louvain: Uystpruyst, 1911–13).

Cunningham, Karen, 'Renaissance Execution and Marlovian Elocution: The Drama of Death', *PMLA*, 105 (1990), pp. 209–22.

D'Andrea, Antonio, 'Studies in Machiavelli and His Reputation in the Sixteenth Century, I: Marlowe's Prologue to *The Jew of Malta*', *Medieval and Renaissance Studies*, 5 (1961), pp. 214–48.

Dabbs, Thomas, *Reforming Marlowe: The Nineteenth-Century Canonization of a Renaissance Dramatist* (Lewisburg: Bucknell University Press, 1991).

Deats, Sara Munson, 'Biblical Parody in Marlowe's *The Jew of Malta*: A Re-Examination', *Christianity and Literature*, 37.2 (1988), pp. 27–48.

—, ed. *Doctor Faustus: A Critical Guide* (London and New York: Continuum, 2010).

Deats, Sara Munson and Robert A. Logan, eds, *Marlowe's Empery: Expanding His Critical Contexts* (Newark, DE: University of Delaware Press, 2002).

—, eds, *Placing the Plays of Christopher Marlowe: Fresh Cultural Contexts* (Aldershot: Ashgate, 2008).

—, Sex, *Gender, and Desire in the Plays of Christopher Marlowe* (Newark, DE: University of Delaware Press, 1997).

Deats, Sara Munson and Lisa S. Starks, '"So Neatly Plotted, and So Well Perform'd": Villain as Playwright in Marlowe's *The Jew of Malta*', *Theatre Journal*, 44 (1992), pp. 375–89.

The decree of the court of Parliament against Iohn Chastel (London, 1595).

Dekker, Thomas, *The Dramatic Works of Thomas Dekker*, ed. Fredson Bowers, 4 vols (Cambridge: Cambridge University Press, 1953).

Dessen, Alan C., 'The Elizabethan Stage Jew and Christian Example: Gerontus, Barabas, and Shylock', *Modern Language Quarterly*, 35 (1974), pp. 231–45.

Donaldson, Peter S., 'Conflict and Coherence: Narcissism and Tragic Structure in Marlowe', in *Narcissism and the Text: Studies in Literature and the Psychology of Self*, ed. Lynne Layton and Barabara Ann Schapiro (New York: New York University Press, 1986), pp. 36–63.

Douglas, Audrey and Peter Greenfield, eds, *Cumberland, Westmorland, Gloucestershire* (Toronto: University of Toronto Press, 1986).

Downie, J. A., 'Reviewing What We Think We Know about Christopher Marlowe, Again', in *Christopher Marlowe the Craftsman: Lives, Stage, and Page*, ed. Sarah K. Scott and M. L. Stapleton (Aldershot: Ashgate, 2010), pp. 33–46.

Downie, J. A. and J. T. Parnell, eds, *Constructing Christopher Marlowe* (Cambridge, Eng.: Cambridge University Press, 2000).

Draya, Ren, 'Silenced Women: Abigail in Marlowe's *The Jew of Malta*', *Publications of the Missouri Philological Association*, 24 (1999), pp. 11–19.

Eliot, T. S. 'Christopher Marlowe', *Selected Essays* (New York, NY: Harcourt, Brace, 1932), pp. 118–25.

—, *Prufrock and Other Observations* (London: Complete Press, 1917).

—, *The Sacred Wood: Essays on Poetry and Criticism* (London: Methuen, 1920).

Elliott, John and Alan H. Nelson (University); Alexandra Johnston and Diana Wyatt (City), eds, *Oxford*, 2 vols (Toronto: University of Toronto Press, 2004).

Ellis-Fermor, Una, *Christopher Marlowe* (London: Methuen, 1927).

Engle, Lars, 'Oedipal Marlowe, Mimetic Middleton', *Modern Philology*, 105 (2008), pp. 417–36.

Eriksen, Roy, 'Insula est Melita: Marlowe's Urban Comedy and the Poetics of Predation', in *Urban Preoccupations: Mental and Material Landscapes* (Pisa: Fabrizio Serra, 2007), pp. 123–42.

Erne, Lukas, *Beyond 'The Spanish Tragedy': A Study of the Works of Thomas Kyd* (Manchester: Manchester University Press, 2001).

—, *Shakespeare as Literary Dramatist* (Cambridge: Cambridge University Press, 2003).

Evans, G. B., gen. ed., *The Riverside Shakespeare*, 2nd edn (Boston and New York: Houghton Mifflin, 1997).

Faini, P., 'Abigail, Jessica e il "tradimento" del padre', in *Le Forme Del Teatro: VII, La posa eroica di Ofelia, Saggi sul personaggio femminile nel teatro elisabettiano* (Rome: Storia e Letteratura, 2003), pp. 79–91.

Farmer, Alan and Zachary Lesser, 'The Popularity of Playbooks Revisited', *Shakespeare Quarterly*, 56 (2005), 1–32.

Farmer, John S., ed., *A New Interlude . . . of Godly Queen Hester*, in *Six Anonymous Plays*, 2nd series (Early English Drama Society, 1906).

Ferguson, D., '"Neither a Borrower nor a Lender Be": Polonius's Borrowings from Marlowe's Barabas', *Conference of College Teachers of English Studies*, 65 (2000), pp. 55–60.

Fitzpatrick, Joan, 'Early Modern Dietaries and the Jews: *The Merchant of Venice* and *The Jew of Malta*', in *Shakespeare's World / World Shakespeares: The Selected Proceedings of the International Shakespeare Association World Congress Brisbane, 2006*, ed. Richard Fotheringham, Christa Jansohn and R. S. White (Newark, DE: University of Delaware Press, 2008), pp. 98–107.

Flosdorf, J. W., 'The *Odi et Amo* Theme in *The Jew of Malta*', *Notes and Queries*, 7 (1960), pp. 10–14.

Foakes, R. A., ed., *Henslowe's Diary*, 2nd edn (Cambridge: Cambridge University Press, 2002).

Freeman, Arthur, 'Marlowe, Kyd, and the Dutch Church Libel', *English Literary Renaissance*, 3 (1973), pp. 44–52.

Freller, T., 'Malta im englischen Drama der Shakespeare-Epoche: Handels-und Reiseverkehr als Ursachen literarischer Phänomene-diskutiert am Beispiel von Christopher Marlowes *The Jew of Malta*', *Anglia: Zeitschrift für Englische Philologie*, 122.3 (2004), pp. 404–34 (English summary).

Friedenreich, Kenneth, *Christopher Marlowe: An Annotated Bibliography of Criticism since 1950* (Metuchan, NJ: The Scarecrow Press, 1979), pp. 1–17.

—, '*The Jew of Malta* and the Critics: A Paradigm for Marlowe Studies', *Papers on Language and Literature*, 13 (1977), pp. 318–35.

Friedenreich, Kenneth, Gill, Roma and Kuriyama, Constance B., eds, *'A Poet & a Filthy Play-maker': New Essays on Christopher Marlowe* (New York: AMS Press, 1988).

Friedman, Alan W., 'The Shackling of Accidents in Marlowe's *The Jew of Malta*', *Texas Studies in Literature and Language*, 8 (1966), pp. 155–67.

Garnet, George, ed. and trans., *Vindiciae, Contra Tyrannos: or, Concerning the Legitimate Power of a Prince Over the People, and of the People Over a Prince* (Cambridge, Eng.: Cambridge University Press, 1994).

Gibson, James M., ed., *Kent*, 2 vols (Toronto: University of Toronto Press, 2002).

Gill, Roma, 'Marlowe and the Art of Translation', in *'A Poet and a Filthy Play-maker': New Essays on Christopher Marlowe*, ed. Kenneth Friedenreich, Roma Gill and Constance Kuriyama (New York: AMS Press, 1988), pp. 327–42.

—, 'Snakes Leape by Verse', in *Christopher Marlowe*, ed. Brian Morris (New York: Hill and Wang, 1968), pp. 133–50.

—, ed., *The Complete Works of Christopher Marlowe, Vol. 4: The Jew of Malta* (Oxford: Oxford University Press, 1995).

Godshalk, W. L., *The Marlovian World Picture* (The Hague: Mouton, 1974).

Goldberg, Dena, 'Sacrifice in Marlowe's *The Jew of Malta*', *Studies in English Literature 1500–1900,* 32 (1992), pp. 233–45.

Grantley, Darryll and Peter Roberts, eds, *Christopher Marlowe and English Renaissance Culture* (Aldershot, Eng.: Scolar Press, 1996).

—, '"What means this shew?"': Theatricalism, Camp and Subversion in *Doctor Faustus* and *The Jew of Malta*', in *Christopher Marlowe and English Renaissance Culture*, ed. Darryll Grantley and Peter Roberts (1996; Aldershot: Ashgate, 1999), pp. 224–38.

Greenblatt, Stephen, *Learning to Curse: Essays in Early Modern Culture* (New York, NY: Routledge, 1990).

—, *Renaissance Self-Fashioning: More to Shakespeare* (Chicago, IL: Chicago University Press, 1980).

—, *Will in the World: How Shakespeare Became Shakespeare* (New York: Norton, 2004).

Greene, Robert, *Perimedes the Blacke-Smith* (1588).

—, *The Plays & Poems of Robert Greene*, ed. J. Churton Collins, 2 vols (Oxford: Clarendon Press, 1905).

Greene, Thomas M., *The Light in Troy: Imitation and Discovery in Renaissance Poetry* (New Haven: Yale University Press, 1982).

Greenfield, Peter, 'Touring', in *The Oxford Handbook of Early Modern Theatre*, ed. Richard Dutton (Oxford: Oxford University Press, 2009), pp. 292–306.

Greg, W. W., *A Bibliography of the English Printed Drama to the Restoration*, 4 vols (London Bibliographical Society, 1970).

—, ed., *Henslowe Papers* (London: A. H. Bullen, 1907).

—, ed., *Henslowe's Diary*, 2 vols (London: A. H. Bullen, 1904–8).

Gurr, Andrew, 'The Great Divide of 1594' in *Words That Count: Essays on Early Modern Authorship in Honor of MacDonald P. Jackson*, ed. Brian Boyd (Newark: University of Delaware Press, 2004), pp. 29–50.

—, *The Shakespeare Company, 1594–1642* (Cambridge: Cambridge University Press, 2004).

—, *Shakepeare's Opposites: The Admiral's Company 1594–1625* (Cambridge: Cambridge University Press, 2009).

—, *The Shakespearian Playing Companies* (Oxford: Clarendon Press, 1996).

—, 'Three Reluctant Patrons and Early Shakespeare', *Shakespeare Quarterly*, 44 (1993), pp. 159–82.

Hadfield, Andrew, *Shakespeare and Republicanism* (Cambridge: Cambridge University Press, 2005).

Hailey, Carter, 'The Publication Date of Marlowe's *Massacre at Paris*, with a Note on the Collier Leaf', *Marlowe Studies*, 1 (2011), pp. 25–40.

Hakim, Rima, *Marlowe on the English Stage 1588–1988: A History of Three Marlowe Plays,* Doctor Faustus, Edward II, *and* The Jew of Malta (Dissertation: University of Leeds, 1990), pp. 105–15, 204–43.

Hamlin, William, 'Misbelief, False Profession, and *The Jew of Malta*', in *Placing the Plays of Christopher Marlowe: Fresh Cultural Contexts*, ed. Sara M. Deats and Robert A. Logan (Burlington, VT: Ashgate Publishing, 2008), pp. 125–34.

Hanusa, Ruth L., 'Killing the Daughter: Judges' Jephthah and *The Jew of Malta*'s Barabas', *Notes and Queries*, 46 (1999), pp. 199–200.

Harbage, Alfred, 'Innocent Barabas', *Tulane Drama Review*, 8 (1964), pp. 47–58.

Harmer, James, 'Toying with Religion in the Prologue to *The Jew of Malta*', *Notes and Queries*, 57.3 (2010), pp. 352–5.

Harraway, Clare, *Re-Citing Marlowe: Approaches to the Drama* (Aldershot: Ashgate, 2000).

Harrison, Thomas P., 'Further Background for *The Jew of Malta* and *The Massacre at Paris*', *Philological Quarterly*, 27 (1948), pp. 52–6.

Healey, Thomas, *Christopher Marlowe* (Plymouth, Eng.: Northcote House in Association with the British Council, 1994).

Heffernan, Carol F., '*The Jew of Malta*: Barabas's "Fine Madness"', *Dutch Quarterly Review of Anglo-American Letters*, 8 (1978), pp. 94–107.

Henry IV, *The Copie of a Letter Sent by the French King to the People of Artoys and Henault* (London, 1595).

Henslowe-Alleyn Digitization Project, dir. Grace Ioppolo (www.henslowe-alleyn.org. uk/index.html)

Henslowe, Philip, *Henslowe's Diary*, 2nd edn, ed. R. A. Foakes (Cambridge: Cambridge University Press, 2002).

Hirsch, Brett D., 'Counterfeit Professions: Jewish Daughters and the Drama of Failed Conversion in Marlowe's *The Jew of Malta* and Shakespeare's *The Merchant of Venice*', *Early Modern Literary Studies*, Special Issue 19 (2009), [n.p.].

Hiscock, Andrew, *The Uses of This World: Thinking Space in Shakespeare, Marlowe, Cary and Jonson* (Cardiff: University of Wales Press, 2004).

Hodge, Bob, 'Marlowe, Marx, and Machiavelli; Reading into the Past', in *Literature, Language, and Society in England, 1580–1680*, ed. David Aers, Bob Hodge and Gunther Kress (Totowa, NJ: Barnes and Noble, 1981), pp. 1–22.

Holmer, Joan Ozark, 'Jewish Daughters: The Question of Philo-Semitism in Elizabethan Drama', in *The Merchant of Venice: New Critical Essays*, ed. John W. Mahon and Ellen Macleod Mahon (London: Routledge, 2002) pp. 107–43.

Hopkins, Lisa, 'Christopher Marlowe and the Succession to the English Crown', *Yearbook of English Studies*, 38.1–2 (2008), pp. 183–98.

—, *A Christopher Marlowe Chronology* (Basingstoke: Palgrave, 2005).

—, *Christopher Marlowe: A Literary Life* (Basingstoke: Palgrave, 2000).

—, '"In a Little Room": Marlowe and *The Allegory of the Tudor Succession*', *Notes and Queries*, 53.4 (2006), pp. 442–4.

—, '"Malta of Gold": Marlowe, *The Jew of Malta*, and the Siege of 1565' *(Re) Soundings*, 1.2 (1997); reprinted http://shura.shu.ac.uk/1294/ <http://shura. shu.ac.uk/1294/> [no pagination].

Hotine, Margaret, 'The Politics of Anti-Semitism: *The Jew of Malta* and *The Merchant of Venice*', *Notes and Queries*, 38.1 (1991), pp. 35–8.

Humphreys, Arthur, '*The Jew of Malta* and *The Merchant of Venice*: Two Readings of Life', *Huntington Library Quarterly*, 50 (1987), pp. 279–93.

Hunter, G. K., 'The Theology of Marlowe's *The Jew of Malta*', *Journal of the Warburg and Courtauld Institutes*, 17 (1964), pp. 211–40.

Hutchings, Mark, 'In Thrace; Brought up in Arabia: *The Jew of Malta* II.iii.131', *Notes and Queries*, 47 (2000), pp. 428–30.

Hyman, Lawrence, 'The Rival Lovers in *The Merchant of Venice*', *Shakespeare Quarterly*, 21 (1970), pp. 109–16.

Ide, Arata, '*The Jew of Malta* and the Diabolic Power of Theatrics in the 1580s', *Studies in English Literature 1500–1900*, 46.2 (2006), pp. 257–79.

Ingram, R. W., ed., *Coventry* (Toronto: University of Toronto Press, 1981).

Ingram, William, *The Business of Playing: The Beginnings of the Adult Professional Theater in Elizabethan London* (Ithaca, NY: Cornell University Press, 1992).

—, *A London Life in the Brazen Age: Francis Langley, 1548–1602* (Cambridge, MA: Harvard University Press, 1978).

James, Heather, 'The Poet's Toys: Christopher Marlowe and the Liberties of Erotic Elegy', *Modern Language Review*, 67 (2006), pp. 103–27.

Johnson, Gerald D., 'Nicholas Ling, Publisher 1580–1607', *Studies in Bibliography*, 38 (1985), 203–14.

Johnson, Richard, *The Golden Garland of Princely Pleasures and Delicate Delights* (London, 1620).

Jones, Robert C., *Engagement with Knavery: Point of View in 'Richard II', 'The Jew of Malta', 'Volpone', and 'The Revenger's Tragedy'* (Durham: Duke University Press, 1986).

Jonson, Ben, *Poetaster*, ed. Tom Cain (Manchester: Manchester University Press, 1995).

Kang, S-J., 'Christopher Marlowe and the Politics of Transgression', *Journal of English Language and Literature / Yongo Yongmunhak*, 48.3 (2002), pp. 639–4 (In Korean; English summary).

Kathman, David, 'Inn-yard Playhouses', in *The Oxford Handbook of Early Modern Theatre*, ed. Richard Dutton (Oxford: Oxford University Press, 2009), pp. 153–67.

Kellner, Leon, 'Die Quelle von Marlowe's *Jew of Malta*', *Englische Studien*, 10 (1987), pp. 80–111.

Kendall, Roy, *Christopher Marlowe and Richard Baines: Journeys through the Elizabethan Underground* (Madison, NJ: Fairleigh Dickinson University Press; Cranbury, NJ: Associated University Presses, 2003).

Kermode, Lloyd Edward, '"Marlowe's Second City": The Jew as Critic at the Rose in 1592', *Studies in English Literature 1500–1900*, 35.2 (1995), pp. 215–29.

—, ed., *Three Renaissance Usury Plays* (Manchester: Manchester University Press, 2009).

Kirschbaum, Leo, *Shakespeare and the Stationers* (Columbus, OH: Ohio State University Press, 1955).

—, 'Some Light on *The Jew of Malta*', *Modern Language Quarterly*, 7 (1946), pp. 53–6.

—, ed., *The Plays of Christopher Marlowe* (Cleveland: World Publishing, 1962).

Kitch, Aaron, 'Shylock's Sacred Nation', *Shakespeare Quarterly*, 59 (2008), pp. 131–55.

Knutson, Roslyn L., *Playing Companies and Commerce in Shakespeare's Time* (Cambridge, Eng.: Cambridge University Press, 2001).

—, 'Toe to Toe Across Maid Lane: Repertorial Competition at the Rose and Globe, 1599–1600', in *Acts of Criticism: Performance Matters in Shakespeare and His Contemporaries*, ed. June Schlueter and Paul Nelsen (Madison and Teaneck: Fairleigh Dickinson University Press, 2005), pp. 21–37.

—, 'What's So Special about 1594?', *Shakespeare Quarterly*, 61 (2010), pp. 449–67.

Kocher, Paul H., *Christopher Marlowe: A Study of His Thought, Learning, and Character* (Chapel Hill: University of North Carolina Press, 1946).

—, 'Contemporary Pamphlet Backgrounds for Marlowe's *The Massacre at Paris*', *Modern Language Quarterly*, 8 (1947), pp. 151–73.

—, 'English Legal History in Marlowe's *Jew of Malta*', *Huntington Library Quarterly*, 26 (1963), pp. 155–63.

Kozuka, T. and Mulryne, J. R., eds, *Shakespeare, Marlowe, Jonson: New Direction in Biography* (Aldershot: Ashgate, 2006).

Kuriyama, Constance Brown, *Christopher Marlowe: A Renaissance Life* (Ithaca, NY: Cornell University Press, 2002).

—, *Hammer or Anvil: Psychological Patterns in Christopher Marlowe's Plays* (New Brunswick: Rutgers University Press, 1980).

Kyd, Thomas, *The Works of Thomas Kyd*, ed. Frederick Boas (Oxford: Clarendon Press, 1901).

Lake, D. J., 'Three Seventeenth-Century Revisions: *Thomas of Woodstock*, *The Jew of Malta*, and *Faustus B*', *Notes and Queries*, 30 (1983), pp. 133–43.

Leech, Clifford, ed., *Marlowe: A Collection of Critical Essays* (Twentieth Century Views) (Englewood Cliffs, NJ: Prentice-Hall, 1964).

Lenker, Lagretta Tallent, 'The Hopeless Daughter of a Hapless Jew: Father and Daughter in Marlowe's *The Jew of Malta*', in *Placing the Plays of Christopher Marlowe: Fresh Cultural Contexts*, ed. Sara Munson Deats and Robert A. Logan (Aldershot: Ashgate, 2008), pp. 63–73.

Lesser, Zachary, *Renaissance Drama and the Politics of Publication* (Cambridge, Eng.: Cambridge University Press, 2004).

— and Peter Stallybrass, 'The First Literary *Hamlet* and the Commonplacing of Professional Plays', *Shakespeare Quarterly*, 59.4 (2008), pp. 371–420.

Levin, Harry, 'Marlowe Today', *Tulane Drama Review* 8, no. 4 (1964), 22–31, reprinted as 'Reconsidering Marlowe', in *Shakespeare and the Revolution of the Times: Perspectives and Commentaries* (New York: Oxford University Press, 1976), pp. 261–73.

—, *The Overreacher: A Study of Christopher Marlowe* (Cambridge, MA: Harvard University Press, 1952).

Lim, Walter S. H., 'Surety and Spiritual Commercialism in *The Merchant of Venice*', *Studies in English Literature*, 50 (2010), pp. 355–81.

Lodge, Thomas. *Wits Miserie, and the Worlds Madnesse* (1596).

Logan, Robert A., intro. and ed., *Christopher Marlowe* (The University Wits Series) (Burlington, VT: Ashgate, 2011).

—, 'Marlowe Scholarship and Criticism: The Current Scene', in *Christopher Marlowe the Craftsman: Lives, Stage, and Page*, ed. Sarah K. Scott and M. L. Stapleton (Aldershot: Ashgate, 2010), pp. 31–44.

—, *Shakespeare's Marlowe: The Influence of Christopher Marlowe on Shakespeare's Artistry* (Aldershot: Ashgate, 2007).

—, 'The State of the Art: Current Critical Research', *'Doctor Faustus': A Critical Guide*, ed. Sara Munson Deats (London, Eng.: Continuum, 2010), pp. 72–95.

Lopez, Jeremy, 'Alleyn Resurrected', *Marlowe Studies: An Annual*, 1 (2011), pp. 167–80.

Lost Plays Database. ed. Roslyn L. Knutson and David McInnis (www.lostplays.org/index.php/Main_Page)

Louis, Cameron, ed., *Sussex* (Toronto: University of Toronto Press, 2000).

Lunney, Ruth, *Marlowe and the Popular Tradition: Innovation in the English Drama Before 1595* (Manchester, Eng.: Manchester University Press, 2002).

Lupton, Julia Reinhard, *Citizen-Saints: Shakespeare and Political Theology* (Chicago: University of Chicago Press, 2005).

—, 'Deformations of Fellowship in Marlowe's *Jew of* Malta', in *Citizen-Saints: Shakespeare and Political Theology* (Chicago: University of Chicago Press, 2005), pp. 51–72.

—, 'The Jew of Malta', in *The Cambridge Companion to Christopher Marlowe*, ed. Patrick Cheney (Cambridge, Eng.: Cambridge University Press, 2004), pp. 144–57.

Lynch, Stephen J., intro. and ed., *Christopher Marlowe: 'The Jew of Malta' With Related Texts* (Indianapolis, IN: Hackett Publishing Company, Inc., 2009).

MacCaffrey, Wallace T., *Elizabeth I: War and Politics, 1588–1603* (Princeton, NJ: Princeton University Press, 1992).

MacCulloch, Diarmaid, *The Reformation* (New York, NY: Penguin, 2005).

Machiavelli, Niccolò, *The Prince* in *Three Renaissance Classics*, ed. Burton A. Milligan (New York: Charles Scribner's Sons, 1953), pp. 3–101.

MacKenzie, Clayton G., *Deathly Experiments: A Study of Icons and Emblems of Mortality in Christopher Marlowe's Plays* (New York: AMS, 2010).

MacLean, Sally-Beth, 'Adult Playing Companies, 1583–1593', in *The Oxford Handbook of Early Modern Theatre*, ed. Richard Dutton (Oxford: Oxford University Press, 2009), pp. 39–55.

—, 'Tour Routes: "Provincial Wanderings" or Traditional Circuits?', *Medieval and Renaissance Drama in England*, 6 (1993), pp. 1–14.

MacLure, Millar, *Marlowe: The Critical Heritage, 1588–1896* (London: Routledge and Kegan Paul, 1979).

Maguin, Jean-Marie, '*The Jew of Malta*: Marlowe's Ideological Stance and the Playworld's Ethos', *Cahiers Elisabéthains*, 27 (1985), pp. 17–26.

Maguire, Laurie, *Shakespearean Suspect Texts* (Cambridge: Cambridge University Press, 1996).

Mahood, M. M., *Poetry and Humanism* (London: Jonathan Cape, 1950).

Malone Society Collections, II.3 (1931, rpt. New York: AMS Press, 1985).

Manley, Lawrence, 'Playing with Fire: Immolation in the Repertory of Strange's Men', *Early Theatre*, 4 (2001), pp. 115–29.

Marcus, Leah S., Mueller, Janet and Beth Rose, Mary, *Elizabeth I: Collected Works* (Chicago: University of Chicago Press, 2000).

Marlowe, Christopher, *All Ovids Elegies: 3 Bookes. By C. M. Elegies by J.D.* (Middlebrough: n.p., n.d).

Marlowe, Christopher and Penley, Samson, *The Complete Plays*, ed. Mark Thornton Burnett (London: J. M. Dent, 1999).

—, *The Famous Tragedy of the Rich Jew of Malta* (London: Printed for I. B. for Nicholas Vavasour, 1633).

—, *The Famous Tragedy of the Rich Ievv of Malta* (London, 1633).

—, *Marlowe's Celebrated Tragedy of* The Jew of Malta; *in Five Acts* (London: Richard White, Sherwood, Neeley and Jones, and T. Earle, 1818).

—, *Marlowe's Poems*. ed. L. C. Martin (London: J. M. Dent, 1931).

—, *The Poems: Christopher Marlowe*, ed. Millar MacLure (London: Methuen, 1968).

—, *The Works of Christopher Marlowe*, ed. C. F. Tucker Brooke (Oxford: Clarendon Press, 1910).

Marston, John, *The Scourge of Villanie* (1598).

Martin, Mathew R., 'Maltese Psycho: Tragedy and Psychopathology in *The Jew of Malta*', *Lit: Literature Interpretation Theory*, 19.4 (2008), pp. 367–87.

— ed., *The Jew of Malta: Christopher Marlowe* (Ontario, Canada: Broadview Press, 2012).

Martin, Randall, 'Anne Dowriche's *The French History*, Christopher Marlowe, and Machiavellian Agency', *Studies in English Literature*, 39 (1999), pp. 69–87.

Masinton, Charles G., *Christopher Marlowe's Tragic Vision: A Study in Damnation* (Athens: Ohio University Press, 1972).

Mateer, David, 'New Sightings of Christopher Marlowe in London', *Early Theatre*, 11.2 (2008), pp. 13–39.

Maxwell, J. C., 'How Bad is the Text of *The Jew of Malta?*', *Modern Language Review*, 48 (1953), pp. 435–8.

McAdam, Ian, 'Carnal Identity in *The Jew of Malta*', *English Literary Renaissance*, 26 (1996), pp. 46–74.

—, *The Irony of Identity: Self and Imagination in the Drama of Christopher Marlowe* (Newark, DE: University of Delaware Press, 1999).

McCabe, Richard A., 'Elizabethan Satire and the Bishops' Ban of 1599', *Yearbook of English Studies*, 11 (1981), pp. 188–93.

McKerrow, R. B., ed., *A Dictionary of Printers and Booksellers in England Scotland, and Ireland, and of Foreign Printers of English Books 1557–1640* (London: The Bibliographical Society, 1968).

McLaren, Anne, 'Rethinking Republicanism: "Vindiciae, contra tyrannos" in Context', *The Historical Journal*, 49.1 (2006), pp. 23–52.

McMillin, Scott, 'The Ownership of *The Jew of Malta*, *Friar Bacon*, and *The Ranger's Comedy*', *English Language Notes*, 9 (1972), pp. 249–52.

McMillin, Scott and Sally-Beth MacLean, *The Queen's Men and their Plays* (Cambridge: Cambridge University Press, 1998).

Melnikoff, Kirk, '"[I]ygging Vaines" and "Riming Mother Wits": Marlowe, Clowns and the Early Frameworks of Dramatic Authorship', *Early Modern Literary Studies*, Special Issue 16 (2007), [n. p.].

—, 'Nicholas Ling's Republican *Hamlet* (1603)', in *Shakespeare's Stationers*, ed. Marta Straznicky (Philadelphia, PA: University of Pennsylvania Press, 2012).

—, intro. and ed., *Robert Greene* (Aldershot: Ashgate, 2011).

Menpes, B. R., 'The Bondage of Barabas: Thwarted Desire in *The Jew of Malta*', *Parergon: Journal of the Australian and New Zealand Association for Medieval and Early Modern Studies*, 20.1 (2003), pp. 65–84.

Menzer, Paul, 'Shades of Marlowe', *Marlowe Studies: An Annual*, 1 (2011), pp. 181–92.

Meyer, Edward, *Machiavelli and the Elizabethan Drama*, Litterarhistorische Forschungan, no.1 (Weimar: Emil Felber, 1897).

Minshull, Catherine, 'Marlowe's "Sound Machevill"', *Renaissance Drama*, n.s. 13 (1982), pp. 35–53.

Moore, Roger E., '"I'll Rouse My Senses, and Awake Myself": Marlowe's *The Jew of Malta* and the Renaissance Gnostic Tradition', *Religion and Literature*, 37.3 (Autumn 2005), pp. 37–58.

Moss, Stephanie, 'Edward Kean, Anti-Semitism, and *The Jew of Malta*', in *Placing the Plays of Christopher Marlowe: Fresh Critical Contexts*, ed. S. M. Deats and R. A. Logan (Aldershot: Ashgate, 2008), pp. 43–59.

Munro, Lucy, 'Marlowe on the Caroline Stage', *Shakespeare Bulletin: A Journal of Performance Criticism and Scholarship*, 27.1 (2009), pp. 39–50.

Murray, John Tucker, *English Dramatic Companies 1558–1642*, 2 vols (Boston and New York: Houghton Mifflin, 1910).

Nashe, Thomas, *Christs teares ouer Ierusalem* (London, 1594).

Newes from Brest (London, 1594).

Nicholl, Charles, *The Reckoning: The Murder of Christopher Marlowe*, revised edn (London: Vintage, 2002).

Nungezer, Edwin, *A Dictionary of Actors* (1929; rpt. New York: Greenwood Press, 1968).

Nuttall, A. D., 'Christopher Marlowe: Iron and Gold', *Comparative Criticism: An Annual Journal*, 24 (2002), pp. 37–51.

O'Neill, Judith, ed., *Critics on Marlowe* (Coral Gables, FL: University of Miami Press, 1970).

O'Rourke, James, 'Racism and Homophobia in *The Merchant of Venice*', *English Literary History*, 70 (2003), pp. 375–97.

Ovid, *Metamorphoses*, trans. Frank Justus Miller, 2 vols (Cambridge: Harvard University Press, 1916).

—, *Tristia [and] Ex Ponto*, trans. Arthur Leslie Wheeler (Cambridge: Harvard University Press, 1924. Reprint 1985).

Oz, Avraham, ed., *New Casebooks: Marlowe* (New York, NY: Palgrave Macmillan, 2003).

Palmer, Barbara D., 'Early Modern Mobility: Players, Payments, and Patrons', *Shakespeare Quarterly*, 56 (2005), pp. 260–305.

Palmer, Daryl. W., 'Merchants and Miscegenation: *The Three Ladies of London, The Jew of Malta*, and *The Merchant of Venice*', in *Race, Ethnicity, and Power in the Renaissance*, ed. Joyce Green MacDonald (London: Associated University Presses, 1997), pp. 36–66.

Parker, John, *The Aesthetics of Antichrist: From Christian Drama to Christopher Marlowe* (Ithaca, NY: Cornell University Press, 2007).

—, 'Barabas and Charles I', in *Placing the Plays of Christopher Marlowe: Fresh Cultural Contexts*, ed. Sara Munson Deats and Robert A. Logan (Aldershot: Ashgate, 2008), pp. 167–81.

Patrons and Performances Web Site, ed. Sally-Beth MacLean and J. Alan Somerset (http://link.library.utoronto.ca/reed/)

Patterson, Annabel, *Censorship and Interpretation: The Conditions of Writing and Reading in Early Modern England* (Madison: University of Wisconsin Press, 1984).

Patterson, Steve, 'The Bankruptcy of Homoerotic Amity in Shakespeare's *Merchant of Venice*', *Shakespeare Quarterly*, 50 (1999), pp. 9–32.

Peavy, Charles E., '*The Jew of Malta* – Anti-Semitic or Anti-Catholic', *McNeese Review*, 2 (1959–60), pp. 57–60.

Peele, George, *The Battle of Alcazar*. Malone Society Reprints (1907).

Penuel, Suzanne, 'Castrating the Creditor in *The Merchant of Venice*', *Studies in English Literature*, 44 (2004), pp. 255–75.

Perry, Curtis, 'The Uneasy Republicanism of Thomas Kyd's *Cornelia*', *Criticism*, 48.4 (2006), 535–55.

Philips, Jerry, 'Cannibalism qua Capitalism: The Metaphorics of Accumulation in Marx, Conrad, Shakespeare, and Marlowe', in *Cannibalism and the Colonial World*, ed. F. Barker, P. Hulme and M. Iversen (Cambridge: Cambridge University Press, 1998), pp. 183–203, 273–6.

Pigman, George W. III, 'Versions of Imitation in the Renaissance', *Renaissance Quarterly*, 33 (1980), pp. 1–32.

Pilkinton, Mark C., ed., *Bristol* (Toronto: University of Toronto Press, 1997).

Poel, William, 'Shakespeare's Jew and Marlowe's Christians', *The Westminster Review*, January, 1909, reprinted in *Shakespeare in the Theatre* (London and Toronto: Sidgwick and Jackson, 1913, reprinted by Project Gutenberg, 2011 <www.gutenberg.org>).

Potter, Lois, 'Marlowe in Theatre and Film', in *A Cambridge Companion to Christopher Marlowe*, ed. Patrick Cheney (Cambridge: Cambridge University Press, 2004), pp. 262–81.

Praz, Mario, 'Machiavelli and the Elizabethans', *Proceedings of the British Academy*, 14 (1928), pp. 49–97.

Priest, Dale G., 'Knave or Fool? Ithamore as Dramatic Paradigm in *The Jew of Malta*', *Explorations in Renaissance Culture*, 8–9 (1982–3), pp. 85–96.

Proser, Matthew N., *The Gift of Fire: Aggression and the Plays of Christopher Marlowe* (New York: Peter Lang, 1995).

Proudfoot, Richard, 'Marlowe and the Editors', in *The Cambridge Companion to Christopher Marlowe*, ed. J. A. Downie and J. T. Parnell (Cambridge, Eng.: Cambridge University Press, 2000), pp. 41–54.

Purcell, H. D., 'Whetstone's *English Myrror* and Marlowe's *Jew of Malta*', *Notes and Queries,* 13 (1966), pp. 288–90.

Rabb, Felix, *The English Face of Machiavelli: A Changing Interpretation, 1500–1700* (London: Routledge and Kegan Paul, 1964).

Ribner, Irving, ed., *Christopher Marlowe's 'The Jew of Malta': Text and Major Criticism* (New York, NY: The Odyssey Press, 1970).

—, *The Complete Plays of Christopher Marlowe* (New York: Odyssey, 1963).

—, 'Marlowe and the Critics', *Tulane Drama Review*, 8 (1964), pp. 211–24.

—, 'Marlowe and Machiavelli', *Comparative Literature*, 6 (1954), pp. 348–56.

—, 'Marlowe and Shakespeare', *Shakespeare Quarterly*, 15.2 (1964), pp. 41–53.

—, 'Marlowe's "Tragicke Glasse"', in *Essays on Shakespeare and Elizabethan Drama in Honor of Hardin Craig* (Columbia: University of Missouri Press, 1962), pp. 91–114.

Riggs, David, 'The Poet in the Play: Life and Art in *Tamburlaine* and *The Jew of Malta*', in *Shakespeare, Marlowe, Jonson: New Directions in Biography*, ed. T. Kozuka and J. R. Mulryne (Aldershot: Ashgate, 2006), pp. 205–24.

—, *The World of Christopher Marlowe* (London: Faber & Faber, 2004).

Rocklin, Edward L., 'Marlowe as Experimental Dramatist: The Role of the Audience in *The Jew of Malta*', in *'A Poet & a Filthy Play-maker': New Essays on Christopher Marlowe*, ed. Kenneth Friedenreich, Roma Gill and Constance B. Kuriyama (New York: AMS Press, 1988), pp. 129–42.

Romany, Frank and Lindsey, Robert, eds, *Christopher Marlowe: The Complete Plays* (New York: Penguin, 2003).

Rosen, Alan, 'Into the Ghetto: Representing Jewish Space in Elizabethan England', *JTD: Journal of Theatre and Drama*, 7–8 (2001–2), pp. 95–104.

Rothstein, Eric, 'Structure as Meaning in *The Jew of Malta*', *Journal of English and Germanic Philology*, 65 (1966), pp. 260–73.

Rowley, William, *A Search for Money, Or The Lamentable Complaint for the Losse of the Wandring Knight, Monsieur L'Argent* (London: Joseph Hunt, 1609).

Rozett, Martha Tuck, *The Doctrine of Election and the Emergence of Elizabethan Tragedy* (Princeton: Princeton University Press, 1984).

Rutter, Carol Chillington, ed., *Documents of the Rose Playhouse* (Manchester: Manchester University Press, 1999).

Rutter, Tom, '*The Jew of Malta* and *The Massacre at Paris*', in *The Cambridge Introduction to Christopher Marlowe* (Cambridge: Cambridge University Press, 2012) pp. 61–78.

—, 'Marlovian Echoes in the Admiral's Men Repertory: *Alcazar, Stukeley, Patient Grissil*', *Shakespeare Bulletin*, 27 (2009), 27–38.

Sales, Roger, 'The Stage, the Scaffold and the Spectators: The Struggles for Power in Marlowe's *Jew of Malta*', in *Christopher Marlowe and English Renaissance Culture*, ed. Darryll Grantley and Peter Roberts (1996; Aldershot: Ashgate, 1999), pp. 119–28.

Salmon, J. H. M., 'Catholic Resistance Theory, Ultramontanism, and the Royalist Response, 1580—1620', in *The Cambridge History of Political Thought 1450–1700*, ed. J. H. Burns and Mark Goldie (Cambridge, Eng.: Cambridge University Press, 1991). Cambridge Histories Online, Cambridge University Press, 26 January 2012.

—, *The French Civil Wars in English Political Thought* (Oxford: Clarendon Press, 1959).

—, *Society in Crisis: France in the Sixteenth Century* (New York: AMS, 1975).

Sanders, Wilbur, *The Dramatist and the Received Idea* (Cambridge, Eng.: Cambridge University Press, 1968).

Scott, Sarah K., '*The Jew of Malta* and the Development of City Comedy: "The Mean Passage of a History"', in *Christopher Marlowe the Craftsman: Lives, Stage, and Page*, ed. Sarah K. Scott and M. L. Stapleton (Burlington, VT: Ashgate, 2010), pp. 91–108.

Scott, Sarah K. and Stapleton, M. L., eds, *Christopher Marlowe the Craftsman: Lives, Stage, and Page* (Aldershot: Ashgate, 2010).

Seaton, Ethel, 'Fresh Sources for Marlowe', *Review of English Studies*, 5 (1929), pp. 385–401.

Segal, Erich, 'Marlowe's *Schadenfreude*: Barabas as Comic Hero', in *Veins of Humor*, ed. Harry Levin (Cambridge, MA: Harvard University Press, 1972), pp. 69–91.

Shakespeare, William, *The First Part of the Contention betwixt the Two Famous Houses of Yorke and Lancaster* (London, 1594).

—, *The Merchant of Venice*, ed. Jay L. Halio (Oxford, Eng.: Oxford University Press, 1993).

—, *The Most Lamentable Romaine Tragedie of Titus Andronicus* (London, 1594).

—, *A Pleasant Conceited Comedie Called, Loues Labors Lost* (London: W.W. for Cuthbert Burby, 1598).

Shapiro, James, *Rival Playwrights: Marlowe, Jonson, Shakespeare* (Chicago, IL: University of Chicago Press, 1991).

—, *Shakespeare and the Jews* (New York, NY: Columbia University Press, 1996).

—, 'Shakespeare and the Jews', in *New Casebooks: The Merchant of Venice*, ed. Martin Coyle (New York, NY: St. Martin's Press, 1998), pp. 73–91.

Shawcross, J. T. 'Signs of the Times: Christopher Marlowe's Decline in the Seventeenth Century', in *'A Poet and a Filthy Play-maker': New Essays on Christopher Marlowe*, ed. K. Friedenreich, R. Gill and C. B. Kuriyama (New York: AMS, 1988), pp. 63–71.

Shepard, Alan, *Marlowe's Soldiers: Rhetorics of Masculinity in the Age of the Armada* (Aldershot: Ashgate, 2002).

—, 'Paying Tribute in Occupied Malta: From Chivalry to Commerce', in *Marlowe's Soldiers: Rhetorics of Masculinity in the Age of the Armada* (Aldershot: Ashgate, 2002), pp. 113–39.

—, '"Thou art no soldier; thou art a merchant": The *Mentalité* of War in Malta', in *Marlowe, History, and Sexuality: New Critical Essays on Christopher Marlowe*, ed. Paul Whitfield White (New York: AMS, 1998), pp. 109–30.

Shepherd, Simon, *Marlowe and the Politics of Elizabethan Theatre* (New York, NY: St. Martin's Press, 1986).

Shuger, Debora Kuller, *The Renaissance Bible: Scholarship, Sacrifice, and Subjectivity* (Berkeley, CA: University of California Press, 1994).

Siemon, James R., intro. and ed., *Christopher Marlowe: 'The Jew of Malta'* (New Mermaids Editions), 3rd edn (London, Eng.: A & C Black, 2009).

—, ed., *The Jew of Malta* (London, Eng.: A & C Black, 1994).

Simkin, Stevie, *Marlowe: The Plays* (Basingstoke: Palgrave, 2001).

—, *A Preface to Marlowe* (London: Longman, 2000).

—, '"A Scattered Nation": *The Jew of Malta* in the Warsaw Ghetto', *On-Stage Studies*, 21 (1998), pp. 31–51.

—, 'Unhallowed Deeds: *The Jew of Malta*', in *A Preface to Marlowe* (Harlow, Eng.: Longman, 2000), pp. 133–67.

Simmons, J. L., 'Elizabethan Stage Practice and Marlowe's *The Jew of Malta*', *Renaissance Drama*, 4 (1971), pp. 93–104.

Sims, James H., *Dramatic Uses of Biblical Allusions in Malowe and Shakespeare, University of Florida* Monographs, Humanities, no. 24 (Gainesville: University of Florida Press, 1966).

Skinner, Quentin, *The Foundations of Modern Political Thought*, vol. 1 (Cambridge, Eng.: Cambridge University Press, 1978).

Slack, Paul, *The Impact of Plague in Tudor and Stuart England* (New York: Routledge, 1985).

Smith, Bruce R., *Shakespeare and Masculinity* (Oxford, Eng.: Oxford University Press, 2000).

Smith, James L., '*The Jew of Malta* in the Theatre', in *Christopher Marlowe*, ed. Brian Morris (New York, NY: Hill and Wang, 1968), pp. 1–23.

Smith, Shawn, 'A Society of One: Reading *The Jew of Malta* through Serres's Theory of Exchange', *Examplaria: A Journal of Theory in Medieval and Renaissance Studies*, 15.2 (2003), pp. 419–50.

Sommerville, Johann P., ed., *King James VI and I: Political Writings* (Cambridge, Eng.: Cambridge University Press, 1994).

Spivack, Bernard, *Shakespeare and the Allegory of Evil: The History of a Metaphor in Relation to His Major Villains* (New York, NY: Columbia University Press, 1958).

Stanivukovic, Goran V., ed., *Remapping the Mediterranean World in Early Modern English Writings* (Basingstoke: Palgrave, 2007).

Stapleton, M. L., 'Christopher Marlowe', in *Oxford Bibliographies Online: British and Irish Literature,* ed. Andrew Hadfield (New York: Oxford University Press, 2012).

—, *Harmful Eloquence: Ovid's 'Amores' from Antiquity to Shakespeare* (Ann Arbor: University of Michigan Press, 1996).

—, 'A *Remedy* for Heywood?', *Texas Studies in Literature and Language,* 43 (2001), pp. 74–115.

—, ed., *Thomas Heywood's 'Art of Love': The First Complete English Translation of Ovid's 'Ars Amatoria'* (Ann Arbor: University of Michigan Press, 2000).

Steane, J. B., *Marlowe: A Critical Study* (Cambridge, Eng.: Cambridge University Press, 1964).

Stevens, Paul, 'How Milton's Nationalism Works: Globalization and the Possibilities of Positive Nationalism', in *Early Modern Nationalism and Milton's England*, ed. David Loewenstein and Paul Stevens (Toronto: University of Toronto Press, 2008), pp. 273–301.

Stewart, Alan, *The Cradle King: A Life of James VI & I* (London, Eng.: Chatto and Windus, 2003).

Straznicky, Marta, *Shakespeare's Stationers* (Philadelphia, PA: University of Pennsylvania Press, 2012).

Sullivan, Ceri, 'Silver in *The Jew of Malta*', *Notes and Queries*, 48.3 (2001), p. 265.

Sullivan, Garrett A. Jr., Cheney, P. and Hadfield A., eds, *Early Modern English Drama: A Critical Companion* (Oxford: Oxford University Press, 2006).

Syme, Holger Schott, 'The Meaning of Success: Stories of 1594 and Its Aftermath', *Shakespeare Quarterly*, 61:4 (Winter, 2010), pp. 490–525.

Tamaizumi, Y., 'Hitsujikai no hen'yo (jo): Marlowe kara Cotton e', *Eigo Seinen / Rising Generation*, 151.5 (2005), pp. 273–77.

Tambling, Jeremy, 'Abigail's Party: "The Difference of Things" in *The Jew of Malta*', in *Another Country: Feminist Perspectives on Renaissance Drama*, ed. Dorothea Kehler and Susan Baker (Metuchen, NJ: Scarecrow Press, 1991), pp. 95–112.

Taylor, George C., 'Marlowe's "Now"', in *Elizabethan Studies and Other Essays in Honor of George F. Reynolds*, University of Colorado Studies, Series B, Studies in the Humanities, vol. 2, no. 4 (Boulder: University of Colorado Press, 1945), pp. 93–100.

Thomas, Vivien and Tydeman, William, eds, *Christopher Marlowe: The Plays and their Sources* (London, Eng.: Routledge, 1994).

Thomson, Leslie, 'Staging on the Road, 1586–1594', *Shakespeare Quarterly*, 61 (2010), pp. 526–50.

Thurn, David, 'Economic and Ideological Exchange in *The Jew of Malta*', *Theatre Journal*, 46 (1994), pp. 157–70.

Tilley, Morris P., *A Dictionary of the Proverbs in England in the Sixteenth and Seventeenth Centuries* (Ann Arbor: University of Michigan Press, 1950).

—, 'Proverbs and Proverbial Allusions in Marlowe', *Modern Language Notes*, 50 (1935), pp. 347–55.

Tkacz, Catherine Brown, '*The Jew of Malta* and the Pit', *South Atlantic Review*, 53.2 (1988), pp. 47–57.

Tobin, J. J. M., 'How Drunken Was Barnadine?', *Notes and Queries*, 50.1 (2003), pp. 46–7.

Tromly, Fred B., *Playing with Desire: Christopher Marlowe and the Art of Tantalization* (Toronto: University of Toronto Press, 1998).

Umunç, H., 'On Her Majesty's Secret Service: Marlowe and Turkey', *Belleten*, 70.259 (2006), pp. 903–18.

Ungerer, Gustav, 'Portia and the Prince of Morocco', *Shakespeare Studies*, 31 (2003), pp. 89–126.

Van Fossen, Richard W., ed., *The Jew of Malta* (Lincoln: University of Nebraska Press, 1964).

Vitkus, Daniel, 'Turks and Jews in *The Jew of Malta*', in *Early Modern English Drama: A Critical Companion*, ed. Garrett Sullivan, Patrick Cheney and Andrew Hadfield (New York, NY: Oxford University Press, 2006), pp. 61–72.

—, *Turning Turk: English Theater and the Multicultural Mediterranean, 1570–1630* (New York: Palgrave Macmillan, 2003).

—, ed., *Three Turk Plays from Early Modern England* (New York: Columbia University Press, 2000).

Webb, David, '"Pageants Truly Played": Self-Dramatization and Naturalistic Character in *The Jew of Malta*', *Renaissance Forum: An Electronic Journal of Early Modern Literary and Historical Studies*, 5.1 (2000).

Weil, Judith, *Christopher Marlowe: Merlin's Prophet* (Cambridge, Eng.: Cambridge University Press, 1977).

Welsh, Robert F., 'Evidence of Heywood Spellings in *The Jew of Malta*', *Renaissance Papers* (1963), pp. 3–9.

Wentersdorf, Karl P., 'The Repertory and Size of Pembroke's Company', *Theater Annual*, 33 (1977), pp. 71–85.

Werstine, Paul, 'Narratives About Printed Shakespeare Texts: "Foul Papers" and "Bad" Quartos', *Shakespeare Quarterly*, 41 (1990), pp. 65–86.

White, Paul W., ed., *Marlowe, History, and Sexuality: New Critical Essays on Christopher Marlowe* (New York, NY: AMS Press, 1998).

Whitney, Geffrey, *A Choice of Emblemes and Other Devises* (Leiden: Christopher Plantyn, 1586).

Wickham, Glynne, Berry, Herbert and Ingram, William, *English Professional Theatre, 1530–1660* (Cambridge: Cambridge University Press, 2000).

Williams, Carolyn D., 'Interview Given by Stevie Simkin, Director of Marlowe's *Jew of Malta*, to Carolyn D. Williams', *Cahiers Elisabéthains*, 55 (1999), pp. 65–73.

Wilson, F. P., *Marlowe and the Early Shakespeare* (Oxford: Clarendon Press, 1953).

Wilson, Richard, 'Another Country: Marlowe and the Go-Between', in *Renaissance Go-Betweens: Cultural Exchange in Early Modern Europe*, ed. W. von Koppenfels (Berlin: de Gruyter, 2005). Also, in *Remapping the Mediterranean World in Early Modern English Writings*, ed. G. V. Stanivukovic (Basingstoke: Palgrave, 2007), pp. 131–56.

—, ed., *Christopher Marlowe: A Critical Reader* (Harlow, Eng.: Longman, 1999).

Wood, James B., *The King's Army: Warfare, Soldiers, and Society during the Wars of Religion in France* (Cambridge, Eng.: Cambridge University Press, 1995).

Woodbridge, Linda, *Vagrancy, Homelessness, and English Renaissance Literature* (Urbana, IL: University of Illinois Press, 2001).

INDEX